Energy as a Sociotechnical Problem

Energy as a Sociotechnical Problem offers an innovative approach to equip interdisciplinary research on sociotechnical transitions with coherence and focus. The book emphasizes sociotechnical problems in three analytical dimensions:

- In the control dimension, contributing authors examine how control can be maintained despite increasing complexity and uncertainty, e.g., in power grid operations or on energy markets;
- In the change dimension, the authors explore if and how change is possible despite the need for stable orientation, e.g., regarding discourses, real-world labs, and learning;
- Finally, in the action dimension, the authors analyze how the ability to act on a permanent basis is sustained despite opaqueness and ignorance, exemplified by the work on trust, capabilities, or individual motives.

Drawing on contributions from engineering, economics, philosophy, political science, psychology, and sociology, the book assembles a range of classic and current themes including innovation, resilience, institutional economics, design, or education. *Energy as a Sociotechnical Problem* presents the ongoing transformation of the energy complex as a multidimensional process, in which the analytical dimensions interact with one another in shaping the energy future. As such, this book will be of great interest to students and scholars of energy transitions, energy science, and environmental social science more generally, as well as to practitioners of energy policy.

Christian Büscher is a senior researcher at the Institute for Technology Assessment and Systems Analysis (ITAS), Karlsruhe Institute of Technology (KIT), Germany.

Jens Schippl is a senior researcher at the Institute for Technology Assessment and Systems Analysis (ITAS), Karlsruhe Institute of Technology (KIT), Germany.

Patrick Sumpf is a research associate at the Institute for Technology Assessment and Systems Analysis (ITAS), Karlsruhe Institute of Technology (KIT), Germany.

Routledge Studies in Energy Transitions
Series Editor: Dr. Kathleen Araújo, Stony Brook University, USA

Considerable interest exists today in energy transitions. Whether one looks at diverse efforts to decarbonize, or strategies to improve the access levels, security, and innovation in energy systems, one finds that change in energy systems is a prime priority.

Routledge Studies in Energy Transitions aims to advance the thinking which underlies these efforts. The series connects distinct lines of inquiry from planning and policy, engineering and the natural sciences, history of technology, STS, and management. In doing so, it provides primary references that function like a set of international, technical meetings. Single and co-authored monographs are welcome, as well as edited volumes relating to themes, like resilience and system risk.

Series Advisory Board

Morgan Bazilian, Columbia University, Center for Global Energy Policy (US)
Thomas Birkland, North Carolina State University (US)
Aleh Cherp, Central European University (CEU, Budapest) and Lund University (Sweden)
Mohamed El-Ashry, UN Foundation
Jose Goldemberg, Universidade de Sao Paolo (Brasil) and UN Development Program, World Energy Assessment
Michael Howlett, Simon Fraser University (Canada)
Jon Ingimarsson, Landsvirkjun, National Power Company (Iceland)
Michael Jefferson, ESCP Europe Business School
Jessica Jewell, IIASA (Austria)
Florian Kern, University of Sussex, Science Policy Research Unit and Sussex Energy Group (UK)
Derk Loorbach, DRIFT (Netherlands)
Jochen Markard, ETH (Switzerland)'
Nabojsa Nakicenovic, IIASA (Austria)
Martin Pasqualetti, Arizona State University, School of Geographical Sciences and Urban Planning (US)
Mark Radka, UN Environment Programme, Energy, Climate, and Technology

Rob Raven, Utrecht University (Netherlands)
Roberto Schaeffer, Universidade Federal do Rio de Janeiro, Energy Planning
Program, COPPE (Brasil)
Miranda Schreurs, Technische Universität München, Bavarian School of Public
Policy (Germany)
Vaclav Smil, University of Manitoba and Royal Society of Canada (Canada)
Benjamin Sovacool, Science Policy Research Unit (SPRU), University of
Sussex (UK)

Titles in this series include:

Energy and Economic Growth
Why we Need a New Pathway to Prosperity
Timothy J. Foxon

Sustainable Energy Transformations, Power and Politics
Morocco and the Mediterranean
Sharlissa Moore

Energy as a Sociotechnical Problem
An Interdisciplinary Perspective on Control, Change, and Action in Energy
Transitions
Edited by Christian Büscher, Jens Schippl, and Patrick Sumpf

For more information about this series, please visit: www.routledge.com/Routledge-
Studies-in-Energy-Transitions/book-series/RSENT

Energy as a Sociotechnical Problem

An Interdisciplinary Perspective on Control, Change, and Action in Energy Transitions

Edited by Christian Büscher, Jens Schippl, and Patrick Sumpf

 Routledge
Taylor & Francis Group
LONDON AND NEW YORK

 earthscan
from Routledge

First published 2019
by Routledge
2 Park Square, Milton Park, Abingdon, Oxon OX14 4RN

and by Routledge
52 Vanderbilt Avenue, New York, NY 10017, USA

First issued in paperback 2020

Routledge is an imprint of the Taylor & Francis Group, an informa business

© 2019 selection and editorial matter, Christian Büscher, Jens Schippl
and Patrick Sumpf; individual chapters, the contributors

The right of Christian Büscher, Jens Schippl and Patrick Sumpf to be
identified as the authors of the editorial material, and of the authors
for their individual chapters, has been asserted in accordance with
sections 77 and 78 of the Copyright, Designs and Patents Act 1988.

British Library Cataloguing-in-Publication Data
A catalogue record for this book is available from the British Library

Library of Congress Cataloging-in-Publication Data
A catalog record for this book has been requested

ISBN 13: 978-0-367-58607-2 (pbk)
ISBN 13: 978-1-138-73582-8 (hbk)

Typeset in Goudy
by Apex CoVantage, LLC

Contents

Figures

Tables

Contributors

Christian Büscher received his Diploma in sociology from Bielefeld University and was member of the post-graduate college "Technology and Society" at the TU Darmstadt, where he finished his doctorate. Currently, he holds the position of senior researcher at ITAS and was project leader within the Helmholtz Alliance ENERGY-TRANS. His main research interests are interdisciplinary risk research as well as environmental and energy-related issues. He has extensive experience in interdisciplinary settings and large research alliances.

Leigh Champagnie successfully completed his M.Sc. in Renewable Energy Engineering at Kingston University, graduating in 2014 before undertaking a Ph.D. at Kingston University's Business School, which he commenced in September 2014. Leigh is currently writing his thesis on the role of institutional entrepreneurs in shaping the renewable energy subfield in the UK during the period 1986–2016.

Florian Diehlmann is a research associate in the risk management unit of the Institute of Industrial Production at the Karlsruhe Institute of Technology (KIT), Karlsruhe, Germany. His research focus is on the supply chains of critical goods with a particular focus on scenario techniques and humanitarian logistics.

Gerhard Fuchs, Dr. phil. in political science, works at the University of Stuttgart (Department of Social Sciences). Before that he served as a Deputy Director of the Department Technology, Organization, Work of the Centre for Technology Assessment in Baden-Württemberg, Stuttgart. His research interests are concentrated on the study of innovation, especially in the fields of new information and communication technologies, local/regional innovation systems, and the development of new industries.

Audley Genus is Professor of Innovation and Technology Management at Kingston University. His research concerns the role of diverse stakeholders in shaping innovation in the renewable energy sector, the contribution of institutional innovation to the transformation of the energy sector, and responsible innovation. Audley leads for Kingston University on the international, multipartner ENERGISE Horizon 2020 project on innovation for sustainable energy.

Matthias Gross is Professor of Environmental Sociology at the University of Jena, jointly appointed by the Helmholtz Centre for Environmental Research – UFZ, Leipzig (Germany), where he heads the Department of Urban and Environmental Sociology. His main areas of research include alternative energy systems, real world experiments and environmental innovation, and ignorance, risk, and the knowledge society.

Rafaela Hillerbrand is a Professor for Philosophy of Science and Technology at the Karlsruhe Institute of Technology (KIT). She holds a Ph.D. in theoretical physics and a Ph.D. in philosophy. Between 2006 and 2008, she held a position as a senior research fellow at the University of Oxford. Before joining KIT, Rafaela Hillerbrand worked as an associate professor at the TU Delft and was head of the interdisciplinary research group eet-ethics for energy technology at the Human Technology Centre at RWTH Aachen University.

Marfuga Iskandarova is a postdoctoral researcher at the Small Business Research Centre, Kingston University. She holds an LLM degree in Law and Sustainable Development (University of Aberdeen) and a Ph.D. in Management Studies (University of Exeter). Marfuga has interests and expertise in the areas of innovation, sustainability, renewable energy, energy policy, and regulation.

Wolfgang Kröger completed his doctorate in Mechanical Engineering at the University RWTH Aachen. From 2003 to 2011, he was Professor and Director of the Laboratory of Safety Analysis of the University ETH Zurich. He is the Founding Rector of the International Risk Governance Council (IRGC). Since 2011, he has been Executive Director of the ETH Risk Center. His recent publications analyze the vulnerability of engineered critical infrastructures and the security of energy supply.

Rolf W. Künneke is Professor of Economics of Infrastructures at the University of Twente, where he was awarded a Ph.D. from the Faculty of Public Administration and Public Policy. He has held academic positions at the Universities of Paris 1 – Pantheon-Sorbonne, the Swiss Federal Institute of Technology – EPFL, the University of Twente (the Netherlands), and Auburn University (USA). In 2011, he coedited the *International Handbook of Network Industries: Liberalization of Infrastructures*, published by Edward Elgar Publishers.

Todd R. La Porte is Professor Emeritus of Political Science at the University of California, Berkeley, where he has been active since 1965. He received his M.A. and Ph.D. from Stanford University (1962), and held faculty posts at the University of Southern California, Stanford University, and the UCB. He teaches and publishes in the areas of organization theory, technology and politics, and the organizational and decision-making dynamics of large, complex, technologically intensive organizations.

Cen Nan received his B. Eng. degree in electrical and computer engineering and M. Eng. degree in oil and gas engineering at Memorial University of Newfoundland, Canada. In 2009, he joined the Lab for Safety Analysis as a Ph.D. student at ETH Zurich. After graduating in 2012, he worked as a research assistant at the Reliability and Risk Engineering Laboratory, ETH Zurich. Since 2017 he has been a senior analyst for quantitative research/risk management of public equities, in a Canadian investment company.

Siegmar Otto, Ph.D., is interested in research of human–environment interaction (e.g., ecological behavior, environmental education), human–technology interaction (e.g., user experience, technology acceptance, psychological aspects of artificial intelligence), data science, and organizational psychology. He is visiting professor at the Division of Business and Organizational Psychology, University of Hohenheim, Stuttgart, Germany, and a researcher at the Institute of Psychology, Otto-von-Guericke University, Magdeburg, Germany.

Wolfgang Raskob is the head of the Accident Consequence Assessment Group of IKET at the Karlsruhe Institute of Technology (KIT), Karlsruhe, Germany. He has developed methods and tools to assist decision makers in dealing with major disasters with a focus on emergency management following nuclear incidents. His key research interests are now the analysis of interdependencies in critical infrastructure, the simulation of countermeasures, and of risk and crisis management.

Jens Schippl studied sociology, geography, and biology at the University of Heidelberg. He holds the position of senior researcher at the Institute for Technology Assessment and Systems Analysis (ITAS), Karlsruhe Institute of Technology (KIT). His research interests focus on sociotechnical processes of change, foresight, and technology assessment in the sectors of mobility and energy. He has worked as the scientific coordinator for the Helmholtz Alliance ENERGY-TRANS.

Frank Schultmann is Chair Professor at the Karlsruhe Institute of Technology (KIT), Germany, and the Director of the KIT's Institute for Industrial Production (IIP) and the French-German Institute for Environmental Research (DFIU). His research interests include sustainable production and logistics, decision support, supply chain management and optimization, systems modelling, project management, technology assessment, and construction management.

Patrick Sumpf holds a B.A. in Political Science and an M.A. in Political Communication from Bielefeld University. He is a project manager and research associate at the Institute for Technology Assessment and Systems Analysis (ITAS), Karlsruhe Institute of Technology (KIT). He defended his Dr. phil. in Media and Communication Studies in 2017 at Mannheim University. His work concentrates on trust research, with a focus on energy and digitalization.

Stefan Wandler is a scientific assistant of the Accident Consequence Assessment Group of IKET at the Karlsruhe Institute of Technology, Karlsruhe, Germany. His field of work is the analysis of interdependencies in critical infrastructure and the development of critical infrastructure models as a part of a multiagent-based simulation in the context of decision support.

Marcus Wiens, Ph.D. in Economics, leads the research unit in risk management at the Institute of Industrial Production at the Karlsruhe Institute of Technology (KIT), Karlsruhe, Germany. His fields of research are economic systems analysis, systemic and behavioral risk management, decision theory, game theory, and experimental economics.

Inga Wittenberg, Ph.D., works as a senior researcher in the Personality and Social Psychology Division at the Otto-von-Guericke University in Magdeburg, Germany. Her research interests include the determinants of proenvironmental behavior as well as energy consumption and related technologies, in particular in the context of the use of renewable energy.

Acknowledgments

First of all, in times of increasing pressure to publish in peer reviewed journals, we are especially grateful for the commitment shown by our contributing authors. They have made it possible for us to be able to conduct this experiment on aligning interdisciplinary research efforts toward commonly shared reference problems and for our idea to come to life in this anthology. The overall notion of sociotechnical problems started to take shape in the inspiring intellectual arena that the Helmholtz Alliance ENERGY-TRANS offered. From 2011 to 2016, ENERGY-TRANS comprised an interdisciplinary group of about 80 researchers from different disciplinary backgrounds who investigated the interfaces and interactions between technical and societal developments in the context of the German *Energiewende* in order to inform the respective policy making (www.energy-trans. de). In particular, a working group whose mission was incorporated in its title – Integrative Key Topic: Analyzing Sociotechnical Systems – pushed forward the investigation into the possibilities for a cognitive integration of sociotechnical concepts. In this regard, we would like to thank Jens Buchgeister and many other colleagues who participated in the workshops we organized over the lifetime of the project.

In 2015 we assembled most of the authors in this book at a workshop in Karlsruhe with the title "Understanding Sociotechnical Problems in Energy System Transformation: Control, Learning, and Actionability as Relevant Dimensions?" Two days of intensive debate about the different approaches that the invited scholars represent and the possibilities of finding problem-oriented points of reference for a comprehensive study of energy transitions induced a great deal of motivation for us to edit the book at hand. Especially the spirit of openness and willingness to learn from each other – combined with good humor and individual humbleness – made it easy for the editors to initiate the endeavor. During this period, we enjoyed the privilege of hosting Todd R. La Porte and Todd M. La Porte as guests at ITAS in Karlsruhe, who stayed for several weeks and took part in the workshop. The intellectually demanding and highly inspiring discussions with them brought us a decisive step forward and made a lasting impression on us.

Our good fortune to be able to realize this anthology has been tremendously supported by Annabelle Harris, Editor for "Environment and Sustainability" at Routledge. With the review process she initiated, we also received a great deal of pointers and recommendations on how to improve the overall project, especially with regard to the book's potential reception by a heterogeneous readership. For this, we want to thank the anonymous reviewers for their efforts. In this connection, Kathleen Araújo, Editor of the Routledge Series "Studies in Energy Transitions," has been a precious consultant in steering the book project in a fruitful direction. Her questions and comments helped us to clarify our intentions and ideas.

The *Institute for Technology Assessment and Systems Analysis* (ITAS) provided financial support for this book project, for which we are also grateful. Mira Klemm provided tremendous support to the editors, especially during the phase of writing the book proposal. Michael Wilson's work on editing the individual contributions has been invaluable to us. With the right balance of pragmatism and accuracy, he polished the language to an extent that jargon is avoided and readability is greatly improved. It goes without saying that any remaining mistakes are our own responsibility.

1 Introduction

Christian Büscher, Jens Schippl, and Patrick Sumpf

Energy transitions as an interdisciplinary problem

In modern society, all human activities rely on energy. Considerable technical and organizational means are directed toward finding sources of energy and providing the continuous allocation of useful energy in mechanical, chemical, or nuclear form. In its original physical meaning, energy enables life, but only temporarily if there is no moment-to-moment provision of utilizable *exergy* (in distinction to nonutilizable *anergy*).[1] The exponential growth of human activities within our planetary sphere is predicated upon the provision, transportation, distribution, and consumption of energy (White 1943; Fouquet 2016). Along this energy supply chain, the irreversible devaluation of (mostly) carbon-based fossil energy resources has sped up dramatically in the last centuries (Fouquet 2009), amounting to 575 quadrillion British thermal units (Btu)[2] worldwide in 2015, according to the International Energy Outlook (IEO 2017). At the same time, the World Energy Outlook (IEA 2017, 4) summarizes: "The world's consumers are not yet ready to say goodbye to the era of oil."

There is a consensus among the majority of scientists that this development causes a change in the climate system that endangers human and other habitats.[3] There is also a consensus that, in order to combat this development, the way in which society metabolizes energy must change with regard to the entire energy complex. As a consequence, energy transitions around the world have been triggered as multilayered, sociotechnical transformation projects that challenge established patterns of technology, business operation, and behavior. The capacity to use renewable energy sources (RES) is widely considered as the new key technology, which provides a major solution to society's manifold problems from our current energy supply, e.g., CO_2 emissions, resource scarcity, dangerous technology, and hazardous waste. The current world energy outlook demonstrates the widespread implementation of RES and the speed of its penetration, even though the dominance of carbon-based fuels still seems to be unbroken (see Figure 1.1).

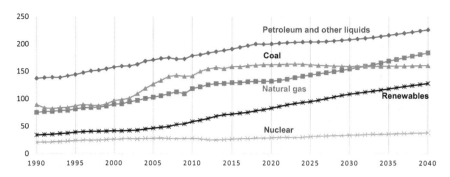

Figure 1.1 World energy consumption by energy source (in quadrillion Btu, history and projections)

Source: (IEO 2017)

In order to gain an understanding of societal transitions and the large-scale diffusion of new technologies, it is not sufficient to turn only to the natural and engineering sciences. The social sciences have generated a great deal of knowledge about the development, innovation, design, diffusion, and usage of technology, as well as about the influence of society on technology and of technology's influence on societal development. As a consequence, the description and analysis of energy transitions as "sociotechnical systems" that include both technical and social elements have become established as a frequent reference point for scholars in this research area. Yet the far-reaching implications of sociotechnical concepts and their inferences for interdisciplinary research involving the social and technical disciplines have rarely been systematically analyzed in the community.

The idea of viewing *energy as a sociotechnical problem* alleviates this gap in research by offering a unique approach to interdisciplinarity aimed at easing the friction encountered in multidisciplinary cooperation, even when it is commonly performed. Instead of employing complementary views, which emphasize definitions shared by different disciplines, we try to achieve a cognitive integration of various disciplines by means of focusing on reference problems in three analytical dimensions: *control, change,* and *action*. By reference problems we do not mean research difficulties (e.g., of a methodological nature), but rather "productive" problems which – in the sense of Bachelard (2002, 25) – precede research and which as such are the cause for research. Consequently, sociotechnical problems are understood as distinct *nuclei* to which disciplinary perspectives are related and subsequently unfold, while possibly maintaining theories and methods that are distinct to respective disciplines.[4] Sociotechnical problems (control, change, and action) are historically invariant, while their manifold solutions are contingent and variable. We will extend this core discussion in the following section.

Existing concepts of sociotechnical systems highlight the multiple, varying relations between heterogeneous elements, which indicates a high level of "organized complexity" (La Porte 2015). In energy transitions, complexity is all-embracing: Different types of power plants (for both conventional and renewable energy sources) are connected to the network by transmission lines, a distribution infrastructure, and smart devices. Moreover, different actors, such as companies, officials, communities, groups, and private persons, are interrelated through rules, contracts, markets, and regulations, alluding to the importance of *institutions* (Fuenfschilling and Truffer 2014; Smith, Stirling, and Berkhout 2005; Carlsson and Stankiewicz 1991, 109). In the multilevel perspective (MLP), the regime (as opposed to niche and landscape) determines social relations by virtue of institutionalized expectations, such as the cognitive rules of scientific observation, agreed upon knowledge, established technical paradigms, and belief systems (Geels 2004, 910; Smith, Stirling, and Berkhout 2005, 1508). In this sense, stable structures and institutions are necessary features of social life, especially in transition periods, providing orientation and enabling action.

In practical terms, the reality of sociotechnical energy systems has long attracted attention with regard to smart grids, energy cooperatives, and electric mobility schemes, for instance. In smart energy grids (or visions thereof), the components are frequently grasped as *cybernetic*, encompassing both humans and technology in an interwoven, all-embracing network. This is particularly visible in conceptions of "prosumers" (producing and consuming energy simultaneously), which emphasize the crucial role of the customer in smart grid designs. Another sociotechnical element in energy systems are (local) cooperatives, which are founded on the decentralized nature of RES-based systems. This involves questions of both system structure and power between bigger, often more centralized players, on the one hand, and challenging, often publicly or citizen-shared cooperatives, on the other. Questions of multilevel governance between larger and smaller energy policy units or issues of affordability, ownership, and energy poverty play along energy cooperative research as well. Finally, one could allude to electric mobility as a sociotechnical development in the transport sector, establishing social innovations (like car sharing) that determine to a large degree how the technology (e.g., electric battery-powered vehicles) is received, especially in an urban context.

In this sociotechnical conglomerate of different actors and components of future energy systems, challenges arise with regard to (a) identifying the relevant knowledge and (b) policy making. With reference to knowledge, one could ask to what extent current empirical trends such as smart grids, energy cooperatives, or electric mobility change the relevant knowledge and data we need to properly assess the dynamics in the field. In smart grids, domains such as engineering, computer science, and social science merge into a new hybrid field some call "energy informatics,"[5] creating new demand for research and university positions. Others wonder if the underlying scenarios combine the right knowledge to make the energy transition happen and speak of a "complexity trap" obstructing its realization (Appelrath, Kagermann, and Mayer 2012). This leads us directly to the second item, which inquires as to the policy-making capacities under these circumstances. Todd R. La Porte has brought up the "unknown knowns"[6] of an emerging technology field such as energy transitions, referring to knowledge which might be known among key players in the field, yet not in the regulatory community. The current situation of uncertainty and reconfiguration in the energy community is likely to embody such a situation, leading to an urgent need for novel types of knowledge management as well as of policy approaches.

These challenges have been tackled by (1) academic research, (2) interdisciplinary research alliances, and (3) universities reacting to the changing environment.

(1) *Academic research:* In recent decades, a vibrant scene of social science and humanities research (SSH) has evolved, tackling a variety of problems left unnoticed by the fields of science, technology, engineering, and mathematics (STEM), including computer science. Regarding SSH research, there is a large body of work to be found from historians, sociologists, economists, or political scientists, among others. While many approaches refer to the relationship between social and technical realities as well as its dynamics and political implications, they emphasize different problems and use dissimilar theories and methods. One of the most dominant research branches is concerned with the transition of one system to another or transformations of existing systems. We can find different attempts to systematize the field, for example, by clarifying the distinct notions of transition and transformation (Child and Breyer 2017), as an overview of definitions, theoretical premises, and methods (Sovacool and Hess 2017), or by evaluating opportunities for interdisciplinary research (Geels, Berkhout, and van Vuuren 2016). Apart from that, many other topics find their way into the view of SSH activities, like research on innovation and the diffusion of technology in society and on the consequences of digitalization such as data safety and privacy, as well as hazard research concerned with the vulnerability and resilience of sociotechnical systems, and economic studies on safeguarding critical transactions in societal infrastructures. Additionally, we find philosophers exploring normative concepts of value design in infrastructure planning, or psychologists looking into the cognitive heuristics of individual persons and their energy behavior. As this is only the tip of the iceberg,[7] many approaches will be mentioned and discussed in the various contributions of this book.

(2) *Interdisciplinary research alliances:* In terms of integrative research alliances targeting sociotechnical change in the energy field, three examples shall be mentioned here. The first is ENERGY-TRANS,[8] a German social science research alliance on energy transitions with the self-declared goal to "investigate the systemic interactions between technology, organization, and behavior in Germany within a European and international context. The research team investigates the interfaces between technical and societal factors that significantly influence the prospects for the envisioned transformation process."[9] A second example moved in a similar direction and was established in Finland: EL-TRAN. "We welcome this initial vision. However, we suggest that Finland lacks a full comprehension of what resource efficiency entails in the context of this transition, what complex policy problems such a society-wide energy transition will involve and generate, and how to respond to them."[10] The alliances' goal is to find these responses, under inclusion of

"societal significance and impact." A third example is the EU-funded project SHAPE ENERGY: "Specifically, it represents a new European platform for energy-related social sciences and humanities (energy-SSH). Energy-SSH has played less of a role to date in shaping (European) energy policy than Science, Technology, Engineering, and Mathematics (STEM) disciplines. In funding this project, the European Commission is supporting better integration of energy-SSH into the policy process."[11]

(3) *Response of universities:* Energy research centers around the world have established interdisciplinary units, not only across the engineering sciences, but also between the SSH disciplines on the one hand and the engineering sciences on the other. The research centers of leading universities have already recognized this need for interdisciplinarity in the energy domain, e.g., Energy Policy Research Group (Cambridge); the Energy Institute (Melbourne University); the Energy and Resources Group (Berkeley); the Sustainable Energy Initiative in the Graduate School of Business, the Precourt Energy Efficiency Center, and the Program on Energy and Sustainable Development (Stanford); the Andlinger Center for Energy and the Environment (Princeton); the Energy Change Institute (Australian National University); the Consortium for Energy Policy Research and Energy Technology Innovation Policy (Harvard); or the Institute of Environment, Energy and Sustainability (at the Chinese University of Hong Kong), just to name a few. Additionally, a complementary trend can be found at some of the most forward-looking technical universities in the US and Europe. Increasingly, they offer multidisciplinary energy minors and undergraduate certificates to all engineering students.

All in all, what is common to all these strands of literature, research alliances, and universities is an understanding of energy as a sociotechnical phenomenon as well as recognition of the ensuing need for *interdisciplinary* comprehension and analysis of energy transitions.

Sociotechnical problems

Understanding sociotechnical processes of change in the energy sector cannot be based on a single perspective or scientific discipline, since far too many different technical and nontechnical factors are involved. Instead, different kinds of knowledge need to be brought together in a meaningful way. However, interdisciplinarity is as much a serious ambition as it is an unfulfilled promise in the current landscape of energy research. The desire to bring researchers of different backgrounds, preferably technical and social, together in new constellations is clearly detectable and constitutes an attempt to work on the problems that the energy transitions have evoked. Yet at the same time, the recipes applied in interdisciplinary contexts frequently lag behind the ambitious goals of participating disciplines, such as to harmonize various researchers' approaches and methods. Our observation is that all too often the energy system is taken apart into its elements and relations, just to attribute certain ensuing responsibilities to different academic disciplines. Engineers perform a modeling calculation of energy demand in a certain region, while sociologists take care of acceptance problems in that neighborhood. Psychologists could figure out the motivations leading to current behavior and find ways to reprogram users accordingly, while economists analyze corresponding incentives. Designers would then help to build appliances and interfaces embodying preferred values, and so on. By decomposing a system like energy in this way, marking clear boundaries for disciplines and their area of expertise, disciplinary gaps are more likely to be widened than lessened. The reason is that in such constellations disciplines tend to overstretch their reach in the overarching research alliance, overburdening their partners with limited perspectives on the matter, preset definitions, theories, terms, and methods. This may result in the hardening of prior gaps and lead only to minor successes that rely on individuals getting along well and potentially giving up scientific positions, causing a stressful tit-for-tat game rich in conflict and disappointment. The likely results of such endeavors are *complementary* views of the energy system.

Our view of the outcome of this rather typical, "interdisciplinary" setting is not a decomposition of energy into elements and relations, but into *problems*, more precisely into *research problems*. The advantage offered by research problems compared to common definitions is that it frees researchers from the need to reach a consensus and opens up avenues to define commonly shared problems instead. These ought to be abstract enough for scholars from the natural, engineering, and social sciences to relate to from their own perspectives. This is exactly why we need to look at the discovery of *sociotechnical* (research) problems, encompassing both technical and social research complexities. As inspiration, we draw on the historian Edwards (2004, 209), who has characterized modern infrastructures as a "linked series of sociotechnical problems." To develop large technical infrastructure systems (Hughes 1987; Mayntz 2009), scientists, engineers, and other scholars have constantly found new solutions to technical and organizational problems. However, these solutions have simultaneously generated new problems in the field. The introduction and implementation of RES in the last decades, for instance, have occurred to replace carbon-dependent energy provision. That fact in itself has created new challenges, notably, for the storage and transportation of electricity, for the coordination of various economic, political, or scientific actors, and for their power relations, as well as for legislative and administrative decision making regarding the installation of the corresponding infrastructures (power plants, physical networks). In this sense, the introduction and implementation of RES have caused cascading problems for multidisciplinary researchers to discover and evaluate.

This idea of *energy as a sociotechnical problem* offers a unique approach for integrative research aimed at easing the friction found in commonly performed interdisciplinary cooperation. Instead of just complementary views, we try to achieve a cognitive integration of various disciplines by utilizing reference problems in three analytical dimensions. In the first dimension we ask how *control* can be maintained despite increasing complexity. In the second dimension

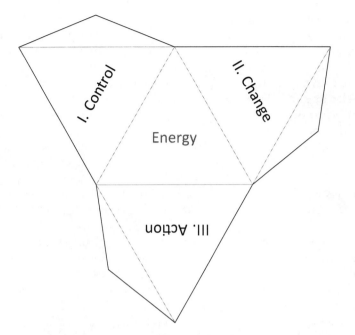

Figure 1.2 Analytical dimensions of sociotechnical problems[12]

we ask how *change* is possible despite the need for a stable orientation. In addition to these well acknowledged research problems, we ask in the third dimension how *action* is sustained despite overwhelming nontransparency. In this sense, we attempt to understand the ongoing transformation of energy systems as a multidimensional process in which the analytical dimensions interact with one another in shaping the energy future. We propose decomposing the whole energy complex into analytical dimensions, as is displayed in Figure 1.2. Folded together, this tetrahedron embodies factual, temporal, and social aspects of the fascinating issue of "energy".

Each of the contributions in Parts I–III of this book highlights specific problems and solutions in one of the three dimensions (not without regard to the other two). In this way, the book as a whole exposes an innovative pathway of analyzing large-scale and dynamic sociotechnical phenomena. Accordingly, the specific characteristics of sociotechnical problems in terms of control, change, and action are:

- They cannot be reduced to the merely technical or strictly social properties of the energy complex;
- They cannot be entirely and definitely solved, and therefore;
- They need to be addressed constantly, again and again, from one period of time to the next.

Overall, this means that issues of sustainment (operating now, tomorrow, and next year) have to be analyzed alongside the issue of sustainability (operating in the next decades for future generations). In any case, policy recommendations have to take into account these peculiarities of long-lasting, large-scale, and dynamic transformations of infrastructures.

In conclusion, sociotechnical problems, and not definitions, serve as reference points for interdisciplinary research. In this book, we bring together different scholars who utilize their theories and methods to contribute to the overall picture of the energy complex.

Authors and chapters

At the beginning, the sociologist Christian Büscher explores the different dimensions of sociotechnical problems by deriving them from the analytical dimension of social meaning (factual, temporal, and social). With the help of social systems theory, he discusses the provision, transportation, distribution, and consumption of energy as a real-time operating complex where different technical and social systems contribute in order to solve sociotechnical problems. Consequently, the goal of this chapter is to expose in depth the cross-cutting sociotechnical problems of *control despite increasing complexity, change in terms of the balance of variety and redundancy,* and *actionability in the face of nontransparency* in a prototypical manner, while aligning these problems with foreseeable changes in the energy realm. In this sense, these discussions provide the structure for the following main parts of the book, each corresponding to a respective dimension.

Part I. Control dimension

The authors concentrate on questions of control in the face of increasing complexity. First, the engineers Wolfgang Kröger and Cen Nan analyze issues of control such as highly dynamic and nonlinear behavior, potential regime shifts, and cascades within and among systems with pathways spreading for disaster. These problems pose significant challenges for operators of large technical systems, especially if the interaction of technical and social variables is further enhanced by introducing more and more smart technology in the realm of energy. Concepts like "vulnerability" and "resilience" are discussed and attempts made to find answers on how to cope with complexity and how to develop principles, as opposed to current practice/strategies (Chap. 3). *Second,* the economist Rolf W. Künneke presents an approach for analyzing the necessary social settings to control critical transactions in energy production, transportation, distribution, and consumption. The basic thesis of the author is that different needs for coordination in the alignment of technical and social operations have to be fulfilled by appropriate social mechanisms. He discusses these needs and solutions in order to safeguard the expected performance of the energy infrastructure (Chap. 4). *Finally,* the economist Marcus Wiens, the engineer Wolfgang Raskob, and their multidisciplinary team of Florian Diehlmann, Stefan Wandler, and Frank Schultmann explore the problems posed by exogenous threats (earthquakes, storms, or flooding) to modern decentralized infrastructures, such as the energy supply, and the means for assessing them. Additionally, the authors take on the task of comparing two vital infrastructures in terms of endogenous hazards, namely energy and finance (Chap. 5).

Part II. Change dimension

This part of the book sheds light on the sociotechnical problem posed by changes in the energy complex where stable orientations (e.g., for institutions) and learning capacities (e.g., for niche developments or experiments) must be analyzed in relation to each other. *First*, the sociologist Matthias Gross highlights the role of "real world experiments," which provide the necessary means for acquiring new knowledge about the interplay between technical innovation and changing individual behavior or organizational reprogramming. He is especially interested in the effects of the inevitable nonknowledge (i.e. ignorance) and surprise, and investigates creative strategies for coping with failures in technical or regulatory designs in the course of the energy transition (Chap. 6). *Second*, the sociologist Gerhard Fuchs considers learning processes and "disruptive innovation" in energy transitions. In doing so, he asks which mechanisms constitute the condition for the emergence of new parties in specific sociotechnical fields, and how these mechanisms can instigate technical and social innovation despite resilient factors in established regimes (Chap. 7). *Third*, the multidisciplinary team of Audley Genus, Marfuga Iskandarova, and Leigh Champagnie present a discourse-institutional approach to transforming energy systems. In particular, they point at the role that language and nondiscursive phenomena play in the constitution of institutions in the context of transition processes. They are especially interested in discursive ways of introducing new organizational forms and energy generation/consumption practices that still have to be legitimized – unlike already established ones (Chap. 8).

Part III. Action dimension

The third part of the book outlines the sociotechnical problem of action, e.g., the ability to sustain the capacity for action despite the increasing nontransparency caused by the changes in the overall energy system design, such as new technology, digitalization, and the burdensome demands placed on a changing lifestyle to achieve more sustainable behavior. *First*, the sociologist Patrick Sumpf introduces the concept of system trust as a vital mechanism for the active participation of "prosumers" in future "smart" energy infrastructures. He draws on the idea that a successful transition requires attention to trust in public, organizational, and transsystemic constellations since there will be different trust relations between service providers and consumers, as well as between organizations involved in the operations of the energy complex. Additionally, he alludes to the positive functions of distrust and the risk of increasing investments in trust (Chap. 9). *Second*,

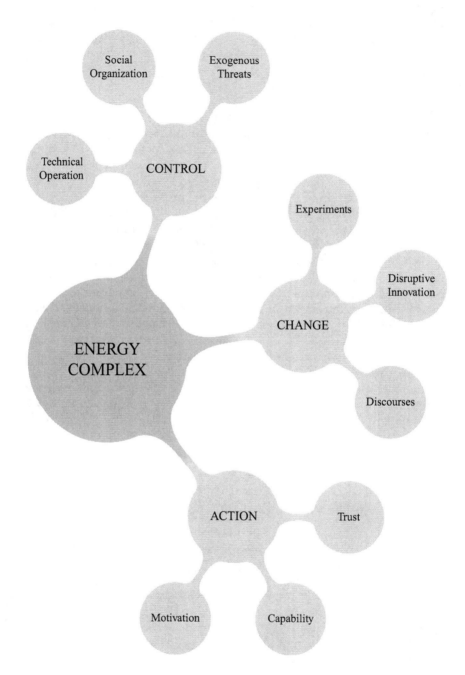

Figure 1.3 Book structure along the three dimensions of control, change, and action

the physicist and philosopher Rafaela Hillerbrand hints at the normative design aspects of future smart grids in order to increase the "capability" of various actors. By not only looking at technical design aspects, the author provides an analysis of the accompanying social innovations. She explores the function of these with regard to how they support us in dealing with uncertainty and nonknowledge in the energy transition, especially in regard to normative considerations. She argues that such innovations are necessary because they provide the framework for stakeholder participation and thus ensure a minimum of procedural justice (Chap. 10). *Third*, the psychologists Siegmar Otto and Inga Wittenberg present an insight into the problem of *motivation* regarding the adoption of new technologies and energy-saving behavior despite various hurdles in the form of "convenience overtures" that render behavioral changes unlikely. They especially look at the long-term possibilities that "education" might offer regarding the generalized shift in individual energy-saving demeanor and thus on slowing down human activities (Chap. 11).

The addendum of the book provides reflections on methodological problems in tackling a research phenomenon of the magnitude of energy transitions. The political scientist and organization researcher Todd R. La Porte reflects on problems of scientific observation of amplified complexity as is the case of the German *Energiewende*. He offers hints at how to control and manage scholarly observation in this case (Chap. 12). Finally, the editors of the book evaluate the fruitfulness of the proposed concept of sociotechnical problems for interdisciplinary research and discuss the ensuing options for policy making (Chap. 13).

The overall structure of the book is visualized in Figure 1.3. This "mindmap" is not an attempt to generate an ontology of sociotechnical problems because it shows only selective research topics. However, if someone develops the urge to do so, this might be a feasible starting point.

Notes

1 *Exergy* is energy transferable into work. *Anergy* equals all energy that is not exergy. The notion of "using" energy actually refers to *devaluation* as the irreversible process of turning *exergy* into *anergy* by energy transport (heat, work, mass) (Wenterodt and Herwig 2014).
2 The number of 575 quadrillion Btu (US based short scale calculation) equals an estimated 1.68×10^{14} kWh. It includes energy generation from all sources, conventional and renewable.
3 See as a source of confirmation: "Scientific consensus: Earth's climate is warming." https://climate.nasa.gov/scientific-consensus/. Accessed 2018/03/21.
4 See, for further inspiration, Luhmann (1994, 459). The author emphasizes the need for commonly shared "paradigms" in transdisciplinary research.
5 See, for instance, the following initiative: www.energieinformatik2018.org/. Accessed 2018/03/21.
6 See the contribution by Todd R. La Porte in this book for some further insights.
7 See for an extended list of research branches in SSH: Annotated Bibliographies of the SHAPE ENERGY platform. https://shapeenergy.eu/index.php/publications/annotated-bibliographies/. Accessed 2018/03/27.

8 The editors of this book worked in ENERGY-TRANS themselves. In the project, we established a working group on analysis of sociotechnical systems that tried to extract system understandings of subprojects. In addition, we learned valuable lessons on interdisciplinarity, which fed largely into the concept of this book.
9 See www.energy-trans.de/english/index.php. Accessed 2018/03/27.
10 https://eltranfi.files.wordpress.com/2016/01/stn-research-plan-public.pdf. Accessed 2018/03/18.
11 See https://shapeenergy.eu/index.php/about/. Accessed 2018/03/18.
12 See for in depth elaboration on these dimensions the contribution by Christian Büscher: "Framing Energy as a Sociotechnical Problem of Control, Change, and Action".

References

Appelrath, Hans-Jürgen, Henning Kagermann, and Christoph Mayer, eds. 2012. *Future Energy Grid. Migration to the Internet of Energy. Acatech STUDY*. Munich.
Bachelard, Gaston. 2002. *The Formation of the Scientific Mind: A Contribution to a Psychoanalysis of Objective Knowledge*. Repr. Philosophy of Science. Manchester: Clinamen.
Carlsson, Bo, and Rikard Stankiewicz. 1991. "On the Nature, Function and Composition of Technological Systems." *Journal of Evolutionary Economics* 1 (2): 93–118. https://doi.org/10.1007/BF01224915.
Child, Michael, and Christian Breyer. 2017. "Transition and Transformation: A Review of the Concept of Change in the Progress towards Future Sustainable Energy Systems." *Energy Policy* 107 (August): 11–26. https://doi.org/10.1016/j.enpol.2017.04.022.
Edwards, Paul N. 2004. "Infrastructure and Modernity: Force, Time, and Social Organization in the History of Socio-Technical Systems." In *Modernity and Technology*, edited by Thomas J. Misa, Philip Brey, and Andrew Feenberg, 185–225. Cambridge, London: MIT Press.
Fouquet, Roger. 2009. "A Brief History of Energy." In *International Handbook on the Economics of Energy*. Cheltenham, UK; Northampton, MA: Edward Elgar.
———. 2016. "Historical Energy Transitions: Speed, Prices and System Transformation." *Energy Research & Social Science* 22 (December): 7–12. https://doi.org/10.1016/j.erss.2016.08.014.
Fuenfschilling, Lea, and Bernhard Truffer. 2014. "The Structuration of Socio-Technical Regimes – Conceptual Foundations from Institutional Theory." *Research Policy* 43 (4): 772–91. https://doi.org/10.1016/j.respol.2013.10.010.
Geels, Frank W. 2004. "From Sectoral Systems of Innovation to Socio-Technical Systems: Insights about Dynamics and Change from Sociology and Institutional Theory." *Research Policy* 33 (6–7): 897–920. https://doi.org/10.1016/j.respol.2004.01.015.
Geels, Frank W., Frans Berkhout, and Detlef P. van Vuuren. 2016. "Bridging Analytical Approaches for Low-Carbon Transitions." *Nature Climate Change* 6 (6): 576–83. https://doi.org/10.1038/nclimate2980.
Hughes, Thomas P. 1987. "The Evolution of Large Technological Systems." In *The Social Construction of Technological Systems: New Directions in the Sociology and History of Technology*, edited by Wiebe E. Bijker, Thomas Parke Hughes, and Trevor J. Pinch, 51–82. Cambridge, MA: MIT Press.
IEA. 2017. World Energy Outlook 2017 (Executive Summary)." Paris: International Energy Agency (IEA). www.iea.org/publications/freepublications/publication/WEO_2017_Executive_Summary_English_version.pdf. Accessed 2018/05/07.

IEO. 2017. "International Energy Outlook 2016-Executive Summary – Energy Information Administration." DOE/EIA-0484(2017). Washington, DC: International Energy Outlook, U.S. Energy Information Administration. www.eia.gov/outlooks/ieo/exec_summ.php. Accessed 2018/05/07.

La Porte, Todd R. 2015. *Organized Social Complexity: Challenge to Politics and Policy*. 2nd ed. Princeton Legacy Library. Princeton, NJ: Princeton University Press.

Luhmann, Niklas. 1994. *Die Wissenschaft der Gesellschaft*. 2nd ed. Frankfurt am Main: Suhrkamp.

Mayntz, Renate. 2009. "The Changing Governance of Large Technical Infrastructure Systems." In *Über Governance. Institutionen und Prozesse politischer Regelung*, 121–50. Schriften aus dem Max-Planck-Institut für Gesellschaftsforschung, Band 62. Frankfurt am Main, New York: Campus.

Smith, Adrian, Andy Stirling, and Frans Berkhout. 2005. "The Governance of Sustainable Socio-Technical Transitions." *Research Policy* 34 (10): 1491–510. https://doi.org/10.1016/j.respol.2005.07.005.

Sovacool, Benjamin K., and David J. Hess. 2017. "Ordering Theories: Typologies and Conceptual Frameworks for Sociotechnical Change." *Social Studies of Science* 47 (5): 703–50. https://doi.org/10.1177/0306312717709363.

Wenterodt, Tammo, and Heinz Herwig. 2014. "The Entropic Potential Concept: A New Way to Look at Energy Transfer Operations." *Entropy* 16 (4): 2071–84. https://doi.org/10.3390/e16042071.

White, Leslie A. 1943. "Energy and the Evolution of Culture." *American Anthropologist* 45 (3): 335–56. https://doi.org/10.1525/aa.1943.45.3.02a00010.

2 Framing energy as a sociotechnical problem of control, change, and action

Christian Büscher

Introduction

The ways of providing energy have changed profoundly in recent decades. Depicted at times as drastic turnarounds – such as with China's "pan-Asia" approach to renewable energy, the (in flux) "Clean Power Plan" in the US, or the German "Energiewende" – political programs worldwide are attempting to foster the development and implementation of technical systems which are able to exploit renewable energy sources (RES).[1] The ongoing process is commonly characterized as the transformation of an existing and currently operating system (Bolton and Foxon 2015; Fouquet 2016) or as the transition from one system to another (de Haan and Rotmans 2011; Geels 2014).

Energy transition programs carry the optimistic expectation of fabricating solutions for a society's energy problems, such as the unsustainable consumption of fossil fuels, increasing CO_2 emissions, and the reliance on dangerous technologies (e.g., nuclear power plants or, as some argue, "fracking"). Grin et al. (2010, 2f.) argue that these fatal trajectories take on the characteristic of "persistent problems," deeply embedded in the structure of social systems. On a more uplifting note, persistent problems are at the same time a cause for innovative practices and structural adaptation leading to system innovation and transitions as a possible *resolution* for those problems. However, the constantly evolving complex of energy provision, as we observe it right now, produces solutions for problems and these "successes" simultaneously generate new problems (Schuitmaker 2012, 1023). Just consider how the introduction and implementation of RES during the last decades has partly replaced carbon-dependent energy provision *and* brought about new challenges for storage and transportation (e.g., for electricity), for the organization of production (market interaction, regulation), and for legislative decision making regarding the installation of corresponding infrastructures (power plants, physical networks, etc.).

The historian Paul N. Edwards argues in the same vein as he depicts large infrastructures not only as solutions for societal problems, but as constant challenges: "The overall [socio-technical] system can be fruitfully described as posing a linked series of socio-technical problems" (Edwards 2004, 209). His argument points in the direction of problems which

- cannot be reduced to either technical or social properties,
- cannot be solved permanently, and
- need to be addressed continuously, i.e., now, tomorrow, next year, and – if we think about "sustainability" – in the coming decades (spanning generations).

In this chapter, the goal is to extend Edwards' idea. For this, multiple dimensions[2] are chosen to highlight specific aspects of the ongoing transition and compare these problems to determine why transition processes reinforce and change the nature of these problems. Existing research from science, technology, and society studies (STS), large technical systems theory (LTS), systems theory, transition, and innovation research, among others, offers a rich body of literature to (tentatively) extract, differentiate, and reduce the many issues to core sociotechnical problems:

The *control* dimension refers to the increasingly complex interaction between technical and social elements, e.g., physical installations and networks with social organization, and the ensuing quest for maintaining control to achieve features such as predictability, security, safety, and efficiency. The *change* dimension focuses on generally shared expectations, e.g., institutions where distinct observers (e.g., actors, parties, persons, agents, and stakeholders) find mutual orientation, and where change is imposed upon or is enacted by the activities of all those involved. The *action* dimension stresses the necessity of making decisions despite the problem of uncertainty and risk. This dimension is especially affected by the consequences of energy transitions because the ensuing structural complexity and institutional change increases nontransparency and challenges our ability to act.

All three dimensions represent – simultaneously – sociotechnical reality in the energy complex. In this sense, they are meant as an analytical heuristic. To this end, they make it possible to emphasize certain aspects which can be exposed and compared to each other.

Table 2.1 Overview of the distinctive problem dimensions

problem dimension	emphasis of	
CONTROL	Structural Aspects	**Relations** of Heterogeneous Elements
CHANGE	Institutional Aspects	**Generalization/(Re) Stabilization** of Social Orientation
ACTION	Operational Aspects	**Absorption of Uncertainty** to Act/Make Decisions

Source: CB

With this multidimensional approach, the perspective of contingency, uncertainty, and risk will be strengthened in order to complement recent research on energy transitions that mostly emphasizes the issues of control and change. The sociotechnical reality as it is unfolding right now in the energy domain entails complicated and complex systems which are subject to change. This enforces the experience of contingency, which has to be contained and absorbed to sustain desired functions and services.[3]

The problem of control

Structures as chains of technical and social events

The notion of a sociotechnical system has been utilized to describe the planned, intended interaction of technical and social elements in order to fulfill specific purposes (Hughes 1983, 5). To perform the intended and planned functions, all the technical and social operations must align "seamlessly" within the system. The medium of technology, as Beckman (1994, 320) argues, is instrumentality in the sense of operative principles of human-led activities. While the form of technology is dependent on the ingenuity of science and engineering, the operative principles are limited to (1) *conservation* (organization to keep from change), (2) *transformation* (organization to enforce change), (3) *storage* (keeping from change of localization), and (4) *transmission* (enforcing change of localization). In complicated technical systems all the principles come into effect simultaneously.

System designers implement the corresponding structures to achieve control of technical operation and social activities, as well as of the interaction of both, specifically to align the actual behavior of a system to its intended behavior (Nightingale et al. 2003, 484). From this point of departure, the term "structure" does not refer to material representations, but rather to the *expectability of events*. Therefore, controlling is observation of the actuality and potentiality of system operation and the corresponding manipulation of operation. The operations involved in controlling are themselves part of the system. For sociotechnical entities, control is dependent on organizational and behavioral patterns. In the early stages of the evolution of electrical power grids, for example, control was the major problem when further rationalization/optimization had to be enforced (Hughes 1983, 367). To achieve economically effective operation, the optimization of the "economic mix" meant aligning physical structures and machine operation with more and more elaborate means of the social organization of production in order to manipulate the system's load factor. This development has been accelerated in recent decades with new means of accessing energy sources. After decades of a few companies operating large, centralized power plant facilities (coal, gas, and nuclear) with a steady output, manifold investors are installing small, decentralized plants that rely on renewable, but volatile, power (Bruns et al. 2010).

Control of complex structures

In the quest for achieving the most economically effective system architecture, system traffic needs to be allocated. Production, and also the control of production, is treated as frequency, i.e., as a chain of events: *a* causes *b*; and *c* controls if *b* is the desired outcome; if not, then *c* actuates *d* to modify *a* to cause *b'*; etc. With modern production technology and electronic data processing, these events happen in complicated chains and in time spans measured in microseconds (Amin 2001, 23). Human cognition can no longer follow this; hence we need complicated models of the system's reality.[4] The physical and organizational structures of a system jointly determine the input – output function and, subsequently, the actual operation. The capacity utilization changes from moment to moment (between full on – idle – full off), as does the internal state, the "load factor," which has to be optimized again and again (see Table 2.2).

The match between potential and actual performance depends on various factors (Nightingale et al. 2003, 486f.).

- The *accuracy* of control: Where more is desired but costly and time-consuming, less accurate models are chosen.
- The *speed of calculation*: If internal states change while control calculates feedback, lags can cause system oscillations and potential failure, thereby reducing the speed of production.
- The balance between local and global control.
- The trade-off between *reliability* and *safety* (Leveson et al. 2009): Control is critical to business, while propagating failures may lead to accidents or catastrophes.

Consequently, social settings for safeguarding critical functions are needed: organization of the supervision (to meter, compare, compensate, and actuate) of operation; the coordination of activities; the limitation of access to the system or network; and turning on or shutting down facilities connected to the overall system (Künneke, Groenewegen, and Ménard 2010, 499).[5] For different system settings, one needs different modes of direct intervention, coordination, and corroboration, to allow for a whole set of differentiated activities, as Künneke, Groenewegen, and Ménard (2010, 502) argue.[6]

Table 2.2 Constituents of system reproduction

SYSTEM	
Structure	Input–output relation
Operation	Capacity utilization (moment-to-moment)
Internal state	Load factor
Rationality	Optimization

Source: CB

The scope of control

The degree of control is vital for the reproduction of systems: "We will speak of production if *some* but *not all* causes that are necessary for specific effects can be employed under the control of a system" (Luhmann 1995, 20). The required degree of control varies significantly depending on the material, social, and temporal scope of a system. Edwards et al. (2007, 12) stress the fact that various technical units and social actors contribute to the functioning of large infrastructures. Control varies depending on the scaling of elements and the relation between elements. Fine-grained, local, and closed technical and social systems allow more control than coarse-grained, regional, and global networks of systems, networks of networks, or webs.

Control problems arise from various endogenous and exogenous changes. Mayntz offers a useful taxonomy for the problem of control in the tradition of large technical systems (LTS) theory. LTS are characterized as networks of heterogeneous technical and social components unified for the purpose of the wide-ranging, inclusive, and permanent provision of services (Mayntz 1993, 98). Mayntz distinguishes social processes from technical processes: the former delineate both the internal organization of work and external regulation, whereas the latter designate internal production/control (Mayntz 2009, 123f.). To complete the picture, we need to add the thesis of infrastructures enabling and/or impacting other infrastructures, and which are coupled with each other while both are changing. Then, we arrive at a simplified model with two variables, first the type of process and, second, the reference to system or environment (Table 2.3):

Table 2.3 Analytical categories for sociotechnical complexes

	ENERGY COMPLEX	
Type of process	SYSTEM(S)	ENVIRONMENT
TECHNICAL	Determination of production	Enabling/Impacting infrastructures
SOCIAL	Organization of production	Regulation/Governance

Source: adapted by CB, based on Mayntz (2009, 124)

With the help of these analytical categories we can now elaborate on some of the most prominent developments in these four categories in a systematic way. Each category highlights specific characteristics of sociotechnical problems in the factual dimension of complexity and control.

(1) *Changes in the determination of production*: Visions of "smart grids" represent a system transformation in favor of decentralized energy generation, which leads to an interwoven network of various energy sources, distributive structures, and storage capacities and which, significantly, requires active

consumers (Ramchurn et al. 2012). In the US and Europe, numerous projects evaluate opportunities to implement innovative technical components, such as digital controls; smart technologies for metering, communications, and automation; smart appliances and consumer devices; peak shaving technologies; and advanced storage technologies (Brown and Suryanarayanan 2009).

(2) *Changes in the organization of production and consumption*: Two-way communication between consumers and suppliers is made possible by smart meters and allows for innovative social arrangements such as new market mechanisms. Corresponding visions are about the widespread linking of households, commerce, and industry into an intelligent system of energy management, so as to improve efficiency, lower CO_2 emissions, and ensure the affordability of electricity (JRC 2011, 35ff.).

(3) *Changes in the regulation of production*: Liberalization of energy markets enforces changes in the regulation of production. The "unbundling" of functional subunits affects the organization of production, i.e., the degree of functional integration of LTS.[7] The proclaimed goal is to create markets and competition despite the obstructions of physical installations (power grids). Economists doubt whether this development will benefit the overall performance of the system (Künneke 2008, 239). Functional differentiation is successful if subunits operate with indifference to the needs of the superordinate system, as recent examples suggest. Many investors can fund renewable energy power plants because the technology is organized at a smaller scale and it is cheaper than coal, gas, or nuclear facilities. Also, the administrative procedure is easier and quicker. As such investments are not made with regard to the overall system performance, *regulative frames constantly require readjusting* in order to align partial interests to the needs of the global system.

(4) *Changes in enabling/impacting infrastructures*: Research on the interdependence of infrastructures investigates how sociotechnical entities enable or impact each other. In terms of progress, intelligent infrastructures are envisioned; in terms of vulnerability or resilience, systemic risks are anticipated. Interdependencies exist

- materially: network installations such as transportation routes with industrial production, or interconnections between different services (Roe and Schulman 2016);
- spatially, i.e., geographically: for example, in dense agglomerations (Büscher and Mascareño 2014; Kraas 2007; Perrow 2007); and
- electronically: e.g., SCADA systems which operate across different sociotechnical systems (Kröger 2017; Moteff, Copeland, and Fischer 2003; Perrow 2011).

A smart electricity system (JRC 2011) with connections to other infrastructures has been heralded as the convergence of infrastructures such as electricity with transportation and the world wide web (internet of everything).

In principle, the control problem remains the same in all these domains "since it is fundamentally indifferent to whether solutions come in the form of hardware, organizations, micro-scale user innovations, or some combination of these" (Edwards 2004, 207). It is only the means that change, providing the basis for advances in speed, volume, and the connectedness of data and information gathering and processing. The increased complexity will weaken the degree of control; the growing variation in the system will generate change (as will be discussed the following section); which increases the degree of opaque operation, and as a consequence, uncertainty in the action dimension (as will be discussed later).

The problem of change

Sustaining functions (redundancy) and enabling change (variety)

The transition from one system to another (or the transformation of a system during operation) implies changes while society is still dependent on the output and services of the system. Therefore, from a factual point of view, the problem is the functioning alignment of social and technical elements, as presented in the previous section. From a social point of view, considering the multitude of social actors, the problem is maintaining a high degree of stable orientation regarding which knowledge, laws, norms, rules, and values are valid in specific situations, or which output one can expect from technical operations. All this changes perpetually, either planned as "reform" or uncontrolled as sociotechnical "evolution."

Structural changes affect the way social actors find mutual orientation in the energy complex. Users expect energy that is reliable, safe, and affordable. This expectation is so deeply entrenched in the industrialized world that the preconditions for its realization come to the forefront only in the case of a failure or an accident. Transitions in energy supply, however, have been rather slow since the industrial revolution (Fouquet 2016). Especially in the carbon decades (the peak periods of extracting energy from coal, oil, or gas), the energy infrastructure was perceived as highly *redundant*. Energy transitions around the world have changed that perception. After decades of successfully deploying the means of energy services according to paradigms, the contingent character of these old paradigms has been exposed.

A system achieves a sharp distinction in complexity from its environment if it can isolate the necessary operations from all the other events which happen simultaneously. That makes redundant operating systems reliable. If transformations occur, and if the degree, scope, and speed of changes reaches an intense *variety*, then complexity is induced (Gallagher et al. 2012, 144). Stable orientations are then jeopardized and the self-organizing capacities of social systems are at stake. Atlan (1974, 300; italics added by CB) concludes:

A self-organizing system is a system redundant enough and functioning in such a way that it can sustain a *decrease in redundancy* under the effects of error-producing factors *without ceasing to function*. [. . .] Self-organization appears as a continuous disorganization constantly followed by reorganization with more complexity and less redundancy.

Both variety and redundancy are indispensable, but too much variety causes volatile, erratic behavior, while too much redundancy causes inertia, lock-ins, and path dependencies (which then sustain redundancy, again). Therefore, the reference problem in the dimension of change can be exposed in the paradoxical necessity to maintain orientation for manifold observers in the field while dramatically changing to become more sustainable.[8]

Transitions challenging high redundancy

Extensive research has tackled *redundancy* regarding stable configurations (Geels 2002), structures (Bolton and Foxon 2015), and institutions (de Haan and Rotmans 2011), on the one hand, and *variety* regarding processes of coevolution, structuration, and institutionalization, on the other hand.

The multilevel perspective (MLP), most prominently, addresses sociotechnical transitions as a relation between redundancy and variety caused by developments on three analytically distinct levels: regime, niche, and landscape (Geels 2004). The concept of regimes expresses the tight coupling of a multitude of actors and organizations, in networks of mutual dependencies, held together through formal and informal relations, such as contracts or trust. Regimes strongly condition social relations by means of institutionalized cognitive and normative expectations, such as cognitive rules of scientific observation, agreed knowledge, established technical paradigms, and belief systems (Geels 2004, 910). Most of all, a regime is reproduced by its constituents and their actions (Smith, Stirling, and Berkhout 2005, 1504). Once they have been established, structures, cultures, and practices function as institutions, for they limit the possibilities and the likelihood of actions (de Haan and Rotmans 2011, 92). These self-referential processes support redundancy and they limit variety.[9]

So the strength of a regime depends on the degree of institutionalization of core elements (Barley and Tolbert 1997, 96). Fuenfschilling and Truffer take a deeper look into different degrees of institutionalization in organizational fields. Competing *field logics* reflect modern society's functional differentiation (into, e.g., economics, politics, science, and law), as the respective field logics challenge each other while enforcing their decision rationales. Consequently, certain behavioral patterns of rather indifferent exploitation of opportunities congeal (Fuenfschilling and Truffer 2014, 776). Many recent studies focus on the *resilience* of sociotechnical constellations to transitions, transformations, and change. Geels, for example, exposes how large utilities in the UK exert political influence, dominate discourses, promise technologies that extend the lifetime of fossil-based energy generation, and activate networks of stakeholders to protect vested interests (Geels 2014). Sovacool refers to a "congealed culture" in the US-based energy infrastructure and claims that the dominant regime limits consumer choice regarding energy supply and therefore established habits and practices are perpetuated (Sovacool 2009). Similarly, Kungl reports that German utilities first exploited the liberalization process (unbundling), but afterwards attempted to block the market entrance of new players (Kungl 2015).

Inducing variety

In social science and humanities research on energy, we find a strong bias toward increasing the degree, scope, and speed of energy transitions. One main feature of transition research is the idea of purposeful transitions in the direction of sustainable development (Rohracher 2008; Verbong and Geels 2007). Scholars propose to unlearn, i.e., to "exnovate," common practices and knowledge in order to learn new ones (Gross and Mautz 2015, 4), to replace dominant "field logics" by more sustainable ones (Fuenfschilling and Truffer 2014), to destabilize regimes (Geels 2014), or to decrease resilience in some parts of the energy domain while increasing it in others (Strunz 2014).

From this point of departure, scholars try to develop strategies that induce more variety in the domains of energy generation, transportation, distribution, and consumption by fostering *niches* or *experiments*.[10] For example, Loorbach proposes three steps: First, readjusting expectation statements about sociotechnical development (including bold visions, long-term perspectives, and collectively shared goals and norms); second, tactically readjusting alternative political, economic, scientific, and legal agendas (including supporting technical innovation, subsidies, legal protection, etc.); and third, operative readjustments by establishing novel practices that have been tested and validated via real world experiments (Loorbach 2010). According to Gross and Mautz (2015, 140), this describes recent transitions: "Research on energy has increasingly turned society into a laboratory – one in which the energy user and non-scientist can potentially play an active part in the experiment."

While it is an intrinsic motivation of economic actors to create and to exploit business opportunities, the call for public policy to enforce change is loud and clear. Like many authors, Weber and Rohracher (2012, 1042) argue that if large sociotechnical infrastructures cannot foster enough variety to stimulate transitions, then state intervention and policy design for goal-oriented transitions is necessary. Lack of investment in research and development or in basic research and the lack of novel insights and inspiration have to be addressed as they pose legitimate access points for policy intervention.

Gallagher et al. highlight that shared or collective expectations can reduce uncertainty and catalyze innovative activity in certain domains.[11] Expectations help actors select technological alternatives from the variety created by knowledge generation activities. The authors also favor public policies for creating collective expectations and/or shaping societal preferences, such as energy efficiency or carbon mitigation (Gallagher et al. 2012, 143).

Balancing redundancy and variety: a functional view

Despite the need for change, stable orientations (such as rules, norms, and routines) are necessary to absorb uncertainty in a complex environment. Innovation research has recognized the functional necessity of absorbing uncertainties in order to realize "economic competence" and generate opportunities, to make educated guesses, maintain flexibility, and learn – in other words, to take risks. At the level of concrete activities in an innovative field or technological system, institutional arrangements are fundamental, be they trust between partners in informal networks, capital markets, fiscal policies, subsidies, insurances, or economic and technology information, or the regulation of markets and technology (Carlsson and Stankiewicz 1991).

Experimenting and learning, the capacity to adapt to change without knowing which future will come true, is often idealized (March and Olsen 1995, 199). However, learning poses many obstacles; it is demanding and risky. How is it possible in large-scale societal settings to control learning? As argued above, the degree of control varies considerably from systems to networks of systems, or networks of networks (i.e., webs). Then the problem posed by the loose and close coupling of experiments arises in order to protect the system from failures and allow for real learning processes. To control the transformation, a balance between tight experiment-reality couplings, which enable innovative, realistic, close-to-the-market benefits, and loose couplings, which disturb the system's operation as little as possible, is required. The right balance is particularly important in the context of critical infrastructures, where large-scale failures may have catastrophic consequences.

Also, what is the correct speed of learning? Recent discussions about transition resistance, regime resilience, and different levels of speed draw a picture of transitions that are slow, uneven, sometimes disruptive, and far from "seamless" (Fouquet 2016; Sovacool and Geels 2016). How to learn correctly? There is always the conflict between societal goals and the individual goals of persons, groups, and organizations. Also, how is it possible to sustain a learning process? March and Olsen, for example, expose "learning traps," where organizations tend to clamp on strategies that have proven successful in the past or to discard learning processes at the first sign of failure because of continuous negative experiences (March and Olsen 1995, 215ff.).

Most of all, it is not always clear who or what is learning/changing. In regard to persons, energy conserving behavior is discussed in terms of providing feedback on energy use, nudging one's intrinsic motivation to use less energy or to choose an alternative technology (Kaiser, Arnold, and Otto 2014).[12] In regard to roles, professional education and academic curricula come to mind where sustainable development issues are increasingly at the core of teaching and education in order to become a mainstream feature of a professional role description for engineers, politicians, and scientists, for instance (Truffer, Schippl, and Fleischer 2017, 5).

The most consequential organizational programs are the object of demands for low carbon economic activities, for sustainability supporting policies, for technical innovation research and development, etc. In the field of renewable energy technologies, Negro et al. address ongoing, continuous "systemic problems," namely problems concerning market structure, infrastructure, institutions, interaction, and capabilities, all of which (as problems) provoke further actions and stimulate system reproduction. Problems stimulate the search for new solutions and, because all solutions are themselves imperfect, create new problems (Negro, Alkemade, and Hekkert 2012, 3838). A striking feature in all these cases is the problem of too much variety, i.e., uncertainty: volatile developments in regulations and subsidies schemes, a shift in policy attention (technical system support changes), misalignment between policy levels, different sectors, and existing and new institutions, contradictory regulations, or lack of support in the most vulnerable times near market introduction (Negro, Alkemade, and Hekkert 2012, 3840).[13]

Like many others in the field, Negro et al. follow a "politics knows best" approach. Politicians are asked to provide the "right" conditions to stimulate the formation of new innovation systems, i.e., reliability, long-term planning and consistency, and flexibility should alternations be necessary (Negro, Alkemade, and Hekkert 2012, 3838).[14] In the field of energy research, there is hardly any debate regarding how politics achieves certainty and confidence on what technology to support, on what strategy to follow through, or when to alter existing regulations or innovation programs. Science might help, but it often instigates more uncertainty than not.

In general, social science research calls for novelty in energy technologies and organization as well as for regulation and smart interconnections to other infrastructures. However, many scholars systematically neglect to investigate the effects of uncertainty if the possible consequences of visions, strategies, or practices are not well known in advance (in terms of being successful regarding the envisioned goals). Moreover, it is necessary to ask how uncertainties will be absorbed in pursuing visions, choosing strategies, and deviating from routine practices. As Gross and Mautz argue, due to the inevitable nonknowledge about the success of the energy transitions, the social actors may be opposed to a learning experience, and such opposition would presumably prevent them from providing active support and involvement (Gross and Mautz 2015, 144).

The problem of balancing redundancy and variety cannot be solved for good, which is rather a continuous process that is carried by the countless actions of participating parties and that, simultaneously, stimulates those actions (coevolution and structural drift). All in all, all the involved actors in a field such as the energy complex experience changing situations molded by different degrees of variety/redundancy (see Table 2.4 for a synopsis). While redundancy, i.e., a stable orientation, allows for action, variety makes learning, innovating, and intelligent adaptation to new circumstances possible. From a global, systemic perspective, the normative goal of sustainability has to be accompanied by measures to ensure that current operation is *sustained*.

Table 2.4 Synopsis of redundancy and variety in sociotechnical complexes

		REDUNDANCY	
		High	*Low*
VARIETY	*High*	Learning organization, Regime-Niche Constellation	Experimental settings, emerging technology fields
	Low	Dominant regimes, path dependency, lock-ins	Low degree of organization

Source: CB

The problem of action

The temporal reality of sociotechnical operations

After having emphasized the structural aspects of control and the institutional aspects of change in the previous sections, the operational aspects of action and decision making within the overall energy complex will be exposed in this section. Here, we do not encounter mere problems of the different time spans of sociotechnical operations, but also of "simultaneity." Both differentiation and simultaneity emburden all energy-related social activities with a high degree of nonknowledge and nontransparency. Therefore, we now turn our attention to problems of enabling action and decision making despite uncertainty and risk (in order to sustain the functions and services of the energy complex).

Technical operations have other frequencies than organizational ones. A sociotechnical system (e.g., power plant, grid infrastructure) enacts and implements its own chronology of events, which is both different from that of the network it is incorporated in as well as from that in other infrastructures and its regulatory environment (see for this differentiation again Table 2.3). For example, Amin (2001, 23) shows how, in the North American power grid, the increasing number of heterogeneous elements and of interactions between these elements generate manifold simultaneously occurring events in varying time spans:

- In regard to technical operation: "System structure monitoring" is a steady state, ongoing technical operation to ensure the equilibrium of inflow/outflow within the net, and without regard to what the source of the electricity is. Split-second events occur in the grid to sustain moment-to-moment control via ICT.
- In regard to organizational decision making: "Load management, load forecasting, and generation scheduling" are hourly/daily social activities. These *decisions* become a mark in the continuous flow of events that can be observed and related to. Power plant operators inform about going online/offline, and grid operators must react accordingly. To do so, they must (re) activate knowledge about the technical conditions and requirements of the

physical grid installation, and about the technical norms, organizational rules, and generalized regulations (like the jurisdiction of the operators) again and again. In order to enable operators to make decisions under conditions of uncertainty about unlikely, but possible, failures, it is essential that the institutionalized structure of the system is generally shared and familiar.

- Regarding long-term processes (decades or longer) such as "power plant site selection, design, construction, environmental impact etc." events as well as structures and institutions are important. The actual investment decisions, siting decisions, license permissions, approvals of operation and alternating subsidies schemes set a mark to which others can and must relate. The anticipation of these events leads to action because all those concerned attempt to prepare and position themselves, i.e., structuration and institutionalization evolve further. Those affected by the decisions need to readjust to new circumstances, and new social dynamics are triggered.[15]

All these events, selected exemplarily with reference to technical, organizational, and societal operation, contribute to the reality of the energy complex. They change the state of the system, which can be observed. The myriad of residual events leading to these visible marks remain *nontransparent* in most cases. Also, these events confirm or refute expectations and, therefore, influence the structure of continuously operating systems (de Haan and Rotmans 2011; Geels 2004, 92).

Distinguishing technical and social operations

In order to carve out the problem of sociotechnical "simultaneity," the distinction between technical and social operations needs to be addressed carefully. Although many scholars in the STS field emphasize how technology is embedded in society[16] or how even technical artifacts themselves are social actors,[17] there are good reasons to recognize a distinction between social realities and technical operations.

Machines achieve the tight coupling of physical, chemical, or biological operation in a "law-abiding way," in order to achieve regularity of behavior (Ashby 2004, 109). In contrast to technical operation (and routinized, quasi-automatic action), *social realities* emerge if actors relate to each other via communication and if the threefold selection of information, utterance, and understanding creates meaningful distinctions in order to maintain communication on an identifiable unity (a system) distinct from all other events (the environment). Social realities have to solve problems of contingency, e.g., the surprise caused by unexpected events, so that structures and institutions can emerge and sustain themselves. Norms, rules, routines, and values, for example, are contingent in their origins, but once they are established they offer stable expectations. Communication, as the basic element of social systems, always inherits the moment of surprise. Every social situation comprised of events brings about a new combination of determinacy and indeterminacy (Luhmann 1995, 291). For its part, technology is supposed to eliminate surprise – technology is the means for planned, repeated, comparable outcomes.

The difference between technical and social realities can be explained by selectivity in the behavior of persons and the contingency, uncertainty, and risk in all social affairs. For example, markets cannot be predicted in the manner that engineers can predict the output of a tremendously complicated nuclear power plant, because markets react to predictions themselves, while power plants do not. Markets are self-organizing dynamic systems (like nontrivial machines, in the sense of Heinz von Foerster).[18] There is an important difference in the modus operandi of technical and social systems. The relation of both types of realities is best described as orthogonal:

> The technical network of energy flow is completely neutral to communication; in other words, information is produced outside the network and can only be disturbed by "noise." Causal relations between technological physics and communicated information are freed of overlap and take the form of structural coupling.
>
> (Luhmann 2012, 180)

In the following, the sociotechnical relation is conceptualized as *structural coupling* of technology and communication, as opposed to operational coupling (Baecker 2011). Structural coupling of social communication and technological operation implies the systematic (nonarbitrary) relation between distinct modi. In this concept, technology is part of the environment of social systems, whose basic element is communication. Communication and technology are orthogonally related to each other. There is punctual, reciprocal conditioning, intervention, or interference, for example in the case of technical distortions and in that of controlling technology (see Figure 2.1). Especially for our case, sociotechnical

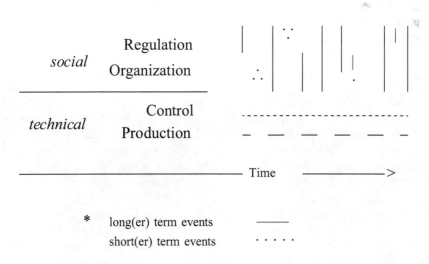

Figure 2.1 Orthogonal relation of technical and social events

Source: CB

infrastructures are latent structures. We know about their existence, but once established they are by and large invisible. "Once here, effective infrastructures appear as timeless, unthought, even natural features of contemporary life" (Jackson et al. 2007, 1). While the idea of orthogonality does not deny the limiting and conditioning effect of technology on action, technology is (not yet) a substitute for communication (Baecker 2011).

The crucial role in influencing the development of future energy systems is meanwhile fulfilled by information and communication technology (ICT). Generally, the increasing implementation of ICT in all areas of modern society comes with the expectation of more transparency, control, efficiency, and productivity. Specifically, the current energy infrastructure is envisioned as becoming more intelligent through more data processing, faster feedback loops, and learning capacities, in order to exploit a more efficient way of organizing the generation, transportation, and distribution of energy (Lösch and Schneider 2016).

The widespread introduction of ICT enhances human capabilities, but also raises new problems. On the one hand, technology offers data processing at enormous speed, vast storage capacity, and almost unlimited connectivity. In this sense, as it exceeds human capabilities by far, it offers both relief from and support for communication. Decades ago, however, Bell (1974, 42) pointed out the downside of this intensification. He exposed the consequences of the increasing use of electronic data processing: an increase in the number of arenas of interaction, of the number of interrelated actors, and of the speed and frequency of transactions. The question was – even at that time – are the existing cognitive and institutional capacities able to cope with an extremely rapidly growing number of events? Therefore, on the other hand, technology itself and subsequently social realities become even more complex and nontransparent, which means that contingency and uncertainty rise accordingly.[19] Society is therefore ever more in need of capacities to absorb uncertainty (March and Simon 1993) and means of coping with exploding amounts of data, information, knowledge – all of which do not exonerate actors from the choices to be made.

Actionability

We currently encounter many factual relationships in the current and developing energy complex between operators of systems, networks of systems, and networks of networks, operators and designers, legislators, controllers, and, in the future, between parts of the general public and all the aforementioned. In these sociotechnical constellations, relationships take on the form of "flat" screens for the user interface, as opposed to the "deep" and complicated structure of the system behind the surface.

Within sociotechnical constellations, operators face the responsibility of maintaining control from moment to moment and in the face of changes in energy supply, i.e., the determination and organization of production as well as the interconnectedness to other sociotechnical systems. Modeling possible failures and threats in order to address vulnerabilities or to increase resilience is a serious challenge.[20] Lack of data hampers informed decision making. Uncertainty must be absorbed by means of distributing risks and responsibilities, legal protection, and informal mechanisms such as trust and confidence. In situations of change, plausible decision programs replace accurate calculation to support decision making (Weick, Sutcliffe, and Obstfeld 2005, 415).

Roe and Schulman (2016, 62) identify this problem of coping with uncertainty with respect to interrelated infrastructures: "What happens when knowledge requirements of an infrastructure's domain of competence are so intensive and demanding that its control operators can't realistically know the other infrastructures they are connected to with the same depth as they know their own systems?" The authors answer that, in order to operate reliably beyond design (planned, intended control), "designers, be they engineers, policy makers, or senior executives, must trust" in the skills and knowledge of those operating facilities from moment to moment (Roe and Schulman 2016, 156).[21]

Visionaries of smart grids propose a two-way data exchange between provider and consumer. Especially consumers are expected to become involved more actively in producing and consuming electricity at the same time. The label "prosumer" (producing and consuming electricity) has become prevalent. Industry is searching for viable business cases and models for smart appliances and prosumer roles, for example "virtual power plants" (Dürr and Heyne 2017), while politicians and administrations are investigating ways of allowing for both innovation and protection of prosumers simultaneously (Covrig et al. 2014, 87). The problem of nonknowledge about the behavior of smart grids may progressively become the most significant issue for all those involved.

As yet, the general public has had only very loose contact to sociotechnical operations, mostly by consuming services. The "audience" of the energy complex must assume the competence of those operating and controlling technical facilities (plants, networks, etc.). The public relies on the knowledge of operators and controllers about the technical and organizational structure and their skill in reliably producing the expected outputs and services. Moreover, it assumes there is an extensive institutionalized set of rules and laws for supervising, for example, safe operation, corresponding market transactions, and access to the services. Social science research, consequently, is looking into data security issues, e.g., setting standards for smart grids to foster trust (Hoenkamp and Huitema 2012) and protect privacy (Cavoukian, Polonetsky, and Wolf 2010).[22]

Trust is not only relevant because of a lack of information and knowledge. It is necessary, moreover, because future and simultaneous events cannot be controlled. This is where the norm of rational calculation of the consequences of actions fails fundamentally and must be supplemented with other social mechanisms such as trust and confidence.[23] Therefore, the problem of nontransparency is not only characterized by the trust addressees' degrees of freedom, the possibility of technical failure, or the lack of information, but rather the necessity to momentarily close the temporal gap to an open future. In this sense, trust is a functional necessity. In order to exploit the opportunities offered by large sociotechnical complexes, such as the energy supply, scholars assume that a whole "architecture of trust" must be in place and sustained (Sumpf 2017).

In a similar vein, philosophers call for decision makers to include nonengineers in the process of designing modern infrastructures in order to increase the "capabilities" of persons to actively participate despite the complicated nature of the designs (Künneke et al. 2015; Ribeiro, Polinder, and Verkerk 2012). In essence, by emphasizing the aspect of system evolution, these authors present a pathway for involvement that is different from debates about participatory proceedings in siting decisions (which often refer to simple "yes," "no," "maybe" alternatives).[24]

Energy consumption is also tackled by technical and social means. The questions as to how to decrease energy use and how to design programs for environmentally sound behavior encourage ideas ranging from feedback systems (Karlin, Zinger, and Ford 2015; Nachreiner et al. 2015) to nudging (Kaiser, Arnold, and Otto 2014), i.e., leading users into desired behavioral frames by means of hardly variable default settings. While feedback is supposed to present users with useful information (via a "simple" interface) to enable them to make informed decisions (rational uncertainty absorption), nudging is supposed to erect some form of behavioral inconvenience, often in the interaction with technology (technical uncertainty absorption). If accepted as is, the nudged decision represents relief; in contrast, the urge to behave otherwise represents a burden. These sociotechnical arrangements – feedback, nudging – also represent a solution to the problem of actionability that creates, again, new problems: Some researchers investigate how energy-efficient behavior in one area can lead to increasing activities in others and, in the end, an even greater consumption of electricity. This phenomenon is discussed in terms of "rebound effects" (Otto, Kaiser, and Arnold 2014).[25]

In conclusion, the problem of actionability – brought about by distinctive time spans of events and the simultaneity of sociotechnical operations – must be tackled all the time by uncertainty-absorbing mechanisms taking the form of social arrangements or with the help of technical devices.

Concluding discussion: temporal solutions for permanent problems

The goal of this theoretical contribution is to reframe "energy" – its provision, transportation, distribution, and consumption – as a threefold sociotechnical problem. In essence, the continued provision and devaluation of energy demands a complex of functions and services,

(1) to which technical and social systems contribute in complicated/complex interrelations (referring to the control aspect),
(2) in which all activities are conditioned by generalized cognitive and normative expectations (referring to the change aspect),
(3) to resolve moment-to-moment sociotechnical problems (referring to the action aspect).

With these sociotechnical problems – highly aggregated and theoretical as they are formulated here – the idea is to offer reference points which can be tackled by the means of the respective disciplines. We have to assume that the abstraction of these problems as presented here is necessary to achieve cognitive integration: On the one hand, this abstraction allows us to keep degrees of freedom in thinking and creating intact because it avoids placing too much burden on strict definitions and methods in other disciplines. On the other hand, however, the description of the sociotechnical problems is – hopefully – specific enough to reveal the mutual interest and to motivate scholars to tackle these with different languages, concepts, terms, and methods.

In the energy realm, one important cross-cutting issue is the continuity and irreversibility of all activities and efforts needed to sustain energy-related functions (which is valid for other vital societal functions as well). For energy science and engineering, that argument is a commonplace: all efforts are directed toward the problem of the *irreversible devaluation of energy*. Every thermodynamic system has a potential for *entropy*. Engineers try to increase the ratio of useful *exergy* (and decrease the ratio of useless *anergy*) in energy transfers to generate useful work/heat. Without interference, any energy flow will irreversibly lead to the dissipation of energy from the system to its ambient. Consequently, every engineering discipline somehow refers to this concept in its effort to optimize the effectiveness of technical devices incorporating heat transfer (in interaction to human action) to tackle sustainability issues (Wenterodt, Redecker, and Herwig 2015).

For all social affairs there is a functionally equivalent problem. Any kind of information or social order will dissipate if not for the reproduction of structure in language (Shannon and Weaver 1963) or in communication systems (Luhmann 1995). Regarding the latter, the problem that is equivalent to entropy is that of contingency.[26] A social structure allows for stable expectations regarding possible events. In a social situation with a conceivable structure, an observer knows what will likely happen next. If and when an observer is not able to predict the next occurrence based on the observation of previous occurrences, then she or he experiences contingency, uncertainty, and risk – or in other words: entropy (Luhmann 1995, 49). Consequently, entropy and contingency can be considered as a reference problem which must be analyzed in multiple dimensions.

Safe, reliable, inclusive, and affordable operating infrastructures must develop and maintain a high degree of social order and organization, with accompanying *complexity in control*, necessary *redundancy balanced with variety*, and sustained *action(ability)*. In sociotechnical configurations, therefore, two glaring characteristics come to the forefront. First, there is the temporality of technical and social events, i.e., providing services/output from moment to moment, even if this often necessitates long-term planning. Second, there is the irreversibility of technical and social events, i.e., the devaluation of energy in any kind of energy transfer on the physical side and the loss of "certainty" in human activities that needs to be absorbed continuously on the social side via communication.

The following contributions will exemplify this argument in depth: (a) the ongoing effort to understand and to control complex sociotechnical systems with engineering means (Kröger and Nan; Wiens et al.) as well as with institutional arrangements (Künneke); (b) the ongoing induction of change despite the need for stability with a continuous interplay of laboratory and real world experiments (Gross), conflicting societal discourses (Genus et al.), and uncertainty-inducing innovation activities (Fuchs); (c) the continuous absorption of uncertainty in social relations (Sumpf), in motivating individual behavior (Otto and Wittenberg), or within the normative deliberations regarding the design of infrastructures (Hillerbrand).

In this chapter, the argument is brought forward that sociotechnical problems remain historically and locally invariant. However, the solutions to these problems change over time and they differ from region to region depending on national policies or geographic conditions as well as on technical standards or local habits, abilities, or means. In this regard, transitions have to be treated as temporary solutions, as they provide a whole new set of technical and social innovations to solve problems and, simultaneously, create new ones. Theoreticians in engineering and social science as well as practitioners in politics and elsewhere will consequently have to be prepared for the new problems.

Notes

1   The International Energy Agency (IEA) envisions that, "With 60 cents of every dollar invested in new power plants to 2040 spent on renewable energy technologies, global renewables-based electricity generation increases by some 8,300 TeraWatt-hours (more than half of the increase in total generation)." The IEA estimates an increase "equivalent to the output of all of today's fossil-fuel generation plants in China, the United States and the European Union combined" (IEEFA 2017, 6).

2   In reference to different dimensions of meaning (factual, social, and temporal) as "world dimensions" (Luhmann 1995, 75), the factual dimension concerns questions of what objects are meant in distinction to something else, which leads in our case to distinctions between system and environment, element and relation, or "energy" and, e.g., "transportation." The temporal dimension concerns questions of present actions viewed in the context of our past experience (i.e., already determined) and of our expectations regarding the undetermined future. The social dimension concerns questions of different perspectives (of ego and alter ego) of interacting observers (actors, stakeholders, parties, persons, organizations, etc.) and the common ground which can be established, such as shared values, norms, and knowledge. Although these dimensions of meaning can be differentiated for analytical purposes; they never appear in isolation (Luhmann 1995, 86).

3   Contingency is understood here such that forms, occurrences, actions, behavior, and decisions are neither impossible nor compulsively necessary. See Luhmann on the relations of complexity and contingency (1995, 25), Mitchell (2009, 13) and on biological contingency, or Rorty (1989) on contingency as a liberal idea of an ironic distance to someone's own beliefs.

4   See especially the contribution by Wolfgang Kröger and Cen Nan in this book, where innovative models of future energy architectures are discussed.

5   If the models of systems used by operators do not align with the actual internal state, then safety problems will occur (Leveson et al. 2009).

6   See also the contribution by Rolf W. Künneke in this book.

7   In Germany, this process is part of a legal framework (§6, 7–10 *Energiewirtschaftsgesetz*) which aims to unbundle vertically integrated organizations into legally and operationally (incl. accounting) separate units (Angenendt, Boesche, and Franz 2011, 118f.).

8   See also the contribution by Gerhard Fuchs in this book.

9 This argument is supported by the observation by Carlsson and Stankiewicz (1991, 95) on how economic change is generated by an "increased *variety* of goods and services over time," and not by a qualitative increase of redundant outputs.

10 See also the contribution by Matthias Gross in this book.

11 On the role of societal discourses in regard to this problem, see the contribution by Audley Genus in this book.

12 See also the contribution by Siegmar Otto and Inga Wittenberg in this book.

13 In this regard Negro et al. are in line with the arguments of innovation system research. Bergek et al. (2008, 422), for example, highlight the functions necessary for the development of innovation fields (e.g., market formation, experimentation, resources, knowledge, and legitimation) and mutually influencing blocking mechanisms (e.g., uncertainty and the lack of standards or educational programs) which should/could be dissolved by political activity.

14 See, e.g., also Gallagher et al. (2012) and Weber and Rohracher (2012).

15 For example, altered business plans and investment strategies regarding the announcement of reforming the EEG in Germany. (Renewable Energy Sources Act – RES Act 2016; www.bmwi.de/EN/Topics/Energy/Renewable-Energy/renewable-energy-sources-act-2016.html.)

16 For an example of the functional equivalence of technical operation and social action: "Technical systems as systems of machineries and free-standing structures performing, more or less reliably and predictably, complex standardized operations by virtue of being integrated with other social processes, governed and legitimated by formal, knowledge-intensive, impersonal rationalities" (Joerges 1988, 24).

17 Most prominent, see Latour's notion of "hybrids": half objects, half subjects (Latour 1993, 112).

18 See also Zio and Kröger (2011, 9ff.) concerning distinguishing between complicated systems (e.g., mechanical watches, aircraft, and power plants) and complex systems (e.g., stock market, internet, and power grid).

19 In this regard, recent discussions address issues of computerized high-speed trading in financial markets. Traders use software agents for transactions to gain information advantages by exploiting temporal margins of split seconds. Here the algorithms "decide" about transactions and traders just observe the results. Nonetheless, research has shown that these sociotechnical operations, where programmers implement rules and rationalities of trading into algorithms, lead to emergent phenomena on a system level: "Society's techno-social systems are becoming ever faster and more computer-orientated. However, far from simply generating faster versions of existing behavior, we show that this speed-up can generate a new behavioral regime as humans lose the ability to intervene in real time" (Johnson et al. 2013, 1).

20 See the contribution by Wolfgang Kröger and Cen Nan in this book.

21 See also the contribution by Patrick Sumpf in this book.

22 Only with mitigated uncertainty that future energy technologies and services are safe from abuse (from tampering with personal information or fraud) will smart meters or, more broadly, smart appliances become successful. The rejection of smart meter technologies by certain users that have already been observed can serve as a warning (AlAbdulkarim, Lukszo, and Fens 2012).

23 In the tradition of Simmel's "leap of faith," Möllering (2006, 356) refers to the fundamental necessity of "suspending irreducible social vulnerability and uncertainty as if they were favourably resolved." The act of "suspension" is indispensable because the evaluation of possible negative consequences must happen prior to monitoring whether the desired outcomes materialize.

24 See for this issue the various contributions in: Devine-Wright (2014) and the contribution of Rafaela Hillerbrand in this book.

25 See also the contribution by Otto and Wittenberg in this book.

26 In formal language, contingency means that occurrences are neither impossible nor
compulsorily necessary.

References

AlAbdulkarim, Layla, Zofia Lukszo, and Theo Fens. 2012. "Acceptance of Privacy-
Sensitive Technologies: Smart Metering Case in The Netherlands." In *Third International Engineering Systems Symposium (CESUN)*. Delft. http://cesun2012.tudelft.nl/
images/5/5e/AlAbdulkarim.pdf.

Amin, M. 2001. "Toward Self-Healing Energy Infrastructure Systems." *IEEE Computer
Applications in Power* 14 (1): 20–8. https://doi.org/10.1109/67.893351.

Angenendt, Nicole, Katharina V. Boesche, and Oliver H. Franz. 2011. "Der energierech-
tliche Rahmen einer Implementierung von Smart Grids." *Recht der Energiewirtschaft* 20
(4–5): 117–26.

Ashby, W. R. 2004. "Principles of the Self-Organizing System." *E:CO* 6 (1–2): 102–26.

Atlan, Henry. 1974. "On a Formal Definition of Organization." *Journal of Theoretical Biology* 45 (2): 295–304. https://doi.org/10.1016/0022-5193(74)90115-5.

Baecker, Dirk. 2011. "Baecker: Who Qualifies for Communication? A Systems Perspective on Human and Other Possibly Intelligent Beings Taking Part in the Next Society."
TATuP 20 (1): 17–26.

Barley, Stephen R., and Pamela S. Tolbert. 1997. "Institutionalization and Structuration: Studying the Links between Action and Institution." *Organization Studies* 18 (1):
93–117. https://doi.org/10.1177/017084069701800106.

Beckman, Svante. 1994. "On Systemic Technology." In *Changing Large Technical Systems*,
edited by Jane Summerton, 311–31. Boulder, CO: Westview Press.

Bell, Daniel. 1974. *The Coming of Post-Industrial Society*. London: Heinemann.

Bergek, Anna, Staffan Jacobsson, Bo Carlsson, Sven Lindmark, and Annika Rickne.
2008. "Analyzing the Functional Dynamics of Technological Innovation Systems:
A Scheme of Analysis." *Research Policy* 37 (3): 407–29. https://doi.org/10.1016/j.
respol.2007.12.003.

Bolton, Ronan, and Timothy J. Foxon. 2015. "Infrastructure Transformation as a Socio-
Technical Process – Implications for the Governance of Energy Distribution Networks
in the UK." *Technological Forecasting and Social Change* 90, Part B (January): 538–50.
https://doi.org/10.1016/j.techfore.2014.02.017.

Brown, H. E., and S. Suryanarayanan. 2009. "A Survey Seeking a Definition of a Smart
Distribution System." In *41st North American Power Symposium, NAPS 2009*.

Bruns, Elke, Dörte Ohlhorst, Bernd Wenzel, and Johann Köppel. 2010. *Renewable Energies
in Germany's Electricity Market: A Biography of the Innovation Process*. Dordrecht et al.:
Springer.

Büscher, Christian, and Aldo Mascareño. 2014. "Mechanisms of Risk Production in Modern Cities." *Nature and Culture* 9 (1): 66–86. https://doi.org/10.3167/nc.2014.090104.

Carlsson, B., and R. Stankiewicz. 1991. "On the Nature, Function and Composition of
Technological Systems." *Journal of Evolutionary Economics* 1 (2): 93–118. https://doi.
org/10.1007/BF01224915.

Cavoukian, Ann, Jules Polonetsky, and Christopher Wolf. 2010. "SmartPrivacy for the
Smart Grid: Embedding Privacy into the Design of Electricity Conservation." *Identity in
the Information Society* 3 (2): 275–94. https://doi.org/10.1007/s12394-010-0046-y.

Covrig, Catalin F., Mircea Ardelean, Julja Vasiljevska, Anna Mengolini, Gianluca Fulli,
and Eleftherios Amoiralis. 2014. "Smart Grid Projects Outlook 2014." EUR – Scientific

and Technical Research Series. Luxembourg: Publications Office of the European Union.

de Haan, (Hans) J., and Jan Rotmans. 2011. "Patterns in Transitions: Understanding Complex Chains of Change." *Technological Forecasting and Social Change* 78 (1): 90–102. https://doi.org/10.1016/j.techfore.2010.10.008.

Devine-Wright, Patrick. 2014. *Renewable Energy and the Public: From NIMBY to Participation.* London; Washington, DC: Routledge.

Dürr, Thomas, and Jean-Christoph Heyne. 2017. "Virtuelle Kraftwerke für Smart Markets." In *Herausforderung Utility 4.0 – Wie sich die Energiewirtschaft im Zeitalter der Digitalisierung verändert*, edited by Oliver D. Doleski, 653–81. Wiesbaden: Springer Vieweg.

Edwards, Paul N. 2004. "Infrastructure and Modernity: Force, Time, and Social Organization in the History of Socio-Technical Systems." In *Modernity and Technology*, edited by Thomas J. Misa, Philip Brey, and Andrew Feenberg, 185–225. Cambridge, MA; London: MIT Press.

Edwards, Paul N., Steven J. Jackson, Geoffrey C. Bowker, and Cory P. Knobel. 2007. *Understanding Infrastructure: Dynamics, Tensions, and Design.* Ann Arbor: DeepBlue.

Fouquet, Roger. 2016. "Historical Energy Transitions: Speed, Prices and System Transformation." *Energy Research & Social Science* 22 (December): 7–12. https://doi.org/10.1016/j.erss.2016.08.014.

Fuenfschilling, Lea, and Bernhard Truffer. 2014. "The Structuration of Socio-Technical Regimes: Conceptual Foundations from Institutional Theory." *Research Policy* 43 (4): 772–91. https://doi.org/10.1016/j.respol.2013.10.010.

Gallagher, Kelly Sims, Arnulf Grübler, Laura Kuhl, Gregory Nemet, and Charlie Wilson. 2012. "The Energy Technology Innovation System." *Annual Review of Environment and Resources* 37 (1): 137–62. https://doi.org/10.1146/annurev-environ-060311-133915.

Geels, Frank W. 2002. "Technological Transitions as Evolutionary Reconfiguration Processes: A Multi-Level Perspective and a Case-Study." *Research Policy* 31 (8–9): 1257–74. https://doi.org/10.1016/S0048-7333(02)00062-8.

———. 2004. "From Sectoral Systems of Innovation to Socio-Technical Systems: Insights about Dynamics and Change from Sociology and Institutional Theory." *Research Policy* 33 (6–7): 897–920. https://doi.org/10.1016/j.respol.2004.01.015.

———. 2014. "The Arduous Transition to Low-Carbon Energy: A Multi-Level Analysis of Renewable Electricity Niches and Resilient Regimes." In *The Triple Challenge for Europe. Economic Development, Climate Change, and Governance*, edited by Jan Fagerberg, Steffan Laestadius, and Ben R. Martin, 91–118. Oxford: Oxford University Press.

Grin, John, Jan Rotmans, and Johan Schot. 2010. *Transitions to Sustainable Development: New Directions in the Study of Long Term Transformative Change.* New York, London: Routledge.

Gross, Matthias, and Rüdiger Mautz. 2015. *Renewable Energies.* London; New York: Routledge.

Hoenkamp, R.A., and G.B. Huitema. 2012. "Good Standards for Smart Meters." In *European Energy Market (EEM), 2012 9th International Conference on The*, 1–6. https://doi.org/10.1109/EEM.2012.6254820.

Hughes, Thomas P. 1983. *Networks of Power: Electrification in Western Society, 1880–1930.* Baltimore; London: The Johns Hopkins University Press.

IEEFA. 2017. "China's Global Renewable Energy Expansion: How the World's Second-Biggest Economy Is Positioned to Lead the World in Clean-Power Investment." Cleveland: Institute for Energy Economics and Financial Analysis (IEEFA). http://ieefa.org/

wp-content/uploads/2017/01/Chinas-Global-Renewable-Energy-Expansion_January-2017.pdf.

Jackson, Steven J., Paul N. Edwards, Geoffrey C. Bowker, and Cory P. Knobel. 2007. "Understanding Infrastructure: History, Heuristics and Cyberinfrastructure Policy." *First Monday* 12 (6). https://doi.org/dx.doi.org/10.5210/fm.v12i6.1904.

Joerges, Bernward. 1988. "Large Technical Systems: Concepts and Issues." In *The Development of Large Technical Systems*, edited by Renate Mayntz and Thomas P. Hughes, 9–36. Frankfurt am Main: Campus.

Johnson, Neil, Guannan Zhao, Eric Hunsader, Hong Qi, Nicholas Johnson, Jing Meng, and Brian Tivnan. 2013. "Abrupt Rise of New Machine Ecology beyond Human Response Time." *Scientific Reports* 3 (September). https://doi.org/10.1038/srep02627.

JRC. 2011. "Smart Grid Projects in Europe: Lessons Learned and Current Developments." Petten: European Commission – Joint Research Centre – Institute for Energy.

Kaiser, Florian G., Oliver Arnold, and Siegmar Otto. 2014. "Attitudes and Defaults Save Lives and Protect the Environment Jointly and Compensatorily: Understanding the Behavioral Efficacy of Nudges and Other Structural Interventions." *Behavioral Sciences* 4 (3): 202–12. https://doi.org/10.3390/bs4030202.

Karlin, Beth, Joanne F. Zinger, and Rebecca Ford. 2015. "The Effects of Feedback on Energy Conservation: A Meta-Analysis." *Psychological Bulletin*. https://doi.org/10.1037/a0039650.

Kraas, Frauke. 2007. "Megacities and Global Change. Key Priorities." *The Geographical Journal* 173 (1): 79–82.

Kröger, Wolfgang. 2017. "Securing the Operation of Socially Critical Systems from an Engineering Perspective: New Challenges, Enhanced Tools and Novel Concepts." *European Journal for Security Research*, 1–17. https://doi.org/10.1007/s41125-017-0013-9.

Kungl, Gregor. 2015. "Stewards or Sticklers for Change? Incumbent Energy Providers and the Politics of the German Energy Transition." *Energy Research & Social Science* 8 (July): 13–23. https://doi.org/10.1016/j.erss.2015.04.009.

Künneke, Rolf W. 2008. "Institutional Reform and Technological Practise: The Case of Electricity." *Industrial and Corporate Change* 17 (2): 233–65. https://doi.org/10.1093/icc/dtn002.

Künneke, Rolf W., John Groenewegen, and Claude Ménard. 2010. "Aligning Modes of Organization with Technology: Critical Transactions in the Reform of Infrastructures." *Journal of Economic Behavior & Organization* 75 (3): 494–505. https://doi.org/10.1016/j.jebo.2010.05.009.

Künneke, Rolf W., Donna C. Mehos, Rafaela Hillerbrand, and Kas Hemmes. 2015. "Understanding Values Embedded in Offshore Wind Energy Systems: Toward a Purposeful Institutional and Technological Design." *Environmental Science & Policy*, 118–29. https://doi.org/10.1016/j.envsci.2015.06.013.

Latour, Bruno. 1993. *We Have Never Been Modern*. New York: Harvester Wheatsheaf.

Leveson, Nancy, Nicolas Dulac, Karen Marais, and John Carroll. 2009. "Moving Beyond Normal Accidents and High Reliability Organizations: A Systems Approach to Safety in Complex Systems." *Organization Studies* 30 (2–3): 227–49. https://doi.org/10.1177/0170840608101478.

Loorbach, Deerk. 2010. "Transition Management for Sustainable Development: A Prescriptive, Complexity-Based Governance Framework." *Governance* 23 (1): 161–83. https://doi.org/10.1111/j.1468-0491.2009.01471.x.

Lösch, Andreas, and Christoph Schneider. 2016. "Transforming Power/Knowledge Apparatuses: The Smart Grid in the German Energy Transition." *Innovation: The European*

Journal of Social Science Research 29 (3): 262–84. https://doi.org/10.1080/13511610.201 6.1154783.

Luhmann, Niklas. 1995. *Social Systems*. Stanford: Stanford University Press.

———. 2012. *Theory of Society – Volume 1*. Cultural Memory in the Present. Stanford: Stanford University Press.

March, James G., and Johan P. Olsen. 1995. *Democratic Governance*. New York: Free Press.

March, James G., and Herbert Simon. 1993. *Organizations*. 2nd ed. Cambridge, MA; Oxford: Blackwell Publishers.

Mayntz, Renate. 1993. "Grosse technische Systeme und ihre gesellschaftstheoretische Bedeutung." *Kölner Zeitschrift für Soziologie und Sozialpsychologie* 45 (1): 97–108.

———. 2009. "The Changing Governance of Large Technical Infrastructure Systems." In *Über Governance. Institutionen und Prozesse politischer Regelung*, 121–50. Schriften aus dem Max-Planck-Institut für Gesellschaftsforschung, Band 62. Frankfurt am Main; New York: Campus.

Mitchell, Sandra D. 2009. *Unsimple Truths: Science, Complexity, and Policy*. Chicago: University of Chicago Press.

Möllering, Guido. 2006. "Trust, Institutions, Agency: Towards a Neoinstitutional Theory of Trust." In *Handbook of Trust Research*, edited by Reinhard Bachmann and Akbar Zaheer, 355–76. Cheltenham, UK: Edward Elgar.

Moteff, John, Claudia Copeland, and John Fischer. 2003. "Critical Infrastructures: What Makes an Infrastructure Critical?" Report for Congress. Washington D.C.: Congressional Research Service – The Library of Congress. http://fas.org/irp/crs/RL31556.pdf.

Nachreiner, Malte, Birgit Mack, Ellen Matthies, and Karolin Tampe-Mai. 2015. "An Analysis of Smart Metering Information Systems: A Psychological Model of Self-Regulated Behavioural Change." *Energy Research & Social Science*, Special Issue on Smart Grids and the Social Sciences, 9 (September): 85–97. https://doi.org/10.1016/j.erss.2015.08.016.

Negro, Simona O., Floortje Alkemade, and Marko P. Hekkert. 2012. "Why Does Renewable Energy Diffuse so Slowly? A Review of Innovation System Problems." *Renewable and Sustainable Energy Reviews* 16 (6): 3836–46. https://doi.org/10.1016/j.rser.2012.03.043.

Nightingale, Paul, Tim Brady, Andrew Davies, and Jeremy Hall. 2003. "Capacity Utilization Revisited: Software, Control and the Growth of Large Technical Systems." *Industrial and Corporate Change* 12 (3): 477–517. https://doi.org/10.1093/icc/12.3.477.

Otto, Siegmar, Florian G. Kaiser, and Oliver Arnold. 2014. "The Critical Challenge of Climate Change for Psychology: Preventing Rebound and Promoting More Individual Irrationality." *European Psychologist* 19 (2): 96–106. https://doi.org/10.1027/1016-9040/a000182.

Perrow, Charles. 2007. *The Next Catastrophe – Reducing Our Vulnerabilities to Natural, Industrial, and Terrorist Disasters*. Princeton: Princeton University Press.

———. 2011. "Software Failures, Security, and Cyberattacks." *TATuP* 20 (3): 41–6.

Ramchurn, S., P. Vytelingum, A. Rogers, and N. Jennings. 2012. "Putting the 'Smarts' into the Smart Grid: A Grand Challenge for Artificial Intelligence." *Communications of the ACM* 55 (4): 86–97.

Ribeiro, P.F., H. Polinder, and M.J. Verkerk. 2012. "Planning and Designing Smart Grids: Philosophical Considerations." *IEEE Technology and Society Magazine* 31 (3): 34–43. https://doi.org/10.1109/MTS.2012.2211771.

Roe, Emery, and Paul R. Schulman. 2016. *Reliability and Risk: The Challenge of Managing Interconnected Infrastructures*. Stanford: Stanford University Press.

Rohracher, H. 2008. "Energy Systems in Transition: Contributions from Social Sciences." *International Journal of Environmental Technology and Management* 9 (2–3): 144–61.

Rorty, Richard. 1989. *Contingency, Irony, and Solidarity.* Cambridge; New York: Cambridge University Press.

Schuitmaker, Tjerk Jan. 2012. "Identifying and Unravelling Persistent Problems." *Technological Forecasting and Social Change* 79 (6): 1021–31. https://doi.org/10.1016/j.techfore.2011.11.008.

Shannon, Claude E., and Warren Weaver. 1963. *The Mathematical Theory of Communication.* Urbana and Chicago: University of Illinois Press.

Smith, Adrian, Andy Stirling, and Frans Berkhout. 2005. "The Governance of Sustainable Socio-Technical Transitions." *Research Policy* 34 (10): 1491–510. https://doi.org/10.1016/j.respol.2005.07.005.

Sovacool, Benjamin K. 2009. "Rejecting Renewables: The Socio-Technical Impediments to Renewable Electricity in the United States." *Energy Policy* 37 (11): 4500–13. https://doi.org/10.1016/j.enpol.2009.05.073.

Sovacool, Benjamin K., and Frank W. Geels. 2016. "Further Reflections on the Temporality of Energy Transitions: A Response to Critics." *Energy Research & Social Science* 22 (December): 232–7. https://doi.org/10.1016/j.erss.2016.08.013.

Strunz, Sebastian. 2014. "The German Energy Transition as a Regime Shift." *Ecological Economics* 100: 150–8. https://doi.org/10.1016/j.ecolecon.2014.01.019.

Sumpf, Patrick. 2017. System Trust – Identity, Expectation, Reassurance. With a Case Study on Trusting the Energy System. Mannheim: PhD Thesis, University of Mannheim.

Truffer, Bernhard, Jens Schippl, and Torsten Fleischer. 2017. "Decentering Technology in Technology Assessment: Prospects for Socio-Technical Transitions in Electric Mobility in Germany." *Technological Forecasting and Social Change.* https://doi.org/10.1016/j.techfore.2017.04.020.

Verbong, Geert, and Frank W. Geels. 2007. "The Ongoing Energy Transition: Lessons from a Socio-Technical, Multi-Level Analysis of the Dutch Electricity System (1960–2004)." *Energy Policy* 35 (2): 1025–37. http://dx.doi.org/10.1016/j.enpol.2006.02.010.

Weber, K. Matthias, and Harald Rohracher. 2012. "Legitimizing Research, Technology and Innovation Policies for Transformative Change: Combining Insights from Innovation Systems and Multi-Level Perspective in a Comprehensive 'failures' Framework." *Research Policy* 41 (6): 1037–47.

Weick, Karl E., Kathleen M. Sutcliffe, and David Obstfeld. 2005. "Organizing and the Process of Sensemaking." *Organization Science* 16 (4): 409–21. https://doi.org/10.1287/orsc.1050.0133.

Wenterodt, Tammo, Christoph Redecker, and Heinz Herwig. 2015. "Second Law Analysis for Sustainable Heat and Energy Transfer: The Entropic Potential Concept." *Applied Energy* 139 (February): 376–83. https://doi.org/10.1016/j.apenergy.2014.10.073.

Zio, E., and W. Kroeger. 2011. *Vulnerable Systems.* Dordrecht: Springer.

Part I

Sociotechnical problem of control

3 Power systems in transition

Dealing with complexity

Wolfgang Kröger and Cen Nan

Introduction

The electric power supply system, designated a critical infrastructure,[1] is being subject to massive technological, organizational, and structural changes (Cohen 2010; Kröger and Zio 2011; Zio 2016): In recent years, there has been tighter integration and surging connectivity. As is commonly agreed, this development is ongoing and pushed by the pervasive use of digital information and communication technology (ICT) and the interdependence within and between connected infrastructure systems and among actors (Aven and Krohn 2014; Nai Fovino et al. 2009). All of these factors are further increasing system complexities to a significant degree (Aven and Krohn 2014). Since the interaction of humans with infrastructure systems (and notably, power systems), both individually and collectively, has made them an essential part of these systems, we need to understand the system as a sociotechnical one and to take more than purely technical factors into account. Moreover, as these systems form and are influenced by their environments, some argue (Heinimann and Hatfield 2017) that they merge into interdependent socio-ecological-technical systems, making them even harder to understand and model. Furthermore, the entire system is living and in transition. Thus, the design and operation need to be linked with ever-changing conditions and domains. The *Energiewende* in Germany and associated developments are nowadays one of the most prominent examples.

This contribution introduces initially the elements and attributes of complexity, second, characterizes bulk electricity supply systems, notably the European high-voltage transmission system, and identifies future trends and related challenges for its reliable operation and planning, third, addresses issues of decision making and system control under conditions of uncertainty and ambiguity and, fourth, develops ideas for reducing the complexity of the power supply system. In the following, it will appraise the status of our ability and of the available analytical tools to understand and model real-world critical infrastructure systems, including the electric power grid, and reflect on any limitations, in particular on our predictive capabilities and the ways to include individual and collective human behavior at varying levels. Case studies are also presented for illustration. Concluding remarks are provided at the end of the contribution.

Approaching complexity and the resulting system behavior

Elements and attributes of complexity

There is no absolute definition of the term "complexity." A characterization of what is complex is however possible in general, such as "something with many parts where those parts interact with each other in multiple ways, culminating in a higher order of emergence greater than the sum of its parts" (according to wikipedia.org)[2] or "if it is not possible to establish an accurate prediction model of system behavior based on knowing the specific functions and states of its individual components" (Aven et al. 2015, 7). It is therefore commonly agreed that the classical methods of deterministic and even probabilistic risk analysis, mainly based on reductionist methods and linear causal event chains without feedback loops, are likely to fail to capture the collective behavior of complex systems and how they interact and form relationships with their human and natural environments.

A complex (adaptive) system has some or all of the following elements and attributes:

- It consists of a large but finite number of interrelated parts/components, that interact with each other in multiple ways, including being interdependent. Parts and types of parts can be physical-engineered, human, logical, or contextual; for example, the Swiss high-voltage transmission network has been mapped by a set of 587 interacting parts ("agents"), either technical or nontechnical in nature (Schläpfer, Kessler, and Kröger 2012).
- It tends to exhibit dynamic and nonlinear behavior, i.e., it is not static, triggering disturbances that often accelerate, and a change of output is not proportional to a change of input.
- It often shows emergent behavior, i.e., larger entities arise through interactions among smaller entities and exhibit properties the smaller ones do not have, e.g., the formation of snowflakes.
- It exhibits positive feedback loops (i.e., no damping or reversing of instabilities) and possible critical tipping points or sudden regime shifts, depending on homogeneity[3] and coupling strength or connectedness (Scheffer et al. 2012; Dobson et al. 2007).[4]
- It is influenced by and adapts to its environment and to management by different kinds of actors, the latter often displaying different rationalities and objectives.
- It is highly sensitivity to initial load and stress conditions and dynamically subject to evolution and growth mechanisms.

Depending on the (inter-) dependencies within and between systems (Rinaldi, Peerenboom, and Kelly 2001), adverse effects may rapidly diffuse directly or indirectly to other components and pathways, facilitating the spread of any disaster: Under the right conditions, small changes in initial conditions or small disruptions can trigger cascades. Their consequences can even reach global dimensions as major system collapses have demonstrated (see also Figure 3.4). Adverse effects often culminate in a higher order of emergence, clearly indicating that collective behavior is more than the sum of its individual behaviors.

Regarding physical-engineered systems, two types of complexity can be distinguished, namely structural and dynamic. The former is intrinsic to system design, and the latter emerges from system operation (and in response to imbalances) (Rinaldi, Peerenboom, and Kelly 2001):

- Structural complexity derives (a) from characteristics such as heterogeneity, scale, and the scale of the connectivity of its components; (b) system architecture (topology and/or logic structure); and (c) divisibility into subsystems and elementary parts.
- Dynamic complexity is manifested "through the emergence of (even unexpected) system behavior in response to changes in the environmental and operational conditions of its components" whereas self-organization is a specific feature capable of reorganizing isolated elements and subsystems into coherent patterns without external intervention.

Both complex and complicated systems entail a large number of interconnected components and are organized in a hierarchy of subsystems. Although there is no absolute definition of the terms, one can however distinguish different meanings. The term "complexity" is composed of the Latin words *com* (= together) and *plex* (= woven) while the word "complicated" entails *plic* (= folded). Thus complexity is characterized by interdependencies within a single infrastructure system and, maybe even more importantly, among them, whereas its layers characterize a complicated system. For an attempt to contrast these terms see Table 3.1.

System boundaries, influencing factors, and limits of predictability

Boundaries are an important element of systems and need to be defined together with the granularity of the system to be analyzed. System boundaries could either reach to the micro (local, component, subsystem), macro (areal, entire system), or large-scale (global, system of coupled systems) level. The power supply system as such can be regarded as a large-scale system and grouped into three constituents from a source, i.e. generation, to transmission, and finally to sinks, i.e. the users or population served, that comprises an essential part of mutually dependent infrastructure systems (see also Figure 3.1). There are a variety of key influencing factors at different levels of systems including their constituents, which range from purely technical (quality, age, stress, etc.) to contextual (operational-organizational, human behavioral, environmental). Those factors are of time scales ranging from short-term control up to long-term strategic decisions. All these elements merge into a network of sociotechnical systems of different spatiotemporal scales (Amin 2002; Little 2004).

Table 3.1 Characteristics of complicated versus complex systems (Kröger and Zio 2011)

Complicated systems (e.g., commercial aircraft, nuclear power plants)	Complex systems (e.g., stock market, power grids, transport networks, www, social networks)
• Large number of highly connected components; frequency-consequence curves tend to follow a normal distribution	• Large number of highly connected components; frequency-consequence curves tend to show "fat tails" and follow power law distributions
• Components have well-defined roles and are governed by prescribed interactions	• Rules of interaction between the components may change over time and may not be well understood
• Structure remains closed and stable over the time; limited range of responses to changes in their environment	• Connectivity of the components may be quite plastic and roles may be fluid; interactions are not obvious
• Low dynamic, mostly linear behavior	• Systems are more open, respond to external conditions and evolve; interact with their environment
• No adaptation; one key defect may bring the system to a halt	• Display organization without a central organizing principle (self-organization/emergence)
• System behaviors are fully predictable	• Inadequate information about the state of the influencing variables; probabilistic rather than deterministic behavior
• Decomposing the system and analyzing sub-parts can give an understanding of the behavior of the whole, i.e. the whole can be reassembled from ist parts ("deductionism")	• High dynamic and nonlinear behavior; sudden regime shifts possible
	• The overall behavior cannot be described simply in terms of their building blocks; the whole is much more than the sum of its parts ("systems approach")

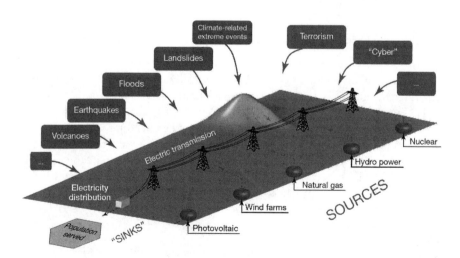

Figure 3.1 Representation of the electricity supply network, grouped into different classes of power generation (sources), high or medium voltage transmission, and medium or low voltage distribution ("sinks") (Komendantova et al. 2016)

Limits on predictability can be reached due to a lack of knowledge, of data, and of adequate tools as well as from an incomplete set of potential disruptions. Further reasons are difficulties of identifying and understanding an unprecedented number of adverse, emerging events and system-specific critical states, and non-transparent interrelationships and consequences of decisions made. Far in excess of these constraints, some argue that there are events or surprising combinations of events that just happen, that is for which there are no means to anticipate or predict them; these are characterized as "unexpected" or "unknown," for which "Black Swans" are a metaphor (Taleb 2007). However, others assume that "unknown events" can be anticipated and predicted if we have sufficient real-time information regarding complex system behavior with adequate time granularity; a metaphor for this concept – which has been successfully demonstrated in the financial sector – is "Dragon Kings" (Sornette and Ouillon 2012).

Characterization of power supply systems and identifiable transitions

Introducing the European high-voltage transmission system

The high-voltage transmission system is part of the electricity supply network that includes a number of grouped elements and is subject to the impact of a range of internal and external events, notably natural hazards (see Figure 3.1 for an illustration).

In Europe, while originally designed to serve a region and to allow for trans-boundary assistance in case of need, the high-voltage transmission (ENTSO-E grid) has been turned into an open system with given energy flow boundary conditions, crossing neighboring countries without a single centralized control. Regional and vertically integrated monopolies are being replaced by an intricate market structure and stressing modes of operation, closer to security levels. The ENTSO-E grid consists of five synchronous large areas, operated by 41 transmission system operators (TSOs) from 34 countries, and serves roughly 534 million citizens with 3,278 terawatt hours consumption and a growing share of cross-border transmission (about 15%, all numbers from 2015, see also Figure 3.2).

The ENTSO-E grid is designed and operated to ensure there is security of supply and reliable operation that is protected against cascade tripping, voltage or frequency collapse, and loss of synchronism. Electric power systems are operated so that any probable single event leading to a loss of a power system element should not endanger the security of the interconnected operation. This N-1 criterion ensures that if one element fails (a line, for example), the redistribution of the flow it was carrying will not overload other lines and cause a tripping cascade (ENTSO-E 2009). N-1 security should be monitored by the TSOs (i.e., the control room operators) at all times for their own systems and some defined parts of adjacent systems. After a disturbance (contingency), each TSO is supposed to return to N-1 compliant conditions as soon as possible, which leaves some flexibility but creates huge pressure in return, depending on the particular situation.

Physical energy flows

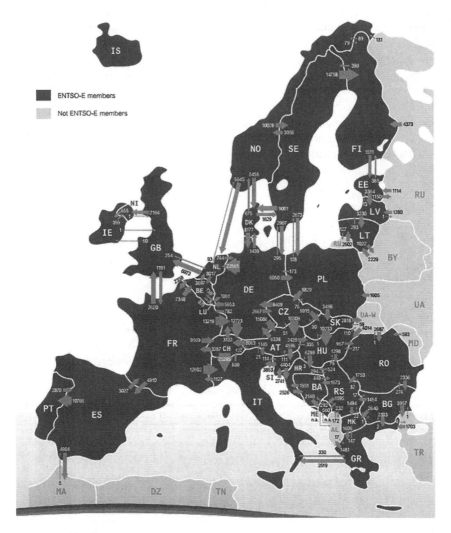

Figure 3.2 The European Transmission System, its spatial extension, and the values for cross-border physical power flow in gigawatt hours

Source: www.entsoe.eu

Lists of contingencies need to be developed by TSOs and taken into account for N-1 security calculations (See also: Kröger and Sansivini 2016).

Historically, this best practice principle has helped make the power system highly reliable. It is nonetheless vulnerable to different degrees. Errant kites, metal chains, and malicious attacks on circuit breakers are several examples of factors that may cause damage to high-voltage transmission lines, while buses are housed within compounds and can be defended more easily (Cuffe 2017). In recent years, the risk of power outages spreading over wide geographic areas has increased. Given the complex behavior of the power grid, it has been argued that the reliability and risk analysis of these systems has to go beyond the conventional approach of decomposition (e.g., fault tree analysis) or cause-and-effect/ causal chain development (e.g., event tree analysis) in order to capture emergent behavior and failure cascades (Eusgeld and Kröger 2008; Liu and Zio 2017).

Evidenced complexity of the power grid

Roughly 100 major outages (blackouts) have happened in the recent past (from mid-1999 to the end of 2015), of which 25 have been selected for further evaluation and characterization (Kröger 2017). Results have confirmed the dominant role that natural hazards play as triggers and emphasized the important role of organizational or contextual factors, while only one outage was triggered by a single technical failure. The cause of about one-third of the major outages has been proven to be the complex behaviors of the affected electricity supply systems, notably dynamics, nonlinearities, and tripping cascades. Furthermore, these major events clearly support the hypothesis that the electric power supply systems in most Western countries constitute a hybrid of social, ecological, and technical elements, i.e., a socio-ecological-technical system (Ferscha et al. 2011; Baxter and Sommerville 2011). Humans involved in the operation of electric power systems are often susceptible to misoperation, making mistakes during the time before the impact of a disruption on the electric power system becomes apparent and while they are still capable of adapting and regaining normal performance levels during the recovery period. They have a direct and instant impact on the performance of these systems (Amin 2002; Little 2004). A number of studies have shown that human errors are the major causes of incidents that occurred in the electric power systems as well as in other infrastructure systems sectors (Johnson and Holloway 2007; Kröger and Nan 2014; Wreathall et al. 2003). This highlights the significance of assessing human performance beyond a pure reliability assessment (Leveson 2004).

All of these major events and incidents manifested the need to include the full range of man-made threats and natural hazards and trigger event scenarios for everything imaginable. An all hazards approach must include technology- and human-related failures, the entire set of natural hazards (see Figure 3.1) and civilian actions (aircraft crash), operational/managerial flaws (e.g., lack of safety culture) and contextual influences (market-related, political, legal or institutional), and – of growing importance – malicious physical and cyberattacks, the latter experienced in the Ukraine on December 24, 2015.

Major changes and identifiable trends

In the recent past, regional and vertically integrated monopolies have been replaced by an intricate evolving market structure, which is generally accompanied by a set of firms following their own interests and rationalities. This has resulted in a lack of an overall view and responsibility for the whole supply chain.

This also leads to modes of operation that the system was originally not designed for. Other major changes include:

- Increasing short-term, cross-border trading (see also the section about the European High-Voltage Transmission System), additionally stressing the physical system and system operator unless it is compensated by better real-time information about the system state.
- Integration of growing shares of intermittent energy sources,[5] notably wind and solar, which are highly dispersedly distributed – dense in remote regions – and beyond our full control because of their massive temporal swings. The use of these sources is strongly dependent on the quality of the weather forecasts and related uncertainties (see Figure 3.3).
- Increasing "smartness" (grids, meters, online monitoring, observation, and control), preferably consisting of decentralized or even cellular structures that have concurrent power generators and consumers ("prosumers") and whose operation is partly controlled by households (whose behavior is unknown). Central units thus exert less control. Smart grids constitute a promising pathway to upgrade and evolve electrical supply systems efficiently and economically to make them fit for the future (Beaulieu, De Wilde, and Scherpen 2016; Scala et al. 2014). They make it possible for distributed renewable energy sources to attain a high market penetration by leveraging their fluctuating stochastic output patterns.
- Intensified security issues, i.e., the potential for detrimental cyberattacks (including manipulation) that take advantage of digital cyber-based information and communication (IC) host technology, which often link domains such as control and trading by using commercial hardware and software and the public internet instead of separate dedicated systems as in the past.

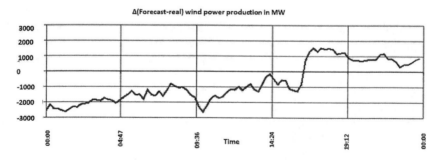

Figure 3.3 Difference between forecast and real wind power production in Germany and Austria on February 16, 2014

Source: EEX (© European Energy Exchange AG)

As indicated before, these changes and transitions could have a negative or a positive impact on the reliability and vulnerability of the transmission grid. It is worth mentioning that an increasing share of different kinds of distributed power sources together with a more decentralized, more loosely coupled structure could increase the heterogeneity and modularity of the grid, thus making critical states (tipping points) and large-scale collapses less probable while local disturbances may become more frequent. Smart grids also permit operators to detect and immediately respond to critical system conditions by continuously assessing the operational state. In case of power interruptions, automated devices speed up service restoration within the affected system section by employing "self-healing" capabilities such as intelligent switches and sensors for power rerouting and network reconfiguration. The observable tendency to increased consumer, even "prosumer" involvement may cause a dramatic shift in the dynamic system evolution, allow for adaptive learning, and even initiate chaotic behavior, counteracting the rigidity of the current grid controlled by a central authority (Zio 2016).

In recent years, the systems have received a number of incremental upgrades improving the efficiency of generation, the operating procedures, and the system security (Chester 2010), while they have been continuously exposed to intensified security issues such as cyberattacks, including manipulation. Future electric power systems will undergo even more technical, economic, and regulatory changes in order to adapt to emerging drivers, e.g., digital IC host technology that employs commercial hardware and software and often the public internet, an extended user involvement (see above) with largely unknown behavior as part of an increasingly fragmented system control, and induced changes in the demand-side management (Welsch et al. 2015). As a consequence, maintaining the stable, reliable, and economic operation of the electric power supply systems and the related decision making are becoming increasingly interesting and challenging.

Decision making under conditions of uncertainty and ambiguity resulting from interdependence and complexity

General remarks

Decisions are usually made at different levels and time scales. They can be at (a) the fairly long-term political-strategic level (e.g., in the EU targeting security, the reliability of supply, and the establishment of an efficient and competitive market, in Germany the *Energiewende*), (b) the medium-term industrial-planning level (e.g., targeting optimal management and the technical-structural development of the network, restructuring and extension of the grid, long-term trading/contracting), or (c) the rather short-term operational level (e.g., grid operators targeting stable and reliable system operation, exchanging information with their neighboring colleagues, inviting consumers to smooth peak loads and reduce costs, conducting short-term power trading).

The transmission grid displays quasistatic behavior under steady-state conditions, i.e., a balance of power generation and consumption without the need for continuous active control. In case of changes or imbalances, the system reacts rapidly as flow redistribution takes place with the speed of light and asks for corrective actions such as a redispatch, load shedding, or increased generation within a short period of time, roughly up to 20 minutes. The length of a grace period depends on various conditions, including the ambient line temperature, which influences line sagging, and load flow. The real status of the system is often hard to monitor, to understand, and to tackle; dependencies within the system itself and on other connected systems are often hidden and hard to identify. Consequently, decisions are significantly affected by uncertainty and ambiguity.[6]

The importance of interdependencies[7] has been proven by numerous past events. One such instance is the Rome telecommunication node failure in 2004. It was triggered by the breakage of a pipe carrying cooling water into an apparatus room, subsequently flooding the floor and causing an array of other vital systems to fail (see Figure 3.4).

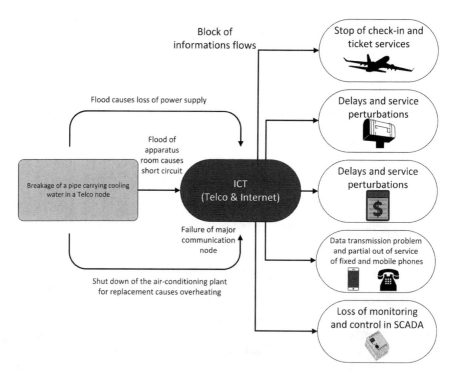

Figure 3.4 Interdependence of coupled networks, demonstrated by the failure of a major telecommunication node in Rome January 2, 2004, and its spread into other systems of social importance, adapted from (Kröger and Zio 2011, 21)

Sources of uncertainties and ambiguities

In the short-term, the sources of uncertainties and ambiguities at the operational level are due to increasing cross-border and short-term trading, lack of full responsibility for the reliable and secure supply of electricity as a "common good" (from the view of implemented unbundling strategy). Further contributions may arise from insufficient or nontransparent information about key system parameters and hidden interdependencies within the respective system and among coupled systems. Inadequate operator training and inadequately defined actions, notably in unforeseen situations, are often mentioned as additional sources. Given the emphasis on future conditions endorsed by political will, we assume that a significantly increased share of renewables will exacerbate, for example, the intermittency of power generation, our inability to control power generation, and our dependence on the accuracy of weather forecasts and anticipated consumer behavior. Without effective countermeasures, these conditions will increase complexity and related uncertainties, while a smarter decentralized grid topology with strengthened islanding capabilities may lead to the opposite.

Illustration of decision making under real conditions

Real-world "complexity" and decision making under conditions of uncertainty can be illustrated by a first example: the *Western European Transmission System Split* on November 4, 2006 (Liu and Zio 2017). The trigger was when two high-voltage lines over the river Ems in northern Germany were switched off to let a cruise liner built at an inland dock pass on its maiden voyage out to sea. The initial action was planned well ahead of time. N-1 calculations were made and provisions taken. But just days before the outage, the shipyard requested that the starting time be brought forward from early morning to late the preceding evening. The neighboring TSOs were not informed as they should have been, and the congestion forecast not updated. When the lines were switched off at 21:39, there was a strong wind infeed and therefore a high load flow to the Netherlands, which in itself was not fatal since the load was taken over by remaining lines, in particular between the substations Landesbergen and Wehrendorf. These substations were operated by two different TSOs, each unaware of different settings at the other end of the line. Based on faulty load flow calculations (empirical evaluation only), the Landesbergen team decided to couple two bus bars, an emergency measure which they expected to reduce the load. Instead the line to Wehrendorf tripped out, followed by a cascade of automatic high-voltage line trippings within 18 seconds, finally dividing the continental European grid into three islands with significant imbalances in each of them (see Figure 3.5). The resulting frequency drops in the Western area caused the supply for 15 million households to be interrupted. Full resynchronization was performed within 38 minutes, and the normal situation was re-established in all the affected European countries in less than two hours.

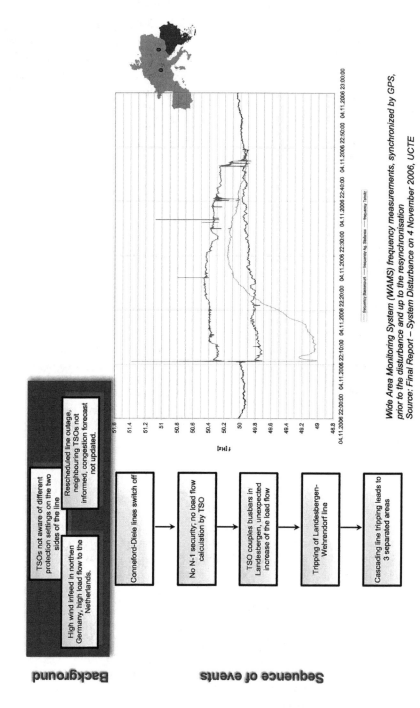

Background

TSOs not aware of different protection settings on the two sides of the line

Rescheduled line outage, neighbouring TSOs not informed, congestion forecast not updated.

High wind infeed in northern Germany, high load flow to the Netherlands.

Sequence of events

Conneford-Diele lines switch off

No N-1 security; no load flow calculation by TSO

TSO couples busbars in Landesbergen, unexpected increase of the load flow

Tripping of Landesbergen-Wehrendorf line

Cascading line tripping leads to 3 separated areas

Wide Area Monitoring System (WAMS) frequency measurements, synchronized by GPS, prior to the disturbance and up to the resynchronisation
Source: Final Report – System Disturbance on 4 November 2006, UCTE

Figure 3.5 Disturbance of the European Transmission System on November 4, 2006: Shown are background, sequence of events, and wide area measurement versus time (Kröger 2017)

Investigations identified two major causes. First, the actual evaluation of N-1 secure conditions was not based on numerical analysis (as requested), and the N-1 criterion was not fulfilled. Second, the regional inter-TSO coordination was inappropriate and no specific attention was given to different settings of protective devices on both sides of one line. Furthermore, five critical factors were identified, all organizational or contextual in nature (including the busbar split in the town of Borken due to maintenance) (Maas, Bial, and Fijalkowski 2007).

As shown by this and other severe events, human operators (TSOs) play a decisive role with regard to contingency management, for which situational awareness, short-term preparedness, and well-timed cross-border coordination are important factors. Appropriate information about important grid parameters, i.e., voltage, frequency, load flow, and synchronization, based on close to real-time monitoring, as well as timely information about longer and short-term power trading are important prerequisites for reducing any perceived complexity and uncertainties when decisions are made under conditions of stress.

The *Italian Power Blackout* may serve as another example. On September 28, 2003, at 3:01 a.m., one of the main north-south transit lines through Switzerland – the Lukmanier line – shut down following a flashover between a conductor cable and an inadequately cut tree. This shutdown resulted in a redistribution of the power flows and a subsequent overload (110%) of another north-south transit line, which, due to a separate flashover, also shut down 24 minutes later, followed by a series of cascading failures of other transmission lines in the border region. At that time, the Italian grid was completely separated from the ENTSO-E network. Despite corrective actions including load shedding (10 GW) as requested by the Swiss TSO – which turned out to be too small and falsely reasoned – the drop in frequency and voltage could not be brought under control and generation plants started to trip, giving rise to a total blackout throughout Italy at 3:27 a.m. (Kröger and Zio 2011, 12).

As these cases demonstrate, the human influence on decision making under real conditions has to become an integral part of any vulnerability assessment of complex systems like the electric power grid. While some suitable methods are available, others are still under development (see the following Section, case study 1, in particular).

Means to better cope with uncertainties and ambiguities

The key goals of maintaining network stability and avoiding tripping cascades will remain in focus in the coming period of time. We hypothesize that the German power supply system – as an integral part of the highly meshed European transmission system – will remain complex, although maybe to a lesser degree, and may continue to exhibit substantial uncertainties and ambiguities. It can be assumed that it is worthwhile to consider means to reduce or better cope with uncertainties and ambiguities mentioned above. The following possibilities appear reasonable:

- Allocate resource buffers, implement physical and functional redundancy or diversity, or at least counter the current trends to reduce them to achieve savings.
- Upgrade the N-1 safety criterion to N-2 to better cope with more than single failures.
- Implement the online monitoring of key parameters to provide real-time information and allow for continuous checking of the N-1/2 safety criterion but realize that this makes the network more vulnerable to remote observation and cyberattacks (Cuffe 2017).
- Ensure sufficient design and operational margins; stay away from (overload) conditions that the system was not designed for; reorganize the system in response to external changes.
- Notice early warning signals, e.g., an increased number of small outages and near misses, inadequate operator responses, and deficits in safety culture.
- Where possible, improve the grid structure and topology to increase the robustness to counter both random failures and targeted attacks.
- Shift the paradigm from the traditional risk concept, which focuses on prevention and mitigation and seeks to harden vulnerable components, to enhance postevent, "soft-landing strategies" (Linkov and Palma-Oliveira 2017), i.e., apply the concept of resilience[8] and, by this means, strengthen the absorptive and adaptive capabilities of the system and promote cost-efficient recovery.

Some argue that changes toward decentralized electric power generation technologies and management strategies can result in higher availability and improved resilience by making it possible to quickly react to short-term demand variations and to redispatch energy feeds to customers (Nan and Eusgeld 2011). Our own investigations basically confirm but slightly modify this general statement (see the following Section, case study 2).

Attractiveness and options to reduce complexity

Based on simulations and learning from the system breakdowns that have occurred, some argue that increasing complexity makes us lose control over the respective systems as a consequence of cascading effects, emerging scenarios, and regime shifts (Helbing 2013) and clearly reach the limits of our capacity to predict vulnerabilities and risks. They propose that strategies be developed to reduce complexity or to better master or balance unavoidable complexity. Furthermore, as a general rule, they claim to reorganize decision making and regulation from top-down to bottom-up.

There is no commonly agreed set of ways and means to reduce complexity and no panacea to master cascades and sudden regime shifts, in particular. Moreover, the aforementioned list of means to better cope with uncertainties and ambiguities does not automatically lead to less complex systems; some of them may even cause just the opposite, such as more sophisticated monitoring/data acquisition and control systems, and a higher degree of redundancy. The following guidelines to restrain or balance the complexity of the electric power system may appear useful:

- Lower the coupling density or decrease connectivity; moreover, develop and implement decoupling strategies, e.g., strengthen "islanding capabilities" to avoid the collapse of an entire system by enhancing the structural system design and/or engineered breaking points to stop cascades (flexible AC transmission system, FACTS).
- Balance automation and human control; relieve humans from unnecessary tasks and duties but keep them in the loop for the unforeseen.
- As connectivity and homogeneity affect the way in which a distributed system with local alternative states responds to changing conditions (see also Figure 3.6), build or reorganize networks with different components (increase

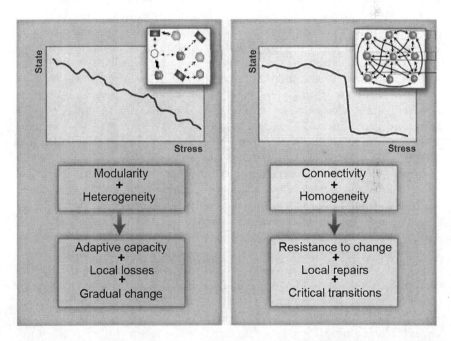

Figure 3.6 The connectivity and homogeneity of the units affect the way in which distributed systems with local alternative states respond to changing conditions ("stress"); incompletely connected, modular, and heterogeneous systems tend to incur local losses and adjust gradually to change. In contrast, highly connected, homogeneous systems are more resistant to change, and local losses tend to be repaired until a critical stress level leads the system to collapse (Scheffer et al. 2012)

heterogeneity) and incomplete connectivity (increase modularity), where appropriate, in order to avoid sudden regime shifts (tipping points) and large-scale breakdowns and to strengthen the absorptive and adaptive capabilities (Scheffer et al. 2012).

- Use modern digital information and communication technology (ICT) to enhance self-awareness, and create self-regulating systems to improve adaptiveness and recovery.
- Strive for robust grid topology, i.e., balance interconnectedness, prevent critical nodes from spreading failures, and optimize structure against the effects of random failures and targeted attacks.

Ability to understand and model critical infrastructure systems

Introduction

To ensure the operability, reliability, and security of dynamic large-scale critical infrastructure systems, e.g., the electric power supply system, and to further optimize the operation of these systems, it becomes essential to understand their behavioral patterns by learning from the past and, in particular, developing and applying analytical modeling and simulation tools. The development of suitable methods is a challenging task due to (a) the elements and attributes of complexity (previously outlined) and the seamless operation of these systems, (b) the lack of sufficiently clear information characterizing failure propagation, and (c) the intricate rules of interaction as a result of their openness and high degree of interconnectedness (Griot 2010; Pederson et al. 2006; Marrone et al. 2013). These systems, sometimes called nondeterministic or "of the 3rd kind" (Heinimann and Hatfield 2017), cannot be analyzed and sufficiently well understood using deterministic approaches based on certainty or using probabilistic methods which take uncertainties into account. Unfortunately, the related classical methods – such as fault trees, based on decomposition, and event trees, based on quasistatic causal chains – and human performance assessment, based on traditional human reliability techniques, often reach their limit.

Currently, a variety of advanced methods, models, and tools have been developed and applied. They can be divided into two categories, namely empirical and predictive (Johansson and Hassel 2010). The empirical approach aims to identify formation mechanisms and patterns of cascading failure, to assist us in learning from the analysis of previous near misses and serious events; the predictive approach mainly refers to modeling and simulating the major characteristics of critical infrastructure systems with the assistance of reasonable simplification. Focusing on advanced methods, mainly for risk analysis, several predictive research methods can be regarded representative and described as follows (Kröger and Zio 2011; Zio and Sansavini 2011; Nan, Eusgeld, and Kröger 2013). They are either structural, topological, or state-related, such as complex network theory, Petri net, and Bayesian net; or phenomenological or functional, such as agent-based or object-oriented modeling; or flow-focused, such as input-output inoperability modeling and system dynamic by nature.

Complex network theory (CNT)

Complex network theory is a widely used method, formed by graph theory, with the goal of understanding the structure of the interactions between components, characterize the topology, and check the vulnerability of the system by removing elements after the real system has been transformed into a graph with nodes and links and the adjacency matrix has been built. The drop in performance is measured by a group of topology-based metrics such as node degree and degree distribution, average and maximum path length, and betweenness centrality or clustering coefficient. Analysis of the topological properties of the network representing critical infrastructure systems can reveal useful information about the system's structure, topological vulnerability, and the level of functionality demanded for its components. However, this method alone lacks the ability to capture uncertain characteristics of critical infrastructure systems due to their inherent complexities and systems' properties when dynamic processes act on the network.

Petri net (PN)

A Petri net is a mathematical modeling language for describing distributed systems. In this approach, components (subsystems) of a system and their states are represented using elements such as places and transitions. The PN approach alone has difficulties modeling critical infrastructure systems quantitatively and often needs to be combined with other methods, e.g., agent-based modeling. Furthermore, the time domain cannot to be taken into account, and it is difficult to model the nonlinear and dynamic behavior of infrastructure systems.

Bayesian net (BN)

A Bayesian net is a probabilistic approach that can be used for modeling system behaviors based on observed stochastic events. This approach is based on a well-defined theory of probability reasoning and provides a strong framework for handling probabilistic events. In recent years, this approach has been applied in the area of dependability analysis of infrastructure systems. One of the major disadvantages of this approach lies in its difficulty in taking time into account.

Input-output inoperability modeling (IIM)

The input-output inoperability modeling approach was originally a framework for studying the equilibrium behavior of an economy by describing the degree of interconnectedness among various economic sectors. It assumes that each system can be modeled as an atomic entity whose level of operability depends on other systems, and that the propagation between them can be described mathematically using the basic Leontief high order mathematical model (Leontief 1986). This approach is capable of analyzing cascading failures and providing a mechanism for determining a dependency measure, and has therefore been widely used for modeling and analysis of critical infrastructure systems (Setola, De Porcellinis, and Sforna 2009). Nevertheless, IIM is a mathematical model which is best known for its application in the area of macroeconomics. Coefficients selected to compute this model are based on knowledge and the experiences of experts, factors which are hard to validate and are insufficient for capturing the complexity of critical infrastructure systems.

System dynamic (SD)

System Dynamic is an approach capable of studying the performance of critical infrastructure systems by using stocks, flows, and feedback loops. The dynamics depend on the structure of the model, time lags, and amplifications that occur through feedback. The approach provides a service-oriented method to analyze the performance of critical infrastructure systems, which can be used to optimize overall system performance. Using this approach, the system behaviors can only be modeled at a relatively abstract level.

Agent-based modeling (ABM)

The agent-based modeling approach is a relatively new approach to simulating systems that are composed of different types of autonomous (technical or non-technical) agents and built with information about a specific location and function as well as about capabilities and behaviors. As a modification and further development of object-oriented modeling (OOM), an ABM hybrid approach is capable of including physical rules in the simulation and emulating the behavior that emerges as a result of individual actions at a global level. It allows the explicit integration of highly nonlinear, time-dependent effects and supports the interdependency assessment process. Furthermore, this approach is capable of conducting a more comprehensive analysis of dynamic system behaviors by "looking into" (modeling) the component level of the studied systems. The ABM approach achieves a closer representation of system behaviors by integrating the spectrum of different phenomena, e.g., generating a multitude of representative stochastic, time-dependent event chains. However, this approach demands that a large number of parameters are defined for each agent, which requires thorough knowledge of the studied systems, including sufficient data.

In general, these methods differ in their capabilities and scope as well as by area of application and objectives. Their targets are mostly vulnerability and risk assessments for existing infrastructure systems with a fixed topological structure and limited to the operational level, although they sometimes extend to the industrial-planning level, e.g., to study the effects of structural-topological changes such as decentralization. The influence on and interaction with the socio-ecological-technical environment is barely treated. Some argue that evaluating vulnerability in power networks using purely topological metrics (like CNT) and not taking physical power flow realities into account can be misleading (Hines, Cotilla-Sanchez, and Blumsack 2010; Eusgeld et al. 2009).

Even quite advanced methods still address interdependencies in a rather simplified way. Scholars have studied critical infrastructure vulnerability taking different types of events into consideration, including (a) random failures, either technical or human in nature, (b) natural hazards and their impact on system components (usually described by fragility curves), (c) malicious attacks (often simulated by simply removing important components), and (d) combinations of the above events (Ouyang et al. 2017). More advanced or novel methods attempting to realistically capture the behavior of complex interdependent critical infrastructures, to include a widened spectrum of triggering events, and to assess modern "smarter" system designs are the object of a worldwide field of active research and development.

There is still a need for developing a comprehensive modeling or simulation approach and a framework capable of achieving a closer representation of critical infrastructure systems and of providing insights into their key behavioral features. In practice, there is still no "one for all" approach and it may be maybe wasted effort to strive for it. Instead, it has proven necessary to integrate different types of modeling approaches into one simulation tool, as a hybrid approach, to fully utilize the advantages of each approach and optimize the efficiency of the overall simulation. In Klein et al. (2007), the PN approach is integrated with the ABM approach to model interdependent infrastructure systems. In Alessandri and Filippini (2012), the authors combine the CNT approach with the SD approach in order to develop a resilience indicator. However, all of these hybrid approaches are not capable of solving one of the key challenges to developing such a simulation tool, namely the ability to create multiple-domain models and for the models to effectively exchange data among themselves (Bloomfield, Chozos, and Nobles 2009; Rome, Langeslag, and Usov 2014). One solution for handling these technical difficulties and meeting these challenges is to distribute different simulation components by adopting the concept of modular design (Kröger and Zio 2011). An experimental simulation test bed is created by adopting the HLA (high level architecture) simulation standard (Nan, Eusgeld, and Kröger 2013; Nan and Eusgeld 2011) and dividing the overall simulation tool into different simulation modules which are domain-specific or sector-specific simulation components. The modules are then combined in a distributed simulation platform, i.e., ABM with other modeling and simulation techniques, such as CNT, SD, Monte Carlo (MC) simulation, fuzzy logic (FL), and finite state machines (FSM).

The comparison of all the approaches (both empirical and predictive) discussed above is summarized in Table 3.2. Three types of approaches, i.e., complex network theory, input-output inoperability modeling, and agent-based modeling, can be considered a modeling approach for representing critical infrastructure systems as judged by their maturity and modeling capacity. Of all these approaches, the hybrid approach seems most promising.

Table 3.2 Comparison of different approaches for modeling critical infrastructure systems

Approach		State space		Multi-domain model	Physical model	Social element model	Analysis type		Outputs		Practical objectives		Recommend to model CI
		Continuous	Discrete				Topological analysis	Functional analysis	System reliability indicators	Identify critical elements	Design optimize	Operation optimize	
Empirical approaches		X		X	X	X	V	V	X	V	X	X	X
Predictive approaches (Modeling & simulation)	CNT	X	V	XX	X	X	V	X	V	V	V	X	*
	PN	X	V	X	X	X	X	V	V	V	V	X	X
	BN	X	V	X	X	X	X	V	V	V	V	X	X
	SD	V	(Frequency)	V	V	X	X	V	V	X	V	X	X
	IM	X	V	X	X	X	X	V	V	X	V	X	*
	ABM	V	V	V	V	V	X	V	V	V	V	V	*
	Hybrid	V	V	V	V	V	V	V	V	V	V	V	**

Source: WK/CN

CNT: Complex network theory PN: Petri-net BN: Bayesian network SD: System Dynamic IIM: Input-output inoperability modeling
ABM: Agent-Based Modeling
X Not recommend
* Recommend
**Highly recommend

Proposing a multilayer hybrid modeling framework

As previously mentioned and based on empirical findings (Luiijf et al. 2009), critical infrastructure systems such as the electric power supply system are highly integrated and interconnected. The operators of these systems must continuously monitor and control them to ensure proper operation and response to congestion (Igure, Laughter, and Williams 2006). These industrial monitoring and control functions are generally implemented using an operational control system (OCS), e.g., a supervisory control and data acquisition (SCADA) system. Their fundamental purpose is to allow users (operators) to collect data from one or more remote facilities and send control instructions back to those facilities (Boyer 2004). The system that is monitored and controlled by the OCS is generally referred to as a system under control (SUC). The monitoring and control function can be executed through dedicated, proprietary communication networks or through a shared, open communication network. The assessment of system performance focuses primarily on the technical aspects, almost ignoring the nontechnical ones, e.g., organizational and human factors (Ferscha et al. 2011; Baxter and Sommerville 2011), which are generally referred to as the human-organizational social system (SS). Yet, a number of studies have shown that the SS is the major cause of accidents that occurred in energy systems as well as in other sectors such as railway, aviation, and maritime infrastructure (Johnson and Holloway 2007; Kröger and Nan 2014; Wreathall et al. 2003). This highlights the importance of properly assessing the performance of the nontechnical aspects of energy systems together with the technical ones to identify vulnerabilities and serve as a basis for appropriate decision making, since changes and transitions within both portions need to be captured.

Research work related to modeling critical infrastructure systems is still at an early stage. Modeling an entire power system as a whole is usually impractical (Ring 2012; Bloomfield, Chozos, and Nobles 2009; Filippini and Silva 2012). Instead, it seems reasonable to take advantage of the structural, physical, and functional diversity of the networks and processes within the system, which can guide its partition into different layers (subsystems) and the choice of the appropriate modeling methods for each layer to fully represent the system behavior and functionalities. In the field of critical infrastructure protection, the hybridization of various modeling approaches has emerged as the most capable means of capturing the complex behaviors of diverse types of infrastructure and assessing their performances under both normal operation and degraded conditions (Beccuti et al. 2012). The results of the hybridization of modeling approaches achieve a high-fidelity representation of infrastructure systems. Nonetheless, the lack of a framework for combining modeling approaches hinders the possibility of analyzing dynamic system behaviors in a heterogeneous network of energy systems.

Motivated by the aforementioned needs, we propose a multilayer, hybrid modeling framework, within which an infrastructure system can be represented by the coupling of interacting subsystems in corresponding layers, i.e., system under control (SUC), operational control system (OCS), and human-organizational social system (SS). The guiding idea of this framework is to develop different subsystem-specific models, to integrate them, to benefit from the strengths of different modeling techniques, and finally to represent system behaviors through the interactions between the layers. The implementation of the proposed multilayer hybrid modeling framework can be divided into three steps: *screening analysis, individual model development,* and *model interaction representation,* briefly introduced below, using the electric power supply system as an example.

Given a system under analysis, the main purpose of first step "screening analysis" is to (a) decompose the system into the relevant subsystems and then (b) select the modeling approach that best captures their characteristics and behaviors. A variety of modeling approaches have been developed and applied (See for more details: Zio and Sansavini 2011; Ouyang 2014), among which agent-based modeling (ABM) seems the most promising due to its ability to represent the complexity and physical reality of any infrastructure system and to its flexibility and adaptability (Kaegi, Mock, and Kröger 2009). The electric power supply system (EPSS) can be viewed as being composed of three interrelated subsystems:

- The SUC represents one technical portion, which includes transmission lines, generators, bus bars, and relays.
- OCS represents another technical portion of the EPSS, comprising the supervisory control and data acquisition (SCADA) system with field instrumentation and control devices (FIDs and FCDs), remote terminal units (RTUs), communication units (CUs), and a master terminal unit (MTU).
- Finally, the SS represents the nontechnical portion of the EPSS, generally responsible for monitoring and processing generated alarms, switching off components at remote substations, and sending commands to remote substations.

Figure 3.7 shows a simplified multilayer representation of the EPSS with the three interacting subsystems and associated elements (components). The entire system is embedded in a socio-political-economic environment, which in principle could also be modeled as a metalevel but which is not included here.

In the second step, i.e., individual model development, subsystem-specific models are individually developed using the modeling approaches selected in step 1. Each model, capable of capturing the characteristics of the related subsystem, can be developed independently of any other peer models. For instance, in order to achieve high-fidelity modeling of technical parts of the EPSS, both functionality (physical laws) and structure (topology) should be taken into consideration. Furthermore, the OCS model needs to be able to process messages among components. Therefore, a hybrid ABM is developed to capture these two subsystems, representing the entire system by dividing it into interacting agents. Each agent is capable of modifying its internal data and behaviors and adapts itself to environmental changes (Chappin and Dijkema 2008; Tolk and Uhrmacher 2010). The model for the social system (SS) should be able to quantify the effects of human performance as well as human behavior, experience, and cognitive capability.

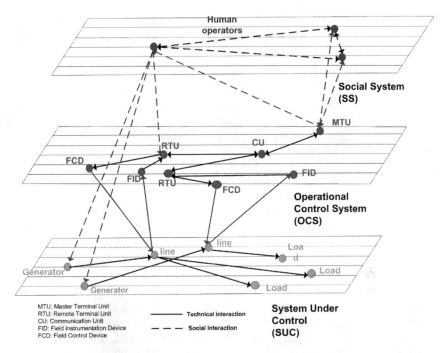

Figure 3.7 The representation of the EPSS using the proposed multilayer hybrid modeling framework. Parallel planes represent different subsystems in corresponding layers, and nodes represent various elements together with the interconnections among them. The elements depend on each other, as depicted by various horizontal (inside a layer) and vertical (between layers) links. The vertical links represent interactions among subsystems. Failure of an element can cascade to other layers and affect the operations of the whole infrastructure system

Source: CN

Motivated by these challenges, an agent-based hierarchical modeling approach is developed.

In the third step, the model interaction representation, variables of each model that are inputs to other peer models are determined. These variables identify the interaction among the subsystems and guide the assembly of the subsystem-specific models. In order to facilitate interoperability of the models and ensure efficient data exchange, the appropriate simulation standards can be used. Several standards that are capable of providing efficient data exchange among different models exist, e.g., high level architecture (HLA), distributed interactive simulation (DIS), and aggregate level simulation protocol (ALSP). Of these standards, the HLA is the most widely implemented and applicable one because it supports simulations made of coupled models (Nan and Eusgeld 2011). In order to exchange identified variables among three models via the HLA simulation standard, a local interface for each model is then developed, which contains HLA-related classes and methods responsible for sending and receiving data to and from other models. The subsystem-specific models are further connected over a local area network (LAN) to the run time infrastructure (RTI) server, which is responsible for the simulation synchronization and communication routing between them.

Representing the human-organizational layer

Modeling human performance and behavior is not a new endeavor. The first human performance related model was developed in the early 1980s by Card, Moran, and Newell (1983). Subsequently, researchers have proposed different approaches aimed at modeling and assessing human performance. According to Laughery, Archer, and Corker (2007), the development of human performance models follows two types of approaches, namely reductionist and first-principle. The former uses the human-system task sequence as the primary organizing structure. Human performance is decomposed into a sequence of tasks. In Lawless, Laughery, and Persenky (1995), this approach is adopted as a means to predict human performance in the control room of a nuclear power plant by decomposing it into a series of subfunctions and tasks. An exemplary framework based on this approach is the cognitive architecture named adaptive control of thought – rational (ACT – R), which models the steps of human cognition by a sequence of production rules (Anderson, Matessa, and Lebiere 1997). The advantage of this framework is its capability to model basic human cognition and to be integrated with other domains of knowledge, e.g., rules, experiences, and learning ability. It is an architecture that can be used to model a wide range of human cognition, including memory retrieval, visual search, and learning physics (Anderson et al. 1998; Salvucci and Anderson 2001). In Lebiere, Anderson, and Bothell (2001), this framework is further employed to develop a human performance model that fulfills a simplified air traffic control task.

In addition to the above top-down approaches with extended task and system analysis, there have been parallel efforts to develop methods to model and assess human performance, e.g., human reliability analysis (HRA). HRA considers the impact of human errors on system risks. It attempts to identify, represent, and quantify human errors and failures for the purpose of determining their contribution to system failures. HRA originates from the probabilistic safety assessment (PSA), where the probability of human failures is required to evaluate the risks to system operations (Sharit 2012). The technique for human error rate prediction (THERP), a first-generation HRA method, is one of the most widely used techniques to date. The goal of THERP is to calculate the probability of the successful completion of activities that are defined as necessary to accomplishing a task. THERP has limitations in human performance analysis because it focuses on errors of omission and intends to characterize each operator action with a binary path, i.e., success or failure. Moreover, the influence of performance shaping factors (PSFs) on human performance is quite poor and heavily based on the assessor's experience (Konstandinidou et al. 2006; Kyriakidis 2009). CREAM (the cognitive reliability error analysis method) is one of the best known second-generation HRA methods; it overcomes the limitations of the previous methods by developing a practical approach to performance analysis and error prediction (Hollnagel 1998). In contrast to other second-generation HRA methods, e.g., a technique for human event analysis (ATHEANA), CREAM presents a consistent error classification system integrating individual, technological, and organizational factors, which can be used both as a stand-alone method for accidental analysis and as part of larger design methods for interactive systems. One of the main features of this method is its integration of a useful cognitive model and framework that can be used in both retrospective and prospective analysis (He et al. 2008).

These three techniques, i.e., reductionist, first-principle, and human reliability analysis, are not mutually exclusive. Although their focus might vary, they can be mutually supportive in any given modeling task. For example, in order to implement an HRA method such as CREAM, a task or an event needs to be divided into a sequence of subtasks using the reductionist approach. On the other hand, implementation of the reductionist approach often needs an accurate representation of behavioral phenomena by basic human behavior models, which requires elements of first-principle approaches. During the last several decades, these three techniques have been widely developed and improved in order to provide an applicable way to assess human performance. However, they present inherent limitations, i.e., the lack of objectivity and the inability to model tasks that consist of highly nested and concurrent cognitive activities. Furthermore, combining them with models representing technical systems is a challenging task. These limitations hinder the possibilities of analyzing the performance of critical infrastructure systems while integrating the human factor in them.

To overcome these limitations, the ABM approach can be adopted because of its ability to represent system complexities and its modeling flexibility and adaptability (Card, Moran, and Newell 1983). Facilitated by these benefits, an agent-based hierarchical modeling approach has been further developed. This approach can be regarded as a more natural way to describe and simulate a system consisting of interacting entities such as those involved in the formation of the human performance, i.e., behavior, experience, cognitive capability, and action (Bonabeau 2002). Advantages of representing these entities as agents are:

- *Ability to represent the complexities of human behavior and performance*: Each individual behavior is nonlinear and cannot be characterized by simply using classic mathematical methods such as differential equations. ABM provides a natural framework for tuning agent complexities, e.g., ability to evolve, degree of rationality, and rules of interactions.
- *Possibility of developing heterogeneous agents*: In general, modeling approaches assume that entities are identical or similar in most aspects. This is particularly common when modeling the technical factors of a system. However, humans may differ in their own preferences and usually do not follow exactly the same rules and perform the same actions, i.e., humans are heterogeneous entities. Using ABM, each agent can operate based on its own preferences and rules of actions.

- *Ability to simulate interactions and rationality*: Interactions among humans and with the environment can be modeled using ABM. The simplest example of this type of interaction is information exchange from one human to another. Interactions can also be much more complicated, e.g., commands issued by a human operator. According to Kahneman (2003), human behavior should be modeled as being bounded rational. ABM is capable of developing bounded rational agents by setting up rules they should follow.
- *Learning ability*: The capability to include the ability to learn into human agents is one of the major features of ABM. This includes both individual and aggregation levels and can be modeled based on its own experience and rules and on interactions with other agents.

Case studies

We have chosen the Swiss high-voltage electric power supply system (EPSS, consisting of 219 transmission lines and 129 substations) to demonstrate the capability of the proposed modeling framework and how characteristics (e.g., vulnerability and resilience) of critical infrastructure systems can be affected by different factors, i.e., human performance and the integration of distributed energy sources.

Case 1: assessment of human influence

(A) PURPOSE AND ASSUMPTIONS

Recent research has revealed that the inadequate inspection and maintenance of SCADA firmware (e.g., inadequate patch management) are the issues most likely to have a significant negative impact on the monitored and controlled system and make it more vulnerable (Rome, Langeslag, and Usov 2014; Nan and Eusgeld 2011). In 2001, a SCADA software error in the Netherlands resulted in natural gas of an incorrect composition being supplied to 26,000 households, leading to the failure of their heating systems for three days (Luiijf et al. 2009). According to the Repository of Industrial Security Incidents (RISI) database, an incorrect SCADA software patch due to human error caused the malfunction of a section of the EPSS in the UK in 2005, as a result of which three power plants lost full operation.[9] Although such incidents, which are mostly due to human error, are fairly rare, the simultaneous malfunction of many SCADA components can cascade and have a large impact.

In this case study, we assume that the EPSS maintenance personnel update the firmware of a group of transducers, supplied by the same vendor, by sending out firmware patches. These transducers (components of the SCADA system) monitor the power flow in power transmission lines. These incorrect patches are sent out by mistake. Consequently, the affected transducers fail to indicate the real value of the monitored variables, which appear larger than the real value. Due to these malfunctions, false overload alarms are generated and sent to the operator in the control center. If the operator recognizes these alarms and handles them successfully, the corrective actions will be performed, i.e., a redispatch is generated. However, if no actions are taken within a certain period of time, it is assumed that the operator has failed to react, and the protection device automatically disconnects the overloaded transmission line to prevent damage to the EPSS.

(B) PARAMETERS AND RESULTS

One of the consequences of the transmission line disconnections is the disruption of the power supply to customers, which can be estimated by calculating the amount of expected demand not served (DNS). One additional performance metric, energy not served (ENS), is further developed, which quantifies the total energy that could not be supplied to the customers due to line disconnections during a certain time interval. The simulation covers two scenarios. In the first scenario (#1), the number of randomly selected field devices that are supplied by the same vendor and receive the wrong firmware update is 30, while this number drops to 20 in the second scenario (#2) (see Table 3.3 for results).

The performance of a human operator is mainly influenced by the number of alarms being handled in the control room, especially the number of simultaneous alarms, which can overwhelm an operator and increase the likelihood of an error. In scenario #1, 37 alarms are triggered; the maximum number of simultaneous alarms is 17. The maximum human error probability is 0.77, indicating the poor performance of the operator. As a consequence, the EPSS becomes more vulnerable since more transmission lines are disconnected and a greater disruption of the power supply is to be expected (ENS = 847 MWh). In scenario #2, the number of affected transducers decreases from 30 to 20, which reduces the number of total alarms to be handled to 26. In this case, the operator performs better, as indicated by the decrease in the maximum human error probability (from 0.77 to 0.41). As a consequence of improved operator performance, the system becomes less vulnerable since fewer transmission lines are disconnected and less power supply disruption is expected (ENS decreases to 397 MW). The influence of human performance on the vulnerability of EPSS can also be demonstrated by examining

Table 3.3 Summary of the validation experiment testing two scenarios

Performability metrics	Scenario #1	Scenario #2
Number of affected SCADA devices	30	20
Maximum human error probability (HEP_{max})	0.77	0.41
Number of total alarms	37	26
Number of maximum simultaneous alarms	17	10
Maximum demand not served (DNS_{max}) in MW	825	397
Energy not served (ENS) in MWh	847	416
Correlation Coefficient (R^2) (HEP and DNS)	0.91	0.87

Source: CN

the correlation coefficient (R^2) between human performance probability (HEP) and demand not served (DNS). The result indicates a strong correlation between HEP and DNS ($R^2 = 0.91$ in scenario #1 and 0.87 in scenario #2).

In this case study, the operator performance degrades when a burst of false overload alarms occur due to the incorrect firmware update, which then affects the system performance and makes the system more vulnerable although it is not the primary cause of failure.

Case 2: Reliability concern regarding the integration of renewable energy sources

(A) PURPOSE AND ASSUMPTIONS

The introduction of decentralized energy generation technologies can result in more energy being available than from traditional, hierarchically managed energy generation systems (Liserre, Sauter, and Hung 2010). The resilience of an electric power supply system could consequently be improved by making it possible to react quickly to short-term variations in demand and by redispatching energy feeds to customers. However, the benefit of implementing decentralized energy generation technologies may be limited by factors such as their highly variable power output and limited capacity. The purpose of this case study is to investigate how decentralized energy generation units, using the wind power system as an example, influence the resilience of the EPSS. The region selected is located in the eastern part of Switzerland, where three electricity distribution substations are installed: Robbia (Sub_{Robbia}), S.Fiorano ($Sub_{SFiorano}$), and Gorlago ($Sub_{Gorlago}$). Figure 3.8 shows the actual demand served by the three substations for a one-week period of time. The simulation starts on Monday and ends on Sunday.

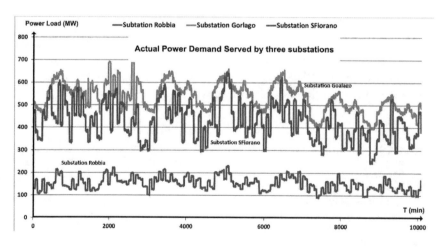

Figure 3.8 The actual power demand served by three substations (the y-axis denotes the power load [MW] and the x-axis denotes the time [min])

Source: CN

This case study assumes that it is possible to install a certain number of wind turbines in the selected region and that there is a sudden increase in the power load demand from customers served by the substation Robbia. This short-term demand variation increases the potential for the corresponding transmission lines to be overloaded, resulting in overload alarms being sent to the control center. For simplicity, we also assume that the operator in the control center fails to react to the overload alarms, thus triggering the corresponding protection devices (e.g., circuit breakers) to automatically disconnect the overloaded lines to prevent permanent damage to the system (EPSS).

(B) PARAMETERS AND RESULTS

In order to minimize the negative impact of this short-term demand variation, wind turbines are installed which can be a means to alleviate the stress exerted on the affected transmission lines by satisfying the power demand locally and without taking power from the EPSS. To assess the resilience of the system, two performability metrics are used. They are the energy not served metric (ENS) (see case study 1 for the definition) and the *average power demand served index* (*APDSI*), defined as the ratio of total actual power load served by all three substations from the EPSS and wind turbines to the total power loads. We have developed different simulation scenarios and tested them by varying the number of wind turbines from 0 to 6 and the capacities of the associated energy production. For the sake of simplicity, the simulation time for each test has been shortened to a randomly selected weekday during the week used for the simulation, and a sudden increase in power demand occurred during the late morning (from 9 to 11 h).

As demonstrated in Figure 3.9, integrating the wind energy production has a large impact on the operation of EPSS if there are variations in the short-term demand for power. With an increasing number of wind turbines, the amount of demand not served (DNS) decreases. The most significant system operation improvement can be observed by comparing the result of scenario 1 (number of wind turbines = 0) with that of scenario 2 (number of wind turbines = 1). When the number of wind turbines is increased further, the additional reduction in the DNS from wind energy is not as large as that achieved in scenario 2.

As shown in Table 3.4, the resilience of EPSS is improved by the introduction of locally generated power, as indicated by both performability metrics, i.e., ENS and APDSI. For example, the ENS value decreases significantly (from 1440 MWh to 756 MWh) and the average power demand served index (APDSI) increases from 0.757 to 0.872 when the number of wind turbines increases from 0 to 1. The same phenomenon can also be observed when using the metric of the line overload probability (the value drops from 0.94 to 0.51.).

The results also indicate the limited incremental improvements in the resilience of EPSS if the number of wind turbines is increased above one, i.e., all three metrics indicate smaller variations if the wind energy production capacity is continuously increased. For instance, the APDSI increases to the range of 0.872–0.900 and line overload probability drops to the range 0.41–0.48.

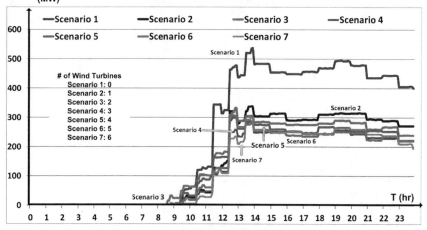

Figure 3.9 Operation of the electricity power supply system under different simulation scenarios. The y-axis denotes the demand not served (MW), and the x-axis denotes time (hours)

Source: CN

Table 3.4 Summary of the overall simulation results under different simulation scenarios

Scenario	# of wind turbines	Wind energy served (MWh)	ENS (MWh)	Line overload probability
1	0	0.00	1440	0.94
2	1	4.99	756	0.51
3	2	10.11	744	0.48
4	3	14.88	630	0.42
5	4	20.32	637	0.41
6	5	24.80	616	0.41
7	6	30.27	595	0.41

Source: CN

The nonlinear relationship between the amount of value variation (i.e., the amount of decreased ENS, the amount of increased APDSI, and the amount of decreased line overload probability) and the number of increased wind turbines is mainly due to the variable and fluctuating nature of wind energy production. As shown in the table, the average energy provided by one wind turbine is 4.99 MWh (the nominal generation capacity of this turbine is 3 MW), which identifies a small generation capacity factor of 7%.

Conclusions

In recent years, critical infrastructures, most notably the electric power supply system, have undergone massive technological, organizational, and structural changes, resulting in growing complexity and mutual dependencies. This development toward a "system-of-systems" has been furthered by the pervasive use of digital information and control systems, which have provided many benefits including real-time information about the system. These in turn have rendered decision making at the operator's level more reliable, but also induced new, mainly cyber-related risks. Because humans interact with critical infrastructures at different levels and in different degrees and ways, it is essential to understand infrastructures as sociotechnical systems that are closely coupled to the environment in which they are operated. Major blackouts have demonstrated the importance of inadequate human performance and the difficulties of making proper decisions under real conditions, often due to a lack of situational awareness and adequate communication.

Complexity is not negative per se. The tighter integration of the formerly loosely connected national and regional power grids have made the power supply to customers more reliable and secure but also made it possible for complex behavior to arise after system disturbances, including cascades and regime shifts. Nowadays, the electric power supply system confronts ongoing major changes and foreseeable trends, e.g., a strong political will for growing the share of energy from intermittent sources ("Energiewende"), an unbundled, competitive European power market, an increasing "smartness" and decentralization accompanied by increased user involvement and fragmentation of system control. These changes, including provision of adequate base-load supply,[10] comprise opportunities and risks and need to be thoughtfully managed. Some argue that with complexity we lose control over our respective systems and reach the limits of being able to predict vulnerabilities, and therefore should find ways to reduce complexity, although some degree of complexity will unavoidably remain.

It seems that some means for achieving less complex systems have become evident, such as increased decentralization, reorganized decision making and regulation from top-down to bottom-up approaches, and finding a balance between modularity and connectivity and between heterogeneity and homogeneity within the grid structure. But we have to be aware that there is no silver bullet, and often there are no solutions without dilemma. For example, by changing the grid structure to become more modular and heterogeneous we may avoid critical transitions and reduce the probability of large-scale collapses but increase the sensitivity to gradual changes and the probability of local losses. Moreover, strong heterogeneity of elements and connections (scale-free networks) translates into a high susceptibility to direct attacks and a low sensitivity to random failures, while homogeneous (small world) networks tend to the opposite. The architecture of complex systems is quite relevant and deserves careful consideration, including multistakeholder processes to fairly balance conflicting factors, interests, and views.

Furthermore, decision making is subject to large uncertainties and ambiguities. Reasonable measures to reduce these, such as increased redundancies and operational margins, have been identified but often contradict mainstream developments, driven by economics and a lack of public risk awareness. At a higher level, unbundling has led to more efficient and transparent markets but also to a loss of responsibility for the whole supply chain and, thus, may be reconsidered.

To recapitulate, managing the transmission of power systems is an extremely challenging endeavor and has to take into account numerous, partly conflicting aspects and factors. Furthermore, scientific evidence is still limited due to the fact that classical modeling approaches and tools for risk analysis, based on reductionism, are likely to fail to capture the behavior of a single complex sociotechnical system, not to mention a network of interacting or interdependent systems. The resilience concept, which is evolving and noteworthy, causes analysts to focus more on flexibility and adaption within their targeted systems (Linkov and Palma-Oliveira 2017).

However, resilience assessment and quantification is less mature than its peer methodology in traditional risk assessment (See for a comprehensive overview: Häring et al. 2017). Therefore, new system approaches and analytical frameworks are needed that are capable of offering a more holistic, multilayer viewpoint. Moreover, the set of natural hazards and man-made threats needs to be widened to include the effects of climate change and intentional malicious attacks (the all hazards/threats approach). Some such methods and tools are available and have been employed but are still in their infancy and need to be further developed.

Notes

1 An infrastructure is termed critical if it "is essential for [. . .] vital societal functions, health, safety, security, economic or societal well-being of people, and the disruption or destruction of which would have a significant impact [. . .] as a result of the failure to maintain those functions." Infrastructure systems are termed European critical infrastructure if their debilitation can effect at least two European countries (EU Member states) (EU Commission 2008).
2 See https://en.wikipedia.org/wiki/Complexity; Accessed 2017/12/07.
3 Homogeneity refers to the similarities in the elements, their interconnections, and their roles within the system structure, often with high-connected core elements and low-connected periphery nodes.
4 See also Figure 3.6 for an illustration.
5 The European Council recently adopted the objective to increase the share of intermittent energy sources (e.g., solar PV, wind turbines, and energy storage) to 20% in the EU by 2020 (da Graça Carvalho 2012).
6 The concept of ambiguity assumes that there are observations of some phenomena which proffer several legitimate interpretations of meaning (Renn and Klinke 2004); the Zika virus may serve as example.
7 The term "dependency" depicts a linkage between two systems through which the state of one system influences the state of the other, whereas interdependency is a bidirectional relationship through which the state of each system is correlated to the state of the other. These linkages can be of different types, e.g., physical, cyber, geographic, or logical (Rinaldi, Peerenboom, and Kelly 2001).

8 The concept of resilience has been developed and explored in various fields. There is no commonly accepted definition yet; in general it is understood as "the ability of a system to resist/absorb the adverse effects of a disruptive force (either sudden (shock) or creeping) with decreasing performance but without collapsing, and the ability and speed to recover and return to an appropriate functionality – by adapting through self-organization and learning and eventually bouncing back or transforming into a different state" (Kröger 2017, 52). The US National Academy of Sciences defines disaster resilience as "the ability to prepare and plan for, absorb, recover from, and more successfully adapt to adverse events" (NAS 2012, 1).

9 See the RISI Online Incident Database (Repository of Industrial Security Incidents; www.risidata.com).

10 Just recently, the US government stated that "the continued loss of base-load power generation with on-site fuel supply [. . .] must be stopped" (according to World Nuclear News on October 2, 2017: www.world-nuclear.org/information-library/country-profiles/countries-t-z/usa-nuclear-power.aspx; Accessed 2017/12/07).

References

Alessandri, Angelo, and Roberto Filippini. 2012. "An Approach to Resilience of Interconnected Systems Based on Stability Analysis." In *Conference on Critical Information Infrastructures Security (CRITIS 12)*. Lillehammer, Norway.

Amin, M. 2002. "Security Challenges for the Electricity Infrastructure." *IEEE Computer Magazine on Security and Privacy* 35 (special issue 4): 8–10. https://doi.org/10.1109/mc. 2002.1012423.

Anderson, John R., Dan Bothell, Christian Lebiere, and Michael Matessa. 1998. "An Integrated Theory of List Memory." *Journal of Memory and Language* 38: 341–80. http://dx.doi.org/10.1006/jmla.1997.2553.

Anderson, John R., Michael Matessa, and Christian Lebiere. 1997. "ACT-R: A Theory of Higher Level Cognition and Its Relation to Visual Attention." *Human – Computer Interaction* 12: 439–62. https://doi.org/10.1207/s15327051hci1204_5.

Aven, Terje, Yakov Ben-Haim, Henning Boje Andersen, Tony Cox, Enrique López Droguett, Michael Greenberg, Seth Guikema, Wolfgang Kröger, Ortwin Renn, and Kimberly M. Thompson. 2015. "SRA Glossary." Council of the Society of Risk Analysis (SRA). www.sra.org/sites/default/files/pdf/SRA-glossary-approved22june2015-x.pdf.

Aven, Terje, and Bodil S. Krohn. 2014. "A New Perspective on How to Understand, Assess and Manage Risk and the Unforeseen." *Reliability Engineering & System Safety* 121: 1–10. https://doi.org/10.1016/j.ress.2013.07.005.

Baxter, Gordon, and Ian Sommerville. 2011. "Socio-Technical Systems: From Design Methods to Systems Engineering." *Interacting with Computers* 23: 4–17. https://doi. org/10.1016/j.intcom.2010.07.003.

Beaulieu, Anne, Jaap De Wilde, and Jacquelien MA Scherpen. 2016. *Smart Grids from a Global Perspective: Bridging Old and New Energy Systems*. Dordrecht: Springer.

Beccuti, Marco, Silvano Chiaradonna, Felicita Di Giandomenico, Susanna Donatelli, Giovanna Dondossola, and Giuliana Franceschinis. 2012. "Quantification of Dependencies between Electrical and Information Infrastructures." *International Journal of Critical Infrastructure Protection* 5: 14–27. https://doi.org/10.1016/j.ijcip.2012.01.003.

Bloomfield, Robin, Nick Chozos, and Phil Nobles. 2009. "Infrastructure Interdependency Analysis: Requirements, Capabilities and Strategy." London: City University, Adelard LLP, Cranfield University. www.adelard.com/assets/files/docs/d418v13_public.pdf.

Bonabeau, Eric. 2002. "Agent-Based Modeling: Methods and Techniques for Simulating Human Systems." *Proceedings of the National Academy of Sciences* 99 (May): 7280–87. https://doi.org/10.1073/pnas.082080899.

Boyer, Stuart A. 2004. *SCADA Supervisory Control and Data Acquisition*. 3rd ed. Research Triangle Park: ISA.

Card, Stuart K., Thomas P. Moran, and Allen Newell. 1983. *The Psychology of Human-Computer Interaction*. London: Taylor & Francis.

Chappin, Emile J. L., and G. P. J. Dijkema. 2008. "Agent-Based Modeling of Energy Infrastructure Transitions." In *Infrastructure Systems and Services: Building Networks for a Brighter Future (INFRA)*, 2008. Rotterdam, Netherlands. https://doi.org/10.1109/INFRA.2008.5439580.

Chester, Lynne. 2010. "Conceptualising Energy Security and Making Explicit Its Polysemic Nature." *Energy Policy* 38 (February): 887–95. https://doi.org/10.1016/j.enpol.2009.10.039.

Cohen, Fred. 2010. "What Makes Critical Infrastructures Critical?" *International Journal of Critical Infrastructure Protection* 3: 53–54. https://doi.org/10.1016/j.ijcip.2010.06.002.

Cuffe, Paul. 2017. "A Comparison of Malicious Interdiction Strategies Against Electrical Networks." *IEEE Journal on Emerging and Selected Topics in Circuits and Systems* 7 (2): 205–17.

da Graça Carvalho, Maria. 2012. "EU Energy and Climate Change Strategy." *Energy* 40 (1): 19–22. https://doi.org/10.1016/j.energy.2012.01.012.

Dobson, Ian, Benjamin A. Carreras, Vickie E. Lynch, and David E. Newman. 2007. "Complex Systems Analysis of Series of Blackouts: Cascading Failure, Critical Points, and Self-Organization." *Chaos: An Interdisciplinary Journal of Nonlinear Science* 17: 026103–026103–13. https://doi.org/10.1063/1.2737822.

ENTSO-E. 2009. "Policy 3: Operational Security." P3. Brüssel: Union for the Co-ordination of Transmission of Electricity (UCTE). https://www.entsoe.eu/fileadmin/user_upload/_library/publications/entsoe/Operation_Handbook/Policy_3_final.pdf.

EU Commission. 2008. "COUNCIL DIRECTIVE 2008/114/EC of 8 December 2008 on the Identification and Designation of European Critical Infrastructures and the Assessment of the Need to Improve Their Protection." *Official Journal of the European Union*. http://data.europa.eu/eli/dir/2008/114/oj.

Eusgeld, Irene, and Wolfgang Kröger. 2008. "Towards a Framework for Vulnerability Analysis of Interconnected Infrastructures." In *Proceedings of 9th International Probabilistic Safety Assessment and Management Conference*, 107–16. Hong Kong.

Eusgeld, Irene, Wolfgang Kröger, Giovanni Sansavini, Markus Schläpfer, and Enrico Zio. 2009. "The Role of Network Theory and Object-Oriented Modeling within a Framework for the Vulnerability Analysis of Critical Infrastructures." *Reliability Engineering and System Safety* Vol.94: 954–63.

Ferscha, Alois, Kashif Zia, Andreas Riener, and Alexei Sharpanskykh. 2011. "Potential of Social Modelling in Socio-Technical Systems." *Procedia Computer Science* 7: 235–7. https://doi.org/10.1016/j.procs.2011.09.051.

Filippini, Roberto, and Andres Silva. 2012. "Resilience Analysis of Networked Systems-of-Systems Based on Structural and Dynamic Interdependencies." Presented at the PSAM 11 & ESREL 2012, Helsinki, Finland.

Griot, Chloe. 2010. "Modelling and Simulation for Critical Infrastructure Interdependency Assessment: A Meta-Review for Model Characterisation." *International Journal of Critical Infrastructure* 6: 363–79.

Häring, Ivo, Giovanni Sansavini, Emanuele Bellini, Nick Martyn, Tatyana Kovalenko, Maksim Kitsak, Georg Vogelbacher, et al. 2017. "Towards a Generic Resilience Management, Quantification and Development Process: General Definitions, Requirements, Methods, Techniques and Measures, and Case Studies." In *Resilience and Risk*, edited by Igor Linkov and José Manuel Palma-Oliveira, 21–80. Dordrecht, The Netherlands: Springer. https://doi.org/10.1007/978-94-024-1123-2_2.

He, Xuhong, Yao Wang, Zupei Shen, and Xiangrui Huang. 2008. "A Simplified CREAM Prospective Quantification Process and Its Application." *Reliability Engineering and System Safety* 93: 298–306. https://doi.org/10.1016/j.ress.2006.10.026.

Heinimann, Hans R., and Kirk Hatfield. 2017. "Infrastructure Resilience Assessment, Management and Governance – State and Perspectives." In *Resilience and Risk. Methods and Application in Environment, Cyber and Social Domains*, edited by Igor Linkov and José Manuel Palma-Oliveira, 147–87. NATO Science for Peace and Security Series C: Environmental Security. Dordrecht: Springer. https://doi.org/10.1007/978-94-024-1123-2_5.

Helbing, Dirk. 2013. "Globally Networked Risks and How to Respond." *Nature* 497: 51–9. https://doi.org/10.1038/nature12047.

Hines, Paul, Eduardo Cotilla-Sanchez, and Seth Blumsack. 2010. "Do Topological Models Provide Good Information about Electricity Infrastructure Vulnerability?" *Chaos: An Interdisciplinary Journal of Nonlinear Science* 20 (033122). https://doi.org/10.1063/1.3489887.

Hollnagel, Erik. 1998. *Cognitive Reliability and Error Analysis Method CREAM*. XIV, 287 S. London: Elsevier.

Igure, Vinay M., Sean A. Laughter, and Ronald D. Williams. 2006. "Security Issues in SCADA Networks." *Journal of Computers and Security* 25: 498–506. https://doi.org/10.1016/j.cose.2006.03.001.

Johansson, Jonas, and Henrik Hassel. 2010. "An Approach for Modelling Interdependent Infrastructures in the Context of Vulnerability Analysis." *Reliability Engineering and System Safety* 95: 1335–44. https://doi.org/10.1016/j.ress.2010.06.010.

Johnson, C. W., and C. M. Holloway. 2007. "A Longitudinal Analysis of the Causal Factors in Major Maritime Accidents in the USA and Canada (1996–2006)." In *The Safety of Systems*, edited by Felix Redmill and Tom Anderson, 85–104. London: Springer.

Kaegi, Manuel, Ralf Mock, and Wolfgang Kröger. 2009. "Analyzing Maintenance Strategies by Agent-Based Simulations: A Feasibility Study." *Reliability Engineering & System Safety* 94: 1416–21. https://doi.org/10.1016/j.ress.2009.02.002.

Kahneman, Daniel. 2003. "Maps of Bounded Rationality: Psychology for Behavioral Economics." *The American Economic Review* 93: 1449–75. https://doi.org/10.2307/3132137.

Klein, Rüdiger, Erich Rome, Césaire Beyel, Ralf Linnemann, and Wolf Reinhardt. 2007. "Information Modelling and Simulation in Large Interdependent Critical Infrastructures in IRRIIS." IRRIS Report.

Komendantova, N., Daniel Kroos, D. Schweitzer, C. Leroy, E. Andreini, B. Baltasar, T. Boston, M. Keršnik, K. Botbaev, and J. Cohen. 2016. "Protecting Electricity Networks from Natural Hazards." Organization for Security and Cooperation in Europe (OSCE). www.osce.org/secretariat/242651.

Konstandinidou, Myrto, Zoe Nivolianitou, Chris Kiranoudis, and Nikolaos Markatos. 2006. "A Fuzzy Modeling Application of CREAM Methodology for Human Reliability Analysis." *Reliability Engineering and System Safety* 91: 706–16. https://doi.org/10.1016/j.ress.2005.06.002.

Kröger, Wolfgang. 2017. "Securing the Operation of Socially Critical Systems from an Engineering Perspective: New Challenges, Enhanced Tools and Novel Concepts." *European Journal for Security Research* 2 (1): 39–55. https://doi.org/10.1007/s41125-017-0013-9.

Kröger, Wolfgang, and Cen Nan. 2014. "Addressing Interdependencies of Complex Technical Networks." In *Networks of Networks: The Last Frontier of Complexity*, edited by Gregorio D'Agostino and Antonio Scala, 279–309. Understanding Complex Systems. Dordrecht: Springer International Publishing.

Kröger, Wolfgang, and Giovanni Sansivini. 2016. "Principles of Disaster Risk Reduction." In *Protecting Electricity Networks from Natural Hazards*, edited by OSCE. Organization for Security and Co-Operation in Europe. Vienna: Organization for Security and Cooperation in Europe (OSCE).

Kröger, Wolfgang, and Enrico Zio. 2011. *Vulnerable Systems*. London; Dordrecht; Heidelberg; New York: Springer.

Kyriakidis, M. 2009. "Focal Report: A Study Regarding Human Reliability within Power System Control Rooms." BABS Report. Zurich: Lab for Safety Analysis, ETH Zurich.

Laughery, K. Ronald, Susan Archer, and Kevin Corker. 2007. "Modeling Human Performance in Complex Systems." In *Handbook of Industrial Engineering*, 2407–44. Chichester: John Wiley & Sons, Inc.

Lawless, M. T., K. R. Laughery, and J. J. Persenky. 1995. "Using Micro Saint to Predict Performance in a Nuclear Power Plant Control Room. A Test of Validity and Feasibility." NUREG/CR-6159. Boulder, CO and Washington, DC: Micro Analysis and Design, Inc. and U. S. Nuclear Regulatory Commission (NRC).

Lebiere, Christian, John R. Anderson, and Daniel Bothell. 2001. "Multi-Tasking and Cognitive Workload in an ACT-R Model of a Simplified Air Traffic Control Task." In *10th Conference on Computer Generated Forces and Behavioral Representation Proceedings*.

Leontief, W. W. 1986. *Input-Output Economics*. 2nd ed. New York: Oxford University Press.

Leveson, Nancy G. 2004. "A Systems-Theoretic Approach to Safety in Software-Intensive Systems." *IEEE Transactions on Dependable and Secure Computing* 1 (1): 66–86.

Linkov, Igor, and José Manuel Palma-Oliveira. 2017. "An Introduction to Resilience for Critical Infrastructures." In *Resilience and Risk. Methods and Application in Environment, Cyber and Social Domains*, edited by Igor Linkov and José Manuel Palma-Oliveira, 3–17. NATO Science for Peace and Security Series C: Environmental Security. Dordrecht, The Netherlands: Springer. https://link.springer.com/chapter/10.1007/978-94-024-1123-2_1.

Liserre, Marco, Thilo Sauter, and John Y. Hung. 2010. "Future Energy Systems: Integrating Renewable Energy Sources into the Smart Power Grid through Industrial Electronics." *IEEE Industrial Electronics Magazine*, 18–37.

Little, Richard. 2004. "A Socio-Technical Systems Approach to Understanding and Enhancing the Reliability of Interdependent Infrastructure Systems." *International Journal of Emergency Management* 2: 98–110.

Liu, Jie, and Enrico Zio. 2017. "System Dynamic Reliability Assessment and Failure Prognostics." *Reliability Engineering & System Safety* 160 (April): 21–36. https://doi.org/10.1016/j.ress.2016.12.003.

Luiijf, Eric, Albert Nieuwenhuijs, Marieke Klaver, Michel van Eeten, and Edite Cruz. 2009. "Empirical Findings on Critical Infrastructure Dependencies in Europe." In *Critical Information Infrastructure Security*, edited by Roberto Setola and Stefan Geretshuber, 5508: 302–10. Lecture Notes in Computer Science. Berlin Heidelberg: Springer.

Maas, Gerard A., Marcel Bial, and Jakub Fijalkowski. 2007. "System Disturbance on 4 November 2006." Final Report. UCTE. ecolo.org/documents/documents_in_english/blackout-nov-06-UCTE-report.pdf.

Marrone, Stefano, Roberto Nardone, Annarita Tedesco, Pasquale D'Amore, Valeria Vittorini, Roberto Setola, Francesca De Cillis, and Nicola Mazzocca. 2013. "Vulnerability Modeling and Analysis for Critical Infrastructure Protection Applications." *International Journal of Critical Infrastructure Protection* 6: 217–27. https://doi.org/10.1016/j.ijcip.2013.10.001.

Nai Fovino, Igor, Andrea Carcano, Marcelo Masera, and Alberto Trombetta. 2009. "An Experimental Investigation of Malware Attacks on SCADA Systems." *International Journal of Critical Infrastructure Protection* 2: 139–45. https://doi.org/10.1016/j.ijcip.2009.10.001.

Nan, Cen, and Irene Eusgeld. 2011. "Adopting HLA Standard for Interdependency Study." *Reliability Engineering and System Safety* 96 (1): 149–59. https://doi.org/10.1016/j.ress.2010.08.002.

Nan, Cen, Irene Eusgeld, and Wolfgang Kröger. 2013. "Analyzing Vulnerabilities between SCADA System and SUC Due to Interdependencies." *Reliability Engineering and System Safety* 113: 76–93. https://doi.org/10.1016/j.ress.2012.12.014.

NAS, ed. 2012. *Disaster Resilience: A National Imperative*. National Academy of Sciences. Washington, DC: National Academies Press. https://doi.org/10.17226/13457.

Ouyang, Min. 2014. "Review on Modeling and Simulation of Interdependent Critical Infrastructure Systems." *Reliability Engineering & System Safety* 121: 43–60. https://doi.org/10.1016/j.ress.2013.06.040.

Ouyang, Min, Min Xu, Chi Zhang, and Shitong Huang. 2017. "Mitigating Electric Power System Vulnerability to Worst-Case Spatially Localized Attacks." *Reliability Engineering & System Safety* 165 (September): 144–54. https://doi.org/10.1016/j.ress.2017.03.031.

Pederson, P., D. Dudenhoeffer, S. Hartly, and M. Permann. 2006. "Critical Infrastructure Interdependency Modeling: A Survey of U.S and International Research." Idaho National Laboratory.

Renn, Ortwin, and Andreas Klinke. 2004. "Systemic Risks: A New Challenge for Risk Management." *EMBO Reports* 5 (S1): S41–46. https://doi.org/10.1038/sj.embor.7400227.

Rinaldi, Steven M., James P. Peerenboom, and Terrence K. Kelly. 2001. "Identifying, Understanding, and Analyzing Critical Infrastructure Interdependencies." *IEEE Control Systems Magazine* 21 (December): 11–25.

Ring, Jack. 2012. "Systems of the Third Kind: Distinctions, Implications, and Initiatives." *INCOSE INSIGHT* 15: 9–12.

Rome, Erich, Peter Langeslag, and Andrij Usov. 2014. "Federated Modelling and Simulation for Critical Infrastructure Protection." In *Networks of Networks: The Last Frontier of Complexity*, edited by Gregorio D'Agostino and Antonio Scala, 225–53. Understanding Complex Systems. Springer International Publishing.

Salvucci, Dario D., and John R. Anderson. 2001. "Integrating Analogical Mapping and General Problem Solving: The Path-Mapping Theory." *Cognitive Science* 25: 67–110. http://dx.doi.org/10.1016/S0364-0213(00)00035-5.

Scala, Antonio, Guido Caldarelli, Alessandro Chessa, Alfonso Damiano, Mario Mureddu, Sakshi Pahwa, Caterina Scoglio, and Walter Quattrociocchi. 2014. "Power Grids, Smart Grids and Complex Networks." In *Nonlinear Phenomena in Complex Systems: From Nano to Macro Scale*, edited by Davron Matrasulov and H. Eugene Stanley, 97–110. NATO Science for Peace and Security Series C: Environmental Security. Springer Netherlands.

Scheffer, Marten, Stephen R. Carpenter, Timothy M. Lenton, Jordi Bascompte, William Brock, Vasilis Dakos, Johan van de Koppel, et al. 2012. "Anticipating Critical Transitions." *Science* 338: 344–8. https://doi.org/10.1126/science.1225244.

Schläpfer, Markus, Tom Kessler, and Wolfgang Kröger. 2012. "Reliability Analysis of Electric Power Systems Using an Object-Oriented Hybrid Modeling Approach." *ArXiv:1201.0552 [Cs].* http://arxiv.org/abs/1201.0552.

Setola, Roberto, Stefano De Porcellinis, and Marino Sforna. 2009. "Critical Infrastructure Dependency Assessment Using the Input-Output Inoperability Model." *International Journal of Critical Infrastructure Protection* 2: 170–8.

Sharit, Joseph. 2012. "Human Error and Human Reliability Analysis." *Handbook of Human Factors and Ergonomics, Fourth Edition*, 734–800.

Sornette, D., and G. Ouillon. 2012. "Dragon-Kings: Mechanisms, Statistical Methods and Empirical Evidence." *The European Physical Journal Special Topics* 205 (1): 1–26. https://doi.org/10.1140/epjst/e2012-01559-5.

Taleb, Nassim Nicholas. 2007. "Black Swans and the Domains of Statistics." *The American Statistician* 61 (August): 198–200. https://doi.org/10.1198/000313007X219996.

Tolk, Andreas, and Adelinde M. Uhrmacher. 2010. "Agents: Agenthood, Agent Architectures, and Agent Taxonomies." In *Agent-Directed Simulation and Systems Engineering*, edited by Yilmaz and Tuncer I. Ören, 73–109. Wiley Series in Systems Engineering and Management. Weinheim, Germany: Wiley-VCH Verlag GmbH & Co. KGaA. https://doi.org/10.1002/9783527627783.ch3.

Welsch, Manuel, Mark Howells, Mohammad Reza Hesamzadeh, Brian Ó Gallachóir, Paul Deane, Neil Strachan, Morgan Bazilian, Daniel M. Kammen, Lawrence Jones, and Goran Strbac. 2015. "Supporting Security and Adequacy in Future Energy Systems: The Need to Enhance Long-term Energy System Models to Better Treat Issues Related to Variability." *International Journal of Energy Research* 39: 377–96. https://doi.org/10.1002/er.3250.

Wreathall, John, Emilie Roth, Dennis Bley, and Jordan Multer. 2003. "Human Reliability Analysis in Support of Risk Assessment for Positive Train Control. Human Factors in Railroad Operations." Washington: U.S. Department of Transportation. https://rosap.ntl.bts.gov/view/dot/8745/dot_8745_DS1.pdf?

Zio, Enrico. 2016. "Challenges in the Vulnerability and Risk Analysis of Critical Infrastructures." *Reliability Engineering & System Safety* 152 (August): 137–50. https://doi.org/10.1016/j.ress.2016.02.009.

Zio, Enrico, and Giovanni Sansavini. 2011. "Modeling Interdependent Network Systems for Identifying Cascade-Safe Operating Margins." *IEEE Transactions on Reliability* 60: 94–101. https://doi.org/10.1109/tr.2010.2104211.

4 Aligning institutions and technologies in energy systems[1]

Rolf W. Künneke

Introduction

Citizens are increasingly able to provide for their own energy needs. They can invest in wind energy that is produced near to their homes, connect to a biogas supply from local farmers, or install solar panels on the roofs of their houses. They are increasingly gaining control over how energy is produced, and when and how it is used. In this way, they even contribute to a cleaner environment and a sustainable energy system. They are becoming "prosumers," i.e., a combination of producer and consumer of energy.

Decentralized power production, close to citizens, is getting increasingly popular. Solar panels and wind turbines are becoming part of the living environment. Germany is a special case in this respect. Since the *Energiewende* (energy transition), there has been a massive increase in the use of sustainable energy production, stimulated by dedicated energy policy programs.[2] Within less than four years, 27 GW of solar panels were installed, which is approximately the complete installed production capacity in a country like The Netherlands. This represents a significant change in the energy provision.

The ongoing technical changes in the energy sector increasingly influence the way energy is provided to citizens. One of the remarkable developments is the growing number of so-called energy communities. These are local initiatives promoting the production of clean energy by using local energy sources. In The Netherlands, there are some 150[3] such communities at the moment, and the number is steadily growing. Typically, these local initiatives are legally organized as cooperatives or foundations, indicating a not-for-profit orientation. Traditionally, electricity is produced by large-scale power plants that are typically operated as a profit-oriented business. Electricity is transported through high-voltage transmission lines over long distances. Finally, it is distributed through low-voltage power grids to the final consumers. This traditional unidirectional provision of power now seems to be being challenged.

The ensuing question is how these changes have an impact on the provision of energy, such that this essential service is provided according to societal expectations. To answer this question, it is important to address the possible interrelations between the technological and institutional specificities that characterize this sector. In the electricity sector, for instance, load balancing is an important issue. The production and consumption of electric power needs to be balanced very carefully. If electricity is fed into the grid in an uncontrolled way, the system will break down. This has significant socioeconomic consequences, since nowadays most social activities depend on an uninterrupted availability of power. The load balancing of electric systems can only be safeguarded by interrelated technological and institutional arrangements. Typically system operators are assigned specific authority to intervene in the operation of electricity systems. They can intervene in the production and the transport of electric energy. The power production of large-scale power plants can be adjusted to the actual power demand. In an emergency, spinning reserves can be activated. Even the power flow in transmission networks can be rerouted to circumvent local failures.

Traditionally, system operators have performed this task of load balancing at the high-voltage level. This was technically effective and economically efficient since electric power was provided by a limited number of large-scale power plants that are directly connected to the high-voltage grid. However, the decentralized provision of power has significantly changed the technical features of the electricity sector. To stay with the example of load balancing, the ability to control the increasing provision of electricity on the low-voltage distribution network poses a challenge. When the supply of solar energy is very high, the amount of locally produced energy could be much higher than the local demand. The surplus power would therefore need to be absorbed by local distribution networks. This causes several technical and institutional problems. Technically, the transformers that connect the distribution grids to the transmission network are only able to transform high-voltage power to low-voltage power, but not vice-versa, which would be technically required in order for the high-voltage network to absorb local energy production. Allowing for bidirectional power flows and transformation is a significant technical reconfiguration of the current power system. From an institutional perspective, system operators only have the authority to intervene in the high-voltage network. This raises several fundamental questions. What are the consequences of this changing technology for the economic organization of local energy systems? Who is responsible for local load balancing? Who must make the necessary investments to further develop innovative local energy systems? Who supervises the local energy providers to ensure the delivery of the required technical quality of power without misusing their local dominant economic position? In other words, the rules and regulations under which these local energy systems can be operated need to be clearly defined. This is the institutional control dimension of changing the energy systems and is concerned with safeguarding the technical and social operations such as system access or the coordination of various actors in the field.

In infrastructure, technological and socioinstitutional change are closely related to each other. They need to fit to each other because an infrastructure will otherwise not be able to provide the expected services. The nature of this interrelationship is only poorly understood (Bauer and Herder 2009; Koppenjan and Groenewegen 2005; Scholten and Künneke 2016). On the one hand, engineers usually focus on the technical aspects of system design and take the socioeconomic organization as given (Faulconbridge and Ryan 2014). On the other hand, economists usually concentrate on the economic organization of infrastructures, without considering or understanding the technical specifics of an infrastructure (Pollitt and Anaya 2015; Joskow 2007). Engineers and economists operate worlds apart. This causes very fundamental problems. Economists might be tempted to believe in the market and trust that new initiatives of decentralized energy production are technically feasible. Similarly, engineers might design very advanced local energy systems without considering who is taking the risk and responsibility of building and operating them.

The above-mentioned changes in the energy sector are illustrative of what is going on in other infrastructures as well. Institutional and technological changes in network infrastructures are driven by the following three developments:

- *Advances in ICT technology*: ICT is an important driver of substantial technical change in all major infrastructures, including communication (internet, telecommunication), energy (electricity, gas, heat), transport (railroads, aviation, public roads), postal services, and water management. Likewise, the institutional changes in these infrastructures are considerable (Kiesling 2015; Glachant 2012).[4] Examples include the development of so-called smart networks, decentralization of the provision of infrastructure services, and the emergence of new services by third parties.
- *Sectorial restructuring*: In past decades, all the major infrastructures have been subject to so-called liberalization, privatization, and reregulation (Finger and Künneke 2011). There is more room for competition and choice for the customer. Infrastructure services like public transportation, energy, and postal services are no longer considered public utilities but rather commercial services. Private sector involvement is stimulated (Kessides 2003).
- *Internationalization and localization*: Infrastructures are increasingly being internationalized. They cross national and regional borders. This creates a need for increased international and inter-regional collaboration and cooperation. The European Union is a good example in this respect. These developments go hand in hand with a further decentralization of infrastructure and the provision of services at a local level, like the above-mentioned examples of prosumers in the energy sector. Hence, the "rules of the game," i.e., the institutions of infrastructures, change significantly, which in turn has consequences for the technological developments and innovations in these sectors (Finger and Laperrouza 2011).

In this chapter, a framework is proposed that highlights interrelations between institutions and technologies in network infrastructures related to safeguarding critical functions. This framework builds on concepts from institutional economics theory (Williamson 1996; Ménard and Shirley 2005). It allows to understand the coordination problems that system operators, regulators, system designer, engineers, politicians, and even citizens have to address regarding the safeguarding of critical functions in order to meet societal expectations. It also addresses the different performance expectations of users and citizens and the different technological and institutional possibilities for respecting them. This chapter is structured as follows. In the next section, the interrelations between technology and institutions are assessed and specified. Following that, the critical infrastructures framework is presented. Finally, the relevance of the critical infrastructure framework to socially responsible innovation is illustrated. A brief summary will conclude this chapter.

Assessing the interrelationship between technology and institutions

The assessment of the interrelations between technology and institutions is based on the four features of infrastructures that are briefly addressed in the following sections.

Infrastructures are sociotechnical systems

Infrastructures are engineering systems that function in a specific social context (Ottens et al. 2006). They perform intended functions, for instance the safe and reliable provision of energy. Human actors purposefully design these systems and monitor and adjust them to meet expectations. There is a close relationship between the technical design and functioning of an infrastructure and the social interactions that safeguard and support these functions. To be sure, not everything in an infrastructure is purposefully planned. Many changes simply evolve as a consequence of unplanned or unexpected activities of infrastructure users. An illustrative example is the development of the wind energy industry in Denmark in the late 1960s (van der Steen, Künneke, and Groenewegen 2008). While the Danish government was stimulating the development of nuclear power production, there were local initiatives for building small wind turbines. These local initiatives became the basis for the current important wind energy industry in Denmark. It is the combination of the technical opportunity for producing power in a different way and the institutional circumstances that allow for these kinds of bottom-up activities. For economists, this means that some deeper understanding about the technical functioning of an infrastructure is needed.

Complementary technical processes require coordination

Complementary technical processes and activities in infrastructure activities need to be coordinated; otherwise the expected performance cannot be provided. For instance, if power is produced at location A, a specific part of the network is needed at a specific time in order to transport it to location B. To allow for these complementary technical processes, certain rules and regulations (i.e., institutions) are required. Hence, the technical and institutional coordination of complementary activities is mutually related. Local energy systems are illustrative in this respect. Figure 4.1 depicts an ideal case of how a local energy system might

Intelligent Gas Network

Liander is building a safe and flexible gas mains network.

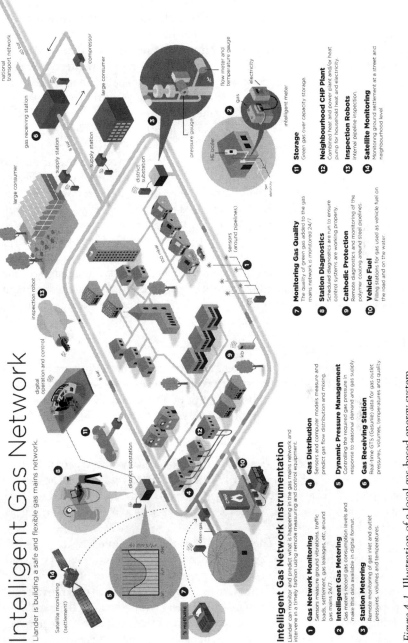

Intelligent Gas Network Instrumentation

Liander can monitor and predict what is happening in the gas mains network and intervene in a timely fashion using remote measuring and control equipment.

① Gas Network Monitoring
Sensors measure ground vibrations, traffic loads, settlement, gas leakages, etc. around gas mains 24/7.

② Intelligent Gas Metering
Gas meters record gas consumption levels and make this data available in digital format.

③ Station Metering
Remote monitoring of gas inlet and outlet pressures, volumes and temperatures.

④ Gas Distribution
Sensors and computer models measure and predict gas flow distribution and mixing.

⑤ Dynamic Pressure Management
Controlling the required gas pressure in response to seasonal demand and gas supply.

⑥ Gas Receiving Station
Real-time GTS (Gasunie) data for gas inlet pressures, volumes, temperatures and quality.

⑦ Monitoring Gas Quality
The quality of green gas added to the gas mains network is monitored 24/7.

⑧ Station Diagnostics
Scheduled diagnostics are run to ensure control systems are working properly.

⑨ Cathodic Protection
Remote diagnostics and monitoring of the polymer coating around steel pipelines.

⑩ Vehicle Fuel
Filling stations for gas used as vehicle fuel on the road and on the water.

⑪ Storage
Green gas over capacity storage.

⑫ Neighbourhood CHP Plant
Combined heat and power plant and/or heat pump for household heat and electricity.

⑬ Inspection Robots
Internal pipeline inspection.

⑭ Satellite Monitoring
Monitoring ground settlement at a street and neighbourhood level.

Figure 4.1 Illustration of a local gas-based energy system

Source: Alliander network company; ©loekweijts.nl

look in the not too distant future. This particular example focuses on the technical features and the coordination required by local gas systems. It is an impressive picture of the many different technical facilities needed for the provision and consumption of energy in local communities. Natural gas is imported from the national transmission network, indicated by the arrow pointing inward in the upper right part of the figure. In addition, the community also relies on locally produced biogas, indicated by a biogas storage facility on the lower left part of the figure. Local houses are equipped with rooftop solar panels, producing electric power. These different facilities for the provision of energy need to be coordinated and balanced with the local energy demand. The figure indicates some residential dwellings, some commercial buildings, and a greenhouse farm. There is even a petrol station that supplies synthetic gas for automobiles. With respect to the supply of biogas, an important need for technical coordination is that related to safeguarding the quality of gas in the local network. This is indicated by different metering devices in the upper left part of the picture. These technical facilities can only be effectively and efficiently operated if certain property rights and decision rights are allocated to different actors, i.e., institutions need to be defined accordingly. Certain actors need to be entitled to monitor and perform the related controls of important system parameters in order for the system to meet the performance expected of it, including security of supply, safety, sustainability, and affordability. In this specific illustration, the network operating company might be entitled to perform the monitoring and control of the local energy system.

Reliable operation depends on critical functions

The assessment focuses on specific technical functions that are required for reliable operation of the infrastructure. There are four categories of critical functions that need to be performed both technically and institutionally, as otherwise the infrastructure might fail, i.e., it would not meet users' expectations (Finger, Groenewegen, and Künneke 2005):

- System control: the system needs to be operated according to certain technical requirements. For gas, this would be a certain caloric value and chemical composition. For electricity, voltage (220 volt) and frequency (50 hertz) are important technical parameters because otherwise appliances will not work or break down.
- Capacity management: The physical capacity of the system needs to be balanced in such a way that the production capacity meets the actual demand. In the case of electricity, load balancing is an important example.
- Interconnection: Networks need to be connected with each other to improve their technical functioning and/or to deliver certain services. Technical reliability can be improved by connecting the local network with the regional or national energy network. In case of an emergency, different sources of power provision are then available.

- Interoperability: Different parts of the technical systems need to be equipped technically to meet the technical requirements of the system. For instance, solar photovoltaic panels need to fulfill certain technical requirements in order to be connected to the electricity network.

Institutions are necessary to support the critical functions

Institutions can be defined as "systems of established and embedded social rules that structure social interactions" (Hodgson 2006). Basically, institutions refer to the formal and informal rules and regulations that influence economic behavior. These rules are needed to structure human interaction. In order to engage in any kind of economic transactions, the participants' rights and obligations of ownership and decision making must be determined. For instance, who owns different facilities within energy networks, such as the production and distribution networks, gas storage facilities, or metering devices? What are the decision rights or obligations of the different participants or actors involved? The allocation and determination of property rights and decision rights determines the monitoring and control of critical functions.

Critical infrastructure framework

The basic idea is that the four critical functions need to be consistently coordinated, technically as well as institutionally, since otherwise the expected infrastructure services will not be provided. In extreme cases, the provision of services might even break down if critical functions are not consistently coordinated. Consistent coordination requires that institutions and technology reinforce or match each other. This is referred to as the alignment of institutions and technology. The case of load balancing in the electricity sector illustrates this approach. To safeguard the technical integrity of electricity systems, the production and use of power needs to be monitored very closely. To satisfy this technical task, a system operator needs to have the appropriate decision-making rights to enforce the necessary controls and interventions. Without suitable institutions, the energy system cannot function according to expectations. Obviously, the problem is to identify the institutions that are appropriate or suitable to support or reinforce technological system requirements.

The alignment of institutions and technologies depends on the objectives and expectations of the users of the infrastructures. Striving for a sustainable energy system implies choices for a specific range of technologies and institutional arrangements. For instance, if there is an excess supply of wind energy that cannot be absorbed by the electricity network, surplus power could be transformed into hydrogen gas at a high cost. In this way the wind power would be utilized in the maximum way possible. Under these conditions, the sustainability of power production would be an important performance criterion. However, if

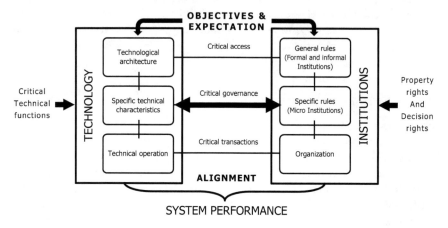

Figure 4.2 Critical infrastructure framework
Source: RK

the societal expectation would be to minimize the costs of the power supply, another trade-off between institutional and technological coordination is appropriate, such as turning off the wind power and using more cost-efficient fossil-fueled power plants as a backup. This example illustrates that the performance expectations shape the applied technology and institutions in an infrastructure.

The objective of the "critical infrastructure framework" (as illustrated in Figure 4.2) is to depict the alignment of the institutional and technological coordination of critical functions in infrastructures to meet societal expectations (see also Ménard 2014). In the illustration, the two columns represent technology and institutions. Technology is described in terms of critical functions, and institutions by property rights and decision rights. The issue of alignment is approached at three different levels of abstraction, i.e., critical access, critical governance, and critical transactions. Figure 4.2 illustrates that the alignment between institutions and technology determines the system performance. The choice of specific technologies and institutions is dependent on the societal objectives and expectations.

Critical access

Critical access refers to the generic design of an infrastructure. At this level, the interrelation between the general rules and the technological architecture of the infrastructure is addressed. At this generic level, the accessibility of the infrastructure determines the institutional and technological coordination of critical functions. Very roughly, a distinction can be made between open access and closed access.[5]

Closed access is associated to a situation in which only dedicated actors or agencies are entitled to monitor and control critical functions within an infrastructure. For instance, the provision of network services is strictly regulated and primarily the task of dedicated network companies. Prior to liberalization, the production and trade of electric power was assigned to dedicated (monopolistic) firms. Under these conditions the coordination of critical functions was the result of directed technical and institutional coordination by these firms. The relevant components of the infrastructure were monitored and controlled in order to safeguard specific anticipated relations between them. These anticipated relations determine the conditions under which an infrastructure can function according to expectations or when it is necessary to intervene in a predetermined or a priori planned way. In other words, possible failures are anticipated as much as possible and the systems are modified before problems occur. In electricity systems, this task is typically delegated to a system operator, such as TenneT in the Netherlands. The technical architecture of a closed access infrastructure can be characterized by centralized hubs that monitor and control the critical functions. The technical relations between the nodes and links are largely predetermined.

Open access refers to infrastructures that are accessible for all the actors and agencies that are willing and able to contribute to its services. For instance, an actor like a private household has invested heavily in decentralized energy production and would like to deliver power to neighbors. The actor might dig cables through the backyards of nearby houses to supply them with electricity. However, by definition an infrastructure requires coordination. For instance, the power quality needs to be safeguarded, and backup facilities need to be available in the case of technical failures. Even in this very simple example, critical functions need to be safeguarded because otherwise the infrastructure will not meet expectations. The means to realize this are fundamentally different from those in a closed access infrastructure. The coordination in an open access infrastructure relies on protocols, standards, or procedures that firms or agencies have to adhere to if they want to participate. To make this spontaneous development of electricity networks possible, the technological architecture would have to be adapted to allow for open access. For instance, the appropriate energy storage facilities would have to be available (for instance batteries for electric vehicles) or actors need to be equipped to balance their individual power needs by technical home management devices. By such a combination of institutions (i.e., general rules) and technological architecture, open access enables *spontaneous* coordination of the components of the infrastructure. The infrastructure evolves according to anticipated and unanticipated combinations of its components, which can result in functions and services that have not been foreseen. Hence, an open access infrastructure can be expected to perform differently than a closed access infrastructure.

This raises two questions: What is the significance of open access and closed access in the critical infrastructure framework? How does it contribute to explaining the interrelation between technology and institutions and the expected performance of an infrastructure? First, the technological and institutional requirements for coordination are fundamentally different as illustrated by the examples. Hence there is an issue of alignment. If an increasing number of citizens decide to become "prosumers," making the system more open, technical changes in the distribution network are required since the local system will otherwise collapse. As indicated earlier, the distribution network needs to be equipped to transport electricity in two directions. A possible surplus would have to be delivered into the high-voltage network and vice-versa. Furthermore, load balancing would have to be performed in the distribution network, and not only in the high-voltage network as is presently the case. These changes result in a different technological architecture of electricity systems, the so-called smart grids.

Second, if the electricity system evolves into an open access system, different drivers for development and innovation would have to be taken into consideration. There would be higher reliance on consumer driven, bottom-up activities (Egyedi and Mehos 2012). This has consequences for system performance. In the case of closed access, a limited number of standardized services can be planned and guaranteed. From a political perspective, this might be attractive for safeguarding social service obligations or national interests. Open access infrastructures, in contrast, are potentially able to provide a broad range of diverse services that are directed toward different groups of users or customers. Hence, by changing the technical or institutional design, different system performances have to be taken into account.

Critical governance

The second level of analysis, i.e., critical governance, is concerned with the requirements for technical and institutional coordination in the specific context of a given infrastructure at a specific location and time. The general rules and technological architecture are taken as given.

From an institutional perspective, the general rules need to be further specified for a given infrastructure in space and time. These specific rules are concerned with the division of tasks with respect to the monitoring and adjustment of the critical functions. One of the questions this concerns is which firms or public or private agents have the authority to monitor or adjust different critical functions? For instance, regulators can be assigned to determine the conditions under which electricity producers or traders can use public networks. A system operator is made responsible for monitoring and adjusting the short-term operation of an electricity system and for intervening in case of an emergency. These so-called meso-institutions create very important conditions for the coordination of critical functions.[6]

From a technological perspective, the analysis of critical functions is focused on the context-specific coordination requirements of a given infrastructure. Critical functions need to be monitored and adjusted according to local conditions and performance parameters. For instance, an electricity system based on hydropower behaves technically different than an electricity system based on offshore wind energy. Wind does not always blow, hence there must be ways to balance the production and consumption of power, for instance by storage of excess energy, alternative means of power production, or demand-side management. In hydropower-based systems, the technical management of the water reservoirs is important for making power available in different seasons of the year. This example illustrates that even within specific infrastructure sectors there are different needs for technical control and system adjustment, as a consequence of which the critical functions pose different technical requirements.

Critical governance is concerned with the alignment of the technological requirements of monitoring and adjustment with the institutional requirements of allocating the tasks of control and intervention between meso-institutions. The increasing interest in decentralized energy production raises several important issues of critical governance. Examples are: How to perform capacity management in decentralized energy systems? What are possible technical solutions for balancing power at the level of single neighborhoods? Power storage in electric vehicles? Is there a need for a local system operator? Who would be assigned to perform this function? A private firm, a publicly owned network operator, or a local cooperative? Who is responsible for the necessary investments in the system? Who assumes the financial risks? At what prices and under which conditions can these facilities be used by households and firms? Without resolving these questions, the large-scale application of decentralized power production is not possible. Even worse, it endangers a safe and secure provision of energy.

An interesting issue in this context is concerned with the unbundling of ownership in electricity distribution networks (Künneke and Fens 2007). Ownership unbundling refers to the allocation of ownership rights between electricity distribution network companies vis-à-vis commercial activities like the production and trade of power. Traditionally, these different economic and technical activities were integrated in individual firms, so-called electric utilities. However, as a consequence of the liberalization of the electricity sector, nondiscriminatory access to distribution networks is required to allow for competition between different electricity providers. Hence, distribution network operators need to operate independently of commercial activities, creating a level playing field. Among other things, this raises the question as to whether distribution network companies should be organized as a private profit-oriented business or as a publicly owned utility that is dedicated to various societal objectives. This is an important issue when it comes to the support of local energy communities. Publicly owned network companies have different incentives for supporting such local energy initiatives compared to privately owned profit-oriented firms. Investments might be necessary to support decentralized energy provision, including investments in bidirectional energy flows between distribution and transmission networks. Such investments might not always be profitable from a private business perspective. Referring to our critical infrastructure framework, it can be expected that different technologies are applied depending on how ownership bundling is substantiated.

Critical transactions[7]

The analysis of critical transactions is focused at the level of technological operation and institutional organization. It is about the coordination of critical functions among different actors who are part of a specific infrastructure. Under these
conditions, the general rules are assumed given, likewise the division of the tasks
regarding control and intervention (i.e., the governance of the sector).

The technical operation of the critical functions needs to be coordinated
throughout the different nodes and links in an infrastructure. Take again the
case of load balancing in the electricity sector. If there is an unexpected failure
of a power production unit, immediate action needs to be taken for large parts
of the system will otherwise break down. Hence several technical activities need
to be coordinated instantly. New sources of power supply need to be identified
and connected to the grid. Possibly also the power flows in the systems need to
be adjusted. The degree of criticality of these technical operations depends on
two aspects:

- The technically acceptable time period to react. In the case of a failure of a
  power plant, the technical balance between the production and consumption of power needs to be reestablished within seconds or minutes, or otherwise there will be serious consequences for the entire system. The longer the
  technically acceptable time period to react, the lower the degree of criticality. For instance, the extension of a network can be planned over a period of
  several years.
- The technical scope of control. Certain critical functions are related to the
  technical control of the entire system, whereas others might be restricted
  to a subsystem (like the regional distribution network) or to the control of
  specific components. For instance, the load balancing of electric power is a
  critical function that has an impact on the entire system. In this sense, the
  degree of criticality is very high. The other extreme of a low degree of criticality would be the development of a super grid in the North Sea that connects the different wind farms in the neighboring countries. This can take
  several decades of planning and design. If the super grid is not completed,
  individual wind farms might be affected as they have no access to this high-
  voltage international transmission network. They could still be operated
  although on the basis on their existing, less efficient and effective network
  connection.

How can these critical transactions be organized? Referring to transaction cost
economics (Williamson 1996), it is possible to identify different modes of organization depending on the degree of criticality of transactions. Figure 4.3 illustrates
different cases of critical transactions. The vertical axis indicates the speed of
adjustment, from very short time periods of seconds to very long ones of decades.
The horizontal axis indicates the scope of control, from system to subsystems to
components.

Critical transactions

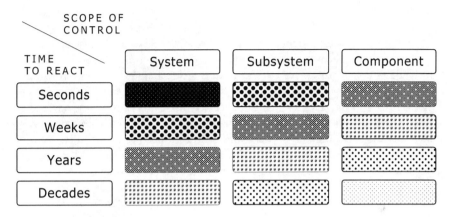

Figure 4.3 Modes of organization to secure critical functions (simplified version of Künneke, Groenewegen, and Ménard 2010, 502)

The upper left cell of the matrix indicates the most critical transaction. This is load balancing in traditional energy systems. Under these circumstances a very specific economic organization (which is indicated as authoritative supervision) is needed to safeguard the critical function. Typically, in an electricity infrastructure there is a system operator with the specific decision-making rights to make the necessary interventions.

Another extreme case of a critical transaction is indicated by the lower right cell of the matrix. This might for instance refer to the above-mentioned development of a super grid in the North Sea. Although some coordination and planning is still needed, there are few restrictions with respect to the safeguarding of critical functions. Hence, there is much room for different modes of organization. For each of these combinations indicated in the matrix, it is possible to specify modes of organization that satisfy the institutional and technological coordination requirements.[8]

Outlook: socially responsible innovation

The critical infrastructure framework allows us to understand and analyze the institutional and technological characteristics of an infrastructure in relation to its expected performance. If the technical characteristics of the electricity infrastructure change, as just outlined, what kind of rules and regulations would support this development? Correspondingly, institutional changes can only be successfully introduced if the technical characteristics of an infrastructure change. If sustainable energy provision is stimulated by different policy instruments as in the case of Germany, there is a strong need to support specific technological changes, including in the development of so-called smart grids or of solar and wind power. Without these technical changes, this policy will not have the intended results and the performance of the infrastructure will not meet expectations.

Analyzing the performance of a complex system like an infrastructure is a challenging task because it is the result of emerging technical systems and institutional arrangements. The critical infrastructure framework contributes to a better understanding of the nature of some interrelations between technology and institutions and to how this is related to the quality of services provided by these systems. It provides a tool for designing institutions in a systematic way to meet societal performance expectations such as robustness, reliability, security, cost efficiency, privacy, and safety (Milchram and Van De Kaa 2017).Take for instance the location of onshore wind turbines close to residential areas. Local residents might be concerned that wind turbines are ugly, pollute the horizon, cause noise, and cast shadows. To address such concerns different technical and institutional alternatives could be investigated that meet different performance expectations. Sometimes ownership rights of the wind turbines are allocated to the citizens living close to them. In this way, citizens are not only confronted by the discomforts of wind turbines, but also receive some benefits. This might contribute toward a different trade-off vis-à-vis the performance expectation of local wind turbines.

The same holds for long-distance power transmission lines. They are needed to transport electric power, for instance from offshore wind parks to the hinterland. There are different technical design options. Cables might be installed underground or above the surface on large poles. The first option is much more expensive but less invasive with regard to the natural living environment of citizens living close to such cables. Cables that are installed above the surface can have a significant impact on their nearby environment. The value of real estate might drop, it might disturb the view, and the electromagnetic radiation might harm the health of people living in the proximity. At the same time, the energy system needs to be technically adjusted to the new needs and requirements of sustainable power production. Obviously, there is tension between this need to transform the energy infrastructure toward more sustainability and the social acceptance of these changes.

In terms of the critical infrastructure framework, social acceptance can be interpreted as the difference between the actual performance of an infrastructure and the expectations of different societal groups (Künneke et al. 2015). Often a lack of social acceptance causes a more serious barrier for an innovative infrastructure than the problems of technical development. The location of onshore wind turbines or the construction of electricity transmission lines are very illustrative examples in this respect. The critical infrastructure framework can be instrumental for approaching the problem of social acceptance from a different perspective. This is related to the idea of value-sensitive design (van de Poel and Kroes 2014) that relates societal acceptance to the embeddedness of societal values in the technical and institutional designs of complex socio-technical systems.

Applying the idea of value-sensitive design to an infrastructure provides interesting perspectives for aligning institutions and technology according to societal expectations. There might be various value-sensitive technical solutions that address concerns of society. For instance, very silent wind turbines can be designed. Or wind turbines might be placed at locations were shadow casting does not cause a disturbance. Another less straightforward option might be to actively involve local residents in the technical operation of wind turbines. An unverified anecdote illustrates this case. A turbine operator placed a switch in the houses near a wind park that enables residents to switch off the turbines when they are disturbed by noise or shadows. As a result, there were no more complaints, and the wind turbines were only occasionally shut down.

The critical infrastructure framework can be useful to investigate more precisely which different constellations of institutions and technology would meet different societal norms and values. This involves a detailed analysis of critical transactions, critical governance, and critical access related to different types of system performance. This results in a consistent set of institutional arrangements and technological characteristics in which societal norms and values are structurally embedded. This is an important contribution to analyzing and identifying responsible innovations in infrastructures. The critical infrastructure framework provides a novel perspective on how to approach responsible innovation and to design complex systems that are acceptable to citizens and users (Scholten and Künneke 2016).

Conclusion

The critical infrastructure framework provides a novel perspective as to how to understand and analyze the changing technological and institutional configurations in the ongoing transition toward sustainable infrastructures. It makes it possible to systematically assess how the performance of an infrastructure is influenced by its changing institutional and technological features. Accordingly, the actual performance can be related to societal objectives and expectations vis-à-vis the infrastructure. This is very useful in identifying socially responsible innovations and the technological and institutional designs of an infrastructure that foster societal acceptance.

Notes

1 An earlier version of this chapter was published as Künneke (2013). The framework presented here is the result of long research collaboration with Prof. John Groenewegen and Prof. Claude Ménard. I am thankful to the editors of this volume for their very helpful comments and suggestions.
2 The effect of this policy is illustrated in a time-lapse video animation: http://enipedia.tudelft.nl/wiki/Videos.

94 *Rolf W. Künneke*

3 See http://nl.lokaleduurzameenergiebedrijven.wikia.com/wiki/Lijst_met_informatie_over_LDEB_in_Nederland.
4 See the contribution by Kröger and Nan in this book.
5 This distinction between open access and closed access systems is inspired by North et al. (2009).
6 The notion of "meso-institutions" was introduced by Ménard (see, for instance, 2017).
7 This section refers strongly to Künneke, Groenewegen, and Ménard (2010).
8 For further specification, please refer to Künneke, Groenewegen, and Ménard (2010).

References

Bauer, Johannes M., and Paulien M. Herder. 2009. "Designing Socio-Technical Systems." In *Philosophy of Technology and Engineering Sciences*, edited by Anthonie Meijers, 601–30. Handbook of the Philosophy of Science. Amsterdam: North-Holland. https://doi.org/10.1016/B978-0-444-51667-1.50026-4.

Egyedi, Tineke M., and Donna C. Mehos. 2012. *Inverse Infrastructures: Disrupting Networks from Below*. Cheltenham, UK; Northampton, MA: Edward Elgar Publishing.

Faulconbridge, Ian R., and Michael J. Ryan. 2014. *Systems Engineering Practice*. Canberra, Australia: Argos Press.

Finger, Matthias, John Groenewegen, and Rolf W. Künneke. 2005. "The Quest for Coherence between Institutions and Technologies in Infrastructures." *Journal of Network Industries* os-6 (4): 227–59. https://doi.org/10.1177/178359170500600402.

Finger, Matthias, and Rolf W. Künneke, eds. 2011. *International Handbook of Network Industries: The Liberalization of Infrastructure*. Cheltenham, UK; Northampton, MA: Edward Elgar.

Finger, Matthias, and Marc Laperrouza. 2011. "Liberalization of Network Industries in the European Union: Evolving Policy Issues." In *International Handbook of Network Industries: The Liberalization of Infrastructure*, edited by Matthias Finger and Rolf W. Künneke, 345–65. Cheltenham, UK; Northampton, MA: Edward Elgar.

Glachant, Jean-Michel. 2012. "Regulating Networks in the New Economy." *Review of Economics and Institutions* 3 (1). https://ideas.repec.org/a/pia/review/v3y2012i1n1.html.

Hodgson, Geoffrey M. 2006. "What Are Institutions?" *Journal of Economic Issues* 40 (1). https://doi.org/10.1080/00213624.2006.11506879.

Joskow, Paul L. 2007. "Chapter 16 Regulation of Natural Monopoly." In *Handbook of Law and Economics*, edited by A. M. Polinsky and S. Shavell, 2: 1227–348. London: Elsevier. https://doi.org/10.1016/S1574-0730(07)02016-6.

Kessides, Ioannis. 2003. "Infrastructure Regulation: Promises, Perils and Principles." *World Bank*, January.

Kiesling, L. Lynne. 2015. "Implications of Smart Grid Innovation for Organizational Models in Electricity Distribution." In *Smart Grid Handbook, 3 Volume Set*, by Liu Chen-Ching, McArthur Stephen, and Lee Seung-Jae. Chichester: John Wiley & Sons.

Koppenjan, Joop, and John Groenewegen. 2005. "Institutional Design for Complex Technological Systems." *International Journal of Technology, Policy and Management* 5 (January): 240–58. https://doi.org/10.1504/IJTPM.2005.008406.

Künneke, Rolf W. 2013. "Critical Infrastructures: Aligning Institutions and Technology." Delft University of Technology. Delft.

Künneke, Rolf W., and Theo Fens. 2007. "Ownership Unbundling in Electricity Distribution: The Case of The Netherlands." *Energy Policy* 35 (3): 1920–30. https://doi.org/10.1016/j.enpol.2006.05.008.

Künneke, Rolf W., John Groenewegen, and Claude Ménard. 2010. "Aligning Modes of Organization with Technology: Critical Transactions in the Reform of Infrastructures." *Journal of Economic Behavior & Organization* 75 (3): 494–505. https://doi.org/10.1016/j.jebo.2010.05.009.

Künneke, Rolf W., Donna C. Mehos, Rafela Hillerbrand, and Kas Hemmes. 2015. "Understanding Values Embedded in Offshore Wind Energy Systems: Toward a Purposeful Institutional and Technological Design." *Environmental Science & Policy*, 118–129. https://doi.org/10.1016/j.envsci.2015.06.013.

Ménard, Claude. 2014. "Embedding Organizational Arrangements: Towards a General Model." *Journal of Institutional Economics* 10 (4): 567–89. https://doi.org/10.1017/S1744137414000228.

———. 2017. "Meso-Institutions: The Variety of Regulatory Arrangements in the Water Sector." *Utilities Policy* 49: 6–19. https://doi.org/10.1016/j.jup.2017.05.001.

Ménard, Claude, and Mary M. Shirley, eds. 2005. *Handbook of New Institutional Economics.* Springer US.

Milchram, Christine, and Geerten Van De Kaa. 2017. "Moral Values as Factors for Social Acceptance of Smart Grid Technologies." Working Paper. Delft University of Technology.

North, Douglass C., John J. Wallis, and Barry R. Weingast. 2009. *Violence and Social Orders: A Conceptual Framework for Interpreting Recorded Human History.* Cambridge; New York: Cambridge University Press.

Ottens, Maarten, Maarten Franssen, Peter Kroes, and Ibo Van De Poel. 2006. "Modelling Infrastructures as Socio-Technical Systems." *International Journal of Critical Infrastructures* 2 (2/3): 133. https://doi.org/10.1504/IJCIS.2006.009433.

Pollitt, Michael G., and Karim L. Anaya. 2015. "Can Current Electricity Markets Cope with High Shares of Renewables? A Comparison of Approaches in Germany, the UK and the State of New York." 1531. Cambridge Working Papers in Economics. Faculty of Economics, University of Cambridge. https://ideas.repec.org/p/cam/camdae/1531.html.

Scholten, Daniel, and Rolf W. Künneke. 2016. "Towards the Comprehensive Design of Energy Infrastructures." *Sustainability* 8 (12): 1291. https://doi.org/10.3390/su8121291.

van de Poel, Ibo, and Peter Kroes. 2014. "Can Technology Embody Values?" In *The Moral Status of Technical Artefacts,* edited by Peter Kroes and Peter-Paul Verbeek, 103–24. Philosophy of Engineering and Technology. Springer, Dordrecht. https://doi.org/10.1007/978-94-007-7914-3_7.

van der Steen, Marianne, Rolf W. Künneke, and John Groenewegen. 2008. "Evolutionary Innovation Systems of Low Carbon Electricity: Insights about Institutional Change and Innovation in the Case of CHP and Wind Energy." In *Innovations for a Low Carbon Economy: Economic, Institutional and Management Approaches,* edited by Timothy J. Foxon, J. Kohler, and C. Oughton, 175–202. Cheltenham, UK: Edward Elgar Publishers.

Williamson, Oliver E. 1996. *The Mechanisms of Governance.* Oxford, New York: Oxford University Press.

5 Exposure and vulnerability of the energy system to internal and external effects

Marcus Wiens, Wolfgang Raskob, Florian Diehlmann, Stefan Wandler, and Frank Schultmann

Introduction

Over the last decade, energy systems in Europe have been subject to a constantly changing technological and regulatory environment as well as to increased external and internal risks. This applies in particular to the German energy system, which is going through a process of major structural change that began at the latest with the beginning of the energy transition. The question raised now is which current and future risks could pose a threat to the safe supply of electricity that we have become used to. Although long-lasting power blackouts are still very rare, their number could increase unless system operators and supervisors are prepared to respond to upcoming risks and system vulnerabilities. In this chapter we first illustrate that even today external, mostly weather-related risks can lead to extensive disruptions in our electricity supply. We also briefly focus on the German energy transition and outline both future challenges and the requirements that a resilient grid must satisfy. In the second part of our contribution, we look at systemic risks from a comparative perspective and compare systemic risk drivers in the energy sector with those in the financial markets. This analysis sheds light on the internal and external vulnerabilities of both systems which – despite major differences – even share some common features with respect to the effects of technological change and the regulatory environment.

Energy system's exposure and vulnerability to external effects

Concerning the topology of electrical power systems, the three-phase AC (alternating current) circuit is the common system worldwide. In the German power system, three subsystems can be distinguished that correspond to different voltage levels (Schlabbach and Rofalski 2008):

- A high-voltage transmission grid (UCTE grid), which connects the large power stations in Europe and which is used to transport energy over large distances. The standard nominal system voltage is 400 kV.
- A 110 kV network, which serves as both a subtransmission grid for regional transportation in rural areas and a regional distribution system for urban population centers.

- A distribution system with nominal voltages of 10 kV to 35 kV, which distributes electrical energy at a regional and local level at different voltage levels. For example, industrial installations are supplied at higher voltage levels (e.g., 10 kV) while 400 V is used for standard tariff customers.

Since the rise of "green energy," power stations have been connected at different voltage levels, ranging from small photovoltaic plants at lower voltage levels to wind power farms at higher voltages. For the remainder of this chapter we use a simplified distinction between the *transmission grid* (high voltage) on the one hand and the *distribution grid* (low voltage) on the other.

Major blackouts in the last 20 years: evidence from the literature and historic incidents in Germany

Over the last 20 years many severe power outages have been reported worldwide (Veloza and Santamaria 2016). Some of them affected more than several million people, in particular in India in 2012 (670 million people), Pakistan in 2006 (160 million people), Turkey in 2015 (70 million people), and Italy in 2003 (57 million people) (see, for example, Veloza and Santamaria 2016; Wu, Chang, and Hu 2017; Rampurkar et al. 2016). Further examples of severe events are incidents in France and Germany in 1998–1999 (Sanson, Rochereau, and Ravail 2000) and others in Münsterland, Germany, in 2005 (Bundesnetzagentur 2006) and Emsland, Germany, in 2006 (van der Vleuten and Lagendijk 2010).

In the following case studies (boxes), we investigate the root causes, the consequences, and lessons learned from two of the above-mentioned power outages, namely France 1999 and Germany (Münsterland) 2005. They represent examples of unforeseen natural disasters and extreme but foreseeable natural external forces.

Case study 5.1: France 1999

Root cause(s): In December 1999, two severe winter storms (Lothar and Martin) crossed France and Germany. Wind speeds were of the highest intensity for about 36 hours. In particular, it was not possible for the national weather services to measure the full impact of Lothar.

Consequences: The storms caused major damage in France, southern Germany, Switzerland, and Italy. About 140 people were killed and about 300 high-voltage transmission pylons damaged. In France, nearly 3.4 million households lost their connection to the grid. Approximately one week later, 500,000 households were still without electricity. The energy provider Electricité de France acquired portable power generators from all over Europe to mitigate the consequences.

Lessons learned: Emergency management procedures were subsequently revised to enable organizations to deal better with the consequences of such an event. The available resources had been inadequate to deal with such severe consequences. This led to the suggestion that better procedures need to be developed to respond to such unforeseeable crisis situations. The electricity grid should be able to withstand such events in a better way, and the use of underground lines should be a matter for discussion. Guidelines should be prepared to inform the public as to how to react to such events.

Case study 5.2: Germany 2005

Root cause(s): A low pressure area caused heavy rainfall at temperatures around 0 C. This resulted in a heavy load of ice on pylons and cables in that area.

Consequences: The ice load resulted in damage to about 80 pylons of the high-voltage transmission lines. This resulted in a longer lasting blackout for about 250,000 people. Short-term outages were reported for Osnabrück, for example, affecting about 600,000 inhabitants in the greater Münsterland region. All households were back to a normal supply of energy after five days.

Lessons learned: Precipitation in the form of ice and snow resulted in extreme loads for pylons and cables that exceeded German regulations. This was confirmed by an independent review. The German supervisory authority, the Bundesnetzagentur, recommended replacing the old pylons and improving the anchoring of cables.

Focal disruptions at critical nodes versus an extensive breakdown at the outer periphery

When analyzing the impact of external shocks on the energy system it is interesting to distinguish between two types of failures. One type has its origin in a vulnerable and critical part of the transmission grid which can be hit by technical failure or cyberattacks (type I), while a second leads to a local breakdown of the distribution grid as a consequence of strong physical forces such as severe weather events (type II), as described in the section on exogenous hazards. In terms of recovery times and durations of these different types of disruptions, current evidence suggests that the second type still poses the greater risk to a stable energy supply.

Although this conjecture is difficult to prove empirically, there are a number of arguments which support this line of reasoning. In type I failures, i.e., a disruption that occurs at a core part of the energy system, the root causes can be localized more easily and quickly. An example could be a disruption due to a failure at a power station or at some critical element of the transmission grid. Furthermore, as soon as the source is identified, it is relatively easy to assess the implications of the disruption in terms of its duration and degree of severity. More importantly, most of these failures are internal ones with mainly technical causes. The prevention and mastery of such events are subject to standardized procedures and technical precautions for coping with overvoltages, insulation coordination, and the protection of equipment. Moreover, standard risk management procedures comprise regular servicing of equipment, maintenance, and the establishment of a restoring capacity, in particular by having critical parts available. As isolated events in the core parts of the energy system, internal failures constitute a risk that is subject to a higher degree of controllability and plannable security.

Conversely, for type II the consequences of external events leading to disruptions in the distribution grid will only become fully apparent after a significant time lag. In many natural disasters the distribution grid is severely affected, which means that the technical maintenance teams need a certain amount of time to inspect the damage before starting to restore power. If the root cause of the disruption is a natural disaster, the circumstances under which the teams have to access the affected parts of the grid may be difficult. In particular, other complicating factors will have to be taken into consideration because the restoration and maintenance logistics will themselves be affected by the very same disruption (e.g., restricted communication and mobility).

All that has been said so far refers mainly to well-known events, in particular to natural disasters. The main argument for a lesser degree of vulnerability of core parts of the system relies on assumptions of a correct prediction and the manageable implementation of recovery capacities in terms of buffer, availability of human resources, and well-designed business continuity routines. This is likely to be the case as most critical infrastructure providers follow high standards for safety and security; such an ambitious level of protection is also feasible because these maintenance and repair operations refer only to the purely technical and logistical part of the recovery phase. However, there are different types of events which may affect the transmission grid in an unexpected way. One reason for this is the potential for *cascading effects* in the transmission grid when isolation fails and high-voltage shocks spill over into other parts of the transmission grid.

As two examples of rather man-made disasters, partly due to mismanagement or ineffective countermeasures, we present two further case studies of power blackouts in Italy in 2003 and Germany (Emsland) in 2006.

Case study 5.3: Italy 2003

Root cause(s): In the morning of September 28, 2003, there was a failure in the Swiss 380 kV line Mettlen-Lavorgo. As a consequence, the Sils-Soazza line also tripped due to an overload (110% load) that caused a flashover with a tree. The Italian system lost its connection to the rest of the European grid as all the other lines were almost simultaneously disconnected by their automatic protection devices.

Consequences: Nearly all of Italy (except Sardinia) lost its connection to the European grid. More than 300 power plants operating in the country were shutdown, resulting in the loss of electricity to about 55 million people. After about 18 hours, service was restored and electricity was again available all over Italy.

Lessons learned: The final report of the investigations suggested that ineffective communication and the lack of an exchange of information contributed to an ineffective response although all the countermeasures had been available to return the system to a secure state. It was suggested that the training of operators, the communication between neighboring TSOs, and the real-time exchange of data be improved. The existing rules should be refined to prevent misinterpretation of the rules.

Case study 5.4: Germany 2006

Root cause(s): To allow the passage of a ship in a canal in northern Germany, the double-circuit 380 kV Conneforde-Diele line was temporarily shut down. However, as the timing of the shutdown was changed at short notice, further power lines tripped as a result of the unforeseen overload.

Consequences: The tripping of several power lines around Emsland resulted in severe imbalances of the power in Europe. This caused a division of the European grid in three distinct areas, namely west, northeast, and southeast. More than 15 million European households lost their connection to the grid. The three areas were resynchronized about 38 minutes later, and the situation returned to normal state for all the households about two hours later.

Lessons learned: The final report suggested that the European grid operators should develop better criteria for interregional communication between the different TSOs. Real-time recording and exchange of information should be strengthened. As the N-1 criterion was not fulfilled, the application of the N-1 criterion in the current handbook should be reviewed. In general, more training and emergency exercises should be encouraged, also including interregional players.

At the time of the events described above, the Union for the Co-ordination of Transmission of Electricity (UCTE) was the organization that operated the largest part of the European transmission grid and was responsible for the harmonization of operational procedures all over Europe.[1] In 2009, these tasks and responsibilities were transferred to ENTSO-E (The European Network of Transmission System Operators for Electricity). As a consequence of the events in Italy in 2003 and Emsland in 2006, chapter 5 on Emergency Operations was revised and a new version was issued in September, 2017 (ENTSO-E 2017). The new handbook addresses lessons learned in the final reports of the events described above, in particular regarding interregional interaction and real-time awareness of the state of the system. In addition to preparedness, restoration to normal conditions was strengthened, and in particular the tasks of the responsible organs were better defined. Training is discussed in chapter 8 of that handbook (ENTSO-E 2008). Even if inter-TSO training is addressed, the extent to which that chapter was revised on the basis of the above-mentioned events is not fully clear. However, the guidelines for all types of training are described and provide the necessary framework for the development of national or TSO-wide training courses.

Internal challenges to managing external risks

Internal risks which affect the reliability of a power system are related to a *loss of power supply stability* or to a *degradation of the condition of the technical infrastructure* (technical resistance and robustness). The first implies increased fluctuations in the amount of available electricity, which increases the requirements for grid protection in two respects. First, the increased system-related complexity and uncertainty challenge long-term planning and forecasting. In spite of technical progress and increased performance, it is indispensable to include a higher fault rate in the system stability calculations. Second, it is important to take precautions which take these fault rates into consideration and which are able to absorb strong fluctuations. Preventive measures of this kind include redundancies, improved grid synchronization, grid expansion, back-up plants, demand management, and improvements in the coordination between network operators.

However, there are also purely technical challenges. Even now there are natural limitations on maintenance. For combinatorial reasons, the number of scenarios taken into consideration in determining the required reserves has to be limited. In addition, it may often be impossible to determine the condition of a component (e.g., a relay) under normal circumstances. It is even conceivable that conducting a stress test is detrimental to the functionality of specific components and that the effect of protective measures on the system is often faded out in the analysis of a scenario (Afgan, Cvetinovic, and Pilavachi 2013). In principle, a main source of danger lies in the fact that not all precautions take sufficient account of the dynamics of a crisis. All of these points will increase in significance in the future due to the ongoing liberalization of the energy market, the energy transition and the accompanying regulations, climate change, and the future structure of the energy markets where smart grids and households as "prosumers" play a more important role.

External effects revisited: the German energy transformation

Centralized vs. decentralized systems

The German *Energiewende* (energy transition) comes with a shift to a higher share of renewable energy sources in the German electricity mix. The Renewable Energy Act ("EEG") is one of the centerpieces of this transition since it details the government's incentives to promote renewable energy. Until 2015, the EEG defined feed-in tariffs for energy generated from renewable sources such as wind power, solar power, or biomass. Starting 2017, the EEG was changed to a tender-based feed-in tariff, in which market mechanisms are supposed to take over and establish economically efficient prices (BMWi 2017). Furthermore, restrictions on possible locations of new power plants ensure that an increasing production is also concordant to the characteristics of the grid infrastructure. These restrictions are indirectly based on the geographical conditions for generating renewable energy – in particular wind power – in Germany.

McKenna, Hollnaicher, and Fichtner (2014) analyzed the potential of onshore electricity generation per total land area at the postal code level. The huge onshore potential in the north – together with a high offshore potential – highlights the need to transport electricity generated in the north of Germany to the south. Figure 5.1 emphasizes this effect, providing an overview of the status of the German Grid Development Plan (Bundesnetzagentur 2017). Even though the final location of some of the new corridors has not yet been finally determined, investments in grid extensions are inevitable.

The *Energiewende* has a vast number of consequences. From a technological point of view for example, Quitzow et al. (2016) mention the necessary adaptations to the grid, the development of energy storage technologies, and the integration of these technologies into the grid as the main challenges. Since some renewables are dependent on energy sources whose availability fluctuates and since there is an increasing number of power producers, there is a strong need

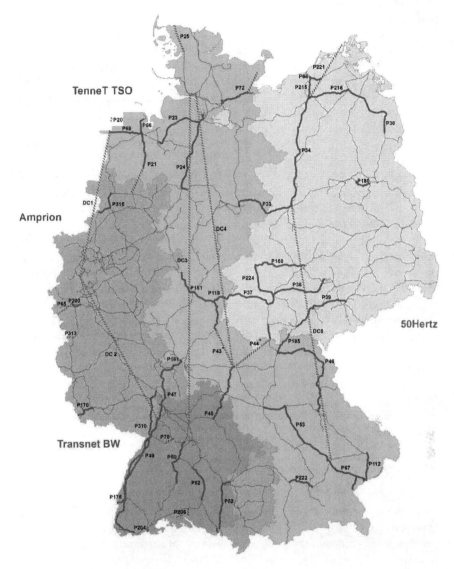

Figure 5.1 Status of the German Grid Development Plan 2017–2030 (Bundesnetzagentur 2017)

for coordination between different energy sources and demand points. Closely related is the concept of "prosumers" ("Producers" + "Consumers"), which means that "consumers produce and share surplus energy with grid and other users" (Zafar et al. 2018). Without strong efforts at coordination, it is not possible to maintain a robust grid.

"Smart grids" aim to solve this issue. The Joint Research Centre of the European Commission, together with the US Department of Energy, defined smart grids as "an upgraded electricity network enabling two-way information and power exchange between suppliers and consumers, thanks to the pervasive incorporation of intelligent communication monitoring and management systems" (Giordano and Bossart 2012). Even though a lot of research has already been conducted, a vast number of the details in this context are still up for debate (see, for instance, Kakran and Chanana 2018).

Exogenous hazards

In a nutshell, the *Energiewende* is leading to a high degree of decentralized energy production, a more complex grid network, and the need for flexibility within this network. However, these effects are not exclusively the result of the *Energiewende* since similar effects can also be seen outside Germany (e.g., the global trend to an increased use of renewable energy in response to global warming). Nevertheless, the proactive way that Germany is proceeding with the *Energiewende* in a comprehensive initiative is unique, and the consequences of this ambitious campaign are difficult to evaluate. We therefore provide a brief assessment of the risks to the grid from extreme weather for the period following the *Energiewende* in the following paragraphs.

As mentioned before, Ward (2013) analyzed the potential effects of climate change on the grid. He introduced six different categories – temperature, wind, ice and snow, lightning, rain and floods, and drought – and identified potential risks to the grid. A holistic discussion of each category in the context of the *Energiewende* would go beyond the scope of this chapter. Therefore, only the two most relevant risks – temperature and strong wind, storms, and hurricanes – will now be briefly assessed.

Temperature

According to Ward (2013), the increasing global temperature requires that just minor adjustments be made to the grid since the effects of the increase can be compared to small increases in power flow. Nevertheless, an increase in temperature is accompanied by a higher probability of flashovers if objects such as trees are very close to the network (Ward 2013). Temperature could therefore increasingly affect the growing grid network, even though the criticality of this risk seems to be rather low.

Wind energy production is very dependent on air density. Increasing temperatures that lead to declining air density subsequently reduce the energy production per wind turbine and could potentially threaten the grid's stability (Pryor and Barthelmie 2013). Even though smart grids take these volatilities into consideration, this kind of weather-related risk cannot be ignored in the period after the *Energiewende*.

Strong wind, storms, and hurricanes

Since wind causes most of the significant power outages, Ward's (2013) analysis of the effects of global warming on the grid is very detailed. These effects could become more severe when the length of the grid network is increased. However, an increase in interconnectivity also improves resilience by providing alternative links if parts of the grid are affected. The same is true for the assessment of the resilience of PV modules as well. Even though additional technical parts are exposed to debris or parts of trees in the case of heavy winds, an increasing number of PV modules could compensate for any destruction more efficiently.

With regard to wind turbines, automatic systems are in place that ensure that the turbines shutdown their production if wind speeds exceed 25 meters per second (or 50 mph). The large number of wind turbines following the *Energiewende* could therefore cause problems if the grid demands (wind) power while the turbines' output is affected by storms.

Apart from the climate risks, some additional challenges are likely to pose a threat to the electricity infrastructure. First, the fluctuation in the energy generation from renewables and the lack of flexibility at traditional power plants are accompanied by the risk of power outages (Fischer et al. 2016). Furthermore, increasing complexity leads to a shift away from generalists to very specialized workers. Finally, cyberattacks on the energy grid also become more likely because the interconnectedness and the high variability lead to a greater need for automated controls, creating additional potential access points for (cyber) terrorists (Wei et al. 2011).

All the uncertainties in regard to the technological and economic parameters mentioned above make it difficult to estimate the success of the *Energiewende* (Servatius, Schneidewind, and Rohlfing 2012). Even though a stakeholder survey in the metropolitan region Bremen–Oldenburg indicated that system operators consider extreme weather risks as too unlikely for them to intensify their adjustments (Goessling-Reisemann et al. 2013), many new risks have to be analyzed and preparatory steps need to be taken to make sure that the *Energiewende* is successful.

Resilience of the energy grid

Resilience of the energy grid is an ongoing topic of discussion.[2] Besides the institutional and operational aspects that are being discussed, for example, in the various ENTSO-E handbooks, technical improvements can be envisaged. Among the items of interest are:

- Hardening of the transmission grid
- Microgrids
- Smart grids with microgrid inclusions

Hardening of the transmission and distribution grid has been intensely discussed in the US as there are much larger deficits there than in Europe (Rehse, Köpp, and Omar 2016). Hardening of the transmission grid often refers to the distribution of energy via underground cables and to improving the structures of pylons and other structures (Panteli and Mancarella 2015). Hardening is often also discussed concerning advanced distributed generation units in the context of the establishment of microgrids (Wu, Chang, and Hu 2017). Microgrids are part of the normal transmission grid but can also be operated as stand-alone islands in case the high-voltage transmission grid is not functioning. A smart grid on the other hand is an "intelligent" grid with a direct connection to communication lines and smart meters, making it possible for the production and consumption of energy to be managed in real time (Momoh 2012; Gharavi and Ghafurian 2011). A microgrid is not necessarily smart, and vice versa a smart grid not necessarily independent, i.e., capable of island operation.

The added value of smart and microgrids with regard to resilience to natural disasters is discussed for example by Yuan (2016), Farzin, Fotuhi-Firuzabad, and Moeini-Aghtaie (2016), and Grünwald (2014). The use of microgrids as a resilient factor to maintain operation of a closed energy island when there are problems in the general transmission grid is appealing. However, such microgrids themselves require an internal energy balance to be maintained. In this respect, the production and consumption of energy has to be taken into consideration. In the framework of the German *Energiewende*, according to which most energy should be produced from renewables by 2050, there are limits on the establishment of microgrids. Wind parks in the North Sea, in particular, are of great importance in the move to renewables. This means that many high-voltage transmission lines are necessary in order to transport the energy to areas in the south of Germany. Furthermore, energy from wind parks is often produced for high-voltage lines and not for the medium voltage grid, which is more relevant for microgrids. To operate microgrids, storage capacities also seem to be important in order to sustain operation even when energy production is limited for some time until the connection to the main transmission grid is restored.

Both smart grids and microgrids may play an important role in ensuring the protection of our critical infrastructure in the case of a longer lasting power blackout. Work has started on investigating the potential of distributing unused energy in smart girds to support the operation of the relevant critical infrastructures in order to ensure for example the continuous operation of health care facilities (Münzberg, Müller, and Raskob 2018). To investigate this, power grid assessments are combined with agent-based simulations to identify those critical infrastructures that require energy and to set up a process to negotiate the distribution of the remaining resources in the best possible way that the overall performance of the system is optimal.

Vulnerability of critical systems: the financial system

Social risks posed by critical infrastructures

As a critical infrastructure the energy system belongs to the group of vital facilities and institutions which provide society with indispensable goods and services. In Germany, the Federal Ministry of the Interior lists nine sectors which represent or entail a critical infrastructure. Apart from energy, these are information and communication, traffic and transport, health, nutrition, finance and insurance, government and administration, as well as media and culture.

In order to understand the prerequisites for a smooth and sustainable functioning of the critical infrastructure it is important to see that basically all critical infrastructures are *interdependent* and that each critical infrastructure is *multidimensional* with respect to its functional requirements. The aspect of infrastructure interdependency implies that any critical infrastructure depends upstream on the input of other critical infrastructures and that downstream it provides output to other critical infrastructures. The second aspect, the multidimensionality, means that each critical infrastructure consists of both technical and social elements. The *technical side* comprises both tangible (physical) and intangible (virtual) elements. For most critical infrastructures the tangible part consists of the physical networks, such as the network of roads, rail lines, or waterways, the electricity grid, or glass fiber optical cable networks. The intangible elements are the transmitted "flows" such as electricity and electrical, electromagnetic, acoustic, or optical signals. Concrete examples are radio waves or the transmission of light and digital signals. When analyzing the impact of external interference on the energy system, most of the research is focused on the technical aspects such as the damage to infrastructure facilities and the degradation of the electromagnet floury (Afgan, Cvetinovic, and Pilavachi 2013). We have already looked at this in the first part of this chapter.

Apart from the technical requirements the *social dimension* of critical infrastructures is also of great importance. By "social" we mean all the instances of human decision making, human interaction, and their underlying institutions which either depend on or have an effect on the smooth functioning of critical infrastructures.[3] The range of stakeholders involved typically comprises

- critical infrastructure providers, in particular those units which are responsible for supervision and control,
- risk and crisis management officials,
- policy makers, in particular regulatory agencies,
- the wider public, in particular regular users of the critical infrastructure.

Among the risks which stem from human decision making and stakeholder interaction we can roughly distinguish between *decision-making biases at an individual or group level* and *incentive structures* which are provided by the *institutional environment.* Decision-making biases can lead to distorted risk perception and finally to a systematic underprovision of protective measures for many reasons. Since the triumphant success of *prospect theory*, there has been a comprehensive account of decision-making fallacies which are related to its three main phenomena, namely loss aversion, framing, and anchoring (Kahneman and Tversky 1979). Furthermore, it is well-known that the perception and evaluation of risks is both selective and subjective, which implies there is a strong emotional and experience-based component in risk assessments and risk decisions (Slovic, Fischhoff, and Lichtenstein 1980; Slovic 1987). In the same way, cognitive limitations can have an influential effect on decisions made under conditions of time pressure, high responsibility, and a high level of complexity of the question. Interestingly, all of these behavioral phenomena are not restricted to laypersons but also apply to experts and can be attenuated or even reinforced by collective decision making in groups and organizations.

Since the breakdown of a critical infrastructure can be a very rare event – even one never experienced by a controller – it is difficult enough for an individual to deal with a risk of disruption even in a static framework. This problem is aggravated when taking a dynamic perspective into consideration. If a critical infrastructure undergoes a significant structural and complex change (*Energiewende*) and in parallel the exposure is gradually increasing (climate change), risk managers face an intricate coincidence of internal and external risks which are difficult to assess in terms of the likelihood of occurrence and impact. In the case of a lack of knowledge, a high degree of ambiguity, and left-skewed risk distributions, decision makers often tend to underestimate extreme events, which constitute a systematic and substantial problem for risk management decisions (Camerer and Kunreuther 1989). Even if risk managers are fully aware of these risks, the struggle to convince superiors to release the necessary funds for increasing the system's resilience can be difficult. While an official budget is fixed and concrete, risks and expected gains in safety appear to be rather speculative, making it quite easy for a manager to "argue it down" and to spend the money for purposes which are easier to prove and hence to justify.

A second category of social elements that influence the performance of critical infrastructures lies in the incentive structure of the decision makers' institutional environment. We use *institution* to refer to the legal, economic, and social rules of the game which shape individual and collective behavior, such as laws and regulations, market-based incentives, social norms, and cultural traditions (North 1991; Crawford and Ostrom 1995).

Market-based incentives and market friction

In the following we concentrate on the influence that market-based incentives exert on the decisions made by a critical infrastructure provider to ensure the system's reliability. Market influence on a critical infrastructure can be manifold. First, there are markets which themselves represent critical infrastructures such as financial markets or supply chains for essential goods and services. Second, some critical infrastructure providers are dominant (in the sense of monopolistic or oligopolistic) players, such as a state-owned or regulated firm. Examples are the Deutsche Bahn for long-distance rail transportation in Germany or regional cable network operators in the case of telecommunications. Finally, even a purely pub-lic infrastructure such as the water system and public emergency services is also linked to markets in its need for employees, equipment, and long-term invest-ments. For the last factor, critical infrastructure providers are on the demand-side of the respective markets. It thus becomes clear that the scope of performance and customer utility and the level of reliability and safety of any critical infra-structure can be directly or indirectly influenced by market conditions.

Before we turn to the specific risks to energy systems and to financial systems that result from misaligned or faulty market incentives, we will briefly outline the possible reasons for economic misallocation in a market economy in gen-eral. Basically, market failure can be due to three main causes: market power including natural monopolies, information asymmetry, and market externalities. *Market power* constitutes a problem because it provides market-dominating firms an incentive to raise prices over competitive levels, which in turn keeps these markets undersupplied and inefficient. A special case of "unavoidable" market power for technical reasons is that of natural monopolies. In the case of a *natural monopoly*, production cannot be divided efficiently between multiple firms, which is mainly due to the prevalence of large networks such as the networks for roads, rail lines, and telecommunication or energy that were mentioned previously. Typ-ical for these networks are high fixed costs together with continuously decreasing average costs due to network effects (in general, the value of a network increases by its size). Among several options for competition authorities, the most common regulatory strategy is *unbundling*, which makes a distinction between the network monopoly itself and the operation of the net. Whereas the former is publicly regulated, the latter allows for competition similar to commodity markets (Kün-neke 2008).

The problem of *information asymmetry* is related to unknown or at least just imperfectly known product quality requirements on the part of markets. The word "asymmetry" indicates that one side of a market has more information about specific and relevant aspects of the market transaction than the other party. Such problems can lead to significant increases in agency costs or even lead to market collapse (Akerlof 1970). Economic theory distinguishes between *ex ante* and *ex post* asymmetries in information. The first refers to a situation before the conclu-sion of a contract and is termed a *problem of adverse selection*. Here, the informed party has an incentive to misrepresent or to exaggerate key characteristics of the transaction such as product quality or competence as these characteristics cannot be directly observed by the dependent party.

The second type of information asymmetry is relevant after the conclusion of a contract which leads to a *moral hazard problem*. In this case, the better informed party has an incentive to reduce the performance level ex post such as the amount of work, care, or quality and will excuse a deficient performance by casting the blame on unfortunate circumstances. Due to information asymmetry, the dependent party is not able to prove there has been a breach of contract in a legally enforceable manner. Both types of information asymmetry are particularly relevant for financial institutions such as insurance companies and banks. For example, credit approval decisions may involve a problem of adverse selection because the bank has to judge the lender's credit worthiness just on the basis of some selective indicators. In the insurance industry, moral hazard is among the main challenges because an insuree has an incentive to reduce the level of care and precautions once the insurance contract has been signed.

The third category of causes which can lead to market friction is that of market externalities. An *externality* is a consequence of an economic activity which affects unrelated third parties. The classical example is pollution caused by the emissions of a factory that spoils the surrounding environment and impairs the business of a nearby fishery or a recreation area. Externalities can also be caused by myopic decisions where long-term consequences are not taken into consideration because they are considered irrelevant by the decision maker. The "affected third parties" are in this case the future generations which have to pay the bill for short-sighted and unsustainable decisions. Economic policy objectives aim to achieve an "internalization" of the external effects so that both costs and benefits will accrue to those parties who decided to incur them.

Endogenous risks in the energy system and the financial system: a comparison

In this section we compare the endogenous risks affecting two critical infrastructures, the energy system and the financial system. Although the internal sources of risk in both systems are quite different, it will become evident that there are not necessarily fewer internal risks in the energy sector but that the risks there are more heterogeneous and different in nature from those in financial markets. Understandably, in the framework of this chapter we concentrate on the most important aspects and develop a focal instead of a detailed account of the two systems because the technical, economic, and social domains of each are very complex. In our view, however, it is both interesting and insightful to compare the risks of two apparently different systems at a high level of abstraction in order to understand the multiple dimensions of sources of risks as well as the broad range of requirements and options for risk reduction.

Basic functions and risks of the financial system

When speaking of "the financial system" we mean the national or global network of lenders (depositors) and borrowers (investors) of funds. The terms "lender" and "borrower" refer to the participants' role on the credit markets while the terms "depositor" and "investor" refer to the economically correspondent role on the capital markets. Financial institutions, such as banks and insurance companies, act as intermediaries and allow funds to be efficiently allocated in the national or global economy. The key function of financial institutions is *risk transformation* (or risk reduction), which implies the balancing of the risk preferences and risk positions of the market participants. This is mainly achieved by risk diversification and risk pooling. Risk diversification makes use of a low correlation (offsetting effect) of a portfolio of risky assets whereas the advantage of risk pooling lies in the possibility to spread the risk over a large group of people. Apart from these mathematical techniques to reduce risk, financial institutions also contribute to risk mitigation by means of their risk competence and by arbitrage and speculation. Both speculation and arbitrage are profitable for an investor if he can outperform the market by having better expertise or information. Speculation implies a price forecast and results in a bet on rising or falling prices. Speculation can have either a stabilizing or a destabilizing effect on market prices, and stabilizing speculation itself is generally seen as a valuable economic activity.

In contrast to speculation, an arbitrage transaction is (nearly) riskless if executed properly. Arbitrage involves the simultaneous buying and selling of an asset at different times or locations in order to profit from price differences. Among the further functions of financial institutions, predominantly banks, are lot-size transformation and maturity transformation. Lot-size transformation refers to the fact that the amounts of credit demanded of borrowers and lenders are generally mismatched. As intermediaries, banks pool these funds and thus have the possibility to provide the desired amounts to both sides of the market. Maturity transformation refers to the option of financial institutions to borrow money on shorter timeframes than they lend money out.

In what follows we briefly describe the most important risks for financial institutions and for the system as a whole. We concentrate on so-called *systemic risks*, i.e., risks which have the potential to trigger a bank run and/or a financial market crash. Basically, the literature distinguishes three types of financial crises (de Haan, Oosterloo, and Schoenmaker 2009): a bank crisis (caused by the insolvency of banks, eventually leading to a bank run), a currency crisis (sharp depreciation of the domestic currency), and a sovereign debt crisis (the government is no longer able to service its debt obligations). These three variants can mutually reinforce each other, e.g., the government's attempt to bail out illiquid banks can increase the public debt. However, our main focus will be on the activities of financial institutions and in particular the banking sector. Likewise, given the objectives and space restrictions of this chapter it is not possible to describe the dynamics of major financial crises in detail, such as the Great Depression in the United States in 1929 or the so-called Subprime Crisis in 2007–2008. We refer the interested reader to the systematic overviews by Reinhart and Rogoff (2009), Allen, Babus, and Carletti (2009), and Sinn (2010).

Given that – as outlined above – information aggregation and risk mitigation are among the key functions of financial markets, it may seem strange at first sight that the reason for most of the financial market failures has been information asymmetry and negligence in the area of risk awareness and thorough risk management. Although every crisis is unique with respect to its initial constellation and its evolution over time, some common patterns can be observed. At the beginning of most banking crises there is a credit boom characterized by an excessive lending spree, an overly optimistic expectation about certain asset prices, and some kind of "gold-rush competition" between the banks which leads to a rather unreflected parallel behavior. A "credit boom" is characterized by a stronger growth in credit than in the GDP. In the case of the crisis in the years 2007–2009, it was the real estate sector which was subject to optimism. In the USA, there had been a permanent increase in housing prices over a nearly ten-year period, which led to the impression that home loans were nearly riskless. The more market participants share such a unidirectional belief about future asset prices, the stronger the speculation which eventually leads to an *asset price bubble* with the asset prices exceeding their fundamental economic value. The exaggerated willingness of banks to provide credit is often reinforced by institutional or sector-specific side effects, such as a strong trend toward deregulation and liberalization on the one hand and the occurrence of financial innovations fostered by technical progress and advances in financial engineering on the other.

When a bank decides on a loan it takes into account the risk posed by the borrower, the available collateral, and some assumptions about future business conditions. There are several ways that this calculation can be easily distorted. First, it is possible that the credit risk is actually higher than presumed because credit assessments made during a boom phase often fall short of the required diligence. The perspective of high profits in combination with competitive pressure leads to parallel behavior (herd behavior), which also provides managers with some kind of mutual assurance that so many actors cannot be wrong if they are all doing the same thing. The incentive to go over the limit is reinforced by the variable remuneration systems with high bonuses, which are common in the banking industry. Second, the value of the collateral can be lower than expected. This is possible if the value of the collateral is not determined under stress conditions but rather under regular (or even overly optimistic) business conditions, which violates an important principle in risk management. For example, if a house price bubble bursts, it is not just the loan that goes into default; the collateral (the value of the house) becomes worthless, too.

The environmental factors, such as deregulation and financial innovation, have an additional cost-decreasing effect on a bank's operations. From a bank's perspective, expanding credit boosts profits for the same level of risk. However, the assumption "for the same level of risk" is just permissible as long as the banks understand the medium- and long-term implications of these structural changes. Taking the example of the subprime crisis, excessive deregulation led to the development of a large and unregulated shadow banking sector where supervision and regulatory requirements were fully absent. And the so-called financial innovations were a double-edged sword, too. In the case of the subprime crisis, the providers of subprime loans (loans with a low credit standing) developed so-called structured products which allowed them to combine good and bad credit risks in "tradable bundles." These constructs are called collateralized debt obligations (CDOs). The CDOs were so complex that hardly any risk manager was able to determine the cash flow of the underlying assets. The fact that only a few banks fully understood these products did not prevent them from buying them.

The motivational drivers were again herd behavior and high profitability, which was mainly due to the *leverage effect*. Loosely speaking, the leverage effect implies that debt-based financing is more profitable than equity-based financing if the return on equity is the ultimate objective criterion. With respect to potential losses, the banks have limited liability, which reinforced this perceived asymmetry between highly profitable chances and highly improbable and limited risks. Financial market insiders report that the financial institutions who developed these products did so with a clear intention to exploit this "illusion of a one-way bet" and their customers' preferences for left-tailed risk distributions (Taleb 2004).

Interestingly, although the main tasks of financial institutions are information aggregation and risk reduction with respect to the parties conducting the transactions in the real economy, informational asymmetry and latent risks *within* the financial sector (i.e., between financial institutions) increased due to environmental uncertainty, product complexity, reliance on imitation strategies, and underestimation of the systemic risk of cascading failures. The very few well-informed banks who understood the "hot potato game" character of the credit bubble not only saw the necessity to get rid of the toxic assets but even had an incentive to exploit their informational advantage at the expense of the stability of the financial system as a whole. Incentives for activities which are designed for the mere purpose of exploiting market participants and which are therefore clearly inefficient from an economic point of view are called *parasitic incentives* (Wiens 2013). If informational asymmetry increases within the financial sector, the opportunity for parasitic incentives increases as well, which ultimately has a destabilizing effect on the system. The risks mentioned so far contribute to the outbreak of a financial crisis, but the dynamics during a crisis lead to a further escalation and cascading effects. In concrete terms, a financial market crisis is accompanied by a strong increase in uncertainty, an increase in asymmetric information worsening the problems of moral hazard and adverse selection, a drastic loss of trust between financial institutions, and market interdependence, which imply the risk that a crisis in one financial market sector will spill over into another.

The importance of psychology and parallel behavior among market participants can cause panic in the market and thus have an accelerating effect on the crisis. For example, under normal conditions banks hold sufficient reserves to cope with withdrawals of deposits but if their customers lose confidence and collectively start to withdraw deposits (bank run) the bank must start to liquidate assets at mostly so-called fire sale prices (de Haan, Oosterloo, and Schoenmaker 2009). From a certain point this process becomes self-fulfilling, i.e., just the fear that the bank *could become* illiquid is enough to make this happen. At the end of a financial crisis there is a sharp contraction in economic activity, a high number of firm insolvencies, and a high level of unemployment.

After the subprime crisis in 2008 regulatory policies were intensified. First and foremost, the G20 group decided on a new framework of bank regulation (Basel III), which should be implemented by 2019. Banks are required to hold a common equity ratio of 4.5%, and banks which are considered to be "systemically relevant" have to meet more restrictive requirements. Furthermore, Basel III defines uniform liquidity requirements. In Germany a law came into force in 2014 which regulates the separation of the proprietary business of banks from customer business. Further regulations focus on the too-big-to-fail problematic, the primacy of owner liability over creditor liability, disclosure requirements for securitization (Basel II.5), more transparency in derivative trading, regulation of high-frequency trade, investor protection, and regulation of remuneration systems.

Comparison of systemic risks: financial sector versus energy sector

Starting with the similarities of the two critical infrastructures from a risk-oriented perspective, it can be said that both sectors have to deal with risks from volatility and extreme risks. In the financial markets, arbitrage, speculation, and information aggregation contribute to the smoothening of price movements (probably with the mere exception of destabilizing speculation). The daily business of financial institutions exerts a market-based incentive for them to reduce price volatility. The task of the energy system is to supply the end user with electricity reliably, i.e., providing the necessary voltages at a constant level of amplitudes. Therefore, in the energy sector the reduction in volatility by means of grid integration or buffering techniques is a technical requirement, and it is becoming an increasing challenge in the context of the energy transformation, as outlined in earlier sections (Sinn 2017). Extreme risks refer to worst case events in both systems. In the financial markets these risks are a bank run, a stock market crash, or a government default, any of which can cause considerable economic and social upheavals. In the energy sector the worst case can either refer to a risky technology that cannot be controlled such as a nuclear meltdown or to a strong disruption of the system as the consequence of which there is a long-lasting power blackout.[4]

Interestingly, in both systems the perception of these extreme risks has changed drastically over the last decade as a result of the subprime crisis in 2007 and the disaster in Fukushima in 2011. Eleven years ago the worst case had been considered highly improbable or even unrealistic given modern expertise and technological progress. These major disruptions in both systems caused strong uncertainty in the population and put politicians under great pressure to act, which became evident in the German *Energiewende*. Even greater was the uncertainty among experts and professional actors in both systems; they were shown their limits and discharged their responsibility in an almost unimaginable manner.[5] In this context philosophers often talk about "hubris" but from our point of view it suffices completely to understand that experts can be subject to distorted risk perceptions (in particular in the context of very rare and extreme risks) and that they also tend to have the biased judgment of an insider. These types of behavioral risk seem to be present in all critical infrastructures.

Both systems are increasingly complex with respect to technological innovation, the number and roles of players, and the regulatory intensity. The high level of complexity and uncertainty in both systems makes it increasingly difficult for the responsible actors to assess risk scenarios and consequences. Moreover, in both systems there is significant economic pressure at work which can dominate long-term risk management objectives.

Apart from the aspects mentioned above there are more differences than similarities between these critical infrastructures with respect to risks. The predominant risks in the financial systems are *behavioral risks* as financial institutions do not just cope with information asymmetry but themselves can easily be subject to the problems of moral hazard and adverse selection. For example, the case of moral hazard is omnipresent if a bank has an incentive to tolerate excessive risks because of limited liability or because it considers itself systemically relevant. The problem of adverse selection can be an accelerating factor during a crisis, such as when it took the form of a drastic loss of trust on the interbank market during the subprime crisis. In general, the distinctive feature of financial markets is the strong influence of psychology and parallel behavior on *professional* transactions. This leads to the risk of self-fulfilling prophecies, which make financial markets vulnerable and prone to exaggeration, rumors, or panic. A specific and very disturbing feature of financial markets is the occurrence of parasitic incentives, which suggests that better informed parties take advantage of the weaknesses of the system and thus contribute to its destabilization.

In contrast, in the energy system the technical dimension plays a predominant role, as does the fact that the energy transformation is part of an intense political and societal debate. Here we find more and in particular more heterogeneous stakeholders, a higher degree of the wider public being affected, and a publicly communicated need for transparent processes and local self-responsibility. In particular, the decision about the future energy mix is potentially vast in scope and far-reaching in its consequences. Critical infrastructure operators are confronted by the fears of the public, e.g., regarding fallout, but also by the classical NIMBY ("not-in-my-backyard") problems. Although the latter are rather "nuisance risks" for the public, to policy makers they represent hard opposition and therefore a high risk of transformation failure. Both energy production and energy distribution require an extensive and visible infrastructure and can therefore easily conflict with various differing ideas and regulatory requirements, e.g., with respect to land use or environmental protection.[6]

In contrast, the current policy and regulatory measures in the financial system are not being given the same attention by the public. Among the private actors of both systems, one gets the impression that it is mainly the actors in the energy system (e.g., the energy supply companies) who are aware of their responsibility for the resilience of the critical infrastructure. In the financial system, important private market mechanisms have failed at their task of reducing intrasystem risk. An example is the role of the rating agencies during the subprime crisis. The rating agencies were subject to a severe conflict of interest and tended to favor ratings instead of carrying out a thorough risk assessment. A phenomenon such as parasitic incentives does not exist in the energy sector although there are some parallels with respect to market manipulation, such as between the Libor scandal (manipulation of the reference interest rate LIBOR on the interbank market in 2011) and the price manipulation on the EEX electricity exchange in Leipzig in 2007. The EEX however should be seen as a hybrid institution, which is part of the energy sector but works like a financial market.

Nevertheless, the energy sector is also strongly affected by energy markets and thus influenced by economic incentives. From an economic point of view, energy markets are quite multifaceted constructs. First, there are the physical grids which represent classical natural monopolies, which have to be regulated since there is no (direct) competition. Second, network roll-out and modification are long-term decisions. The mixture of political, social, and technical risks in the energy sector complicates the decision-making process for long-term investments which are necessary for grid expansion and grid modification. With respect to operation of the grid and the sale of electricity, the energy market represents a so-called narrow oligopoly for which there is a corresponding risk of collusion. Third, add to this the new and mostly not yet competitive types of technology which have to be subsidized for a certain time period. When this period of subsidies comes to an end, many suppliers will face a hard struggle. A current example as to how negligence regarding infrastructure investment and renewal can backfire on a whole region is Puerto Rico. In 2017 Puerto Rico was hit by the hurricanes Irma and Maria, the latter being one of the strongest storms in the Caribbean. Due to the impact of the storms and flooding, Puerto Rico lost nearly its entire electricity supply, and the recovery took months. However, the energy infrastructure was known to be unsustainable and outdated for a long time. Even before the disaster, modest winds could cause a power blackout that lasted several days. The utility provider in Puerto Rico, PREPA, filed for bankruptcy several months before the disaster, a fact which illustrates that the problems – resulting in fatalities and the suffering of the population – are obviously a failure of governance and management, not primarily of the hurricanes.

Finally, one last feature that perhaps all types of critical infrastructure have in common deserves to be mentioned: the aspect of *international collaboration on system governance and regulation*. For the financial markets a large part of the regulatory program mentioned above was initiated by the G20 group, which requires a strong commitment on behalf of each partner country. Regulating global markets can only make sense if at least the largest countries are willing to enforce the rules of the game. Ensuring this for the global financial markets is extremely difficult because firms will easily identify the weakest part of the regulatory landscape and exploit these to their advantage, a phenomenon which is called regulatory arbitrage. Although there are no such extreme drivers to circumvent the measures protecting the energy system, there is a strong need for coordination between the interdependent subsystems. As the cases of Italy in 2003 and Emsland in 2006 show, the need for international coordination is still underestimated. As was described further above, the UCTE, as the organization responsible for coordinating operational procedures in Europe, took a variety of measures to improve preparedness and awareness, restoration, and training. In March, 2018, an incident took place which further raised attention not only to the need for cooperation in the energy sector but also to the need for commitment and probably even for sanctions. There was a shortage due to a deficient provision of energy, which had the consequence that electrically powered clocks were affected. Curiously enough, the reason for this underprovision was a political conflict in the Balkans between Serbia and Kosovo, both of which use the same grid, which is connected to the high-voltage European grid. Kosovo had used more power than it generated and Serbia, which is in charge of grid management, was not able to balance this out. The European grid lost 113 gigawatt-hours of energy. As a consequence, the frequency of the power grid was not stable, falling slightly under 50 Hz, which in turn affected the precision of digital clocks.

Summary and outlook

In this chapter we have analyzed the vulnerability of the energy system to disruptions from external and internal causes. The first finding was that external, in particular weather-related, events mainly affect the distribution grid. Management of the transmission grid is of greater relevance if very strong shocks spill over to other parts of the high-voltage grid – an event which requires more preparation but above all more cooperation and training among the European grid operators. We illustrated these issues with reference to four cases.

The subsequent section dealt with future challenges to the energy system in Germany with respect to the German energy transformation. The analysis shows that the structural vulnerability of an energy system will increase in the future although the smart grid can be one interesting option for increasing the system's resilience. Finally, we compared the risks of the energy system to those of the financial system, which is a rather unorthodox approach to comparing systems. One can conclude that the financial system is more strongly characterized by internal risks, behavioral risks, and even parasitic incentives, which partly raises doubt as to the ability of the financial market institutions to meet their obligations as key actors in a critical infrastructure. However, at the level of governance and regulation much has been done since the subprime crisis in 2007 and 2008 in order to reduce the risks at a systemic level.

Both systems are characterized by a high degree of uncertainty and complexity in terms of players, sectors, regulations, and technology. For the energy sector the dimension of political and social risks is of increasing importance, which indicates that socioeconomic risks should be taken into account in addition to technology-oriented ones. A systematic comparison of different types of critical infrastructure from a risk-oriented perspective can deliver valuable insights for many reasons. First, identification of similar risk drivers in two apparently very different systems means there is much to suggest that these factors can be considered as rather general risk factors and that they can be used for a cross-system risk management approach. Such general risk factors will predominantly be related to sources of risk which are independent from specific domains but rather closely related to the way humans perceive and evaluate risk (e.g., extreme, left-skewed risks) and to typical failures to overcome collective risks in an organizational context (e.g., problems of regulation and coercion). Second, even if there are many differences between the risks in the two systems, we cannot take it for granted that these risks will also remain unrelated in the future. For example, since the liberalization of the energy markets competitive pressure and market forces have played an increasingly important role, and risk managers with cross-system expertise would have a better chance to identify the increasing importance of incentive-based systemic risks. Finally, and related to the last argument, a consequence of critical infrastructures becoming more and more interdependent is that the need for integrative approaches for assessing and managing risk across systems is going to increase in the future.

Notes

1 For further information see www.entsoe.eu/news-events/former-associations/ucte/Pages/default.aspx. Accessed 2018/03/29.
2 See the contribution by Kröger and Nan in this book.
3 See the contribution by Künneke in this book.
4 In 2007, the former president of the ifo institute in Munich, Hans-Werner Sinn, used an interesting energy-metaphor to describe the extent of the financial crisis at the time. He said that at the peak of the crisis we were on the eve of a meltdown of the global financial system.
5 See the contribution by Fuchs in this book.
6 See the contribution by Hillerbrand in this book.

References

Afgan, Naim H., Dejan B. Cvetinovic, and Petros A. Pilavachi. 2013. "Catastrophe of Power Transmission System." *Energy and Power Engineering* 05 (08): 498. https://doi.org/10.4236/epe.2013.58054.

Akerlof, George A. 1970. "The Market for 'Lemons': Quality Uncertainty and the Market Mechanism." *The Quarterly Journal of Economics* 84 (3): 488–500. https://doi.org/10.2307/1879431.

Allen, Franklin, Ana Babus, and Elena Carletti. 2009. "Financial Crises: Theory and Evidence." *Annual Review of Financial Economics* 1 (1): 97–116. https://doi.org/10.1146/annurev.financial.050808.114321.

BMWi. 2017. *Renewable Energy Sources Act (EEG 2017)*. www.bmwi.de/Redaktion/EN/Downloads/renewable-energy-sources-act-2017.pdf?__blob=publicationFile&v=3.

Bundesnetzagentur. 2006. "Untersuchungsbericht Über die Versorgungsstörungen im Netzgebiet des RWE im Münsterland." Bonn. www.bundesnetzagentur.de/SharedDocs/Downloads/DE/Sachgebiete/Energie/Unternehmen_Institutionen/Versorgungssicherheit/Berichte_Fallanalysen/Bericht_12.pdf?__blob=publicationFile&v=2.

———. 2017. "Bedarfsermittlung 2017–2030: Bestätigung des Netzentwicklungsplans Strom für das Zieljahr 2030." Netzentwicklungspläne 2017–2030 und Umweltbericht. 2017. www.netzausbau.de/bedarfsermittlung/2030_2017/nep-ub/de.html.

Camerer, Colin F., and Howard Kunreuther. 1989. "Decision Processes for Low Probability Events: Policy Implications." *Journal of Policy Analysis and Management* 8 (4): 565–92. https://doi.org/10.2307/3325045.

Crawford, Sue E. S., and Elinor Ostrom. 1995. "A Grammar of Institutions." *American Political Science Review* 89 (3): 582–600. https://doi.org/10.2307/2082975.

de Haan, Jakob, Sander Oosterloo, and Dirk Schoenmaker. 2009. *European Financial Markets and Institutions*. Cambridge: Cambridge University Press. https://doi.org/10.1017/CBO9780511806230.

ENTSO-E. 2008. "Policy 8: Operational Training." Brussels: Union for the Co-ordination of Transmission of Electricity (UCTE). www.entsoe.eu/fileadmin/user_upload/_library/publications/entsoe/Operation_Handbook/Policy_8_final.pdf.

———. 2017. "Policy 5: Emergency Operations." Brussels: Union for the Co-ordination of Transmission of Electricity (UCTE). www.entsoe.eu/Documents/Publications/SOC/Continental_Europe/oh/170926_Policy_5_ver3_1_43_RGCE_Plenary_approved.pdf.

Farzin, H., M. Fotuhi-Firuzabad, and M. Moeini-Aghtaie. 2016. "Enhancing Power System Resilience Through Hierarchical Outage Management in Multi-Microgrids." *IEEE Transactions on Smart Grid* 7 (6): 2869–79. https://doi.org/10.1109/TSG.2016.2558628.

Fischer, W., J.-Fr. Hake, W. Kuckshinrichs, T. Schröder, and S. Venghaus. 2016. "German Energy Policy and the Way to Sustainability: Five Controversial Issues in the Debate on the 'Energiewende.'" *Energy*, Sustainable Development of Energy, Water and Environment Systems, 115 (November): 1580–91. https://doi.org/10.1016/j.energy.2016.05.069.

Gharavi, H., and R. Ghafurian. 2011. "Smart Grid: The Electric Energy System of the Future [Scanning the Issue]." *Proceedings of the IEEE* 99 (6): 917–21. https://doi.org/10.1109/JPROC.2011.2124210.

Giordano, Vincenzo, and Steven Bossart. 2012. "Assessing Smart Grid Benefits and Impacts: EU and U.S. Initiatives." Luxembourg: European Commission, Joint Research Centre; US Department of Energy, National Energy Technology Laboratory.

Goessling-Reisemann, Stefan, Jakob Wachsmuth, Sönke Stührmann, and Arnim Gleich. 2013. "Climate Change and Structural Vulnerability of a Metropolitan Energy System the Case of Bremen-Oldenburg in Northwest Germany." *Journal of Industrial Ecology* 17 (December). https://doi.org/10.1111/jiec.12061.

Grünwald, Reinhard. 2014. "Moderne Stromnetze als Schlüsselelement einer nachhaltigen Energieversorgung." *TAB Arbeitsbericht Nr.162.* https://www.tab-beim-bundestag.de/de/pdf/publikationen/berichte/TAB-Arbeitsbericht-ab162.pdf

Kahneman, Daniel, and Amos Tversky. 1979. "Prospect Theory: An Analysis of Decision under Risk." *Econometrica* 47 (2): 263–92. https://doi.org/10.2307/1914185.

Kakran, Sandeep, and Saurabh Chanana. 2018. "Smart Operations of Smart Grids Integrated with Distributed Generation: A Review." *Renewable and Sustainable Energy Reviews* 81 (January): 524–35. https://doi.org/10.1016/j.rser.2017.07.045.

Künneke, Rolf W. 2008. "Institutional Reform and Technological Practise: The Case of Electricity." *Industrial and Corporate Change* 17 (2): 233–65. https://doi.org/10.1093/icc/dtn002.

McKenna, Russel, Simon Hollnaicher, and Wolf Fichtner. 2014. "Cost-Potential Curves for Onshore Wind Energy: A High-Resolution Analysis for Germany." *Applied Energy* 115 (February): 103–15. https://doi.org/10.1016/j.apenergy.2013.10.030.

Momoh, James. 2012. *Smart Grid: Fundamentals of Design and Analysis.* 1 edition. Hoboken, NJ: Wiley-IEEE Press.

Münzberg, Thomas, Tim Müller, and Wolfgang Raskob. 2018. "A Future-Oriented Agent-Based Simulation to Improve Urban Critical Infrastructure Resilience." In *Urban Disaster Resilience and Security*, 261–84. The Urban Book Series. Springer, Cham. https://doi.org/10.1007/978-3-319-68606-6_16.

North, Douglass C. 1991. "Institutions." *Journal of Economic Perspectives* 5 (1): 97–112. https://doi.org/10.1257/jep.5.1.97.

Panteli, M., and P. Mancarella. 2015. "The Grid: Stronger, Bigger, Smarter?: Presenting a Conceptual Framework of Power System Resilience." *IEEE Power and Energy Magazine* 13 (3): 58–66. https://doi.org/10.1109/MPE.2015.2397334.

Pryor, S. C., and R. J. Barthelmie. 2013. "Assessing the Vulnerability of Wind Energy to Climate Change and Extreme Events." *Climatic Change* 121 (1): 79–91. https://doi.org/10.1007/s10584-013-0889-y.

Quitzow, Leslie, Weert Canzler, Philipp Grundmann, Markus Leibenath, Timothy Moss, and Tilmann Rave. 2016. "The German Energiewende – What's Happening? Introducing the Special Issue." *Utilities Policy* 41 (August): 163–71. https://doi.org/10.1016/j.jup.2016.03.002.

Rampurkar, Vaishali, Polgani Pentayya, Harivittal A. Mangalvedekar, and Faruk Kazi. 2016. "Cascading Failure Analysis for Indian Power Grid." *IEEE Transactions on Smart Grid* 7 (4): 1951–60. https://doi.org/10.1109/TSG.2016.2530679.

Rehse, Susanne, Merle Köpp, and Jaro Omar. 2016. SMART CITY. Zielmarktanalyse USA 2016. Ostküste, Schwerpunkt New York City mit Profilen der Marktakteure. New York: German American Chamber of Commerce.

Reinhart, Carmen, and Kenneth S. Rogoff. 2009. *This Time Is Different. Eight Centuries of Financial Folly*. Princeton: Princeton University Press. https://press.princeton.edu/titles/8973.html.

Sanson, Gilles, Olivier Rochereau, and Bruno Ravail. 2000. "Evaluation Des Dispositifs de Secours et d'intervention Mis En Oeuvre à l'occasion Des Tempêtes Des 26 et 28 Décembre 1999: Rapport d'étape de La Mission Interministérielle."

Schlabbach, Juergen, and Karl-Heinz Rofalski. 2008. *Power System Engineering: Planning, Design, and Operation of Power Systems and Equipment*. Weinheim: Wiley-VCH.

Servatius, Hans-Gerd, Uwe Schneidewind, and Dirk Rohlfing, eds. 2012. *Smart Energy: Wandel zu einem nachhaltigen Energiesystem*. Berlin Heidelberg: Springer-Verlag.

Sinn, Hans-Werner. 2010. *Casino Capitalism. How the Financial Crisis Came About and What Needs to Be Done Now*. Oxford; New York: Oxford University Press.

———. 2017. "Buffering Volatility: A Study on the Limits of Germany's Energy Revolution." *European Economic Review*, Combating Climate Change. Lessons from Macroeconomics, Political Economy and Public Finance, 99: 130–50. https://doi.org/10.1016/j.euroecorev.2017.05.007.

Slovic, Paul. 1987. "Perception of Risk." *Science* 236 (4799): 280–85. https://doi.org/10.1126/science.3563507.

Slovic, Paul, Baruch Fischhoff, and Sarah Lichtenstein. 1980. "Facts and Fears: Understanding Perceived Risk." In *Societal Risk Assessment*, 181–216. General Motors Research Laboratories. Boston, MA: Springer. https://doi.org/10.1007/978-1-4899-0445-4_9.

Taleb, Nassim Nicholas. 2004. "Bleed or Blowup? Why Do We Prefer Asymmetric Payoffs?" *Journal of Behavioral Finance* 5 (1): 2–7. https://doi.org/10.1207/s15427579jpfm0501_1.

Veloza, Olga P., and Francisco Santamaria. 2016. "Analysis of Major Blackouts from 2003 to 2015: Classification of Incidents and Review of Main Causes." *The Electricity Journal* 29 (7): 42–9. https://doi.org/10.1016/j.tej.2016.08.006.

Vleuten, Erik van der, and Vincent Lagendijk. 2010. "Transnational Infrastructure Vulnerability: The Historical Shaping of the 2006 European 'Blackout.'" *Energy Policy*, Energy Security – Concepts and Indicators with regular papers, 38 (4): 2042–52. https://doi.org/10.1016/j.enpol.2009.11.047.

Ward, David M. 2013. "The Effect of Weather on Grid Systems and the Reliability of Electricity Supply." *Climatic Change* 121 (1): 103–13. https://doi.org/10.1007/s10584-013-0916-z.

Wei, D., Y. Lu, M. Jafari, P. M. Skare, and K. Rohde. 2011. "Protecting Smart Grid Automation Systems Against Cyberattacks." *IEEE Transactions on Smart Grid* 2 (4): 782–95. https://doi.org/10.1109/TSG.2011.2159999.

Wiens, Marcus. 2013. *Vertrauen in der ökonomischen Theorie: Eine mikrofundierte und verhaltensbezogene Analyse [The Concept of Trust in Economic Theory]* . Münster: LIT Verlag.

Wu, Yuan-Kang, Shih Ming Chang, and Yi-Liang Hu. 2017. "Literature Review of Power System Blackouts." *Energy Procedia*, Power and Energy Systems Engineering, 141 (December): 428–31. https://doi.org/10.1016/j.egypro.2017.11.055.

Yuan, W., J. Wang, F. Qiu, C. Chen, C. Kang, and B. Zeng. 2016. "Robust Optimization-Based Resilient Distribution Network Planning Against Natural Disasters." *IEEE Transactions on Smart Grid* 7 (6): 2817–26. https://doi.org/10.1109/TSG.2015.2513048.

Zafar, Rehman, Anzar Mahmood, Sohail Razzaq, Wamiq Ali, Usman Naeem, and Khurram Shehzad. 2018. "Prosumer Based Energy Management and Sharing in Smart Grid." *Renewable and Sustainable Energy Reviews* 82 (February): 1675–84. https://doi.org/10.1016/j.rser.2017.07.018.

Part II

Sociotechnical problem of change

6 Real-world experiments as generators of sociotechnical change

Matthias Gross

Introduction: experiment and sociotechnical change

Nonrenewable fossil fuels have made possible what we today call the modern world. Perhaps any notion of modernity cannot make sense without a good understanding of energy production as part of "industrial civilization," which has been characterized by the widespread use of powered machines in society since the industrial revolution. This revolutionary shift from agricultural to mainly fossil fuel–based forms of production has also been referred to as the "great experiment" (Blumler 2008). Given that the nonrenewable resources on which this shift has been based are becoming more and more difficult and costly to extract, it may be safe to say that the next great experiment will be one in which the transition to alternative resources is the crucial task. Whether these alternatives are renewable only (sun, geothermal, wind etc.) or also include synthetic oils or oils made during gas-to-liquid and coal-to-liquid processes is a question that cannot be addressed here – and cannot be answered at all at this time given the major uncertainties regarding the feasibility of all new forms of technology. In any case, our civilization cannot continue to exist in its current form without an uninterrupted supply of energy. The issue of energy can be understood in sociological terms as the lynchpin of the way sociotechnical change is set to develop in the twenty-first century: Given that the expansion of renewables will not occur proportionately to the phase-out of traditionally produced fuel-based energy, the transition from a mainly fossil fuel-based energy system to a world of renewable energy will require not just technological change but also sociocultural transformation (Gross and Mautz 2015, 32–48).

Understood in this sense, experiments and unexpected sociotechnical changes share some crucial similarities. An experiment can be defined in the most general sense as a cautiously observed venture into the unknown. An experiment is deliberately arranged to generate an unknown or uncertain outcome. Rheinberger (1997) has even argued that what makes the procedural basis for an experiment work is that it is deliberately arranged to generate surprises. The surprising effects derived from an experimental set up can be seen as the driver behind the production of new knowledge, not least because surprises help the experimenter to become aware of their ignorance or nonknowledge. At least in hindsight it has been the unexpected results of experiments that have been a most important source for learning from "failure." The crucial difference is that such "surprises" in a laboratory experiment are welcomed and can even be considered as successes, whereas in contemporary processes of energy transition they normally are not. In the real world, surprises are often considered failures, which are to be avoided, of course.[1] Put differently, one thesis might be that the Renewable Energy Sources Act (EEG), a series of German laws that provided incentives and feed-in tariffs to encourage the generation of renewable electricity, will work properly, but a realistic expectation is (or perhaps: should be) that things will go wrong and that the EEG will need to be amended or perhaps even undergo fundamental changes.

Given that the acknowledgement of ignorance is a crucial element in processes of experimentation, ignorance cannot be thought of simply as the absence of knowledge or even as antiknowledge. If this were the case, it would clearly be judged to be an undesirable condition. Scholars in many disciplines have recently begun to challenge this negative assumption, exploring the ways in which ignorance can be more than simply the obverse of knowledge. Such inquiries have demonstrated that ignorance has a social and political life of its own (for an overview, see Smithson 2015). They have pointed out that in many areas of social life individuals often need to act in spite of (sometimes) well-defined ignorance, or what Georg Simmel termed nonknowledge (*Nichtwissen*) – the possibility of becoming knowledgeable about one's own ignorance (Gross 2012). Unlike the notion of ignorance, nonknowledge refers to knowledge about what is not known but is reasonably well defined. Nonknowledge constitutes a more precise form of the unknown. It can thus be used when describing how decisions are made that have an uncertain outcome, just as it can also point to mechanisms of control relating to what ought (or ought not) to be known. Nonknowledge will thus be referred to in the following when discussing the experimental strategies involved in advancing toward a post-fossil fuel and (hopefully) renewable energy society along with the inevitable knowledge gaps they entail.

The present challenge is to effect a sociotechnical transition to a low energy society based on alternative sources of energy and on sustainable patterns of consumption. Whereas the first industrial experiment was a fossil fuel revolution, the next "great experiment" will need to be based on a sociotechnical transition to the use of renewable energy. The view that the laboratory needs to be justified to those stakeholders outside the lab correlates well with contemporary observations that many of the risks entailed by research processes are increasingly being displaced onto society, making citizens part of a large scale experiment or several small scale ones (Shapo 2009; Stilgoe 2015; van de Poel, Asveld, and Mehos 2018). If we go one step further in this line of thinking and say that the experiment is conducted in the wider society, then we have a shift that decenters the laboratory as the privileged location of science. Such a view suggests that the laboratory experiment can be understood as a subordinated extension of a real-world experiment taking place in society. Rather than excluding outside influence and ensuring control of boundary conditions, a real-world experiment can only be an innovative generator of change when it is open to surprises. Such surprises are to be understood as a key part of the experiment taking place in the real world. The question as to what is part of the experiment and thus what is inside or outside the space where the experiment takes place is something to be defined in the course of the experimental process. According to this understanding, the experimental processes taking place in and with society should be considered the everyday, or the real world, experiment. Thus, experiments in the real world are, in a sense, the real and true experiments, and the laboratory experiment is a temporarily consequence of it.

In order to show what such real-world experiments can look like I will reconstruct recent research processes connected with geothermal energy to illustrate that experimental practices take place in many spots and that much of the laboratory research being conducted only takes place once the experiment is underway and it has become apparent what kind of research is required. This appears to be important because, given geothermal energy's relative novelty as a source for generating electricity in many countries, it is a field characterized by unavoidable unknowns and uncertainties. The question then arises how to move forward. In a first step I will suggest that the experiments conducted outside the laboratory can essentially be understood as a way of making strategic use of well-defined ignorance. I will build on the idea of locating the unexpected elements of experiments at the core of geothermal technologies. In contrast to approaches that externalize ignorance by analyzing risk assessments, I will suggest, in a second step, how the unexpected aspects of knowledge production can be analyzed using the notion of "experimentality." In a third step, I will discuss issues connected to perceived ignorance that are transferred – relocated – to closed laboratories.[2] Finally, I will reflect on questions of the acceptability and democratic governance of such experimental processes and their possibilities and limits to cope with the increasing uncertainty and often unavoidable ignorance that complicate conditions for the transition to renewable energy.

Coping with uncertainty in energy transitions

Risk, experiment, and innovation

The main purpose of the concepts of risk developed since the second half of the twentieth century has increasingly been to make the future predictable by means of probability calculations, thereby rendering it amenable to human intervention and planning. Understood in this fashion, risk can be seen as a way of rationalizing an uncertain future. Although many different concepts of risk exist, I hypothesize that when either scientists or lay people talk about risks, it would in many cases be empirically and theoretically more useful and meaningful to frame decisions, utterances, and practices in terms of different shades of ignorance. In other words, I argue that it is more often the things that are not known that are most important for decision makers and thus more important for empirical analysis. This position abandons the view that ignorance is necessarily detrimental and points instead to the broader challenges and (in some cases) the merits of not knowing as well as to the ways in which ignorance might even serve as a productive resource. This idea can be linked nicely with the notion of experiments taking place in the world outside the traditional sphere of science (Berry 2015; Gross 2016a; Schwarz 2014). Taking this line of thought further, in order to be able to act in an experimental setting, the actors involved need to agree on what is not known and to take this into account in future planning. They need to decide to act in spite of (sometimes) well-defined ignorance – or what I will call "nonknowledge" – to indicate the symmetry between the known and the unknown (Gross 2016b). The aim here is therefore to specify ignorance so that it can be used in a meaningful and constructive way. While having faith in control of ecological systems and social processes implies an ability to act only when everything is known in advance, an "experimental approach" makes it possible to accommodate different factors despite the presence of gradations of the unknown. This calls for a notion of an experimental society that is based on a conceptualization of social processes as experimental endeavors undertaken to cope with the structural complexity and surprising dynamics of modern social life – in other words, a modern society conducting experiments on itself. Whereas experimentation used to be a term that did not have a clearly positive connotation when referring to learning in policy making, recent observers seem to have detected a change toward a more experimental type of political regulation and decision making. They have sometimes referred to a new mode of governance in an experimental society (Evans, Karvonen, and Raven 2016; Gross 2010; Overdevest, Bleicher, and Gross 2010). A truly experimental approach, however, needs to be understood as one that, first, knowingly moves into the unknown by trying to specify what is unknown as clearly as possible (e.g., hypothesis building) and, then, uses unavoidable failures or mishaps as a basis for learning. To put it in more general terms, sudden unexpected changes that make the experimenters aware of their own ignorance (a falsified hypothesis) provide the impetus for new knowledge to foster innovation and creativity.

Digging deeper: the case of geothermal energy operations

Although the use of geothermal energy represents but one small part of many countries' energy transitions from fossil fuel- and/or nuclear-based forms of energy production to renewable ones, its experimental context could be seen as a model for other areas of the much larger experiment comprising the shift toward sustainability. Some of the uncertainties involved in tapping geothermal energy are especially prevalent when it comes to using a new drilling technology in order to probe downward into geothermal reservoirs up to five kilometers below the Earth's crust. After all, for most deep wells there are no preexisting data on which to base reliable modeling (Vienken et al. 2014). In this sense, moving forward and downward in geothermal engineering can only be done where even an expert works under conditions of nonknowledge, where experience, intuition, and perhaps even good guesswork skills may be crucial. Furthermore, geothermal energy is different from any other energy source because at the beginning of a geothermal power project the size of the investment is the main measure of the unknown. The exploration phase and the test drillings are based on processes of probing gingerly toward success – or indeed failure. After an initial stage of investigation (often involving geological studies conducted by the company involved but more usually involving data available only from the literature) the "relevant developer [. . .] will have to decide whether to continue developing the project or not and whether to assume the risks of the next phase" (Bloomquist, Lund, and Gehringer 2013, 253). The authors go on to note: "Computer models that accurately take into account this source of uncertainty to quantify the tradeoffs with competing resources have yet to be developed" (Bloomquist, Lund, and Gehringer 2013, 266). Consequently, Giardini (2009, 849) succinctly sums up the current situation of geothermal energy utilization in the following terms: "From their outset, EGS [enhanced geothermal system] projects need to be thought of both as pilot projects with scientific unknowns and as commercial ventures with technological and financial risks." Despite the many uncertainties and unknowns – which include the contamination of groundwater due to drilling, the question of long-term liabilities, and other technical hurdles – the prospects of achieving new knowledge by conducting research on new remote-control technologies and simulation tools designed for use in the geological substrata are increasing.

In the next section I will briefly outline how actors cope with unavoidable nonknowledge and surprising events while moving downward through the geological layers of the Earth. I will outline two examples of "raising" a laboratory after an experiment has already started. The first example is drawn from the context of geothermal drilling practices and the associated testing of the behavior of components in geochemical fluids, carried out in laboratories separated from the actual real-world experiment in society. The second example is drawn from focus group meetings involving stakeholders associated with geothermal projects – an example of relocating human subjects to a laboratory-like setting.[3]

Establishing laboratory sites during an experiment

Exploring geological and physical conditions: coping with nonknowledge among stakeholders

In many drilling operations for geothermal wells the drilling assembly (as in gas and oil drilling) is crammed full of electronic devices for controlling the direction of the drilling. The high-tech electronics and operational tools, however, only work well up to about 150 degrees Celsius. Furthermore, the drilling technologies that have been adapted from gas and oil drilling need to convey much greater volumes of liquid than in conventional oil drilling, so that the diameter of the boreholes in geothermal drilling is much larger. This makes the drilling equipment subject to a high rate of failure at high temperatures (Glassley 2010, 135–52). However, economically efficient geothermal power plants in countries whose geothermal sources are not as favorable as those in Hawaii or Iceland only become a sensible option at temperatures above 150 degrees. In the Handbook of

Best Practices for Geothermal Drilling, this problem is described in these words: "The difficulties inherent in directional drilling are aggravated in geothermal wells because both the electronic tools used to control and survey the well trajectory and elastomer elements in the motors are susceptible to malfunction at high temperatures" (Finger and Blankenship 2010: 46; see also Grimm et al. 2014). In cases such as these, drilling is often continued with corrections made ad hoc during operation. These include decisions with regard to determining the exact position of the measuring instrument in the drilling assembly (close to the bit at the bottom of the string or further away), which is precisely when the measurements should be made (given that each measurement is not only a cost factor but is also an important issue that affects the general usability of the data), and to safeguarding the electricity supply to the measuring devices. Scientists and engineers often point to the experience-based processes involved in such decisions, where adjustments in one area of the drilling operation prompt changes in another. Tapping geothermal energy thus takes place in a realm that is beyond the existing knowledge (e.g., peer reviewed publications) of the scientists and engineers involved; then, however, they have potential to turn into "successful" projects without anyone knowing exactly why.

The exploration phase of a geothermal project (when the geology and the geophysical condition of the subsurface are investigated) and the access phase (involving drilling and logging) both take place out of the public's sight (beneath the surface of society per se). Geothermal projects are associated with nuisance levels of noise and with risks related to seismic activity triggered by the disturbance of rocks caused by reservoir engineering. These risks can affect buildings and any infrastructure above ground (Grimm et al. 2014; Mukuhira et al. 2013) and have triggered public protests that have led to the cancelation of projects and a general decline in the social acceptance and media presentation of the technology in recent years (Bleicher and Gross 2016; Stauffacher et al. 2015).

During a drilling project involving geothermal water loops, hydraulic experiments are performed in the well to assess the long-term functionality of the engineered reservoir. Any measurements are carried out in situ in order to observe the performance of the modified zones. However, only a few meters away from the real world experiment an on-site laboratory is set up. This is a classical science laboratory designed for detailed geochemical investigations in case any unusual finds or obstacles are encountered underground. Thus, the real-world experiment does not seem to be able to exist without a laboratory experiment. Indeed, all the novel experimental processes taking place in the world of engineering are then downscaled back into the closed world of the laboratory. The activities done there include classification of fluids in terms of their geological properties, determination of the chemical composition of the geothermal fluid during operation, and analysis of the accompanying gases. Other in situ laboratories are used to test hydraulic stimulation techniques in different sedimentary and volcanic rocks. In other words, the systematic investigation required to make any statements about geothermal engineering to a concerned public can only be done post hoc in the laboratory. In the case of geothermal drilling, then, the debate about possible risks and gaps in our knowledge is shifted from the real world to the context of the laboratory. This often means, for instance, that a group of engineers is asked to lay bare to a concerned public what is known and what is not known about how a real-world experiment close to residential buildings might influence factors such as the soil and the groundwater table. This is a difficult but crucial issue.

Exploring political conditions: public participation and nonknowledge

This brings us to the second example, where stakeholders (concerned citizens, engineers, and decision makers) are moved into a laboratory delineated as distinct from the real-world experiment. Alexander Bogner has referred to these types of participatory experiments as a "form of participation organized by professional participation specialists, taking place under controlled conditions and largely without reference to public controversies, political participation demands, or individual concerns" (Bogner 2012, 519). Whereas Bogner focused on citizen conferences on stem cell research, I will point to a study on citizen involvement in a small town in Saxony in the Ore Mountains close to the borders of the German state of Thuringia and the Czech Republic. Here, a real-world experiment in geothermal drilling and the plan to build an adjacent power plant led to the laboratory-like "isolation" of concerned citizens in a location well away from their everyday lives (a conference hall in a small health resort). This was designed to ensure that the participants are able to speak and act freely and without incurring any consequences in the "participation laboratory," just as their natural scientist counterparts used to do in a classical laboratory, where the consequences of lab activities are only noticeable inside the laboratory.

One reason for organizing such a participatory process is that major knowledge gaps exist in the public's perceptions of the subterranean environment. The invisibility of geothermal operations deep in the ground, especially, has the potential to foster suspicion and fear, which is often seen as an obstacle to geothermal drilling and technology diffusion as well as to the communication of the benefits of the new technology. The intention is to lift the veil of invisibility in the lab-like situation and for investors and engineers to strategically present the drilling and heat exchanging technologies in order to bring light into the debate.

The actual participatory process was organized by experts from two major German research institutions. The invitation to this laboratory was sent out via the local and regional media and advertised as a place to get first-hand information on geothermal drilling and power generation. The participants who eventually agreed to take part were not selected by any method that guaranteed representativeness but on a first come, first served basis. This basically meant that everybody who felt he or she needed some information or wanted to discuss issues of concern and their "way of seeing" the issue was welcomed. Thus, the laboratory was not set up to pacify protest (although this was a possibility that could have happened) but rather to see how a public group reacts to problematic issues such as knowledge gaps and how it considers issues of uncertainty in such settings. A newspaper clipping in the major daily of the region, the *Freie Presse* (with over 250,000 copies sold on a subscription basis alone, it is the largest newspaper in Saxony), reported on the laboratory. The reports, however, clearly pointed to the information-based character of the event, even to the extent of beating the drum for the topic. The exact purpose of assembling this group was thus not clearly communicated for the intention was for experts to inform people and for all the participants to debate the acceptable and unacceptable uncertainties. The actual laboratory meeting, which lasted almost a full day, followed the focus group method. This method has recently been praised as a way of providing specific data on social groups and is framed as a process involving natural interactions in artificial situations.

The topics discussed in this laboratory-like participatory situation were straightforward. They mainly focused on perceptions of seismic risks, the relation of geothermal drilling to contemporary fracking technologies, the possible economic incentives for the region, and the role of geothermal energy in the overall plan to establish renewable sources of energy in Germany and Europe. Thus, although protest-based interventions by civil society groups continue to play a role in governance processes regarding engineering, ecology, and technology, in this case we see a form of "invited participation," where potential participants have to be convinced by local media (newspapers, advertisements, and information on bulletin boards) to participate in a lab-like situation in which they are allotted a "place sitting down at roundtable discussions." Here, then, participation involves "retreating from society into the lab" (Bogner 2012, 522). This lab may then become a place where stakeholders sit together around a table and discuss whether the procedures in question are worth "trying out" (a term often used among stakeholders in geothermal drilling operations) or not. This also includes that scientists and engineers explain to stakeholders and decision makers why some things cannot be known any better within a certain time frame. This in turn makes it clear that it is important to start work in order not to fritter away time. Waiting for a risk analysis often means doing exactly this, however. In other words, acknowledging ignorance must not be misunderstood as a failure of expertise but as a normal process in the production of experimental knowledge (Gross 2010).

Limits of participation and mutual understanding

Much of the discussion and research on public participation harbors a rather romantic view of grassroots democracy and participatory processes. This conceptualization that participation is inherently "good" is problematic because it is based on the assumption that the emergence of mistrust and of a lack of acceptance results from badly communicated results of science. However, and at least indirectly, such a view also implies that increasing transparency regarding science will inevitably help minimize the development of public protest. Needless to say, a critical public may not even be prepared to accept participation as a tool for decision making in many cases. Even more so, as (Bogner 2012, 510) has shown, citizens are sometimes simply not interested, and they almost have to be dragged into the (participation) laboratory because their input and knowledge are needed. The participation procedure in the case discussed here, however, can be understood as lab activity since the results of this engagement process (so far) have not had any real consequences for policy making in the world outside the laboratory. In short, participation in the lab contributed to legitimizing the larger real-world experiment simply by enabling the lab to take place. However, it can be said that without the laboratory-like participation process in a democratic society the real-world experiment of geothermal energy operation would not be complete due to the lack of the legitimization that the lab provided.

In order to engage meaningfully in such experiments and to cope with non-knowledge and uncertainty, the stakeholders involved need to develop openness toward the possibility of redefining their goals in the course of iterative discussions. Experiments of this kind are most likely to be conducted when knowledge gaps are clearly defined. This may be during phases in the drilling process in which a judgment must be made about whether any of the perceived knowledge gaps can be reduced by conducting further geological investigations or acquiring new data for modeling, or whether only a "learning while doing" strategy is conceivable. In this way, decision making that is based on a stock of nonknowledge discussed in participatory lab experiments would not be considered mere irresponsible tinkering but would rather be based on a shared sense of justifiable (reasonable) ignorance that has been acknowledged and clearly defined (and perhaps even consensually agreed upon) so that the experiment can continue.

Taking the experiment (back) into the laboratory?

As we have seen by looking at the example of geothermal energy, it is the (real world) experiment that seems to be there first while the situation that requires clarification by a laboratory is determined post hoc. In the realm of geothermal energy utilization it can be shown that experimental practices occur in many places while the laboratory and the social actors from outside the institutional spheres of science come into the picture only after the start of the experiment when, for instance, stakeholders are invited to participate in laboratory-like settings or the geochemical specificities of fluids are tested. In real-world experiments, hazards and obstacles often become apparent only after the technology has been tested or stakeholders have been "invited" to the laboratory.

Experts' conversations with stakeholders in laboratory settings can thus be understood as being just as important a part of real-world experiments as are the laboratory investigations of the scientists involved. They certainly constitute an important part of the effort to harness geothermal energy and perhaps of the energy transition from fossil fuels to renewable ones in general. Such a transition entails altering permits (administration) and changing plans (engineering companies and research institutes). This seems to encourage the development of innovative strategies and to make full use of the potential and resources of the actors involved to achieve a common goal. Furthermore, new knowledge may emerge from unexpected events, which in post hoc defined laboratories can help to further specify our ignorance, so that we can consciously take the limits and boundaries of our knowing into account when acting or planning. Thus, real-world experiments are designed to cope with unknowns by anchoring them – albeit sometimes only briefly – in a traditional laboratory. In order to legitimize the real-world experiment, it sometimes seems that some critical components are moved into the laboratory so that they remain without consequence. If the laboratory part of the real-world experiment fails, then the overall process cannot be continued. Thus, the world of the classical science laboratory and the necessary containment of this world behind laboratory walls – whether for stakeholder workshops or for scientists' activities – still exists today, albeit initiated by a real-world experimental process whose participants include geothermal energy companies, scientists, engineers, and concerned citizens. Only the traditional sequence from laboratory research to application in the real world seems to have been switched around, that is, the experimental set up is there first and is sometimes even independent of a clearly defined laboratory that comes into play later.

The unavoidable unknowns and uncertainties from such experiments are relocated to corresponding "laboratories" outside the actual experiments. Depending on the type of uncertainties and unknowns, these laboratories may be either traditional science labs or the laboratory-like participation of stakeholders from outside the realm of science – or both. It can be said, then, that alternative energy research on the subterranean environment, as discussed in this chapter, demonstrates a trend whereby research processes are started in the real world and the issues they raise are displaced from the context of the real-world experiment into the more closed world of a (variously configured) laboratory. Real-world experiments thus provide justification for lab activities. From this perspective, lab experiments are post-positioned microvariants of real-world experiments in and with society. In this sense, the risk-laden production of new knowledge via real-world experimentation fosters a practice of shifting the context of discovery in society into post hoc defined laboratories of justification.

Outlook: real-world experiments and sociotechnical change

The acquisition of new knowledge often leads to the perception of new horizons concerning what is not known. This development is fostered by the increasing pressure placed on science to promote applications as we know from the debates on postacademic (Ziman 2000) and postnormal science (Funtowicz and Ravetz 1993) and from the numerous debates on transdisciplinary and program-oriented research programs (Bergmann et al. 2013; Gross and Stauffacher 2014; Stauffacher et al. 2013); it is also based on what has been termed the mode 2 stage in science and knowledge production (Gibbons, Nowotny, and Scott 2001). When it comes to planning and handling processes of moving into such new modes of energy production, however, it is still common for both policy makers and scientists to officially state that decisions are based on known and observable "facts." This leads to a gap between official rhetoric and the situation of practitioners on the ground, for whom dealing experimentally with ignorance has become a state of normalcy.

Furthermore, if it appears meaningful to characterize contemporary modern societies as exhibiting a trend toward more experimentality, then real-world experimentation and the acknowledgement of nonknowledge are set to become more important than ever before. It would mean moving away from an orientation on previous experience and historical extrapolations in nature, technology, and society (e.g., risk assessments) and shifting instead toward prospective and temporary notions of what is known and unknown. This may be in line with what has been termed the "proactionary" imperative in innovation and sociotechnical change (Fuller and Lipińska 2014; More 2005), but it harbors a few challenges that need to be addressed. The actors involved need to agree that no other means are reasonably available (with regard to time, funding, and the results to be expected) to gain knowledge about a certain issue that seems desirable (Gross 2017). In addition, and perhaps even more importantly, the possibilities for stopping an experiment need to be clarified beforehand. Finally, and this may be the most pressing and problematic issue, a fair distribution of benefits and hazards needs to be addressed, as do moral and ethical issues (van de Poel et al. 2018). However, this is easier said than done. In a democratically anchored version of real-world experiments, this also means that as many people as possible need to benefit from it. Again, this may sound feasible in theory, but a wide range of different framings are needed to offer at least a basis for achieving a better understanding of the potential benefits in practice. The task, then, becomes one of experimentally reformulating different understandings so that public perspectives are incorporated at the outset and form part of the imagined pathways.

Despite the discourse on experimentalism in some areas of research and practice, official rhetoric calls for more certainty and more safety measures. After all, the precautionary principle is well established in everyday thinking. Decision making based on nonknowledge would then be regarded as irresponsible tinkering – which it can certainly sometimes be – but to at least an equal measure it appears as an inevitable fact that should not be excluded from official statements. Despite this, real-world decision making in a strictly regulated bureaucracy seems, quite paradoxically, to foster a positive engagement with ignorance and surprise because in clearly defined spatial and temporal settings the experimental activities can be rendered an accepted part of an adversarial society, since they define legal spaces for failure, mishaps, and (unavoidable) risk taking.

This, of course, may also invite corporations or individual actors with unsavory motives to not taking this precaution, but just takes chances, because of a desire to achieve an outcome (Gross 2016c). This may be a reason why experimental strategies are mostly found in sociotechnical projects, such as the ones discussed in this volume. In this sense, experimentality is not a romantic idea of incrementalism, of muddling through, or of some type of adaptive management where actors passively adapt to changing external conditions ("roll along with the punches"); instead it demonstrates in a stark manner that dealing with unknowns can become a reality not by choice but by necessity and initiate sociotechnical change. One is tempted to speculate that at a local or regional level experimental strategies may thrive best when there are strict state regulations in place that provide the "proactionary" freedom to experiment and also to fail (Gross 2017).

In the end, an important prerequisite for an experiment to successfully fail is that the actors involved are prepared to make the decision to proceed despite the existence of ignorance. There must also be public debate and the existence of citizens prepared to accept transformation and disruption. This includes a culture of acknowledging nonknowledge, of anti-blame and rejecting finger pointing, and of clarifying the benefits of moving into the unknown. This needs to be done to conceptualize sociotechnical change and the problems inherent in it as part of a larger experimental avenue taken by science and engineering in the twenty-first century.

Notes

1 For an attempt to categorize different forms of surprise in science and in everyday life, see Gross (2010, 34–47).
2 The cases I focus on in this article are based on two interdisciplinary projects on geological substrata at the Helmholtz Centre of Environmental Research (UFZ) in Leipzig, Germany. The summaries I present are based on field notes and interviews conducted during excursions to drilling sites, geothermal energy workshops, focus group discussions, and meetings with decision makers and stakeholders. For further details and other results of these research projects not discussed here, see Bleicher and Gross (2015, 2016) as well as Gross (2013; 2015, 2016a).
3 This and the following two sections draw heavily on (Gross, 2016a). Further details on geothermal drilling such as adventurous strategies for moving into the unknown can be found in (Gross, 2015). Different sociotechnical "cultures" of using shallow geothermal heat at the household level are discussed in (Bleicher and Gross, 2016).

References

Bergmann, Matthias, Thomas Jahn, Tobias Knobloch, Wolfgang Krohn, Christian Pohl, and Engelbert Schramm. 2013. *Methods for Transdisciplinary Research: A Primer for Practice*. Frankfurt am Main: Campus Verlag.

Berry, Dominic. 2015. "The Resisted Rise of Randomisation in Experimental Design: British Agricultural Science, c.1910–1930." *History & Philosophy of the Life Sciences* 37: 242–60.

Bleicher, Alena, and Matthias Gross. 2015. "User Motivation, Energy Prosumers and Regional Diversity: Sociological Notes on Using Shallow Geothermal Energy." *Geothermal Energy* 3: 1–12.

Bleicher, Alena, and Matthias Gross. 2016. "Geothermal Heat Pumps and the Vagaries of Subterranean Geology: Energy Independence at a Household Level as a Real World Experiment." *Renewable & Sustainable Energy Reviews* 64: 279–88. https://doi.org/10.1016/j.rser.2016.06.013

Bloomquist, Gordon, John Lund, and Magnus Gehringer. 2013. "Geothermal Energy." In *The World Scientific Handbook of Energy: Materials and Energy*, 3, edited by Gerard M. Crawley, 245–73. World Scientific Publishing.

Blumler, Mark A., 2008. "The Fossil Fuel Revolution: A Great, and Largely Unrecognized, Experiment." *Pennsylvania Geographer* 46: 3–21.

Bogner, Alexander, 2012. "The Paradox of Participation Experiments." *Science, Technology & Human Values* 37: 506–27. https://doi.org/10.1177/0162243911430398

Evans, James P.M., Andrew Karvonen, and Rob Raven. (Eds.), 2016. *The Experimental City*, Routledge Research in Sustainable Urbanism. London; New York: Routledge, Taylor & Francis Group.

Finger, John, and Doug Blankenship. 2010. *Handbook of Best Practices for Geothermal Drilling*, Sandia Report. Albuquerque, New Mexico: Sandia National Laboratories.

Fuller, Steve, and Veronika Lipińska. 2014. *The Proactionary Imperative: A Foundation for Transhumanism*. UK: Palgrave Macmillan.

Funtowicz, Silvio O., and Jerome R. Ravetz. 1993. "Science for the Post-Normal Age." *Futures* 25: 735–55.

Giardini, Domenico. 2009. "Geothermal Quake Risks Must Be Faced." *Nature* 462: 848–49. https://doi.org/10.1038/462848a

Gibbons, Michael, Helga Nowotny, and Peter Scott. 2001. *Re-Thinking Science: Knowledge and the Public in an Age of Uncertainty*, 1st ed. Cambridge, UK: Polity.

Glassley, William E. 2010. *Geothermal Energy: Renewable Energy and the Environment*, Energy and the Environment. London: CRC Press.

Grimm, Manuel, Ingrid Stober, Thomas Kohl, and Philipp Blum. 2014. "Schadensfallanalyse von Erdwärmesondenbohrungen in Baden-Württemberg." *Grundwasser* 19: 275–86. https://doi.org/10.1007/s00767-014-0269-1

Gross, Matthias 2010. *Ignorance and Surprise: Science, Society, and Ecological Design*. Cambridge, MA: MIT Press.

Gross, Matthias 2012. "'Objective Culture' and the Development of Nonknowledge: Georg Simmel and the Reverse Side of Knowing." *Cultural Sociology* 6: 422–37. https://doi.org/10.1177/1749975512445431

Gross, Matthias 2013. "Old Science Fiction, New Inspiration: Communicating Unknowns in the Utilization of Geothermal Energy." *Science Communication* 35: 810–18. https://doi.org/10.1177/1075547012469184

Gross, Matthias 2015. "Journeying to the Heat of the Earth: From Jules Verne to Present-day Geothermal Adventures." *Engineering Studies* 7: 28–46. https://doi.org/10.1080/19378629.2014.997738

Gross, Matthias 2016a. "Give Me an Experiment and I Will Raise a Laboratory." *Science, Technology, & Human Values* 41: 613–34. https://doi.org/10.1177/0162243915617005

Gross, Matthias 2016b. "Risk as Zombie Category: Ulrich Beck's Unfinished Project of the 'non-knowledge' Society." *Security Dialogue* 47: 386–402. https://doi.org/10.1177/0967010616645020

Gross, Matthias 2016c. "Layered Industrial Sites: Experimental Landscapes and the Virtues of Ignorance." In *Restoring Layered Landscapes: History, Ecology, and Culture*, edited by M. Hourdequin, and D.G. Havlick. Oxford; New York: Oxford University Press.

Gross, Matthias 2017. "Shaping New Horizons: Proactionary Attitudes, Precautionary Principles, and the Experimentalities of Science in Society." In *Imagined Futures in Science, Technology and Society*, edited by Gert Verschraegen, Frédéric Vandermoere, Luc Braeckmans, and Barbara Segaert. Routledge Studies in Science, Technology and Society. London; New York: Routledge, Taylor & Francis Group.

Gross, Matthias and Rüdiger Mautz. 2015. *Renewable Energies*. London, New York: Routledge.

Gross, Matthias, and Michael Stauffacher. 2014. Transdisciplinary Environmental Science: Problem-oriented Projects and Strategic Research Programs. *Interdisciplinary Science Reviews* 39: 299–306. https://doi.org/10.1179/0308018814Z.00000000093

More, M. 2005. The Proactionary Principle. http://www.maxmore.com/proactionary.html. Accessed 2016/08/26.

Mukuhira, Yusuke, Hiroshi Asanuma, Hiroaki Niitsuma, and Markus O. Häring. 2013. Characteristics of Large-Magnitude Microseismic Events Recorded During and After Stimulation of a Geothermal Reservoir at Basel, Switzerland. *Geothermics* 45: 1–17. https://doi.org/10.1016/j.geothermics.2012.07.005

Overdevest, Christine, Alena Bleicher, and Matthias Gross. 2010. The Experimental Turn in Environmental Sociology: Pragmatism and New Forms of Governance. In *Environmental Sociology: European Perspectives and Interdisciplinary Challenges*, edited by Matthias Groß and Harald Heinrichs, 279–94. Heidelberg: Springer.

Rheinberger, Hans-Jörg, 1997. *Toward a History of Epistemic Things: Synthesizing Proteins in the Test Tube*. Stanford: Stanford University Press.

Schwarz, Astrid E., 2014. *Experiments in Practice, History and Philosophy of Technoscience*. London: Pickering & Chatto.

Shapo, Marshall S., 2009. *Experimenting with the Consumer: The Mass Testing of Risky Products on the American Public*. Westport, CT: Praeger.

Smithson, Michael, 2015. Ignorance Studies: Interdisciplinary, Multidisciplinary, and Transdisciplinary. In *Routledge International Handbook of Ignorance Studies*, Routledge International Handbooks, edited by Matthias Gross, and Linsey McGoey, 385–99. London; New York: Routledge, Taylor & Francis Group.

Stauffacher, Michael, Vicente Carabias-Hütter, Ruth Förster, Patricia Fry, Marcus Hall, Andreas Kläy, Christoph Kueffer, Harry Spiess, Patrick Wäger, and Claudia Zingerli. 2013. Engagement für inter- und transdisziplinäre Forschung zur nachhaltigen Entwicklung. *Gaia* 22: 142–44.

Stauffacher, Michael, Nora Muggli, Anna Scolobig, and Corinne Moser. 2015. Framing Deep Geothermal Energy in Mass Media: The Case of Switzerland. *Technological Forecasting and Social Change* 98: 60–70. https://doi.org/10.1016/j.techfore.2015.05.018

Stilgoe, Jack, 2015. *Experiment Earth: Responsible Innovation in Geoengineering*. London, New York: Routledge, Taylor & Francis Group.

van de Poel, Ibo, Lotte Asveld, and Donna C. Mehos. (Eds.) 2018. *New Perspectives on Technology in Society: Experimentation Beyond the Laboratory, Emerging Technologies, Ethics and International Affairs*. Abingdon, Oxon; New York: Routledge.

Vienken, Thomas, Sophie Schelenz, Karsten Rink, and Peter Dietrich. 2014. Sustainable Intensive Thermal Use of the Shallow Subsurface – A Critical View on the Status Quo. *Groundwater* 53: 356–61. https://doi.org/10.1111/gwat.12206

Ziman, John M. 2000. *Real Science: What It Is and What It Means*. Cambridge; New York: Cambridge University Press.

7 Learning and disruptive innovation in energy transitions

Who causes which constraints in the German electricity transition?

Gerhard Fuchs

Introduction

In Germany, more than 36% of the electricity used in 2017 was harvested from renewable energy (RE) sources. While in the 1990s the contribution of mainly old RE stagnated, since the beginning of the new century we can observe a remarkable dynamic of growth in the area of new RE (solar, wind, and biomass) (Fettke and Fuchs 2017). Given that the present chapter will develop a sociological perspective on these developments, the figures concerning energy sources should be used as a starting point to discuss the question of whether the social practice of electricity production and distribution has changed in the same way as the technical features. The increase in the use of specific types of technology does not automatically need to be connected with changes in the ways we are dealing with specific problems, with changes in the type of actors involved in addressing the problem being examined, or with changes in the position of these actors within a field. The dominant car producers, for example, for a long time continuously introduced new forms of technology in their production processes and products, but essentially their position as dominant players did not change and our ways of dealing with mobility also did not undergo dramatic revaluation.

In the relevant literature, processes in which technologies and technological applications are involved are very often analyzed in terms of changes in sociotechnical systems, highlighting the specific connection between the features of technologies and the way they are promoted and used in social contexts. Sovacool and Hess (2017) have recently published a paper in which 14 different approaches to the study of sociotechnical systems are presented. The aim of this chapter is not to present an additional analytical approach to the study of sociotechnical systems and their transformation. It rather attempts to build on established concepts in sociological theory and to apply them to the problems we are interested in. "Established" in this context means that linkages to discussions in general social theory have been made. The rationale behind this is to avoid a fragmentation of the debate in which each researcher employs his or her favorite concept, maybe a self-developed one, which may be valid only for specific fields or problems. Rather than helping us try to explain and discuss developments in the social world, such fragmentation would lead us into conducting a debate about concepts.

Empirically the chapter will use the case of the German electricity transition to assess the extent to which the social practice on which the transition is based has changed. It will analyze what has happened to the actors engaged in the practice, their position in the field, and the mechanisms responsible for the changes. Thinking about mechanisms has a long history in the social sciences. The most important classic to quote is probably Robert K. Merton, who was concerned with answering the question "How did certain events come about?" This led Merton to focus on mechanisms and theories suitable for answering such questions (Merton 1968). Mechanism-based explanations (a) differ from covering-law explanations, (b) do not attempt (unlike functionalist or structuralist explanations) to abstract from the actions of social actors, and (c) go beyond quantitative correlation analysis between variables (Mayntz 2004). Merton did not give a precise definition of "mechanism." One of the many more recent definitions was developed by Hedström (2005). It characterizes mechanisms as consisting of entities (with their properties) and the activities that these entities engage in, either by themselves or in concert with other entities. These activities bring about change, and the type of change depends on the properties of the entities and the way in which the entities are organized spatially and temporally. Real actors are treated as entities.

The chapter will proceed as follows. In the next section, the theoretical framework will be introduced. Based on these considerations, four phases in the development of the German electricity transition will be distinguished. A concluding section will return to the general questions posed in the introduction. The main aim will be to show that the electricity transition in Germany is an emergent process with few features of linearity.

Sociological theory and transitions

The above-mentioned reference to established concepts in social theory that we are attempting to establish may actually be somewhat misleading. Over the last couple of years, there has been an intensive discussion in sociology about how to deal with the problem of change. It seems to be generally acknowledged that in the past sociology was primarily concerned with static structures and regularities, i.e., social facts. The problem of change, on the other hand, was given short thrift. Insofar we are in a sense still at the beginning of introducing change into sociological theory. Abbott (2016), for example, is concerned with the principles of a processual sociology; Padgett and Powell (2012) investigate the origin and development of new organizations and markets, for example;[1] and Fligstein and McAdam (2011, 2012) are developing a field theory combining aspects of stability and change in social relations. All these authors share the idea that structures and institutions should not be treated as something given and, as such, constraining, but as something that comes into existence, develops, and eventually might dissolve again. Martin (2009) makes it clear that such an approach does not mean turning sociology into history. If I look upon structures and institutions as processes, I will naturally be treating them as being transient, coming from somewhere, having a certain configuration in the present, which will be different in the future. We will, however, look for generic principles that tell us how structures are formed and stabilized and how they may eventually be destroyed again. This turns the attention of the researcher away from a traditional concern with "why" questions, putting mechanisms and "how" questions in the foreground (White 2008).

In this sense, what we are interested in is to look at the practice of electricity production and distribution, assess whether this practice has changed, and look for the mechanisms responsible for a possible change. Concentrating our attention on electricity production and distribution has both conceptual and empirical reasons. In spite of the fact that there is a lot of talk about energy transitions as a whole, this whole is a conceptual idea rather than an empirical fact. If we look at energy-related activities in Germany (but we could also look elsewhere, see, e.g., McAdam and Schaeffer-Boudet [2012] on the USA), we will quickly see that the various energy-related activities reflect the fact that different principles, different regulations, and different actors are involved. Insofar there is no unity and no common institutional background that can be meaningfully detected with regard to energy-related activities as a whole.[2]

Conceptually, if we want to assess whether institutional frames for actors have changed, we do need to pick actors who are engaged in a similar, comparable type of activity. With respect to institutions, one often finds a reference to the "rules of the game" in the literature. This implies that if we want to look at institutions, we will have to study actors who are playing according to a common framework. Politicians who decide upon new regulations concerning wind parks are not in the same game as people who are trying to set up a wind park. Of course, they influence each other, but they need not be potentially aware of one another and the frameworks by which they are guided in their endeavors can be very different.[3] Decisions about energy contracting involve still other actors, both among the decision makers as well as among the users. Each is in a different game. However, as Scharpf (1997) has argued, the number of different types of games that can be played by real actors is limited, turning our attention again toward the issue of mechanisms.

Furthermore, we have to be aware of the fact that, at least in Germany, climate-related activities are successful to a very different extent. The present government (January 2018) openly says that the climate goals for 2020 have to be abandoned. In this context, RE is a success story, while in many other areas (e.g., traffic, mobility) little progress has been made. We should insofar be careful about making a general assessment about energy transitions based on electricity alone or making one that overlooks their fragmented emergent character.

Having thus cleared the way, we can assume that a social practice revolves around a common understanding of what is going on in a field. There are actors who wield more or less power in influencing the practice; we will call them incumbent and challenger actors, respectively. There is a common set of rules, defining legitimate actions and a broad interpretative framework that individual and collective actors share to make sense of what others within the field are doing. This all happens within an environment that is constantly changing and posing new challenges to the participating actors. An eminent part in this environment is played by political actors, who set the regulatory framework. Changes in practices are advanced by challenger actors coming either from outside the established fields or from disadvantaged "niches" within the field. In order to be able to change an established practice, challengers need to be able to take advantage of changes in the surrounding environment that will help them – properly framed – to delegitimize existing practices.

Learning is done along the lines of improving an established practice. Developing new practices or changing them substantially involves unlearning, which is promoted by the challengers and potentially forced on the incumbents. Such a process of unlearning is conceived of as disruptive innovation. Slightly modifying the stance of Padgett and Powell (2012), who distinguish between innovation and invention, we can say: *incremental innovations* improve on existing ways of doing things, while *radical innovations* change the ways things are done. Based on this we can determine that an incremental innovation in the field of electricity generation aims at improving the existing ways and procedures (fossil fuel- and nuclear power-based electricity generation by established actors) and at gradually adapting to new demands coming from the environment (more RE installations). Radical innovation is concerned with new ways of generating electricity, engages new actors, and builds new networks.

Institutional transformation

Analyzing processes such as electricity transitions makes us think about periods of time. Determining periods or distinguishing between different phases of development in a process has always included some element of arbitrariness. This is indicated by questions such as where to start and where to end, and how to avoid the impression that the present state of affairs is to be considered the logical outcome of a development full of contingent events. If I write a study in 2018 rather than in 2017, the process results might be quite different, and it would be ludicrous to assume that the logical conclusion of the activities of the year 2017 will necessarily be what comes into existence in 2018. Clearly if we want to retrace a process, the elements highlighted need to be connected to one another, in order to show the flow, but as mentioned before we should not suggest that the flow has been without alternatives (Abbott 2001).

A relational approach fully incorporates at least two types of actors or agencies occupying different positions within the social space or field and bound together in a relationship of mutual dependence or struggle. In this way, we distinguish at the beginning of the electricity transition process between the incumbent actors, dominating the field, and the challengers, at the fringes or even outside of the field, who are eager to disturb the dominant field practices. The roots of the dominant system of electricity generation and distribution in Germany in the 1990s – our starting point – differ from those of the RE movement, which we consider as the challengers. Insofar we have two processes running parallel for some time. Nevertheless, they have one common reference point: the discussion about nuclear energy. The dominant industrial and political actors for a long time considered nuclear energy to be an important building block of the German electricity system. A social movement against nuclear energy, however, led to a stop of construction plans, and especially after the Chernobyl accident the anti-nuclear sentiment won broad public support. The successful attribution of a threat to nuclear energy and later on to climate change was achieved by the challengers. Actors associated with the threat were the big energy companies and parts of the government(s). The anti-nuclear power movement had also demonstrated that mobilizing can be effective and successful.

In their efforts to mobilize, RE actors were also developing a collective attribution of opportunity, by developing the idea that RE and a new decentralized system of energy generation and distribution would help in coping with the threats to the environment.

The success of the movement and the specific German way of dealing with problems (e.g., as opposed to that in the UK or France), however, depended on specific changes in the environment of the movement. Thirty years of social movement research have affirmed the important role that favorable "political opportunities" play in shaping the emergence and development of contentious politics (Kriesi 2004). Insofar we will try to trace the development of the German electricity transition along the lines of changes in political power constellations. The changes in power constellations, of course, do not immediately or necessarily translate into changes in social practices. Nevertheless, they influence opportunity structures in the sense that the changed composition of the government did go along with changing attitudes toward RE deployment.

Phase 1 (–1998): building niches and developing markets

In the 1990s, there was a straightforward consensus regarding who acts legitimately and how legitimate activities in the field of electricity generation and distribution are to be conducted. The dominant idea was that electricity generation has to rely on fossil fuels and nuclear energy. Electricity is to be produced in big power plants, owned by actors able to make capital-intensive long-term investments. Electricity, produced some distance from the points of consumption, has to be transported via big cross-country grids to the end user. Before electricity markets were formally liberalized in 1998, the German electricity sector was organized on the basis of a "natural monopoly." The market was shaped by nine vertically integrated public utilities, which provided electricity within specific territorially fixed boundaries (Bontrup and Marquardt 2010, 20f). Insofar there was no competition. The nine companies mainly served as the backbone for 80 regional supply companies and about 900 municipal utilities. Some of the regional suppliers also possessed production capacities. Most of the municipal utilities, however, held little or no production capacity at all and concentrated on matters of distribution. This setup reflected the decentralized way the electricity system in Germany had developed historically and the typical quasi-corporatist organizational setup for public services to be found elsewhere as well (e.g., post, telecommunications, and social insurance).

Except for some large companies who owned power plants to help operate their production units, independent energy producers were generally considered to be illegitimate. Owners of decentralized RE systems usually did not get permission to connect their installations to the grid. The regulatory basis for this was the German Energy Act (EnWG) of 1935. The law guaranteed the supply monopoly for supposedly economic reasons. It was primarily justified by the argument that regional monopolies would enable the production of power at the lowest costs. For the dominant actors in this period, learning meant extending the reach of their business models to the former German Democratic Republic (GDR) and preparing for liberalization. In their optimization efforts, they were not searching for new technological options.[4] Anyway, why would they consider it necessary to abandon a successful legitimate practice? They were busy with further developing their advantaged position in the field.

The search for new technological options did take place elsewhere: in the RE movement. The origins of this movement can be found mainly in the anti-nuclear power movement and to a lesser extent in protest movements against big industry/big government projects. Some members of the movement were scientists who were eager to develop alternatives to nuclear energy; many others were (organized) activists, who were willing to build experimental installations. An important window of opportunity for these groups opened following the rising electoral successes of the Green Party in the 1980s and 1990s, which eagerly picked up the energy issue. In some communities where the green movement was strong, experiments were conducted with local energy solutions, operating with different organizational and technological mixes. There was little direct competition between incumbents and challengers, which were not yet considered to be relevant. The incumbents, however, did lobby politicians, obstruct RE programs, and use the courts to stop RE development.

Political decision makers at the federal level were also mainly concerned with organizing the electricity system in the former GDR and preparing for liberalization, an issue especially advanced by the European Commission. Attitudes toward RE were reluctant and haphazard. Less by persuasion than as a sign of being open to the public mood against nuclear energy, technology-based support programs for small wind turbines were first introduced in the late 1980s (Neukirch 2010), which were later extended to solar energy; both were funded by the ministry for education and research (as opposed to the ministry of economic affairs, which was concerned with liberalization, market framework, and nuclear energy). The introduction of a first Feed-In Law in 1990 constituted an important milestone; this was the result of a compromise between different political groups ahead of an important federal election.

The opponents of RE considered the program to be too small and unimportant to be relevant and actually believed that it would demonstrate that RE is not viable in Germany. They therefore let it pass. For the supporters of RE, it was a major success, a symbol for successful collective action. Now the independent operators of turbines got the guarantee that utilities not only had to connect their installations to the general grid, but that they were also obliged to pay fixed tariffs for the energy supplied. The Feed-In Law helped the German wind energy market to grow in the early 1990s. Photovoltaic operators received the same tariffs as turbine operators. However, the tariff for photovoltaics was far too low to be economically viable. In addition, in 1991 the "1000-roofs program" (Mautz, Byzio, and Rosenbaum 2008, 53) was launched. This program could not have had more than a small effect. It led to a capacity of 5.3 MWp of installed photovoltaics in 1993 (Jacobsson and Lauber 2006, 265). Although more users were waiting in line to get a loan, the program was discontinued.

In the mid-1990s, however, there was general insecurity about the future stance of the government toward RE. The then minister of environmental affairs, Angela Merkel, proclaimed in the mid-1990s that it is not conceivable that RE will play any significant part in the future German electricity mix. Nevertheless, the 1990s proved to be a period in which RE actors could experiment with various designs, build up public support for RE, and extend the advocacy coalition. Using the language of transition theory, one could say that RE activities in this period were (not necessarily protected) niche activities, while coalition formation took place on a much broader scale.

When we talk about the stance of "the government" or even of the state toward RE, we have to be aware that this is a simplification and most probably theoretically as well as empirically false. Many analyses of the relationship between the state and supporters or challengers (such as social movements or other states) assume that states are more or less unified actors. They therefore imagine that the state confronts an opponent and, mindful of its own interests and resources, takes actions that are likely to allow the state, as the state, to realize its goals. This is not true in an empirical sense and leads to errors due to its conceptual vagaries. Specific individuals do the acting. Sometimes they valiantly attempt to be mere agents of something else, but even then it is quite rare for it to be clear to impartial analysts, or even to the actors themselves, whom they represent (the state, the government, the nation, the people, their party, the voters, those who voted for them, their protectors? or their immediate supervisors, to mention several possibilities). More generally, states are assemblages of actors pursuing their own goals at the same time, since they are responsible to other claimants. The federal government consists of different ministries sometimes pursuing opposing aims (economics vs. the environment). Even within the ministries, there are different stances toward specific problems (e.g., support for solar), which leads to new winners and losers when there is a change in the composition of the government. Over time finally, the government is dominated by different parties, which may also change their attitudes toward contested issues. At times, it might be useful to treat corporate actors like government agents, but we have to be aware of the impreciseness of this, especially if we want to work out theories on why and how "the" state acts or does not act in a specific way.

Phase 2 (1998–2008): the politics of layering

The second phase from 1998 to 2008 is dominated by the formation of a new federal government and a dynamic development concerning both incumbent actors and challenging niche actors. The main disputes in this phase were concerned with the issue of the legitimacy of the different energy sources (coal, nuclear, renewables). In our case, this meant that the interpretation of what is a legitimate action became layered depending on which subfield it was taking place in. Yet there was not yet an impression of a general crisis. Let us look at the details.

The year 1998 featured a change in government from a conservative one to one controlled by a coalition of the Social Democratic Party (SPD) and the environmentally focused Green Party (Bündnis 90/Die Grüne). Under their leadership, important but also slightly conflicting regulatory decisions were passed. Following an EU market directive aiming at liberalizing the European energy markets, an amendment to the Energy Economy Law (EnWG) was put into effect in 1998. Monopolistic structures were dismantled, and the law now required that electricity suppliers separate their business activities along the supply chain by maintaining separate accounts for their business activities in generation, transmission, and distribution as well as for nonelectricity activities.

Furthermore, demarcation agreements between energy suppliers were banned, while at the same time third-party access to their power grids had to be ensured. As a result, the regional monopolies held by the power companies were formally limited to the operation of the electricity grids. Competition was thus introduced as a new element in the field of electricity distribution. In 2005, the EnWG was again significantly amended. The two main changes were: (1) both grid access and network charges were regulated by the newly established *Bundesnetzagentur* (Federal Network Agency) and (2) legal unbundling was enforced (Bontrup and Marquardt 2010, 31). This meant that a new market framework had been put in place for the established utilities, new governance units had been established, and the incumbent firms had to adapt and to learn to act in a somewhat competitive market.

Liberalization supported strong concentration in the market. A wave of mergers changed the playing field from one in which eight vertically integrated energy companies were operating to one in which the "Big 4" (RWE, E.ON, EnBW, and Vattenfall) were loosely competing against one another. The Big 4 acquired shares in smaller regional suppliers as well as municipal utilities. The latter were affected by the competition with private energy suppliers, which resulted in considerably lower profits, in turn affecting the municipal budgets and capacity to subsidize, for example, public transport. Hence, many of them were swallowed by the Big 4 or began to refrain from producing energy. By 2005, the shareholder structure of more than 100 municipal energy companies had changed. The market share of the Big 4 subsequently amounted to 82% of the electricity production capacity and 90% of electricity generated in 2003 and 2004 (Bundesnetzagentur 2007, 60). The expansion of the incumbents on the domestic market, however, was eventually stopped by cartel authorities because of concerns about a lack of competition. Going abroad then became an important new growth strategy for the major companies.

With respect to RE, two[5] important regulatory changes were implemented. Eventually they contributed to far-reaching changes in the balance of power in the field. In 2000, the Renewable Energies Law (EEG) was passed. It provided incentives for investments in renewable energy generation by obliging grid operators to give priority to connecting such facilities. It also guaranteed a consistent minimum payment for the electricity produced for a period of 20 years and thus ensured investment and planning security. In contrast to the Feed-In Law of 1990, the level of financial support was held flexible depending on the maturity of the different technologies. This especially included much higher remuneration for photovoltaic installations, making this technology economically feasible for the first time[6] (Hoppmann, Huenteler, and Girod 2014). Furthermore, unlike the Feed-In Law, the EEG did not directly exclude utilities from receiving benefits. In the end, the EEG helped boost the expansion of renewable energy from 6.6% of the electricity generated in 2000 to 14.5% in 2008.[7] For our purposes, it is equally important to note that the specification of the actors who can legitimately produce electricity in this expansion had changed significantly. Now new types of actors, i.e., ones in addition to the established utilities, were allowed to generate electricity and connect to the grid. Consequently, new types of legitimate social practices evolved beyond certain limited niches.

Implementation of the EEG in 2000 – which became the most important support mechanism for renewable energy – was only possible due to the broad coalition of actors supporting it via different channels. The federal law was inspired by local feed-in tariffs that had been introduced over the 1990s in cities like Aachen, Freising, or Hammelburg, which provided legitimacy and ammunition for federal policy entrepreneurs like the SPD politician Hermann Scheer (Fuchs and Wassermann 2012). It was additionally supported by the lobbying activities of a broad advocacy coalition – consisting of NGOs like Eurosolar, Förderverein Solarenergie, and Greenpeace, but also industrial associations and even one incumbent utility (Preussen Elektra) – which intensified pressure on federal policymakers (Jacobsson and Lauber 2006, 267). Besides ecological arguments, this coalition pointed to the economic benefits of RE. They highlighted the first mover advantages of an early adoption of renewable energy and the benefits for the national economy from the growth of the RE industries. Furthermore, they claimed that the electricity market was distorted, since the prices for electricity from fossil sources did not include the external costs resulting from environmental pollution and climate change. Because of this, renewables would be much cheaper than its opponents were claiming (Hirschl 2008, 193). As the renewables industries grew in size and professionalization (e.g., photovoltaic module producers, wind-turbine manufacturers) as well as due to the increasing contribution to regional value creation (especially in eastern Germany), there was growing support from previously critical parts of the SPD and the CDU (Lauber and Jacobsson 2016). Admittedly, they promoted renewables more for economic reasons than for ecological ones.

In parallel, it was decided to phase-out nuclear power plants. Following the *Atomkonsens* (consensus agreement on atomic energy) of 2000, the Atomic Energy Act was amended in 2002. The amendment stipulated an end to the construction of new nuclear power plants and limited the running time of the existing ones. After the 1998 election, the red-green government had put the phase-out of nuclear power at the center of their coalition agreements and directly started negotiations with the incumbent utilities. These negotiations led, two years later, to the nuclear consensus (*Atomkonsens*) mentioned above, which in turn formed the basis of the 2002 amendment to the Atomic Energy Act. The whole process took some time due to conflicts among the coalition parties; while the Green Party was advocating an immediate phase-out, the Social Democrats were in favor of a more moderate approach, taking the interests of the incumbent energy providers into account. Eventually the SPD prevailed (Lobo 2011, 218f). However, the struggles about nuclear energy again heated up as, at the end of the red-green coalition in 2005, incumbents saw a chance of achieving a repeal of the phase-out decision. They began to promote nuclear power as being important for the German energy supply. They stressed the security of nuclear power, and its importance for climate change mitigation as well as for the security of supply. They highlighted the benefits for the national economy and the opportunity to finance the switch to a renewable energy future by utilizing the profits made from nuclear energy. They also claimed that nuclear power plants would be much more flexible than generally assumed and would thus be perfect partners for renewable energy.

It has to be added that, in 2000, the red-green government published a climate protection program that aimed to achieve a 25% CO_2 reduction by 2005 compared to 1990 and 10% use of renewable electricity in 2010. In 2002, the climate change target was confirmed, while the renewable electricity target was scaled up to 12.5% by 2010 and 60% in 2050 (Jacobsson and Lauber 2006). In 2002 the Green Party was able to achieve a transfer of the competence for renewable energy from the Ministry of Economic Affairs to the Ministry for Environmental Affairs, thus extending their influence on the issue of renewables (Jacobsson and Lauber 2006, 268f). The ministry of economics was part of a tradition that looked very suspiciously at the development of renewables and had always had a strong affinity to the nuclear power industry.

The actors representing the vision of a decentralized energy supply developed strongly and successfully. Mautz, Byzio, and Rosenbaum observed that the professionalization, stabilization, and differentiation of decentralized actors and diffusion networks increased and the general "social opening" of the electricity sector proceeded further – although the developments differed for the various types of technology (Mautz, Byzio, and Rosenbaum 2008, 83). In the case of wind power, the number of economically motivated actors rose. This led to a further professionalization of the sector while at the same time the actors' scope of action narrowed. The spectrum of actors engaged in photovoltaics remained broad. Mautz and Rosenbaum differentiate four main types of actors involved in electricity generation in this period: homeowners, citizen action groups, private investors, and farmers. Biogas formed the main driver throughout the period. For all the renewable technologies, the multiplier function of civil society actors was important. The activities in the RE sector were thus still being driven forward by decentralized and less organized actors. In contrast to the situation in phase one, the framing that was used to legitimize the initiatives changed. While in phase 1 ecological motives were predominant, in phase 2 economic arguments of various sorts began to dominate both the discourse and the efforts of the initiatives to achieve legitimation.

The developments in phase 2 led to two different fields within electricity generation. On the one hand there was the liberalized electricity market, dominated by the big four utilities relying on fossil fuels and nuclear energy. The new market environment allowed them to grow significantly by swallowing smaller competitors and realizing benefits of scale. On the other hand, there was the RE sector, which was regulated by different principles and which was populated by different actors. Here we found mainly small entrepreneurs, individual citizens, farmers, and cooperatives, who unlike the actors in the traditional field were not looking to optimize their business strategies, but who were struggling to build a new market framework that would allow them to act profitably. The motivating forces for many of these actors, however, were not primarily economic motives, but the intention to change the electricity system.

The learning trajectories of the two actor groups were thus very different. Direct competition between the two groups did not take place. Especially the RE group did not have significant problems from internal competition. The market for RE was developing quickly, and new actors were coming in on a continuous basis. As Lawrence and Phillips (2004, 706) have argued, institutional entrepreneurship in emerging fields is likely to be associated with rapid imitation and relatively little conflict. The immediate effects of institutional entrepreneurship in emerging fields are likely to be highly uncertain and therefore the strategies of institutional entrepreneurs are more likely to be emergent than intended. Unlike in the old field, hierarchies were not present and no single actors were in a position to dominate the fragmented field. This effect is not one only visible in this area. Lawrence and Phillips (2004, 704f.) have claimed that changes in macro-cultural discourses (e.g., the stance toward nuclear energy and climate change) will in general have a greater impact on the emergence of new institutional fields when they are easily accessed and legitimate to participants in the emerging field.

Even without direct economic competition, the incumbents continued their opposition to RE. They used two main delegitimation strategies. (1) They claimed that German energy policy disregarded economic issues in a one-sided manner and favored ecological concerns unilaterally. They painted a gloomy picture of an impending deindustrialization and a shrinking competitiveness of the German economy. (2) They engaged in direct lobbying activities to get rid of the EEG or at least to alter it to their advantage. These lobbying activities were strengthened in the aftermath of the end of the red-green government in 2005.[8]

Yet there was still no significant reorientation of business models. The incumbents started to establish separate business divisions for RE. In 2007, RWE founded "RWE Innogy" and Vattenfall bundled its activities in the generation of climate-neutral electricity in "Vattenfall Europe New Energy." At a group-wide level, Vattenfall created the subdivision "Wind" in their business group "Pan Europe" as part of its 2009 restructuring. In 2008, E.ON founded "E.ON Climate and Renewables" and EnBW launched "EnBW Renewables." The main activities, however, were not taking place in Germany, but in other countries in which the companies had been strengthening activities in phase 2.

Phase 3 (2009–2013): transformation and disruptive innovation

Important regulatory changes were again introduced in phase 3. Phase 3, however, was dominated by global developments external to the field, which eventually led to a significant crisis in the field. The success of RE had enticed many other countries to develop national industries. This was especially true in China, which began to produce cheap equipment and export it vehemently. The ensuing price competition proved detrimental to many German producers. This, however, affected not only the producers, but also the RE advocacy coalition. As mentioned previously, the actors who had supported RE for economic reasons, based especially on structural policy arguments, began to lose interest, especially since a newly formed federal government (2009) made it clear that it would not support the ailing industry. The big utilities also ran into problems. Internal growth in Germany was limited by competition laws. The internationalization of their business proved to be largely a failure in the aftermath of the finance crisis. Growth prospects were thus dim. Finally, the Fukushima catastrophe had an important and decisive impact on electricity-related issues. Old and new actors were now forced into direct competition. With RE leaving their niche, formerly hidden conflicts and parallel developments in a differentiated field became increasingly apparent and obvious once the technology mix began to be shaped more and more strongly by high shares of RE, which especially at peak times increasingly displaced conventional energy sources in the electricity mix. The incumbents thus had to face a direct attack on their market position. This was the end of layering and established business practices.

Things turned nasty in phase three, which we can consider to start with the formation of the conservative-liberal coalition in 2009. As mentioned before, the main developments were not directly linked to the formation of the new government, but to the fact that there was a significant change in the way that problems were addressed. From the beginning, the liberal party demanded that the system supporting RE had to be dismantled. Even if they were not successful in this, it set the tone for the ensuing discussions. Instead of promoting RE, the government extended the running times of the existing nuclear power plants and reversed the compromise on atomic energy that the red-green government had negotiated. Now the ministry for economic affairs was headed by a member of the FDP, which had always been critical of the EEG and had always favored more market-oriented governance instruments like a quota regime.[9] Although the ministry for economic affairs could not formalize this policy, it at least opened the door for critical discussions about the EEG, stressing arguments made for example by the German Monopoly Commission (Monopolkommission 2013) and the European Commission (European Commission 2013).

This phase of the transformation was primarily characterized by contradictory political and regulatory developments, unstable coalitions among different actors in the field, and new conflicts and struggles. The new insecurity and contradictions became obvious in 2010. On the one hand, the government amended the Atomic Energy Act and extended the lifetime of nuclear power plants (Deutscher Bundestag 2010a, 2010b). Hence, for a short period it seemed as if the incumbent energy providers had scored an important victory against the challengers. But the situation was not that clear because at the same time the German government published a new energy concept which set highly ambitious development targets for RE, according to which the RE share of the electricity mix was now supposed to increase to 35% in 2020, to 50% in 2035, and to 80% by 2050 (BMWi and BMU 2010). One year later, however, the nuclear power coalition faced a clear backlash: In the aftermath of the Fukushima accident, the government then reinvigorated the nuclear phase-out (BMWi 2011) and the so-called Energy Transition decision was passed. The political decision reflected the general mind-set of the German population. There has always been a strong opposition to nuclear power (Europäische Kommission 2008), and this rejection increased substantially after the Fukushima accident. Furthermore, the population explicitly supported the German energy transition and especially the idea of building a more decentralized infrastructure and distributed power generation (TNS Emnid 2013). Moreover, due to bad experience and scandals related to radioactive waste and the search for respective repositories, the population mistrusted the big power companies and was explicitly in favor of RE (Scheer, Wassermann, and Scheel 2012).

On the other hand, the political coalition supporting RE began to crumble. The German RE industry suffered severely from cheap, mainly Chinese, imports. The bulk of the industry disappeared again, and along with it the hopes of local and state politicians for economic rewards. The government was not providing assistance but was rather supporting a process which it called "market adaptation." The farmers' association began to lobby against RE because it was afraid that the economic success of energy farmers would undermine their main business of lobbying for subsidies for regular farmers. The old political coalition of red-green supporters of RE was excluded from power and even within the SPD the supporters of RE lost influence as concern over job losses in the heavily unionized old utilities grew. This all led to regulatory amendments, which generally tried to make life for RE more difficult, especially for small, decentralized units. Instead of support for small units, private households, and farmers, for example, bigger installations like off-shore wind and solar parks became the new beneficiaries (Unnerstall 2017).[10]

These developments were not derailed by the energy transition decision. It signified another turnaround in the nuclear energy question, but no new policies to foster RE deployment were designed. This is a phase of vibrant contention because the incumbent energy providers were running into deep trouble. Following the global financial crisis, most of the foreign investments they had made in order to continue a deliberate growth strategy proved to be no longer economically viable. Growth in the German market was not an option due to the increasing role played by RE (the incumbents were not investing in RE in Germany) and finally the energy transition decision had made it obvious that the old business models would not work any longer. The incumbents nevertheless still tried to defend the status quo by making piecemeal institutional adjustments. They now claimed that they intended to become an active part in the energy transition by providing the backbone for it. Hence, their assessment of RE finally shifted. They intensified their investments in RE. Yet according to a study by Trend Research (Maron, Klemisch, and Maron 2011), only 6.5% of all the renewable plants in Germany in 2010 were operated by the big four companies and most of this share came from hydroelectric power. Nevertheless, the position of the incumbents had definitely changed. They were now picturing themselves as (reliable) partners for the RE actors, as "project enablers" or "system integrators" for prosumers, communities, municipal utilities, or project developers. The competence that RE actors were lacking and the support for the transition period until RE was fully deployed were to be delivered by the incumbents.

Phase 3 thus ended with a curious situation. On the one hand, the movement for RE had now finally achieved its aim and the switch to the use of RE formally received the support of all the major parties. Use of the term "transformation" to describe this phase thus seems to be justified, even if the transformation was not the result of conscious planning and strategy. On the other hand, the movement and the support coalition for RE were disintegrating.

The group of actors interested in electricity nevertheless continuously broadened and became more heterogeneous over time. Especially newly founded municipal utilities started to act as new competitors, were explicitly criticizing incumbents, and were investing in RE (Berlo and Wagner 2013).[11] Traditional challenger actors such as green electricity providers built up strategic partnerships with these new actors, for example by providing them with green electricity products. There were also new types of cooperation between the newly founded municipal utilities and citizen energy cooperatives. Furthermore, many of these actors continuously searched for and developed new ideas and solutions to contribute to the new challenges encountered in the third phase. The trend toward municipalization in this third phase can not only be observed in the new founding of municipal utilities and their investment activities in RE, but also in the trend toward the municipalization of distribution networks. The background for this is that 60% of the German electricity network concessions were up for renegotiation between 2010 and 2015. In just the first two years of this period the ownership of 190 distribution networks changed hands in spite of heavy resistance by the incumbents (Berlo and Wagner 2013, 70ff). Besides municipalization, a growing number of regions and villages were committing themselves to a 100% supply of renewable energy (Fuchs and Hinderer 2016). This usually goes

Table 7.1 Ownership structure of RE installations in Germany (2010)

Technology		Ownership							
		Private citizens	Farmers	Banks + funds	Project developers	Municipal utilities	Industry	Four major utilities	Others (contractors, internat. utilities)
	Wind	51,5	1,8	15,5	21,3	3,4	2,3	2,1	2,2
	Biogas	0,1	71,5	6,2	13,1	3,1	0,1	0,1	5,7
	Biomass	2,0	0	3,0	6,9	24,3	41,5	9,6	12,7
	PV	39,3	21,2	8,1	8,3	2,6	19,2	0,2	1,1

Source: Maron, Klemisch, and Maron (2011)

hand in hand with the establishment of new electricity- and heat-related organizations with little or no involvement by the old industrial actors.

Apart from intensifying investments in RE projects, and voicing open support for the government, incumbents continued to run strategies to delegitimize support for activities in RE. Their attention in this phase turned to the rising costs of the electricity transition, which due to the specific German financing setup had to be paid by individual consumers. The incumbents were successful in convincing politicians to lower the EEG tariffs by painting a dire picture of a cost explosion and by stressing the bad effects of this on the national economy. Furthermore, they tried to reframe the issue of rising electricity prices as an antisocial development and claimed that it was especially the poor households that had to shoulder the costs of the energy transition project (INSM 2012).

In some respects, these fears were justified (Tews 2014; VZBV 2013). Part of rising electricity prices was caused by the EEG surcharge. Whereas the size of the EEG surcharge had been negligible, between 2009 and 2010 it doubled and between 2009 and 2013 it increased by a factor of 6. The reason behind this increase, however, was not only a general increase in the overall amount of support for renewables, but also the fact that the government released an increasing proportion of industry from the obligation to pay the EEG charges, which then had to be paid by private consumers. Furthermore, the EEG surcharge was expanded to cover additional responsibilities such as paying for the grid extension. Due to the nonfunctioning competition on the electricity markets, the big utilities were in a position to pass on these increases directly to the consumers. Any discussion about a fundamental reorganization of the funding regime for the electricity transition (e.g., tax based) and its advantages and disadvantages was sidelined.

Phase 4 (2013–2017): *constructing new market frameworks*

In phase 4, the generation of electricity based on RE became the new normal. Having reached a share of almost 25% in 2013, it was no longer a niche phenomenon, but an integral part of the field of electricity generation. In addition, a thoroughgoing trend toward decentralization has made decisions on electricity-related issues urgent matters of public debate (Unnerstall 2017). Insofar it is no wonder that the RE movement collapsed. A movement needs an opponent against whom it mobilizes. In this case it had become official government policy to base the energy supply on renewables, and there seems to be no future for nuclear energy. Besides these technology-oriented decisions, a lot of questions nevertheless still require answers. How will a future market operate? Who will be able to participate legitimately in field-related activities? What will be the fate of the old utilities? What will be the role of small-scale installations and their owners? Insofar as layering was an important mechanism in phase 2, and open contention was in phase 3, they have been replaced in phase 4 by integration.

An initial aim of the new coalition between the conservative parties (CDU/CSU) and the Social Democrats at the beginning of this phase (2012) was to better influence RE deployment. The government's intention to make RE growth more manageable had failed for several years. The government regularly had to upgrade projections because the growth of installations was much quicker than had been anticipated. In phase 4 the system for providing support for RE was changed in order to finally stop the quick expansion of RE and to save the incumbents. A new regulatory initiative was passed in 2014 for the first time that explicitly mandated upper limits for the expansion of RE. This was especially targeted at bioenergy and solar energy. Various new instruments were introduced to achieve this aim, among them most prominently the requirement for an actor to participate at an auction in order to obtain a permit to install photovoltaic modules; this was subsequently expanded to also apply to the construction of wind turbines. Now only the winners at the auction were to get permission to build installations and connect them to the grid. This measure was accompanied by various other new regulations, which generally were specifically aimed at making life more difficult for decentralized, less professional initiatives. The ministry of economic affairs, which had conceived these measures, had now regained full responsibility for electricity-related issues, sidelining both the ministry for environment and the ministry for research and education. Access to policymakers now became even more limited for RE actors than in phase 3. While writing the new regulations the incumbent utilities were regularly contacted and their input acknowledged, but RE actors were hardly addressed. Besides the changing political priorities, it has to be acknowledged that in contrast to the old incumbents, the actor constellation in the RE field is rather fragmented. The different types of actors involved and their different organizational and technological set-ups make it difficult to formulate common goals and to mobilize for them. This reflects the inequality in the initial distribution of resources among RE actors.

Nevertheless, the one development in this phase that most clearly demonstrates that things had changed has surely been the organizational breakup of the two major utilities EON and RWE. In order to increase their chances for survival in a new environment, both companies have split their activities into two parts, one becoming responsible for the old activities (e.g., power plants), while the other one was supposed to tackle new issues such as RE. This should allow for more differentiated and successful learning processes. While the companies responsible for the old stuff were lobbying for capacity markets and the public financing of so-called reserve power plants (to be paid for by the surcharge on RE), the new organizations were busy expanding cooperation with actors in the RE field. In spite of the fact that the incumbents always favor bigger and centralized solutions, the present setup of RE installations makes it necessary for the incumbents to cooperate with local, urban, and/or regional actors. The competence needed to participate successfully in auctions for solar and wind installations can be better garnered by the big organizations, but in the auctioning process local approval of the respective installations is required, which is hardly possible without engaging in some kind of cooperation with locally based organizations. Another area in which the incumbents are trying to become more active is services. They all now offer the sale, installation, and maintenance of decentralized electricity generating units and storage equipment for domestic use, services concerning energy efficiency and building maintenance, smart home and smart meter solutions, e-mobility services, and various support schemes to help

RE actors come to grips with the new EEG regulations. At first sight, these activities might not appear dramatic, but in fact they signal a turnaround in the way these organizations develop their business plans and develop relations to customers. In the past, electricity was treated as a standardized mass product for an anonymous client. Now the customer has to be addressed with individualized solutions, and the good electricity is a mere by-product. This requires significant unlearning both on the management side and on that of employees. No wonder that all the big utilities have replaced their management team since 2012.

The biggest loser in this game has been people interested in installing photovoltaic modules. As early as in phase 3, the utilities and parts of the government held solar energy to be primarily responsible for the run-away development in the RE field. Regulations were then especially aimed to discourage the enthusiasm for solar energy. This was done so effectively that by 2017 Germany had not reached the (starkly reduced) envisioned growth rate for photovoltaic installations for the fourth year running.

Conclusion: the transformation of a field

We started this chapter by asking whether the practice of electricity generation and distribution has changed during the years under discussion. We can easily answer this question positively. The characteristics of "legitimate" action in this field have changed substantially. Electricity generation increasingly takes place in decentralized units, which are often very small to medium in scale. The operators are no longer solely the established utilities, but include a host of different actors with a variety of motives. These new actors can be individual citizens just as easily as big investment funds. The incumbent utilities have survived, but they are struggling to find their place and are attempting to redefine their role in the field. RWE and EON have each broken up, creating separate units for dealing with new technology. They want to position themselves as system integrators and traders rather than primarily as the producers of electricity.

The framing has changed as well. It has become generally accepted that the generation of electricity is an important element of climate change policies, the objective of which is both to reduce the amount of coal and gas that is used and to remove nuclear energy from the electricity mix altogether. Nevertheless, the field is far from having attained a stable structure. Among the challenger actors, few have managed to attain a powerful position. The old actors have been weakened, but they have not been replaced by a group of new influential actors. This has given the incumbents time to try to redefine their role in the field in order to retain a commanding position. They have been supported by various measures implemented by the present and previous governments. Whether they will be successful in doing this remains to be seen, especially given the fact that their most important resource, i.e., big power stations, are becoming increasingly obsolete, which makes learning as well as unlearning paramount tasks.

The mechanisms that produced this result were first of all the successful efforts at mobilization by the RE actors. They shared a view of a new electricity system in which the old utilities with their centralization strategy and big power stations had no role. For a long time the incumbents opposed such ideas, hardly envisaging any alternative futures until confronted by the political decisions following Fukushima. They relied on their well-established relationships with political decision makers and on fueling fears about the consequences of changes to the status quo. As early as in 1990, they had claimed that the electricity system would collapse if even only a few decentralized generating units with flexible inputs were connected to the grid. This argument can still be heard today. Since the growth of RE cannot be stopped, it is now used as a justification to subsidize old power plants in order supposedly to guarantee a stable supply of electricity for periods when the sun or wind are not sufficient. In more general terms, we have found evidence that new frames and forms of action within a field usually originate in invader or challenger groups. RE actors successfully developed new frames and forms of action and built broad coalitions to fashion a new set of cultural understandings that have reorganized the interests and identities of members in the field.

The energy transition in Germany can best be conceived of as an emergent phenomenon, coming about essentially as a bottom-up event and consisting of various more or less interrelated activities in a new ecology of fields. These activities were especially motivated by different ideas about the importance of renewable energy and the organizational architecture of a new electricity system (Fettke and Fuchs 2017). While the incumbent energy providers were slow to adapt to changing institutional environments (Kungl and Geels 2016), pressure was exerted by actors such as local initiatives, who at least for an intermediate period of time exerted significant influence on the development of the German energy transition (Fuchs and Hinderer 2016).

Notes

1 "We economists, political scientists and sociologists have many theories about how to choose alternatives, once these swim into our vision. But our theories have little to say about the invention of new alternatives in the first place" (Padgett and Powell 2012, 1).

2 In a project comparing activities in Germany in the areas of wind energy, power to heat coupling, energy contracting and intelligent infrastructures (Fuchs 2017) this was determined very clearly.

3 In the negotiations on forming a new federal government in late 2017, regulations on renewable energy were used as bargaining chips for reaching concessions in other areas, like immigration.

4 On the differentiation between optimizing and searching (as a characteristic of innovative firms), see Lazonick (2005).

5 Furthermore, a follow up to the 1,000-roof program of the 1990s was implemented, namely the 100,000-roof program of 1999.

6 The law was amended in 2004, 2009, 2012, 2014, and 2016/17 in addition to some minor amendments in between. Hoppmann et al. (2014) offer a vivid description of the early political concerns behind the several adjustments of the law (with a focus on solar energy). They present the development of renewable energy policy as a trial and error process rather than one following a master plan.

7 Data from the AG Energiebilanzen (www.ag-energiebilanzen.de/)

8 For a more detailed analysis see Hirschl (2008): 169, 195 and Suck (2008).

9 The ministry for environmental affairs, responsible for the issue of RE, and still (reluctantly) supporting the EEG, was run by the CDU.

10 We will not discuss the issue that the attempts to dampen the expansion of RE were largely unsuccessful in this phase. In 2009 RE accounted for about 16% of the German electricity supply, in 2011 this share increased to 20%, and at the end of 2013 it was almost at 25% (Unnerstall 2017).
11 Municipalization was an important trend in this third phase. Whereas only 13 municipal utilities were founded between 2005 and 2008, the number of new foundings rose to 59 between 2009 and 2012 (Berlo and Wagner 2013, 17).

References

Abbott, Andrew. 2001. *Time Matters: On Theory and Method*. Chicago: University of Chicago Press. www.press.uchicago.edu/ucp/books/book/chicago/T/bo3643810.html.
———. 2016. *Processual Sociology*. Chicago: University of Chicago Press.
Berlo, Kurt, and Oliver Wagner. 2013. "Stadtwerke-Neugründungen Und Rekommunalisierungen: Energieversorgung in Kommunaler Verantwortung." Sondierungs Studie. Wuppertal: Wuppertal Institut für Klima, Umwelt, Energie GmbH. https://wupperinst. org/uploads/tx_wupperinst/Stadtwerke_Sondierungsstudie.pdf.
BMWi. 2011. *Der Weg zur Energie der Zukunft – sicher, bezahlbar und umweltfreundlich*. Berlin: BMWi – Bundesministerium für Wirtschaft und Energie. www.bmwi.de/Redaktion/ DE/Downloads/E/energiekonzept-2010-beschluesse-juni-2011.html.
BMWi, and BMU. 2010. *Energiekonzept für eine umweltschonende, zuverlässige und bezahlbare Energieversorgung*. Berlin: BMWi – Bundesministerium für Wirtschaft und Technologie, BMU – Bundesministerium für Umwelt, Naturschutz und Reaktorsicherheit. www.bmwi.de/Redaktion/DE/Downloads/E/energiekonzept-2010.html.
Bontrup, Heinz-Josef, and Ralf-Michael Marquardt. 2010. *Kritisches Handbuch der deutschen Elektrizitätswirtschaft: Branchenentwicklung, Unternehmensstrategien, Arbeitsbeziehungen*. Berlin: Edition Sigma.
Bundesnetzagentur. 2007. *Monitoringbericht 2007*. Bonn: Bundesnetzagentur für Elektrizität, Gas, Telekommunikation, Post und Eisenbahnen. www.bundesnetzagentur. de/SharedDocs/Downloads/DE/Allgemeines/Bundesnetzagentur/Publikationen/Berichte/2007/Monitoringbericht2007Id12086pdf.pdf?__blob=publicationFile&v=2.
Deutscher Bundestag. 2010a. *Gesetzentwurf der Fraktionen der CDU/CSU und FDP: Entwurf eines elften Gesetzes zur Änderung des Atomgesetzes*. Berlin: Deutscher Bundestag. http://dip21.bundestag.de/dip21/btd/17/030/1703051.pdf.
———. 2010b. *Gesetzentwurf der Fraktionen Der CDU/CSU und FDP: Entwurf eines zwölften Gesetzes zur Änderung des Atomgesetzes*. Berlin: Deutscher Bundestag. http://dip21. bundestag.de/dip21/btd/17/030/1703052.pdf.
Europäische Kommission. 2008. *Spezial Eurobarometer 300: Einstellungen der europäischen Bürger zum Klimawandel*. Brüssel: TNS Opinion & Social.
European Commission. 2013. *State Aid: Commission Opens In-Depth Inquiry into Support for Energy-Intensive Companies Benefitting from a Reduced Renewables Surcharge*. Brussels: European Commission. http://europa.eu/rapid/press-release_IP-13-1283_en.htm.
Fettke, Ulrike, and Gerhard Fuchs. 2017. "Incumbent-Challenger-Interaktionen und die Veränderungen im Markt für Stromerzeugung und -verteilung in Deutschland." In *Die Energiewende aus wirtschaftssoziologischer Sicht*, edited by Sebastian Giacovelli, 15–43. Wiesbaden: Springer VS. https://doi.org/10.1007/978-3-658-14345-9_2.
Fligstein, Neil, and Doug McAdam. 2011. "Toward a General Theory of Strategic Action Fields." *Sociological Theory* 29 (1): 1–26. https://doi.org/10.1111/j.1467-9558.2010.01385.x.
———. 2012. *A Theory of Fields*. New York: Oxford University Press.

Fuchs, Gerhard. 2017. *Lokale Impulse Für Energieinnovationen – Bürgerwind: Bürgerwind, Contracting, Kraft-Wärme-Kopplung, Smart Grid*. Wiesbaden: Springer Vieweg.

Fuchs, Gerhard, and Nele Hinderer. 2016. "One or Many Transitions: Local Electricity Experiments in Germany." *Innovation: The European Journal of Social Science Research* 29 (3): 320–36. https://doi.org/10.1080/13511610.2016.1188683.

Fuchs, Gerhard, and Sandra Wassermann. 2012. "From Niche to Mass Markets in High Technology: The Case of Photovoltaics in Germany." In *Innovation Policy and Governance in High-Tech Industries: The Complexity of Coordination*, edited by Johannes Bauer, Achim Lang, and Volker Schneider, 219–44. Berlin und Heidelberg: Springer. https://doi.org/10.1007/978-3-642-12563-8_10.

Hedstrom, Peter. 2005. *Dissecting the Social: On the Principles of Analytical Sociology*. Cambridge: Cambridge University Press. https://doi.org/10.1017/CBO9780511488801.

Hirschl, Bernd. 2008. *Erneuerbare Energien-Politik: Eine Multi-Level Policy-Analyse mit Fokus auf den deutschen Strommarkt*. Wiesbaden: Springer VS. //www.springer.com/de/book/9783835070240.

Hoppmann, Joern, Joern Huenteler, and Bastien Girod. 2014. "Compulsive Policy-Making: The Evolution of the German Feed-In Tariff System for Solar Photovoltaic Power." *Research Policy* 43 (8): 1422–41. https://doi.org/10.1016/j.respol.2014.01.014.

INSM. 2012. *Das EEG belastet vor allem Geringverdiener. Pressemeldung*. Berlin: INSM – Initiative Neue Soziale Marktwirtschaft GmbH. www.insm.de/insm/Presse/Pressemeldungen/EEG.html.

Jacobsson, Staffan, and Volkmar Lauber. 2006. "The Politics and Policy of Energy System Transformation: Explaining the German Diffusion of Renewable Energy Technology." *Energy Policy, Renewable Energy Policies in the European Union*, 34 (3): 256–76. https://doi.org/10.1016/j.enpol.2004.08.029.

Kriesi, Hanspeter. 2004. "Political Context and Opportunity." In *The Blackwell Companion to Social Movements*, edited by David A. Snow, Sarah A. Soule, and Hanspeter Kriesi, 67–90. Malden, MA; Oxford, UK; Carlton, AU: Blackwell Publishing Ltd. https://doi.org/10.1002/9780470999103.ch4.

Kungl, Gregor, and Frank W. Geels. 2016. "The Destabilisation of the German Electricity Industry (1998–2015): Application and Extension of a Multi-Dimensional Framework." Working Paper 2016. Stuttgarter Beiträge Zur Organisations- Und Innovationsforschung, SOI Discussion Paper. Stuttgart: University of Stuttgart, Institute for Social Sciences. http://hdl.handle.net/10419/148335.

Lauber, Volkmar, and Staffan Jacobsson. 2016. "The Politics and Economics of Constructing, Contesting and Restricting Socio-Political Space for Renewables – The German Renewable Energy Act." *Environmental Innovation and Societal Transitions* 18: 147–63. https://doi.org/10.1016/j.eist.2015.06.005.

Lawrence, Thomas B., and Nelson Phillips. 2004. "From Moby Dick to Free Willy: Macro-Cultural Discourse and Institutional Entrepreneurship in Emerging Institutional Fields." *Organization* 11 (5): 689–711. https://doi.org/10.1177/1350508404046457.

Lazonick, William. 2005. "The Innovative Firm." In *The Oxford Handbook of Innovation*, edited by Jan Fagerberg, David C. Mowery, and Richard R. Nelson, 29–55. Oxford: Oxford University Press. https://doi.org/10.1093/oxfordhb/9780199286805.003.0002.

Lobo, Kai R. 2011. *Die Elektrizitätspolitik Und Ihre Akteure von 1998 Bis 2009 – Eine Strategische Politikfeldanalyse*. Dissertation: Freie Universität Berlin.

Maron, Helene, Herbert Klemisch, and Bernhard Maron. 2011. *Marktakteure Erneuerbare-Energien-Anlagen in der Stromerzeugung*. Köln: Klaus Novy Institut (KNI). www.forschungsradar.de/studiendatenbank/studie/detail/marktakteure-erneuerbare-energien-anlagenin-der-stromerzeugung.html.

Martin, John L. 2009. *Social Structures*. Princeton: Princeton University Press.

Mautz, Rüdiger, Andreas Byzio, and Wolf Rosenbaum. 2008. *Auf dem Weg zur Energiewende : die Entwicklung der Stromproduktion aus erneuerbaren Energien in Deutschland ; eine Studie aus dem Soziologischen Forschungsinstitut Göttingen (SOFI)*. Göttingen: Univ.-Verl. Göttingen. http://nbn-resolving.de/urn:nbn:de:0168-ssoar-272915.

Mayntz, Renate. 2004. "Mechanisms in the Analysis of Social Macro-Phenomena." *Philosophy of the Social Sciences* 34 (2): 237–59. https://doi.org/10.1177/0048393103262552.

McAdam, Doug, and Hilary Schaffer-Boudet. 2012. *Putting Social Movements in Their Place: Explaining Opposition to Energy Projects in the United States, 2000–2005*. Cambridge: Cambridge University Press.

Merton, Robert K. 1968. *Social Theory and Social Structure*. New York: Free Press.

Monopolkommission. 2013. *Sondergutachten 56. Energie 2013: Wettbewerb in Zeiten der Energiewende. Sondergutachten Der Monopolkommission Gemäß § 62 Abs. 1 EnWG*. Berlin: Monopolkommission.

Neukirch, Mario. 2010. *Die internationale Pionierphase der Windenergienutzung*. Dissertation: Georg-August-Universität Göttingen. https://ediss.uni-goettingen.de/handle/11858/00-1735-0000-0006-B5F4-5.

Padgett, John F., and Walter W. Powell. 2012. "The Problem of Emergence." In *The Emergence of Organizations and Markets*, edited by John F. Padgett and Walter W. Powell, 1–29. Princeton: Princeton University Press.

Scharpf, Fritz Wilhelm. 1997. *Games Real Actors Play: Actor-Centered Institutionalism in Policy Research*. Boulder, CO: Westview Press.

Scheer, Dirk, Sandra Wassermann, and Oliver Scheel. 2012. "Stromerzeugungstechnologien auf dem gesellschaftlichen Prüfstand: Zur Akzeptanz der CCS-Technologien." In *Akzeptanzforschung zu CCS in Deutschland: Aktuelle Ergebnisse, Praxisrelevanz, Perspektiven*, edited by Katja Pietzner and Diana Schumann. München: Oekom-Verlag.

Sovacool, Benjamin K., and David J. Hess. 2017. "Ordering Theories: Typologies and Conceptual Frameworks for Sociotechnical Change." *Social Studies of Science* 47 (5): 703–50. https://doi.org/10.1177/0306312717709363.

Suck, André. 2008. *Erneuerbare Energien Und Wettbewerb in Der Elektrizitätswirtschaft. Staatliche Regulierung Im Vergleich Zwischen Deutschland Und Großbritannien*. Wiesbaden: Springer VS. www.springer.com/de/book/9783531158266.

Tews, Kerstin. 2014. "Energiearmut – vom politischen Schlagwort zur handlungsleitenden Definition." In *Im Hürdenlauf zur Energiewende*, 441–9. Wiesbaden: Springer VS. https://doi.org/10.1007/978-3-658-06788-5_28.

TNS Emnid. 2013. *Emnid-Umfrage zur Bürger-Energiewende. Ergebnisse einer repräsentativen Meinungsumfrage des Forschungsinstituts TNS Emnid im Zeitraum 23.09. – 25.09.2013 im Auftrag der Initiative „Die Wende – Energie in Bürgerhand"*. Berlin: Bündnis Bürgerenergie e.V. http://100-prozent-erneuerbar.de/wp-content/uploads/2013/10/emnid-umfrage-B%C3%BCrgerenergie.pdf.

Unnerstall, Thomas. 2017. *The German Energy Transition: Design, Implementation, Cost and Lessons*. Berlin, Heidelberg: Springer-Verlag.

VZBV. 2013. *Energiewende: VZBV fordert Entlastung für Verbraucher*. Berlin: VZBV – Verbraucherzentrale Bundesverband. www.vzbv.de/pressemitteilung/energiewende-vzbv-fordert-entlastung-fuer-verbraucher.

White, Harrison C. 2008. *Identity and Control. How Social Formations Emerge*. 2nd ed. Princeton: Princeton University Press.

8 Energy system transformation and inertia in the UK

A discourse-institutional perspective

Audley Genus, Marfuga Iskandarova, and Leigh Champagnie

Introduction

The nature of effective approaches for realizing the transition to sustainable energy systems remains a matter of some debate, a dialog which is rehearsed in the chapters of this book and beyond. For some commentators what is required is more thoroughly "transformative" change; addressing the energy subsystem is merely one part of a nexus of activities, practices, and actors in society, which need a radical rethink individually and in toto. In any case, contributors in their various ways are concerned with how to understand and realize effective challenges to institutionalized modes of energy and wider sustainability governance, models of production, and consumption practices. The size of the task here appears larger when one properly recognizes both the relations between local initiatives and wider culture and society, and the paradoxical lives to which citizens active in "niche" sustainability innovations are also subject, in which they are reproducers of prevailing norms and values, which may underpin unsustainable energy system-related practices (Genus 2016). This institutional inertia is what the "new economics," attempts to embed more sustainable energy, and other societal subsystems and practices are up against (Cohen, Brown, and Vergragt 2013). This chapter provides evidence that institutional momentum favorable to such sociotechnical developments is achievable, though it may be patchy, both temporally and spatially.

This chapter takes an approach in which institutional analysis is to the fore, complemented by an appreciation of discourses of energy and within society in general. These need to be understood in relation to the processes which hold prevailing technical and socioeconomic arrangements and ways of thinking in place, and to those which constitute more or less fundamental change. The approach has been extended to more explicitly recognize and account for institutional entrepreneurship, meaning the process by which certain actors create new institutional arrangements, or through which existing institutional rules and processes shape the possibilities available to entrepreneurial or innovative actors. The core elements of this perspective have been presented and published elsewhere, for example, in relation to institutional change (Genus 2012) and discourse institutions (Genus 2014, 2016). The present chapter will therefore only briefly present the approach here, which it does in the following section. Subsequently, the third section considers evidence of institutional change and inertia within the energy "field," focusing on data taken from research conducted by the authors in relation to developments in the UK over the past three decades (since the late 1980s). In particular, this research involved interviews undertaken between 2014 and 2016 with over 60 government, industry, commercial, and community actors relevant to policy making and to the generation and technical administration of electricity from renewable and nonrenewable sources on and off-grid in the UK. The fourth section then moves on to consider implications of this research for understanding and effecting policy for energy transformation and institutional design, while summarizing the work of the chapter and its significance to energy system research and policy.

Approach: institutions, discourse, and entrepreneurship

Institutions have been variously defined across the social sciences. Two common definitions are (1) valued, stable, and recurring patterns of behavior (Huntington 1965) and (2) "organized, established procedures" (MacIver 1931, 16). In other words, institutions are "the rules of the game" (Jepperson 1991, 143). Institutional environments are characterized by individual organizations conforming to these rules (Jepperson 1991), with institutions constraining behavior due to procedures associated with three institutional pillars: regulative, normative, and cultural-cognitive processes (Scott 2008). Institutions are transmitted by carriers such as routines, artifacts, relational systems, and symbolic systems (Scott 2008). Institutions are based on rules, structures, schemes, routines, and norms, which – once they become institutionalized and diffused – are the basic requirements for organizations and individuals to gain legitimacy and support (Scott 2005; Suchman 1995). Institutions therefore provide meaning and stability to social life (Scott 2008).

Institutions are resilient, multifaceted social structures, comprised of social activities, symbolic elements, and material resources (Scott 2008). In spite of the connotation of stability (Scott 2008), resistance to change (Lawrence 2008), durability (Meyer 2008), and persistence (Holm 1995), institutions are susceptible to change (DiMaggio 1988). Therefore it must be recognized that institutional analyses cannot be confined to explanations of stability. Institutions have a higher propensity to change when they are characterized by internal contradictions (Greenwood and Suddaby 2006; Seo and Creed 2002; Zilber 2002) and uncertainties (Déjean, Gond, and Leca 2004) because these constraints motivate actors to engage in "collective action to reconstruct the field" (Hardy and Maguire 2008; Seo and Creed 2002).

One may contrast "old" institutionalism with the neoinstitutional and contemporary thinking about institutions which inform this chapter. The conceptual foundations of old institutionalism can be traced to the works of Veblen (1899), Weber (Camic, Gorski, and Trubek 2005), Commons (1931), Parsons (1937), and Durkheim (1964). Collectively, these contributors invoked notions of "institution" to determine the sequences of social, economic, and political behavior and of change over time (Hinings and Tolbert 2008), offering a model of rational behavior and path dependency (Garud, Hardy, and Maguire 2007). Although this early work usefully explained how political behavior is scripted by the formal rules of the institutional setting (Battilana 2004), old institutionalism overlooked the role of organizations in the process (Scott 2008), provided "answers that were largely descriptive," and was so abstract that it lacked "explanatory punch" (Powell and DiMaggio 1991, 2).

Selznick (1948) was arguably the first analyst to break from the traditional view of institutions by postulating that individuals within organizations can hold multiple goal sets, making it difficult for employees and organizations to have the same implicit, rational objectives. From an economics perspective, Coase (1937, 1960) and Williamson (1975, 1985) used institutions as the primary unit of analysis to demonstrate that institutions arise and persist when they provide benefits which are greater than transaction costs. The expansion of the "new" institutionalism took root during the late 1970s and early 1980s with the publication of the seminal works of Meyer and Rowan (1977), Meyer and Hannan (1979), and DiMaggio and Powell (1983).

Although there are variations across disciplines, all strands of neoinstitutionalism share a common critique of atomistic accounts of social processes (Barley 2008). In sociology, neoinstitutionalism emphasizes the way in which institutional life establishes normative behavior, conventions, and taken-for-granted practices which shape and influence behavior (Powell and DiMaggio 1991). While these early works had their merits, they focused too strongly on institutional isomorphism in organizational analysis (Barley 2008), tending to ignore the role of agency, power, and interest in the process (Garud, Hardy, and Maguire 2007). In order to break from this overly structuring view of institutions, DiMaggio (1988, 14) formally introduced the notion of institutional entrepreneurship, declaring that "new institutions arise when organized actors with sufficient resources see in them an opportunity to realize interests that they value highly."

Institutional entrepreneurship is a complex, multifaceted practice (Garud, Hardy, and Maguire 2007; Leca and Naccache 2006). A rich stream of research (Wijen and Ansari 2007; Garud, Jain, and Kumaraswamy 2002; Lawrence, Hardy, and Phillips 2002) has shown that it involves institutional entrepreneurs using intervention strategies to dislodge existing institutional practices (in mature fields), introduce new ones, and then ensure that they become widely adopted and taken for granted by other actors in the field (Hardy and Maguire 2008). This may take the form of employing strategies such as lobbying governments for new or revised regulations (Jolly and Raven 2015; Walker, Schlosser, and Deephouse 2014) or of assuming technical and market leadership (Fligstein 1996; Maguire, Hardy, and Lawrence 2004), or may involve professional associations persuading their members to standardize new procedures (Greenwood, Suddaby, and Hinings 2002). Institutional entrepreneurs lead efforts to frame issues and problems, mobilize constituencies, identify political opportunities, and command collective attempts to instill new beliefs, values, and norms into social structures (DiMaggio 1988). They also seek to influence other actors to participate in their institutionalization projects (Greenwood, Suddaby, and Hinings 2002), for example, through mimicry (Hargadon and Douglas 2001), by shaping related discourses (Garud, Hardy, and Maguire 2007), and by theorizing (Greenwood, Suddaby, and Hinings 2002).

Institutional entrepreneurship is a highly discursive process. As certain contributors have shown (Garud, Jain, and Kumaraswamy 2002; Seo and Creed 2002; Benford and Snow 2000), institutional entrepreneurs provide legitimizing accounts of their institutionalization projects by framing their intended changes in such a way that they engender collective action (Creed, Scully, and Austin 2002). Relatedly, researchers (Greenwood, Suddaby, and Hinings 2002; Strang and Meyer 1993) have explored how institutional entrepreneurs identify a problem in existing practices and use theorization to justify new ones as a solution. Theorization involves two main tasks: (1) specifying a general organizational failing for which an innovation is the solution; and (2) justifying the innovation (Greenwood, Suddaby, and Hinings 2002). In practice, theorization may involve institutional entrepreneurs engaging in agenda-setting activities to promote their preferences and priorities and producing texts (e.g., press releases, reports, website materials, speeches, and interviews) to assist in making sense of their intended solutions (Greenwood, Suddaby, and Hinings 2002). By so doing, institutional entrepreneurs aim to confer legitimacy (Greenwood, Suddaby, and Hinings 2002). From a critical discourse point of view one can understand the potential and difficulties of effecting institutional change in terms of uneven social relations between institutional entrepreneurs and others as they produce, interpret, and consume text (e.g., in relation to the arguments of policy makers, incumbent energy firms, or civil society opponents of renewables) amidst broader and deeper social currents. The next section presents findings from the research bearing on the transformation of and institutional entrepreneurship within the field of energy in the UK.

Evidence of institutional inertia and change in the UK energy field

There is evidence that institutional change has occurred in the UK since the late 1980s within the field of energy provision and the renewable energy subfield, manifest largely as changes in formal legislation, regulations, and incentive schemes and norms concerning the role and conduct of industry protagonists. Views diverge on the extent of institutionalization. One view holds that the field of energy has changed considerably and has evolved from relying almost solely on hydrocarbons and nuclear power, to a more mixed composition involving a much greater proportion of renewable energy. With particular regard to the renewable energy subfield there is a feeling that the subfield has evolved from a community populated by a few "geeky" pure play renewable energy players responsible for small-scale renewable energy deployment, to a highly professional

Table 8.1 Renewable electricity generation in the UK by renewable source 1990–2015

	1990	2000	2010	2014	2015
Onshore wind	0	9.1	27.9	28.8	27.4
Offshore wind	0	0	12.0	20.7	20.8
Solar	0	0	0	6.2	9.1
Hydro	89.7	51.5	14.0	9.1	7.5
Landfill gas	1.7	22.2	19.4	7.7	5.9
Other bioenergy	8.6	17.2	26.7	27.2	29.3
Total (%)	100	100	100	99.7*	100

Source: BEIS (2016)

*Does not sum to 100 due to rounding

subfield credited with the widespread diffusion of renewable energy generation technologies.

The data on electricity supplied partly supports this view (though note that electricity is a much smaller element of UK primary fuels production and primary and final energy use than either petroleum or natural gas (BEIS 2016). In the late 1980s renewables accounted for less than 2% of the total electricity supplied in the UK (DECC 2014b), whereas in 2015 renewables accounted for nearly 25% of the electricity generated (BEIS 2016). Table 8.1 provides a breakdown of electricity generated in the UK by renewable energy source. An indication of the changes now occurring in the electricity supply is represented by the fact that for the first time, on June 7, 2017, solar and wind each generated more electricity than did gas and coal plants combined, and the renewables total at midday accounted for over 50% of the UK total electricity supplied (Harrabin 2017).

The consensus view of informants in our research is that the field of energy provision has not been changed radically since the late 1980s. In spite of the liberalization and privatization of the electricity market, the UK remains reliant on hydrocarbons and nuclear power for the overall energy supplied and used. This view is supported by data showing that in 2015 "low carbon" sources accounted for 16.5% of the total energy supplied in the UK (see Table 8.2). About half (7.9%) of this was from nuclear power and a third (5.5%) from bioenergy, the sustainability of which is not universally accepted (BEIS 2016; see for a critique of the carbon emissions impact of bioenergy: Brack 2017).

The UK energy field is portrayed as being in a state of protracted flux, with certain technologies being favored during particular periods. For instance, gas became the most prominent generation technology with the onset of the "dash for gas" in the 1990s, while coal had played a central role prior to that point. Fossil fuels have continued to dominate the overall energy generation in the UK, with centrally generated electricity being favored over distributed electricity generation. The principal justification that has been given for this is that a

Table 8.2 Contribution of low carbon energy to total UK primary energy (in percentages, selected years 2000–2015)

	2000	2010	2015
Nuclear	8.4	6.3	7.9
Wind	0	0.4	1.8
Hydro	0.2	0.1	0.3
Bioenergy	0.9	2.6	5.5
Transport fuels	0	2.6	0.5
Other	0	0	0.4
(%) contribution of low carbon energy to total UK primary energy production	9.4	10.1	16.5

Source: BEIS (2016)

centralized grid allows the system to operate safely given the existing infrastructure while being more predictable and controllable. Fundamentally, distributed electricity generation requires changes to distribution networks, which would be challenging given the existing electricity system, e.g., requiring new technologies and business models.

To understand these developments, an account of how the UK energy field and renewable energy subfield have coevolved in recent years could take as its point of departure the liberalization of the energy market (1989), which spawned the establishment of Ofgem (the Office of Gas and Electricity Markets). Other critical events at this time include the introduction of the Non-Fossil Fuel Obligation (1990), which obliged district network operators (DNOs) in England and Wales to purchase a certain amount of their electricity from renewable energy sources. A catalyst for the growth of renewables was the legal requirement that the UK provide at least 15% of its energy from renewable energy sources by 2020, with the Department of Energy and Climate Change (DECC) being established in 2008 to deliver this target.

For the period since the late 1980s, there is evidence of institutional change contributing to establishing the subfield of renewable energy in the UK. Apart from those mentioned in the previous paragraph, regulative or formal measures include: the UK microgeneration strategy and community energy strategy; targets, including climate change goals and the carbon budget; funding mechanisms such as the feed-in tariff; ethical/green finance; enterprise investment schemes; and green bonds. Among the new standards and certification schemes established to regulate and police the subfield are the Microgeneration Certification Scheme (MCS) and the Renewable Energy Consumer Code (RECC). A plethora of new types of contractual arrangements has been put in place, including contracts for difference (CfD) and engineering procurement construction (EPC).

In terms of the normative pillar of institutions, one may consider factors connected with professional pride, moral conduct, or the proper role of protagonists. A central theme concerns the idea that agents in the energy/renewable field feel that they (or the organizations they work for) ought to contribute to making the world "greener." Another perspective of this involves moral conduct; for example, renewable energy entrepreneurs or environmental activists may feel that they have right on their side or that they are doing good on behalf of the Earth or future generations. In this vein, for some of our respondents, involvement in renewable energy becomes associated with the morality and ethicality of actively working to secure both a sustainable economy in which energy generation and use is less polluting than hitherto, and a society in which there is a prospect of growing the role for locally or community-owned and/or decentralized power generation.

In a mundane way, there is the matter of what it means to work in a professional way in relation to energy/renewable energy generation. Interviewees in our research point to a tension between the accepted ways of operating in the energy field and the practices of some, especially community, renewable energy organizations. These concern organizational processes and structures. Some new funding mechanisms have been established as investment vehicles, partly intended to help renewable energy entrepreneurs overcome their lack of reputation. Yet, within the subfield of renewable energy these are thought not to be sufficiently adapted to the characteristics of investments in renewable energy, which provide steady but rather slow returns. New entrants attempting to generate community or local renewables have often had to become engaged in partnerships with larger organizations in order to acquire the kinds of funding, resources, or expertise that they have lacked.

Considerations of this type discussed above go to the heart of what it might mean to transform energy in the UK. For some this means a greatly enhanced role for renewable, community, and off-grid energy supply, pointing to developments in what are seen as exemplar countries such as the *Energiewende* in Germany, which has seen significant growth in localized energy provision. In the UK (or more specifically England, since the devolved administrations of the UK may have different arrangements and experience in this regard) there appears to be tension regarding what counts as community renewable energy. This tension is at its root a discursive struggle implicated with institutionalization of more or less challenging models of community energy. Thus one sees variety, with many initiatives involving shared community ownership, in which there is partnership between community groups and commercial developers, and the "community" (local residents/activists) is offered the opportunity to share in the ownership of commercially developed renewable energy projects. Such shared ownership models fit the state's vision of community energy as set out in the then Conservative-Liberal Democrat coalition government's policy (DECC 2014a). Other initiatives maintain a purer "green" and energy democracy agenda and a localized orientation, which have the potential to mount a radical challenge to the mainstream of energy supply and use, and thus to realize a thoroughgoing energy transformation.

Some of the ways in which (community) renewable energy seeks to build capa-bilities that may further institutionalization are by building networks among sim-ilar organizations to enable them to share their experience and to learn from each other to improve organizational processes and how to negotiate dealings with others (e.g., suppliers, local government, and grid operating companies). The establishment of a national representative body (Community Energy England and its Community Energy Hub)[1] helps to build and to support these networks, as well as to provide a voice in national debates concerning renewable and commu-nity energy as well as energy policy per se. Another important aspect is to develop a bank of evidence on the impact of community renewable energy, the contents of which can be used as persuasive data that can be employed in arguing the case for community renewables and continued state support for it.

The need for such argumentation to buttress the case for renewable energy or community renewables may be considered in terms of the prevailing dominant discourses around energy supply and security. In the UK this can be summed up by the phrase "keeping the lights on," which has become a shorthand way of expressing national energy policy priorities. In the discourse on energy, citi-zens are portrayed as passive consumers. Energy consumers are therefore subjects for whom policy makers attempt to deliver "affordable" energy and competitive markets rather than active energy citizens who are expected and expect to lead or participate in local electricity generation initiatives. Moreover as users they come to experience the use of energy as the consumption of a remotely supplied and invisible good, not one that they need to have a hand in for sustainability reasons. More broadly, a culture of NIMBYISM ("not in my backyard") and an antipathetic media are quick to present the limitations of individual renewable energy technologies or of "cowboy" suppliers or installers. In many cases refer-ence will be made to the intermittency and variability of renewables (especially where onshore wind is concerned). There will typically be less consideration of systemic energy questions, framed in the context of the scientific knowledge and international commitments concerning human-made climate change. For these kinds of reasons, community-driven renewable energy is far from being accepted as a "given," and is thus only partially institutionalized and only in ways which are relatively unchallenging to conventional energy generation and use.

Proponents of an energy transformation have had to argue for renewables and distributed energy generation in the face of deep-seated cultural assumptions regarding the energy supply and the role of energy users and, more generally, in relation to active citizenship in a world where individual consumption, not col-lective action, is the ultimate expression of identity. This has involved appeals to the utility of renewable energy, i.e., to meet climate goals. It often takes the form of authorization, in which protagonists make appeals to the authorized nature of the activity they seek to promote. Here, newcomer renewable energy generators have been able to argue for the legitimacy of their investments and incentives and allowances received, on the basis that the activity was sanctioned by the state and was a good fit with local or national policies. Of course, this legitimacy is brought into question once state support is reduced or diminished, as has been the case in the UK since the financial year 2015/16, when the government heavily reduced incentives to small-scale renewable generators.

Renewable energy entrepreneurs engage in telling "good news" stories about the pioneering achievements of themselves or their firms. Examples from our fieldwork include: the development of the UK's first and Europe's largest floating solar farm; being the first domestic consumer to capitalize on the feed-in tariff; the design of a new device for reducing refrigeration loading capacities to facilitate renewable energy systems; being responsible for the first inner-city property renewable project on social housing; being the first community crowdfunding platform to be authorized by the Financial Services Authority; establishing the first industry-led Sustainability Fuel Register; installing the first residential Archimedes screw hydropower scheme in the UK; and developing and operating an innovative elevated tower wind turbine. The following section discusses the findings in relation to the implications of the work for research and policy pertaining to the transformation of energy provision.

Concluding discussion

Renewable energy remains a highly promising rather than an established organizational subfield in the UK, part of a wider energy field which continues to be dominated by fossil fuels and nuclear power, which is not a renewable resource though controversially classified as "low carbon" in UK energy policy. Thus it could justifiably be argued that the UK energy system has not been transformed, although it has certainly been the subject of much change over the past 30 years. There are several reasons for this incomplete institutionalization or lack of transformation. These are summarized in the paragraphs below.

First, the most evident explanation for the lack of a thoroughgoing transformation of the energy system in the UK lies in the instability and inconsistency of the policies of state agencies vis-à-vis issues of state vs. public control in the energy sector, of national and international commitments, and of concerns relating to climate change mitigation, carbon emission reductions, and energy security, resilience, and affordability. The evidence from the interviews in the research undertaken by the authors suggests that informants believe that had the state energy and climate change department, established in 2008 and closed in 2016, been more fully and permanently institutionalized, it might have contributed to creating enduring, powerful formal and other institutions capable of promoting, growing, and embedding renewable energy (Scott 2013; Hoffman 1999).

Second, contradictory institutional arrangements within the field of energy provision may have affected the transformative potential and agency of actors in its subfield and consequently institutional entrepreneurship therein (Battilana, Leca, and Boxenbaum 2009; DiMaggio 1988). As the findings show, the renewable energy subfield has only attained partial institutionalization (Powell 1991). In contrast, the overarching field of energy provision is highly institutionalized, as is the fossil fuels subfield (Greenwood and Suddaby 2006). And whether one speaks of renewable energy or not, the UK energy supply remains oriented toward feeding inputs into a national centralized grid.[2]

Third, one of the important findings of this research was that multiple actors were unable or unwilling to deinstitutionalize debilitating (from the point of view of lowering carbon emissions) but prevailing institutional logics based on a vision of UK energy as primarily provided by fossil fuels and nuclear. An essential precursor to institutional and field-level organizational change is theorization (Greenwood, Suddaby, and Hinings 2002). This is because theorization provides compelling rationales for the adoption of institutional change (Lawrence and Suddaby 2006). The most significant deinstitutionalization project in the field of energy provision in the UK is based on the theorization that coal is a failing (and not a "clean") technology, one that belongs to the past. However such a process has not been extended to all fossil fuels, nor to nuclear. Competing institutional logics may have therefore limited field-level institutional change; at root, excessive variety in logics has not been helpful. As the findings show, the most intense wave of institutional entrepreneurship in the emerging renewable energy field was triggered after the Department of Energy and Climate Change (DECC) was formed and initiated a number of measures to promote renewable energy. In addition to spurring growth, it also strengthened the institutional logic that the UK should provide its energy from renewable energy sources because of its environmental credentials (Thornton and Ocasio 2008). The findings suggest, though, that the transformative effect of such growth is muted because the partially institutionalized renewable energy subfield is embedded within the more highly institutionalized field of energy provision, which has a stronger and different institutional logic. This is based on the centralized grid supply of electricity and favors larger scale units of operation than might be the case for a truly alternative approach (Sine, Haveman, and Tolbert 2005).

Fourth, the lack of a common meaning system among the institutional entrepreneurs may have precluded institutional change in the field of energy provision. As this study has established, three main categories of actors have acted as institutional entrepreneurs: state agencies such as DECC, renewable energy practitioners/activists, and incumbent energy practitioners. Yet although these actors practised as institutional entrepreneurs (DiMaggio 1988; DiMaggio and Powell 1983), they had divergent goals: the state promoted natural gas, nuclear energy, and offshore wind for the UK's future energy needs; the incumbents (primarily fossil fuels) and renewable energy practitioners/activists have grown the renewable energy subfield. The findings also show that there were divergent renewable energy goals across UK member countries because some aspects of renewable energy policy have been devolved (Cabinet Office 2002). These disparate goals may have limited field-level institutional change because institutional entrepreneurship is largely a collective strategy (DiMaggio 1988; Hardy and Maguire 2008; Jolly and Raven 2015).

Despite the divergence in goals, the findings suggest that a multiactor brand of institutional entrepreneurship has shaped the emerging renewable energy subfield in a number of ways. Thus regulative institutions, created predominantly by the state, have regularized and constrained behavior within the subfield (Meyer and Scott 1983). For example, DECC played a dichotomous role by introducing policies such as national incentive schemes to kick-start the renewable energy market and then modified these to constrain growth. This finding is significant because institutional entrepreneurs are generally portrayed as valiant warriors who provide desirable outcomes (Battilana, Leca, and Boxenbaum 2009). Further, the normative institutions created by the incumbent practitioners shaped the subfield by specifying how things should be done in the domain. For instance, one of the most impactful renewable energy schemes was the conversion of one of the UK's largest coal-fired powers to sustainable biomass. Moreover, renewable energy practitioners mainly acted as institutional entrepreneurs by normatively professionalizing the subfield; activists play a prominent role in legitimizing renewable energy, emphasizing moral, ethical, and environmental arguments to justify it.

It seems that in emerging subfields such as renewable energy, multiple actors are likely to act as institutional entrepreneurs because of the complexity of the field configuration (Wooten and Hoffman 2008; Dacin, Goodstein, and Scott 2002). For instance, the state might create regulative institutions such as national renewable energy targets, while the incumbents and renewable energy practitioners/activists might create normative institutions such as the conventions of the field and new business models, respectively. However, since renewable energy has only really started to emerge in the past decade, there has until comparatively recently been a shortage of established patterns or leaders for newcomers to emulate in the subfield (Maguire, Hardy, and Lawrence 2004). One side effect of this has been a tendency to rely on institutionalized authorities, such as the state, to be the default sources of institutional change (Jepperson and Meyer 1991; DiMaggio 1988).

Fifth, the research has shown that some of the triggers for institutional entrepreneurship in the energy field and subfields discussed above differ from those in the prevailing literature. Contrary to the commonly held view that elite actors are least likely to envision institutional change because they are privileged by existing institutional arrangements (Hardy and Maguire 2008; Greenwood and Suddaby 2006), this study found that these central agents readily initiated change. In the 1990s and 2000s this was with the aim to meet national and international climate change commitments, but in the 2010s this was part of a package of "austerity" measures following the financial crisis of 2008, as well as based on the precept that earlier interventions, taken by a Labour government rather than a Conservative one, have in a sense worked too well and that some renewable technologies should now be able to stand on their own two feet financially. Similarly, although it is commonly proposed that peripheral actors are most likely to enact institutional change (Greenwood, Suddaby, and Hinings 2002), this study found that some renewable energy practitioners or activists were unable to initiate their change projects because their agentic power was low (Fligstein 2001). That said, the findings provide substantive evidence that these institutional entrepreneurs have been able to argue for and instigate (or get instigated) a number of formal and normative changes in rules governing renewable energy in the UK. These changes have altered the character of energy provision though appear to stop short of thoroughly transforming the field (DiMaggio 1988).

The institutions created by institutional entrepreneurs have shaped the renewable energy subfield considerably and especially in the 2000s by reducing uncertainty and providing a degree of structure for the field (North 1990; DiMaggio 1988; Giddens 1984). In spite of this, they may ultimately prove to have limited impact on the field of energy provision, partly owing to the instability and incoherence of rules regimes and partly owing to deep-seated cultural values in UK society (at least in English society) which seem to work against certain renewable energy technologies, most notably onshore wind, and the broader scale commitment to active energy citizenship and the idea of decentralized, locally led or owned renewable energy generation and use.

Summary

The chapter has highlighted factors which may facilitate or impair the transformation of energy systems, focusing on the emergence of a renewable energy subfield in the UK since the late 1980s. Its findings have been informed by work undertaken by the authors on projects investigating institutional entrepreneurship and questions of legitimacy, in relation to the growth of energy generation from renewable sources and new business models such as those connected with community energy initiatives. Fundamentally, the chapter underscores the role of multiple actors engaging to varying degrees both in institutional entrepreneurship favorable to transformative change and in strategies inimical to fundamental change or preservative of the status quo. The nature and (in)consistency of state policies may be critical to both tendencies but over and above this it is important to recognize the role of exemplar organizations and business models in legitimizing and hence garnering support for renewable energy. They symbolize and enact what a sustainable energy future might look like, and can substantiate a discourse of transformation, albeit one which will have to contend with other narratives of energy in the future, including those which continue to validate the status quo or the contribution of incumbents.

Notes

1 http://hub.communityenergyengland.org/
2 Note, however, that recent developments include consultation on changes to the UK power networks, which could eventually result in an infrastructure better able to accommodate more distributed energy (UK Power Networks 2017).

References

Barley, Stephen R. 2008. "Coalface Institutionalism." In *The SAGE Handbook of Organizational Institutionalism*, edited by Royston Greenwood, Christine Oliver, Kerstin Sahlin, and Roy Suddaby, 491–518. London: SAGE Publications Ltd.

Battilana, Julie. 2004. "Foundations for a Theory of Institutional Entrepreneurship: Solving the Paradox of Embedded Agency." Paper presented at the European Group for

Organizational Studies (EGOS) Conference, Ljubljana, Slovenia. www.hbs.edu/faculty/
Pages/item.aspx?num=41107.

Battilana, Julie, Bernard Leca, and Eva Boxenbaum. 2009. "How Actors Change Institutions: Towards a Theory of Institutional Entrepreneurship." *The Academy of Management Annals* 3 (1): 65–107. https://doi.org/10.1080/19416520903053598.

BEIS. 2016. *UK Energy in Brief 2016*. London: BEIS – Department for Business, Energy
and Industrial Strategy. www.gov.uk/government/uploads/system/uploads/attachment_
data/file/540135/UK_Energy_in_Brief_2016_FINAL.pdf.

Benford, Robert D., and David A. Snow. 2000. "Framing Processes and Social Movements: An Overview and Assessment." *Annual Review of Sociology* 26: 611–39. https://
doi.org/10.1146/annurev.soc.26.1.611.

Brack, Duncan. 2017. "The Impacts of the Demand for Woody Biomass for Power and
Heat on Climate and Forests." Research Paper. London: Chatham House. www.
chathamhouse.org/sites/files/chathamhouse/publications/research/2017-02-23-impacts-
demand-woody-biomass-climate-forests-brack-final.pdf.

Cabinet Office. 2002. "The Energy Review." A Performance and Innovation Unit Report.
London: Cabinet Office, Performance and Innovation Unit. www.gci.org.uk/Documents/
TheEnergyReview.pdf.

Camic, Charles, Philip S. Gorski, and David M. Trubek, eds. 2005. *Max Weber's Economy
and Society: A Critical Companion*. 2nd ed. Stanford: Stanford University Press.

Coase, Ronald H. 1937. "The Nature of the Firm." *Economica*, New Series, 4 (16):
386–405.

———. 1960. "The Problem of Social Cost." *The Journal of Law & Economics* 3: 1–44.

Cohen, Maurie J., Halina Szejnwald Brown, and Philip J. Vergragt, eds. 2013. *Innova-
tions in Sustainable Consumption: New Economics, Socio-Technical Transitions and Social
Practices*. Advances in Ecological Economics. Cheltenham, UK; Northampton, MA:
Edward Elgar Publishing.

Commons, John Rogers. 1931. "Institutional Economics." *History of Economic Thought Articles*
21: 648–57.

Creed, W. E. Douglas, Maureen A. Scully, and John R. Austin. 2002. "Clothes Make the
Person? The Tailoring of Legitimating Accounts and the Social Construction of Identity." *Organization Science* 13 (5): 475–96. https://doi.org/10.1287/orsc.13.5.475.7814.

Dacin, M. Tina, Jerry Goodstein, and W. Richard Scott. 2002. "Institutional Theory and
Institutional Change: Introduction to the Special Research Forum." *The Academy of
Management Journal* 45 (1): 45–56. https://doi.org/10.2307/3069284.

DECC. 2014a. *Community Energy Strategy*. London: DECC – Department of Energy and
Climate Change. www.gov.uk/government/uploads/system/uploads/attachment_data/
file/275163/20140126Community_Energy_Strategy.pdf.

———. 2014b. *UK Energy in Brief 2014*. London: DECC – Department of Energy and
Climate Change. www.gov.uk/government/uploads/system/uploads/attachment_data/
file/350941/UK_Energy_in_Brief_2014_revised.pdf.

Déjean, Frédérique, Jean-Pascal Gond, and Bernard Leca. 2004. "Measuring the Unmeas-
ured: An Institutional Entrepreneur Strategy in an Emerging Industry." *Human Relations* 57 (6): 741–64. https://doi.org/10.1177/0018726704044954.

DiMaggio, Paul J. 1988. "Interest and Agency in Institutional Theory." In *Institutional
Patterns and Organizations: Culture and Environment*, edited by Lynne G. Zucker, 3–22.
Cambridge, MA: Ballinger Publishing Co.

DiMaggio, Paul J., and Walter W. Powell. 1983. "The Iron Cage Revisited: Institutional
Isomorphism and Collective Rationality in Organizational Fields." *American Sociological
Review* 48: 147–60.

Durkheim, Émile. 1964. *The Rules of Sociological Method*. New York: Free Press.

Fligstein, Neil. 1996. "Markets as Politics: A Political-Cultural Approach to Market Institutions." *American Sociological Review* 61 (4): 656–73. https://doi.org/10.2307/2096398.

———. 2001. "Social Skill and the Theory of Fields." *Sociological Theory* 19 (2): 105–25. https://doi.org/10.1111/0735-2751.00132.

Garud, Raghu, Cynthia Hardy, and Steve Maguire. 2007. "Institutional Entrepreneurship as Embedded Agency: An Introduction to the Special Issue." *Organization Studies* 28 (7): 957–69. https://doi.org/10.1177/0170840607078958.

Garud, Raghu, Sanjay Jain, and Arun Kumaraswamy. 2002. "Institutional Entrepreneurship in the Sponsorship of Common Technological Standards: The Case of Sun Microsystems and Java." *The Academy of Management Journal* 45 (1): 196–214. https://doi.org/10.2307/3069292.

Genus, Audley. 2012. "Changing the Rules? Institutional Innovation and the Diffusion of Microgeneration." *Technology Analysis & Strategic Management* 24 (7): 711–27. https://doi.org/10.1080/09537325.2012.705122.

———. 2014. "Governing Sustainability: A Discourse-Institutional Approach." *Sustainability* 6 (1): 283–305. https://doi.org/10.3390/su6010283.

———. 2016. "Sustainability Transitions: A Discourse-Institutional Perspective." In *Handbook on Sustainability Transition and Sustainable Peace*, edited by Hans Günter Brauch, Úrsula Oswald Spring, and Jürgen Scheffran, 527–41. Hexagon Series on Human and Environmental Security and Peace. Springer. https://doi.org/10.1007/978-3-319-43884-9_24.

Giddens, Anthony. 1984. *The Constitution of Society: Outline of the Theory of Structuration*. Cambridge, UK: Polity Press.

Greenwood, Royston, and Roy Suddaby. 2006. "Institutional Entrepreneurship in Mature Fields: The Big Five Accounting Firms." *The Academy of Management Journal* 49 (1): 27–48. https://doi.org/10.2307/20159744.

Greenwood, Royston, Roy Suddaby, and C. R. Hinings. 2002. "Theorizing Change: The Role of Professional Associations in the Transformation of Institutionalized Fields." *The Academy of Management Journal* 45 (1): 58–80. https://doi.org/10.2307/3069285.

Hardy, Cynthia, and Steve Maguire. 2008. "Institutional Entrepreneurship." In *The SAGE Handbook of Organizational Institutionalism*, edited by Royston Greenwood, Christine Oliver, Roy Suddaby, and Kerstin Sahlin, 198–217. London: SAGE Publications Ltd. https://doi.org/10.4135/9781849200387.

Hargadon, Andrew B., and Yellowlees Douglas. 2001. "When Innovations Meet Institutions: Edison and the Design of the Electric Light." *Administrative Science Quarterly* 46 (3): 476–501. https://doi.org/10.2307/3094872.

Harrabin, Roger. 2017. "Renewables Provide More Than Half UK Electricity for First Time." *BBC News*, 2017. www.bbc.com/news/business-40198567.

Hinings, C.R., and Pamela S. Tolbert. 2008. "Organizational Institutionalism and Sociology: A Reflection." In *The SAGE Handbook of Organizational Institutionalism*, edited by Royston Greenwood, Christine Oliver, Roy Suddaby, and Kerstin Sahlin, 473–90. London: SAGE Publications Ltd. https://doi.org/10.4135/9781849200387.

Hoffman, Andrew J. 1999. "Institutional Evolution and Change: Environmentalism and the U.S. Chemical Industry." *The Academy of Management Journal* 42 (4): 351–71. https://doi.org/10.2307/257008.

Holm, Petter. 1995. "The Dynamics of Institutionalization: Transformation Processes in Norwegian Fisheries." *Administrative Science Quarterly* 40 (3): 398–422. https://doi.org/10.2307/2393791.

Huntington, Samuel P. 1965. "Political Development and Political Decay." *World Politics* 17 (3): 386–430. https://doi.org/10.2307/2009286.

Jepperson, Ronald L. 1991. "Institutions, Institutional Effects, and Institutionalism in Organizational Analysis." In *The New Institutionalism in Organizational Analysis*, edited by Walter W. Powell and Paul J. DiMaggio, 143–63. Chicago: University of Chicago Press.

Jepperson, Ronald L., and John W. Meyer. 1991. "The Public Order and the Construction of Formal Organizations." In *The New Institutionalism in Organizational Analysis*, edited by Walter W. Powell and Paul J. DiMaggio, 204–31. Chicago: University of Chicago Press.

Jolly, Suyash, and Rob Raven. 2015. "Collective Institutional Entrepreneurship and Contestations in Wind Energy in India." *Renewable and Sustainable Energy Reviews* 42: 999–1011. https://doi.org/10.1016/j.rser.2014.10.039.

Lawrence, Thomas B. 2008. "Power, Institutions and Organizations." In *The SAGE Handbook of Organizational Institutionalism*, edited by Royston Greenwood, Christine Oliver, Roy Suddaby, and Kerstin Sahlin, 170–97. London: SAGE Publications Ltd. https://doi.org/10.4135/9781849200387.

Lawrence, Thomas B., Cynthia Hardy, and Nelson Phillips. 2002. "Institutional Effects of Interorganizational Collaboration: The Emergence of Proto-Institutions." *Academy of Management Journal* 45 (1): 281–90. https://doi.org/10.2307/3069297.

Lawrence, Thomas B., and Roy Suddaby. 2006. "Institutions and Institutional Work." In *The SAGE Handbook of Organization Studies*, edited by Stewart R. Clegg, Cynthia Hardy, Thomas B. Lawrence, and Walter R. Nord, 2nd ed., 215–54. London: SAGE Publications Ltd. https://doi.org/10.4135/9781848608030.

Leca, Bernard, and Philippe Naccache. 2006. "A Critical Realist Approach to Institutional Entrepreneurship." *Organization* 13 (5): 627–51. https://doi.org/10.1177/1350508406067007.

MacIver, Robert Morrison. 1931. *Society, Its Structure and Changes*. New York: Ray Long and Richard R. Smith.

Maguire, Steve, Cynthia Hardy, and Thomas B. Lawrence. 2004. "Institutional Entrepreneurship in Emerging Fields: HIV/AIDS Treatment Advocacy in Canada." *Academy of Management Journal* 47 (5): 657–79. https://doi.org/10.2307/20159610.

Meyer, John W., and Michael T. Hannan. 1979. *National Development and the World System: Educational, Economic, and Political Change, 1950–1970*. Chicago: University of Chicago Press.

Meyer, John W., and Brian Rowan. 1977. "Institutionalized Organizations: Formal Structure as Myth and Ceremony." *American Journal of Sociology* 83 (2): 340–63.

Meyer, John W., and W. Richard Scott. 1983. *Organizational Environments: Ritual and Rationality*. Thousand Oaks, CA: SAGE Publications Ltd.

Meyer, Renate E. 2008. "New Sociology of Knowledge: Historical Legacy and Contributions to Current Debates in Institutional Research." In *The SAGE Handbook of Organizational Institutionalism*, edited by Royston Greenwood, Christine Oliver, Roy Suddaby, and Kerstin Sahlin, 519–38. London: SAGE Publications Ltd.

North, Douglass C. 1990. *Institutions, Institutional Change and Economic Performance*. Political Economy of Institutions and Decisions. Cambridge: Cambridge University Press.

Parsons, Talcott. 1937. *The Structure of Social Action*. New York [u.a.]: McGraw-Hill.

Powell, Walter W. 1991. "Expanding the Scope." In *The New Handbook in Organisational Analysis*, edited by Walter W. Powell and Paul J. DiMaggio, 183–203. Chicago: University of Chicago Press.

Powell, Walter W., and Paul J. DiMaggio. 1991. "Introduction." In *The New Institutionalism in Organizational Analysis*, edited by Walter W. Powell and DiMaggio, 1–38. Chicago: University of Chicago Press.

Scott, W. Richard. 2005. "Institutional Theory." In *Encyclopedia of Social Theory*, edited by George Ritzer, 409–14. Thousand Oaks, CA: SAGE Publications, Ltd. https://doi.org/10.4135/9781412952552.

———. 2008. *Institutions and Organizations: Ideas and Interests*. 3rd ed. Thousand Oaks, CA: SAGE Publications Ltd.

———. 2013. *Institutions and Organizations: Ideas, Interests and Identities*. 4th ed. Thousand Oaks, CA: SAGE Publications Ltd.

Selznick, Philip. 1948. "Foundations of the Theory of Organization." *American Sociological Review* 13 (1): 25–35.

Seo, Myeong-Gu, and W. E. Douglas Creed. 2002. "Institutional Contradictions, Praxis, and Institutional Change: A Dialectical Perspective." *Academy of Management Review* 27 (2): 222–47. https://doi.org/10.5465/AMR.2002.6588004.

Sine, Wesley D., Heather A. Haveman, and Pamela S. Tolbert. 2005. "Risky Business? Entrepreneurship in the New Independent-Power Sector." *Administrative Science Quarterly* 50 (2): 200–32. https://doi.org/10.2189/asqu.2005.50.2.200.

Strang, David, and John W. Meyer. 1993. "Institutional Conditions for Diffusion." *Theory and Society* 22 (4): 487–511.

Suchman, Mark C. 1995. "Managing Legitimacy: Strategic and Institutional Approaches." *Academy of Management Review* 20 (3): 571–610. https://doi.org/10.5465/AMR.1995.9508080331.

Thornton, Patricia H., and William Ocasio. 2008. "Institutional Logics." In *The SAGE Handbook of Organizational Institutionalism*, 99–128. London: SAGE Publications Ltd. https://doi.org/10.4135/9781849200387.

UK Power Networks. 2017. "Future Smart. A Smart Grid for All: Our Transition to Distribution System Operator." Consultation Report. London: UK Power Networks. www.ukpowernetworks.co.uk/internet/en/about-us/documents/FutureSmart_Consultation-Report_.pdf.

Veblen, Thorstein. 1899. *The Theory of the Leisure Class: An Economic Study of Institutions*. New York: MacMillan.

Walker, Kent, Francine Schlosser, and David L. Deephouse. 2014. "Organizational Ingenuity and the Paradox of Embedded Agency: The Case of the Embryonic Ontario Solar Energy Industry." *Organization Studies* 35 (4): 613–34. https://doi.org/10.1177/0170840613517599.

Wijen, Frank, and Shahzad Ansari. 2007. "Overcoming Inaction Through Collective Institutional Entrepreneurship: Insights from Regime Theory." *Organization Studies* 28 (7): 1079–100. https://doi.org/10.1177/0170840607078115.

Williamson, Oliver E. 1975. *Markets and Hierarchies, Analysis and Antitrust Implications : A Study in the Economics of Internal Organization*. New York: Free Press.

———. 1985. *The Economic Institutions of Capitalism: Firms Markets, Relational Contracting*. New York: Free Press.

Wooten, Melissa, and Andrew J. Hoffman. 2008. "Organizational Fields: Past, Present and Future." In *The SAGE Handbook of Organizational Institutionalism*, edited by Royston Greenwood, Christine Oliver, Roy Suddaby, and Kerstin Sahlin, 129–48. London: SAGE Publications Ltd. https://doi.org/10.4135/9781849200387.

Zilber, Tammar B. 2002. "Institutionalization as an Interplay Between Actions, Meanings, and Actors: The Case of a Rape Crisis Center in Israel." *Academy of Management Journal* 45 (1): 234–54. https://doi.org/10.2307/3069294.

Part III

Sociotechnical problem of action

9 The energy system and trust

Public, organizational, and transsystemic perspectives

Patrick Sumpf

Introduction

Precisely 50 years ago, Niklas Luhmann introduced the idea of "system trust" (Luhmann 1968). He was convinced that trust in a modern society is not conceivable as trust in individual persons but rather as trust in corporate societal sectors – like the *energy system*. The dependence of modern civilization on this sort of trust has also occupied major sociological theorists such as Giddens (1990) and Coleman (1990), yet has rarely progressed. Today, trust in systems is more significant than ever given current empirical developments such as global energy transitions and the introduction of data-intense smart grids. Very likely, these transitions will encompass more active involvement by consumers and industrial grid contributors alike. New technologies, business models, and organizational patterns have emerged already, and further substantial change is heralded for the mid and long term (Appelrath, Kagermann, and Mayer 2012; B.A.U.M. Consult 2012; Ramchurn et al. 2012). This applies to both private and commercial domains, where risks such as power outages, bottlenecks, hacking, financial burdens, and business espionage are common expectations (ZfK 2015). Anti-smart meter movements (e.g., in the Netherlands)[1] or self-supply through power plant construction (e.g., in Germany)[2] are past reactions to this and expressions of distrust. In order to act in the face of these growing perceptions of risk, trust is an indispensable bridging resource. Trust bridges perceived risks by securing *actionability* among trustors, i.e., securing their capacity to make decisions and act despite possible uncertainties along the way. Actionability – and therefore trust – may thus become highly demanded yet scarce resources in future energy systems, which are likely to rest increasingly on trust instead of control due to boosts in complexity.[3]

While Giddens predominantly follows the Luhmannian perspective of individuals trusting a system, Coleman alludes to "systems of trust" (Coleman 1990, 188ff) and enriches the debate by stressing trust-building within and between different social systems such as politics and finance. With reference to sociotechnical energy systems,[4] we can pick up this idea and ask about the nature of the different trust relations in the energy sector. Besides consumers trusting the energy system, organizations in the energy economy mobilize and uphold/dismiss a range of trust relationships with other organizations. Furthermore, organizations appear as a trustee of trusting clients and citizens, a role rarely scrutinized (compare La Porte and Metlay 1996; SEAB 1993). Going beyond some of the existing literature on trust in the energy realm, this chapter seeks to explore different levels and arenas of trust in, through, or within the energy system and its conditions and consequences. In particular, three views are presented that encompass *public, organizational,* and *transsystemic* trust. Insights on these issues can help to progress in both energy and trust research by paying tribute to the increasing role played by trust despite the limited systematic study of it. Accordingly, an attempt is made to recalibrate how trust operates in systemic contexts such as the energy supply; alongside this, inferences are drawn for the success and failure of energy transitions. This is deeply tied to trust's permanent role as a trigger/inhibitor of actionability in energy systems, which is a focus of this chapter.

As an overall framework, I will introduce the sociology of trust and its functions in the following section. Thereafter, I will present the three perspectives on trust in energy systems both theoretically and empirically. The first perspective deals with *public trust in the energy system* as related to consumer perspectives on trusting the energy system. In the second major section, I will shift the focus to *trust between organizations* and discuss how the problem of subsidiarity will create new hierarchies between energy organizations and their trust relations. Last, I will allude to *transsystemic trust* between collective societal sectors such as politics and the economy, furthered by an insurance-based future energy system that likely depends on backup capacities of electricity. Finally, there is a conclusion section.

The sociology of trust and its functions

I want to present a focused introduction of trust research mainly based on sociological contributions pertaining to the realities of system trust. Without neglecting the need or relevance of mental trust antecedents and psychological research, one can emphasize the sociological impact of trust:

> We see that the primary function of trust is sociological rather than psychological, since individuals would have no occasion or need to trust apart from social relationships. In addition, we would like to argue that, like its function, the bases on which trust rests are primarily social as well.
>
> (Lewis and Weigert 1985, 969)

This statement is particularly valid for trust in systems. Being a "collective cognitive reality" (Lewis and Weigert 1985, 970) with primary social functions, bases, and consequences, it is no coincidence that every author with a major contribution to system trust is a sociologist (Barber 1983; Coleman 1990; Giddens 1990; Lewis and Weigert 1985; Luhmann 1979; Simmel 1978). This reality leads us directly to the core of (system) trust research, which is grounded in the need of *bridging double contingency*[5] (Luhmann 1979). The very reason why Lewis and Weigert allude to trust's primary functions and bases as being social (rather than mental) is related to contingencies in the process of communication: Neither alter nor alter ego know how their counterpart is going to respond to their offers of communication (e.g., rejecting, asking for reasons, or alluding to bad timing) – *and both of them know about this.*[6] This double contingency situation (Parsons 1964) leads to surprises and the unpredictability of social processes,[7] i.e., to perceptions of uncertainty and risk among decision makers, both private and commercial. These irreducible social parameters of uncertainty and risk are absorbed by trust in that trust suppresses potential surprises and errors of prediction by decision makers in a way that allows for an as if everything-goes-according-to-plan approach (Möllering 2006b).

Accordingly, leading (sociological) scholars have described trust as "a gamble, a risky investment" (Luhmann 1979, 24) that shadows alternate future developments that trustors deem unfavorable, while in absolute terms they remain correspondingly probable. In this way, trust can be regarded as an "illusion" (Luhmann 1979, 32) in that it is *suspending irreducible social vulnerability and uncertainty as if they were favourably resolved*" (Möllering 2006a, 356; emphasis added). This act of "suspension," Möllering's core theoretical concept, is at the heart of trust research. Suspension of disbelief and doubt transforms perceived risk into imagined certainty in that it makes people act as if the future was certain (Luhmann 1979; Möllering 2006b). Consequently, suspension touches upon the temporal dimension of social reality, as it requires transformation of imagined futures into the present as a foundation for decisions of trust or distrust. In this temporal (or operational) dimension of present trust-based decision making, suspension entails the effect of generating *actionability*, i.e., the capacity to act among trustors: "trust, by the reduction of complexity, discloses *possibilities for action* which would have remained improbable and unattractive without trust – which would not, in other words, have been pursued" (Luhmann 1979, 25; emphasis added).

Based on these elaborations, it is evident and shared in the research community that trust operates as an action enhancer (Strulik 2007), just like its functional equivalent of distrust. Distrust not only constrains certain actions (namely those that are to be avoided or circumvented), but also mobilizes action toward trajectories of less complexity, while potentially magnifying these behavioral patterns. Imagine a consumer distrustful of nuclear energy who avoids electricity from these sources and might move away from a nuclear plant to escape radiation, thus constraining (i.e., limiting) yet concentrating (i.e., mobilizing) actions simultaneously. The application of trust *or* distrust in overcoming or giving in to certain risk perceptions relating to energy (like radiation) is generally possible in both directions, yet with quite different consequences for the social process and energy system performance.

Applying trust encompasses a renunciation of control, i.e., letting things go without (personal) scrutiny. Distrust, on the other hand, usually involves some form of (at least imagined) control over the object trustors are suspicious of, often through complete avoidance or, quite the reverse, through very differentiated assessments. Whatever the case, social designs of either trust or distrust can have their roots in (a) intentional choices of trustors going one way or the other while both possibilities are actually feasible or manageable, or (b) system complexities reaching levels where possibilities of factual control become more and more unlikely. The latter leaves trustors few choices as to whether to trust or distrust since reliance on external sources – often due to social complexity[8] – can hardly be prevented. Model a could be an organizational cultural scheme, for instance, where managers would rather trust their staff to perform certain tasks without too much control and scrutiny until delivery of the final outcome is due. The case of energy represents more elements of model b, where factual control of systemic processes seems to allow less potential for intervention: Both consumers (comprehending how electricity is generated and reaches one's home, fully understanding how home-based technology works, and comprehending tariff structures) and professional operators (gathering information across energy-related sectors to uphold grid frequencies [security of supply], monitoring decentralized energy generation, and comprehending price mechanisms on stock markets) see themselves confronted by a "complexity trap" (Appelrath, Kagermann, and Mayer 2012). This is not to say that control and scrutiny of processes is factually impossible in every case, but that the transaction costs for conducting these operations increase rapidly – as do the demands on time and skill – in part now but more so in smart future grids (Sumpf 2017). Consumers are supposed to dedicate more attention to what happens "behind the power outlet" and businesses are supposed to communicate and network even more with neighboring actors, even if that entails cooperation between previously disconnected branches such as engineering, computer science, and the social sciences. The merging of different knowledge sets and empirical sectors (energy technology, internet technology, and communication management) in practice is what creates the basis for the "smart grid," making the social organization of energy systems (interaction, coordination, and communication) a permanent priority.

This nexus of control, information flows, communication patterns, and reliance on others is decisive for both the cohesion of social (and sociotechnical) systems and the study of trust. Trust and distrust are the social mechanisms securing the ease of cooperation (Misztal 1996; Lane and Bachmann 1998) and success of complex system management, and they offer conceptual tools that help describe the current transition efforts of energy systems. The social component of energy systems, which consists of processes of communication, is regulated decisively by the mobilization, alteration, or absence of either trust or distrust, with consequences for the overall system. In essence, we can deduce three aspects for the following analysis that the study of trust in energy systems is supposed to deliver: (i) creating sensitivity for the social dimension of energy systems, which relates to communication, action, and decision-making patterns among consumers and organizations; (ii) discover the action-enabling effects of trust-building in the realization of future energy systems, just like the possible paralysis in the opposite case; and (iii) understand the systemic dimension of trust/distrust, along with elaborations on normativity such as the benefits and risks associated with trust and distrust. These aspects will be mirrored against the requirements for successes and failures of energy transitions at three levels: public trust in the energy system, trust between organizations, and transsystemic trust. Methodologically, I rely on document analysis, expert interviews, and theoretical considerations of trust.

Varieties of system trust

Based on the prior elaborations, there are three situations where the special status of systems plays an incomparably crucial role in processes of trust: (1) the trust by individuals, groups, and organizations toward a system (Simmel 1978; Luhmann 1979; Giddens 1990); (2) systems of trust (Coleman 1990) or system-specific trust architectures (Strulik 2011); and (3) transsystemic trust between social systems (Strulik 2011; Schweer and Siebertz-Reckzeh 2014). While the first category has received the most scholarly attention in the trust community and mostly occupies an exemplary status regarding system trust, this discussion includes research avenues for the other two categories, which have been somewhat underrepresented so far. The next three sections, therefore, will describe each of these cases of system trust in more detail by combining insights from both energy and trust research.

Public trust in the energy system

This original idea of system trust is commonly described as a routine mechanism of social life, investing trust in complex, opaque, and often overwhelming structures beyond trust in persons – an aspect which is strongly related to transformations of premodern (Giddens 1990) or stratified (Luhmann 1979) societies into modern societies. Crucially, it involves reliance on processes of which one personally lacks the knowledge to evaluate and involves substantial trust in strangers, i.e., people whom one is not familiar with (Giddens 1990, Zucker 1986). Luhmann (1979) exemplifies his idea of system trust by referring to trust in symbolically generalized media of communication such as money, power, or truth: Here, the trustor is confronted with expectations toward the functioning of an economic, political, or scientific "system" which enables certain transactions in these particular realms where the communication media are effective. These systemic trust processes are accompanied by trust in "symbolic tokens or expert systems" (Giddens 1990, 33), food systems (Sumpf 2013), the financial system (Strulik 2007), or virtual systems (König and Sumpf 2018). In general, researchers target the general public as an aggregate of single individuals (laypersons, the lay public) who are considered the subject of trust and the systems mentioned as collective entities which are their trustees (e.g., Schubert, Meyer, and Möst 2015). The question is whether trust in "the system" as such (Sumpf 2017) or trust relations between the public and organizations such as the US Department of Energy (DOE), nuclear plants, or supervisory institutions are implied (compare SEAB 1993; La Porte and Metlay 1996).

In this connection, one of the substantive contributions to trust and energy is made by a special issue of the journal *Energy Policy* on "the role of trust in managing uncertainties in the transition to a sustainable energy economy" (Bellaby,

Eames, and Flynn 2010). Several authors examined questions of trust in the energy system concerning different levels and themes. In close relation to the prior themes, they discovered the following levels of systemic trust:

- Trust between citizens and authority – expert or political – with respect to benefits and risks of any new technology required.
- [. . .] Trust around change in consumption practices involving energy.

(Bellaby, Eames, and Flynn 2010, 2614)

Since "authority" and "practices" (Bellaby, Eames, and Flynn 2010) are both social concepts that apply to more than individual persons, trust in them or through their enactment can be regarded as being systemic rather than personal. This remains true even if individual people (like politicians, scientists, or personal friends) embody or represent these concepts and roles for individual trustors. This cements the original conception of public trust in a system that, with regard to energy supply, hinges on citizens' relationships with experts and politics and on sociotechnical patterns of behavior. Accordingly, trust relationships of citizens with the energy system have been initially analyzed in the research community, for instance with reference to the roles of consumers, investors, and those affected by energy-related, public decision making (Büscher and Sumpf 2015). In relation to energy, characteristic for the public level of trust is the frequent description of increasing *interactivity* with the system: In all three roles of consumers, investors, and those affected, private and commercial actors alike face growing demands of reflexivity and awareness about electricity as a scarce and volatile resource. While businesses have always had a share of their attention directed toward energy consumption (mainly as a more or less substantial cost driver), private households can be described as having a "taken for granted" attitude when it comes to electricity provision (Shove and Warde 1998). For multiple reasons (low prices, complicated topic, and little appeal), most western consumers have gotten used to the convenient nonstop delivery of energy with no questions asked:

> The fact is that mature technological systems reside in a naturalized background, as ordinary and unremarkable to us as trees, daylight, and dirt. Our civilizations fundamentally depend on them, yet we notice them mainly when they fail, which they rarely do.
>
> (Edwards 2004, 185)

This situation, according to prevailing visions, is about to change more or less drastically: Both private consumers and commercial actors are expected to intervene more in markets in order to increase the shares from renewable energy sources (RES) and contribute to innovations that secure successful smart grid operation in the future. Concrete measures entail the use of smart meters and other appliances for home owners and tenants, as well as participation in stock and capacity markets for commercial users. Overall, more decentralization and feed-in from RES from both private and business owners is an objective along with mechanisms for supplying emergency capacities in the case of RES volatility (BMWi/BMU 2011; BMWi 2015). While this generally pertains to both the private and the business world, average users of electricity are the party less prepared in this respect. First, their degree of previous attention to this subject has been lower (see above), and second, public debate across the EU, e.g., in Germany, initially classified private households as less significant due to profitability shortfalls stemming from load-shifting activities. Current EU communications signal a self-declared mix of technology and business opportunities and of cost burdens for smart grid clients, further pushing "consumer empowerment" in this field (European Commission 2015, 3). Given the swift penetration of smart meters in economies in Europe (JRC 2011) and the US (Depuru, Wang, and Devabhaktuni 2011), for instance, debates about the cost–benefit relation and data security seem to pose temporary rather than constant obstacles to this development. Consequently, even though the motto of modern capitalism is to "keep it simple," average consumers are more and more likely personally to be involved in a system they once observed from the outside. This is equally valid for more skeptical countries like Germany, where a representative of a leading German environmental association in an expert interview[9] said: "And I can truly imagine how (and that is why I´m still, nonetheless, not completely cutting off communication) in the end, the private household will finally really be able to play a greater role through its marketing demand."

While the exact degree of private household involvement in smart grids is still being contested and business models are targeting easy and convenient solutions (Khala, Sumpf, and Büscher 2014), the scenario described on the foregoing pages hardly implies business as usual for electricity clients. This is particularly valid considering their current status of alienation with regard to the topic. Current and growing demands for interactivity in markets, with technologies, and in new demanding social arrangements (e.g., virtual power plants, energy communities, and prosumer activities) lead to consumer *action (trust)* and *inaction (lack of trust, distrust)* serving as a cornerstone of the energy transition. The motivation and ensuing actionability of private clients and businesses develop into a political category that needs systematic attention by decision makers, both political and commercial. This would secure consideration of the central social challenge posed by digitally driven energy transitions, replacing the prominent yet old system-oriented discussion of "social acceptance" (Kasperson and Ram 2013). While the latter usually targets the local acceptance of physical infrastructure phenomena (compare Büscher and Sumpf 2015), trust research opens up avenues for analyzing decision making and technology usage on and around new market constellations.

Due to the progressive innovations in the electricity sector that are not primarily related to physical infrastructure but to the reorganization of patterns of communication and markets in decentralized microgrids, the conceptual value of acceptance seems little helpful in describing system–client relations. How are we going to accept or oppose a whole market? How are we going to accept or oppose demand-response programs in smart grids when our own dynamic participation is required? It is evident that the smart grid is not about changes in a single technology alone (like the deployment of smart meters) that can be accepted or declined, but about much finer grained relationships of consumers with the system (compare Todt 2011). Trust research is an opportunity for social science energy researchers to analyze communication and behavior patterns around these emerging challenges in order to determine the actionability potential among trustors. This potential crucially affects the success or failure of energy transitions in that it regulates the trust–distrust mix among consumers. From a normative viewpoint, a mix of both resources is favorable since trust cannot alone be regarded as a positive resource, nor can distrust be branded negatively. Both trust and distrust have positive (enactment and support of cooperation/healthy suspicion) and negative functions (blind trust/paranoia), which results in the necessity of multilayered, differentiated trust analyses (Lumineau 2017). Increasingly, the outcomes of the trust–distrust mixes will determine the actions of energy consumers, and analyses of this kind will similarly grow in importance and in their impact on the research community, energy business, and policy making.

A final, more conceptual question for trust research is how to model trust in "abstract systems" (Giddens 1990, 87) under the premises outlined so far. In order for research results to achieve a high level of validity and for the research to come to terms with what it means to trust/distrust the energy system, differentiated perspectives on system–element relations are necessary. This primarily pertains to the question about system representation for trustors. Do energy consumers perceive a coherent system with an identity strong enough for them to form a trusting relationship with it? Or do single element relations with (dominant) system components prevail (e.g., providers)? This leads to the ultimate question of whether and how such a system could possibly be represented by its perceived elements, such as utilities organizations, so that experiences with the latter are generalized onto the system (compare Sumpf 2017). First results indicate that the public is split in this respect, so that only parts of the population can be expected to form genuine systemic trust relations in the energy field (Sumpf 2017). This has consequences for the design of consumers' complex trust environment with energy, especially given the current and coming changes. In order to exploit the utmost rationality of the smart grid, it seems advantageous for clients to form systemic trust relationships, thus considering the repercussions their actions (e.g., investment, electricity use/withdrawal, self-generation, consumption reflexivity, and increased backend knowledge) might have within that system. While the need for a reduction in complexity through trust (Luhmann 1979) does not vanish (e.g., reducing information bases for action among client–provider relations), the threshold of information processing capacity is probably shifted to a higher level due to the demanding smart grid developments. This moves attributions of decision making and being exposed, of intention and blame, as well as of cause and effect into new directions for consumer and business relations with the system.

Trust between organizations in the energy system

In contrast to many other forms of trust, the existence and operation of trust in organizations has almost become a domain that has been taken for granted in trust research (Kramer and Tyler 1996; Lane and Bachmann 1998; Kramer and Cook 2004; Gillespie 2012). This is partly due to the fact that we are dealing with a social address of trust in this case that can even appear as a trustor, not only a trustee – "Trust Within *and* Between Organizations" was in fact the title of a book by Lane and Bachmann (Lane and Bachmann 1998, emphasis added). When one talks about a "system" or about "impersonal" trust, trust in organizations plays a major role in the debate (e.g., Zucker 1986; Shapiro 1987; Benseler et al. 2003; Strulik 2007). In the case of trusting the energy system, for instance, organizations such as regulatory agencies, the government, facility operators, or utilities companies are frequently mentioned (Bellaby, Eames, and Flynn 2010; Greenberg 2014). Apart from the trust relations between the public and such organizations that are often implied, Bellaby, Eames, and Flynn (2010, 2614) allude to an "investigation of trust between producers, distributors and regulators of the energy system." Referring back to the end of the preceding section, we can thus draw the important distinction between trust *in* and *between* organizations in the energy sector: While the first case (*in*) involves public actors either trusting an organization directly or generalizing that experience onto the whole system, the latter (*between*) is reserved to interorganizational, professional relations within the energy system.

Another important addition is the perspective of organizational trustees in gaining trust and confidence from either (individual) public or corporate trustors (compare SEAB 1993; La Porte and Metlay 1996). This view is underrepresented in trust research, which emphasizes how trust is formed, upheld, and altered from the viewpoint of trustors, but which rarely systematically analyzes these conditions for *trustees* such as businesses or regulatory organizations.[10] Without the capacity to fully explore this research field here, we can allude to the necessity of directing attention to the systematic study of trustees. As a result, in this section we are neither limited to trustor perspectives nor to the public realm, which is often characterized by problems of knowledge asymmetries between laypersons and experts. Instead, we move toward the processes within systems: "Trust mechanisms do not relate only to the connections between laypersons and experts: they are also bound up with the activities of those who are 'within' abstract systems" (Giddens 1990, 87).

The actors within the system are predominantly professional organizations, even though the number of (potentially individual) decentralized, private actors is likely to increase in the mid and long term (Ramchurn et al. 2012; Amin and Giacomoni 2012; B.A.U.M. Consult 2012). The trust relationships between these professional organizations, i.e., the "producers, distributors and regulators" (Bellaby, Eames, and Flynn 2010, 2614), are of vital importance for both the social and technical functioning of the energy system. In particular, trust is meaningful between control room operators (e.g., regulators) and producers of energy (e.g., generation facilities and plants) as well as distributing units. Due to the crucial 50 Hertz equilibrium[11] that electricity grids need to maintain stable demand–supply ratios, control rooms rely on accurate information concerning the momentary electricity loads in the grid that are provided by producers and distributors (Döring 2013). Trust that this information is accurate and valid for inferring the necessary technical conclusions is the basis for determining the overall success and rationality of the system and the security of supply. Another, more general case of interorganizational coordination concerns liaison between political and economic organizations about executing the energy transition in the first place. Document study of reports by the government, its agencies, and nonprofit organizations in Germany reveals how delegation of responsibility and disparate temporal horizons between energy sector organizations differ,[12] both of which are decisive factors for building trust/distrust. These two cases – the *social dynamics of control rooms* and the *political-economic coordination between energy organizations* – will be discussed under consideration of the current transition efforts and their consequences for trust.

Social dynamics of control rooms

The approval and coordination patterns between different corporate actors will gain in importance following the transition to smart energy grids. According to Roe and Schulman (2016), knowledge shortages of control room operators are likely to increase:

> What happens when knowledge requirements of an infrastructure's domain of competence are so intensive and demanding that its control operators can't realistically know the other infrastructures they are connected to with the same depth as they know their own systems? Does this mean that there must be a control room of control rooms to address interconnectivity issues related to reliability across systems?
>
> (Roe and Schulman 2016, 61f)

Toward the end of their book, the authors (Roe and Schulman 2016, 156) conclude that the designed reality of novel sociotechnical systems usually results in a stronger reliance on trust instead of certainty, especially with regard to executive management (designers, regulators) and control rooms (operators, producers). This development is very likely attached to the multisectoral design of smart grids, encompassing at least elements of mechanical engineering, digital infrastructure, and patterns of social self-organization (Appelrath, Kagermann, and Mayer 2012; BMWi 2015).

The multitude of sectors, organizations, and action layers in future energy systems leads to a fundamental restructuring in the way both the field and its analysis will and should be organized. In an expert interview,[13] a German energy economist referred to the idea of *subsidiarity* to explain future organizational patterns in the energy sector. In the midst of transitions to smart grids, the future system will be based much more firmly on (real-time) data from clients through smart meters than currently. A central result of the new data-based energy system will be the ensuing question of access, storage, and usage of that data by the different corporate actors involved in the process (European Commission 2015). Who will be responsible for handling all this sensitive consumer data? Will it be the smallest possible unit (i.e., the local utilities company) or perhaps a centralized agency (as the largest possible unit)? This subsidiarity question – i.e., which entity at what level of system scaling (local to federal) will be responsible and conduct access management – has the potential of turning into a major debate in the transition phase and thereafter. With regard to trust, it will be decisive to establish the relevant communication patterns between the countless organizations involved in making secure and smart renewable energy provision a reality. Thus, whether a future control room or a distributing unit will have to request information[14] from data bases at a federal agency or will have direct access to it is another issue situated between certainty (controlling information oneself) and trust (relying on external partners). In any case, the patterns and chains of communication within the system that determine what information is available from and for whom and at what point will regulate the levels of control, reliance, and dependence on others and will therefore react sensitively to the degree of trust and distrust between organizations.

Political-economic coordination between energy organizations

Trust and distrust between organizations also characterize the political landscape steering the energy transition in close coordination with business actors and NGOs. The massive synchronization process between local, regional, state, and federal levels involves countless organizations exerting a stronger or a lesser impact, which offers insight into patterns of trust, suspicion, and control. In the German case, for instance, this means that the federal government (BMWi/BMU 2011; BMWi 2015) creates "the necessary basis in law" for the operation of smart grids, yet delegates the concrete tasks for its execution, such as the definition of standards and interfaces for smart meters, to a subsidiary organization, the *Bundesnetzagentur* (BNetzA), the federal German network agency (BMWi/BMU 2011, 19f). BNetzA, on the other hand, has published a highly recognized paper on distinguishing smart grids from "smart markets" (BNetzA 2011), where a tendency to delegate responsibility to markets is visible: "The energy future requires that participants in the market take greater responsibility and that there is an increase in negotiated solutions. The grid should play rather a serving role and is to be separated from competitive activities as much as possible" (BNetzA 2011, 8; translation PS). The relationship and chains of delegation between the federal government and the BNetzA can be regarded as analogous to those between executive management and control room operators, as another quote from Roe and Schulman illustrates:

> We return then to the key point that large sociotechnical systems cannot be designed to be "damned foolproof" and that highly reliable systems are managed to be reliable beyond design. If they were operated only according to

design, they wouldn't be managed with the resilience needed for reliability. That means designers, be they engineers, policy makers, or senior executives, *must trust and facilitate the skills of control room operators* to add the necessary resilience to the engineered foundations of high reliability. [. . .] this is in no way assured when top-level officials introduce major technological innovations into the real-time operations of infrastructure control rooms.

(Roe and Schulman 2016, 156; emphasis added)

It seems that *en passant* the authors have alluded to trust as the vital resource that makes a division of labor possible, that allows designers and operators to interact, and that guarantees policy makers are able to delegate operative work to an agency specializing in matters of grid control and supervision. Given the increases in complexity in energy systems sketched out in the section on public trust above, one can imagine the rising importance of trust in this facilitation process between decisive organizations in the energy sector to keep the system running according to the set design standards. These standards amplify the role of trust in the energy transition and in future systems. Due to the massive need for coordination and liaison between grid actors ([intra-]political and [intra-]economic), trust becomes a highly valued resource that determines success or failure of the envisioned system design. The smart grid, which provides the foundation for data generation and dissemination between organizations, and the decentralized feed-in of electricity, which needs to be calculated anew at every moment to guarantee grid stability, are two powerful drivers of this development. An absence of trust or an emergence of distrust could exert critical influence on system performance, creating possible vulnerabilities in the social sphere of energy systems. A systematic study of trust between organizations in the energy sector that includes sophisticated theories and methods as well as empirical evidence is thus now appropriate in social science energy research.

This angle of research covers another underappreciated source of influence on interorganizational trust relations, that is, the *time horizon of organizations* in relation to the energy transition goals. In the context of the previous example of the German federal government and the BNetzA, one can find quite distinct ways of dealing with temporality in analyzing the policy papers on the *Energiewende* (BMWi/BMU 2011; BNetzA 2011). While the government envisions long-term goals of supply security and increasing the RES share to 80% by 2050 (BMWi/ BMU 2011, 3ff), the BNetzA displays a rather short- and mid-term perspective by discussing the possibilities of realizing smart markets under the current legal framework (BNetzA 2011, 9; 46f). While the BNetzA by no means ignores long-term visions, it applies a much more careful step-by-step approach that emphasizes the means of realization and the foundations of the technoeconomic system. In this way, both organizations create their own "system-internal time" (Luhmann 1995, 309) that affects their degree of concretization (government: rather low; BNetzA: rather high) of possible actions and the radius of anticipation. By projecting rather generalized goals for RES and the climate in a distant future, the German federal government follows a political rationality of bold yet abstract visions which can be achieved one way or the other, by embracing certain values or others, by adopting certain policies and measures or others, and so on. The BNetzA, on the other hand, as an administrative body, formulates expectations that are much more grounded in the past and present (legal framework, the way that the system used to be operated, and how it operates now) and only dares to look into the horizon of the immediate future.[15]

The synchronization of these differing time horizons as central variables controlling the way such organizations operate is a challenge for social science researchers on energy. As a trust researcher, the connection to temporality and expectations is significant because trust can be described as "maintaining a state of *favourable expectation* toward the actions and intentions of more or less specific others" (Möllering 2006b, 356; emphasis added). In the words of Lewis and Weigert, "[t]rust exists in a social system insofar as the members of that system act according to and are secure in *the expected futures* constituted by the presence of each other or their symbolic representations" (Lewis and Weigert 1985, 968; emphasis added).

As a consequence, the hypothesis that trust and distrust between these organizations are of special significance given that *in concert* they realize what we call the "energy transition" is not far-fetched. On the contrary, trust's function can yet again be discovered in securing the synchronization of "expected futures" (Lewis and Weigert 1985, 968) between relevant actors in the field. This harmonization of expectations in the form of the development of trust/distrust takes place in every other present, thus enabling actionability or forms of paralysis among stakeholders. The systemic process of collective management between the numerous organizations involved in the *Energiewende* has long been treated with conventional wisdom rather than with social science expertise, which is why a perspective of organizational trust could be beneficial for its analysis. Ultimately, the aim would be to analyze trust/distrust equilibria in order to avoid system breakdowns and crises as early as possible, along with the frequently cited "complexity trap" (Appelrath, Kagermann, and Mayer 2012). The emergence of trust and distrust in systems can be interpreted as being either positive or negative: While trust's negative counterpart can be entitled *blind trust* or *overconfidence*, distrust's positive part is a *healthy suspicion*, potentially uncovering flaws in the distrusted object. As a consequence, the analysis should not focus on "appropriate" trust or distrust, but on a systemic management of both resources, functioning as a sort of sensor instrument that detects the "social system condition" in terms of actors' action capacity and the direction it is taking. Its scope would be a clearer analysis of the perspectives of organizational actors relating to expectation trajectories and time horizons. Such an analysis could complement "roadmap" (e.g., BDEW 2013) or "scenario" (e.g., Appelrath, Kagermann, and Mayer 2012) concepts for energy transitions, for instance, which are frequent reference points in the discourse yet partly lack integration of sophisticated social science concepts.

Transsystemic trust: politics and the energy economy

The concept of "transsystemic trust" (Strulik 2011, 247) is a rather abstract concept whose full power can only be unfolded by conducting an empirical-practical substantiation. Apart from individuals or organizations awarding trust or being trusted, transsystemic trust refers to functional systems at the societal level (like politics or the economy) as possible trustors and trustees. To some degree, Bellaby, Eames, and Flynn (2010, 2614; emphasis added) seem to have alluded to this form of trust in mentioning "the *high level issue of trust* between states that must be party to agreements involving global energy futures." Although "states" could be interpreted as organizations, they also represent the political system and refer to a more abstract level of social reality than does, for instance, "the government." With regard to global finance and the latest crises, Strulik (2011, 247) has observed an emergent level of "transsystemic trust constitution" above the regular level of system trust that is related to the development of mutual expectations between social systems and their fulfillment or disappointment. From a theoretical point of view, we thus move from trusting a system and finding trust within systems to identifying *trust between systems*.

Strictly speaking, interorganizational trust can be interpreted as trust between (organizational) systems as well, which is why transsystemic trust is limited to the more abstract level of functional systems of society such as politics, the economy, or science (Strulik 2011, 247f). In the case of the financial crises around 2008, for instance, the guarantees that states announced to support system-relevant actors like banks or hedge funds in the financial sector confirmed the expectation that it is safe to conduct risky behavior in the financial system (Strulik 2011, 247f). This system trust of the economy in itself that is reinforced through its trust in the political system (e.g., the support for potentially failing businesses) is such an example of *transsystemically* formed trust, i.e., mutual expectation management between societal systems that leads to trust/distrust in each other and eventually in themselves and their own affirmation of actions. It also contains a reference to the mechanism of "trust intermediation" (Coleman 1990, 188ff; Strulik 2011, 247), in this case conducted through politics as a moderator for economic system trust.

Transsystemic forms of trust can similarly be found in the energy field. Schweer and Siebertz-Reckzeh (2014, 231f), for instance, discover that "an example for a transsystemic action context would be the so-called energy transition, a relatively abstract construct which, by including different interests and inventories of knowledge and expertise, does not allow for an overview of all actions of each individual protagonist." In their view, accordingly, "the transsystemic level now resorts to complex action contexts, that make it nearly impossible to relate trust to specific individuals or systems" (Schweer and Siebertz-Reckzeh 2014, 231). By integrating Strulik's concept into their own, differing framework, the authors do not directly consider transsystemic trust as an "emergent form of trust" (Strulik 2011, 248). Yet their approach illustrates the usefulness and appeal of the concept in particular with reference to the example of energy, concluding that "the consideration of a transsystemic component in addition to the personal and systemic components of trust is increasingly necessary" (Schweer and Siebertz-Reckzeh 2014, 239).

In the original vein of Strulik's idea, however, it is possible to find first hints of emergent, transsystemic trust-building with regard to the relationship between politics and the energy economy. In interviews with German experts on the challenges facing the future energy system, an *insurance-based* system logic was mentioned.[16] This insurance is related to the necessity of maintaining backup electricity capacities in the face of potential RES shortages due to their volatile patterns of generation (e.g., wind or solar). In contrast to the current state, where generation can be more or less centrally controlled, an insurance-based system would alter the trust relations between politics and the energy economy dramatically. In order to guarantee system safety and continuous energy provision, public agencies will have to organize sufficient reserve capacities of electricity generation for emergency situations. Since this cannot be done by the agencies themselves (BMWi 2015), economic actors are required to provide these capacities for the state. Even for the "normal operation" mode of the future system, mechanisms such as "capacity markets" (Bhagwat, de Vries, and Hobbs 2016) are being discussed as a tool for the internal economic allocation of electricity loads, where they are needed in order to guarantee the security of supply (SoS) in a volatile, RES-based system. These coordination patterns between the political and the economic systems allude to transsystemic trust relations. Politics trusts the economy that sufficient capacity shifting and reservation is executed to (1) secure everyday functioning of markets and (2) provide the necessary backup capacities the state needs to exert grid control in cases of bottlenecks/power outages in order to fulfill its role as guarantor of SoS (BMWi 2015). In return, the energy economy trusts that a certain legal framework will be upheld by the political system in order to solidify investment expectations (BDEW 2013). In both cases, services are provided that neither one can produce on their own yet crucially depend on to fulfill an overarching purpose (provision of electricity). In the future of energy supply, this trust relationship will be more delicate than in the past since the normal and emergency modes of functioning of the energy system potentially rely on it.

Finally, I want to stress the latter aspect. Many assumptions regarding the actual deployment of capacity markets and reserve capacities have not yet been fully determined, so that definite statements cannot be made at this point. Still, a promising angle of research was presented that allows for transsystemic analysis by emphasizing the nature of political-economic relations from a *systemic* point of view, in contrast to an *organizational* point of view that was introduced in the preceding section. On the one hand, the system and level of organization interact in that organizations appear as attribution points for trust or even congruent representatives of systems (like "the government" for politics or an association or dominant company for "the economy"). This is inevitable insofar as organizations embody the only addressable system components (besides persons) since they have communication capacity (Luhmann 2012, 145) – an important function for the sanctioning of trust. Still, on the other hand, functional systems of society form their own emergent reality – also for the purpose of trust-building – that is uncoupled from individual/organizational attributions in that functional systems form a background horizon for communication processes within and between them, which allows actors to ascribe action capacity to systems as well (Sumpf 2017). In empirical reality, this occurs when we speak of delegating responsibility to "the political system" or to "science" as collective contexts without clarifying the exact personal or organizational address. These attributions have consequences for the social process and the continuation of communication and are therefore no less valid than attributions to entities with communication capacity such as persons or organizations. For the study of energy transitions and future system conditions, this avenue of research is worth further illumination.

Conclusion

Trust in the energy system is relevant in three varieties: public trust in the energy system, trust between organizations, and transsystemic trust. Trust unfolds its cohesive power at three levels of the system, namely as trustee, within the system, and between different social systems, by letting consumers make decisions, by bringing energy organizations together, and by mediating relations between the energy economy and politics. In all three realms, trust creates the ties that are necessary to keep the system running, a circumstance whose importance is increasing under the current changes to low-carbon transitions and smart grids. Trust lets people act with the system, lets organizations rely on each other in complex information networks, and lets systems build up favorable expectations under the impression that the trustee will provide services they cannot generate by themselves. Due to rising system complexity and ensuing coordination requirements, energy actors are prone to lack either time or ability to scrutinize system processes on their own, which implies that knowledge is increasingly replaced by trust in the presumed knowledge of others. Given this likely acceleration of trust operations, we should expect that the future energy system and its client relations will rely more on trust than the current one and that this will affect all three systemic trust domains. In consequence, this lets the "dark side" of trust emerge (Skinner, Dietz, and Weibel 2013) because a lack of knowledge or control always bears the risk of disappointment. Besides forging cooperation, the inherent trait of trust is risk (Strulik 2011), which is most powerful where large amounts of trust are invested, as in smart grid constellations. The less this trust is backed by verified knowledge, the greater the risk that is looming in the background as the flipside of the trust that is given. In order to exploit the full potential of trust as a moderating resource in this process, its reflection as distrust (as healthy suspicion) should be included. An answer to these current challenges could take the form of intelligent, systematic trust management that takes the distribution of both trust and distrust into consideration and that consequently can serve as a social sensor mechanism for policy makers, business, and academia. It could provide the data necessary to analyze both system trust and the energy transition in its overarching, societal framework.

Notes

1 See von Schomberg 2013.
2 Personally conducted interview with an energy economist from a German university department (2013). The economist said that energy-intensive German companies contemplate building their own power plants out of distrust toward the German energy policy. The interview was conducted as part of the project "Systemic Risks in Energy Infrastructures" of the Helmholtz-Alliance Energy-Trans.
3 To say that the reliance on trust is growing is not a normative statement that favors trust over distrust, for instance. What it means is to stress that relations of trust are going to have a much more decisive function in future energy systems than is the case today since trust can be the enabler of new business models – as distrust could be their obstacle. Intuitively, one could mention trust in the safety of nuclear power plants in earlier energy systems as a trust issue of similar relevance. Yet this sort of trust–distrust connection of consumers to the system was (a) usually limited to once-in-a-lifetime decisions toward accepting–opposing a generating technology, (b) affected a limited number of people suspicious of the technology, and (c) did not directly influence system operations. One can ask what effect on the energy system and its processes the protests of a certain part of the population had besides creating political resonance. The smart grid, in contrast, connects consumer actions directly to system operations (compare Büscher and Sumpf 2015).
4 See the contribution by Christian Büscher in this book.
5 "Something is contingent insofar as it is neither necessary nor impossible; it is just what it is (or was or will be), though it could also be otherwise" (Luhmann 1995, 106).
6 This applies to systems through *attributions* of contingency, either by actors with communication capacity who represent the system (persons, groups, organizations) or by an attribution of action capacity to the system as such. See the section about trans-systemic trust above for further details.
7 See the contribution by Christian Büscher in this book for further insights on how social processes are separate from technical processes in this respect.
8 See the contribution by Todd R. La Porte in this book.
9 Personally conducted interview with a renewable energy expert from an environmental association (2013); translation PS. The interview was conducted as part of the project "Systemic Risks in Energy Infrastructures" of the Helmholtz-Alliance Energy-Trans.
10 This is of course different in the practical world, where public relations agencies try hard to establish the good reputation and trustworthiness of organizations. Yet from a theoretical point of view, especially highlighting system trust, this perspective has not received much attention, in particular when overarching issues like societal stability or system functioning are targeted (as in SEAB 1993, for instance).
11 Electricity systems rely on a stability of these frequencies – like 50 hertz in Europe or 60 hertz in the US (Neidhöfer 2011) – in order to secure grid functions and avoid bottlenecks and outages. These can occur through an imbalance in demand and supply, e.g., through a surplus of electricity generation. In the German grid, experts speak of the "50.2 Hz problem" when the frequency increases to 50.2 Hz and parts of the supply that caused the increase (e.g., growing photovoltaic capacities) are shut down, causing potential power failures (Döring 2013).
12 Thanks to Neo Khala for some valuable hints in this regard.
13 Personally conducted interview with an energy economist from a German university department (2013). The interview was conducted as part of the project "Systemic Risks in Energy Infrastructures" of the Helmholtz-Alliance Energy-Trans.
14 This information is ultimately used for balancing the demand–supply equilibrium in the grid as described above and therefore serves the security of supply.

15 The list of organizations and their time horizons in the energy sector could be lengthened, for instance, by including associations, interest groups, and nonprofits, which can also be shown to deal very differently with time. A noteworthy perspective is that of the German Association of Energy and Water Industries (BDEW), which formulates a *conditional program* of operation: Implementation of smart grids can only be targeted and potentially realized if the goals of the energy transition are translated into cost–benefit schemes (BDEW 2013).

16 Personally conducted interview with an energy economist from a German university department (2013). The interview was conducted as part of the project "Systemic Risks in Energy Infrastructures" of the Helmholtz-Alliance Energy-Trans.

References

Amin, S. Massoud, and Anthony M. Giacomoni. 2012. "Smart Grid – Safe, Secure, Self-Healing: Challenges and Opportunities in Power System Security, Resiliency, and Privacy." *IEEE Power & Energy Magazine* 10: 33–40.

Appelrath, Hans-Jürgen, Henning Kagermann, and Christoph Mayer, eds. 2012. *Future Energy Grid. Migration to the Internet of Energy. Acatech STUDY.* Munich.

Barber, Bernard. 1983. *The Logic and Limits of Trust.* New Brunswick: Rutgers University Press.

B.A.U.M. Consult, ed. 2012. *Smart Energy Made in Germany. Interim Results of the E-Energy Pilot Projects towards the Internet of Energy.* Munich, Berlin.

BDEW. 2013. "BDEW Roadmap – Realistic Steps for the Implementation of Smart Grids in Germany." German Association of Energy and Water Industries. www.bdew.de/media/documents/Pub_20130211_Roadmap-Smart-Grids_english.pdf. Accessed 2018/08/01

Bellaby, Paul, Malcolm Eames, and Rob Flynn. 2010. "The Role of 'trust' in the Transition to Sustainable Energy." *Energy Policy*, The Role of Trust in Managing Uncertainties in the Transition to a Sustainable Energy Economy, Special Section with Regular Papers, 38 (6) (June): 2613–14. https://doi.org/10.1016/j.enpol.2009.03.066.

Benseler, Frank, Bettina Blanck, Reinhard Keil, and Werner Loh, eds. 2003. "Deliberation, Knowledge, Ethics – Forum for Deliberative Culture (Erwägen, Wissen, Ethik)" 14 (2): 323–90.

Bhagwat, Pradyumna C., Laurens J. de Vries, and Benjamin F. Hobbs. 2016. "Expert Survey on Capacity Markets in the US: Lessons for the EU." *Utilities Policy* 38 (February): 11–17. https://doi.org/10.1016/j.jup.2015.11.005.

BMWi. 2015. "Baustein für die Energiewende: 7 Eckpunkte für das 'Verordnungspaket Intelligente Netze.'" Berlin: Bundesministerium für Wirtschaft und Energie.

BMWi/BMU. 2011. "The Federal Government's Energy Concept of 2010 and the Transformation of the Energy System of 2011." Berlin: German Federal Ministry of Economics and Technology; Federal Ministry for the Environment, Nature Conservation and Nuclear Safety.

BNetzA. 2011. *'Smart Grid' und 'Smart Market'. Eckpunktepapier der Bundesnetzagentur zu den Aspekten des sich ändernden Energieversorgungssystems.* Bonn: Bundesnetzagentur.

Büscher, Christian, and Patrick Sumpf. 2015. "'Trust' and 'Confidence' as Socio-Technical Problems in the Transformation of Energy Systems." *Energy, Sustainability and Society* 5:34: 1–13. https://doi.org/doi:10.1186/s13705-015-0063-7.

Coleman, James S. 1990. *Foundations of Social Theory.* Cambridge: Harvard University Press.

Depuru, Soma S. S. R., Lingfeng Wang, and Vijay Devabhaktuni. 2011. "Smart Meters for Power Grid: Challenges, Issues, Advantages and Status." *Renewable and Sustainable Energy Reviews* 15 (6): 2736–42.

Döring, Michael. 2013. "Dealing with the 50.2 Hz Problem." Modern Power Systems.Com. 2013. www.modernpowersystems.com/features/featuredealing-with-the-50.2-hz-problem/. Accessed 2018/05/07.

Edwards, Paul N. 2004. "Infrastructure and Modernity: Force, Time, and Social Organization in the History of Socio-Technical Systems." In *Modernity and Technology*, edited by Thomas J. Misa, P. Brey, and A. Feenberg, 185–225. Cambridge, MA; London: MIT Press.

European Commission. 2015. "Delivering a New Deal for Energy Consumers." Brussels: COMMUNICATION [COM(2015) 339] FROM THE COMMISSION TO THE EUROPEAN PARLIAMENT, THE COUNCIL, THE EUROPEAN ECONOMIC AND SOCIAL COMMITTEE AND THE COMMITTEE OF THE REGIONS.

Giddens, Anthony. 1990. *The Consequences of Modernity*. Stanford: Stanford University Press.

Gillespie, Nicole. 2012. "Measuring Trust in Organizational Contexts: An Overview of Survey-Based Measures." In *Handbook of Research Methods on Trust*, edited by Fergus Lyon, Guido Möllering, and Mark Saunders, 175–88. Cheltenham: Edward Elgar Publishing.

Greenberg, Michael R. 2014. "Energy Policy and Research: The Underappreciation of Trust." *Energy Research & Social Science* 1 (March): 152–60. https://doi.org/10.1016/j.erss.2014.02.004.

JRC. 2011. "Smart Grid Projects in Europe: Lessons Learned and Current Developments." Petten: European Commission – Joint Research Centre – Institute for Energy. https://ses.jrc.ec.europa.eu/sites/ses.jrc.ec.europa.eu/files/publications/smart_grid_projects_in_europe_lessons_learned_and_current_developments.pdf. Accessed 2018/08/01.

Kasperson, Roger E., and Bonnie J. Ram. 2013. "The Public Acceptance of New Energy Technologies." *Daedalus* 142 (1): 90–96. https://doi.org/10.1162/DAED_a_00187.

Khala, Neo, Patrick Sumpf, and Christian Büscher. 2014. "'Wir sind das Smart Grid' – Zu einer aktuellen Debatte unter InformatikerInnen." *Technikfolgenabschätzung – Theorie und Praxis* 23 (3): 118–21.

König, René, and Patrick Sumpf. 2018. "Hat der Nutzer immer Recht? Zum inflationären Rückgriff auf Vertrauen im Kontext von Online-Plattformen." *Soziale Welt, Sonderband "Digitale Soziologie"* (forthcoming).

Kramer, Roderick M., and Karen S. Cook eds. 2004. *Trust and Distrust in Organizations – Dilemmas and Approaches*. Russell Sage Foundation Series of Trust. New York: Russell Sage Foundation.

Kramer, Roderick M., and Tom R. Tyler eds. 1996. *Trust in Organizations: Frontiers of Theory and Research*. Thousand Oaks, CA: SAGE Publications Ltd.

La Porte, Todd R., and Daniel S. Metlay. 1996. "Hazards and Institutional Trustworthiness: Facing a Deficit of Trust." *Public Administration Review* 56 (4): 341–47. https://doi.org/10.2307/976375.

Lane, Christel, and Reinhard Bachmann eds. 1998. *Trust Within and Between Organizations: Conceptual Issues and Empirical Applications*. Oxford: Oxford University Press.

Lewis, J. David, and Andrew Weigert. 1985. "Trust as a Social Reality." *Social Forces* 63 (4) (January): 967–85. https://doi.org/10.1093/sf/63.4.967.

Luhmann, Niklas. 1968. *Vertrauen. Ein Mechanismus der Reduktion sozialer Komplexität.* Stuttgart: Enke Verlag.

———. 1979. *Trust and Power*. Chichester: Wiley.

———. 1995. *Social Systems*. Stanford: Stanford University Press.

———. 2012. *Theory of Society, Volume 1*. Stanford: Stanford University Press.

Lumineau, Fabrice. 2017. "How Contracts Influence Trust and Distrust." *Journal of Management* 43 (5): 1553–77. https://doi.org/10.1177/0149206314556656.

Misztal, Barbara. 1996. *Trust in Modern Societies: The Search for the Bases of Social Order*. Chichester: Wiley.

Möllering, Guido. 2006a. "Trust, Institutions, Agency: Towards a Neoinstitutional Theory of Trust." In *Handbook of Trust Research*, edited by Reinhard Bachmann and Akbar Zaheer. Cheltenham: Edward Elgar.

———. 2006b. *Trust: Reason, Routine, Reflexivity*. Amsterdam: Emerald Group Publishing.

Neidhöfer, Gerhard. 2011. "50-Hz Frequency. How the Standard Emerged from a European Jumble." *IEEE Power and Energy Magazine* 9 (4): 66–81. https://doi.org/10.1109/MPE.2011.941165.

Parsons, Talcott. 1964. *The Social System*. New York: The Free Press/Macmillan.

Ramchurn, Sarvapali D., Perukrishnen Vytelingum, Alex Rogers, and Nicholas R. Jennings. 2012. "Putting the 'Smarts' into the Smart Grid: A Grand Challenge for Artificial Intelligence." *Communications of the ACM* 55: 86–97. https://doi.org/10.1145/2133806.2133825.

Roe, Emery, and Paul R. Schulman. 2016. *Reliability and Risk: The Challenge of Managing Interconnected Infrastructures*. Stanford: Stanford University Press.

Schubert, Daniel Kurt Josef, Thomas Meyer, and Dominik Möst. 2015. "Die Transformation des deutschen Energiesystems aus der Perspektive der Bevölkerung." *Zeitschrift für Energiewirtschaft* 39 (1): 49–61. https://doi.org/10.1007/s12398-015-0146-3.

Schweer, Martin, and Karin Siebertz-Reckzeh. 2014. "Personal, Systemic and Transsystemic Trust: Individual and Collective Resources for Coping with Societal Challenges." In *Mindful Change in Times of Permanent Reorganization*, edited by Guido Becke, 225–43. Berlin, Heidelberg: Springer.

SEAB. 1993. "Earning Public Trust and Confidence: Requisites for Managing Radioactive Wastes." Final Report of the Secretary of Energy Advisory Board (SEAB) Task Force on Radioactive Waste Management. Washington, DC: U.S. Department of Energy, Secretary of Energy Advisory Board (SEAB).

Shapiro, Susan P. 1987. "The Social Control of Impersonal Trust." *American Journal of Sociology* 93 (3): 623–58. https://doi.org/10.1086/228791.

Shove, Elizabeth, and Alan Warde. 1998. "Inconspicuous Consumption: The Sociology of Consumption and the Environment." Published by the Department of Sociology, Lancaster University. www.comp.lancs.ac.uk/sociology/papers/Shove-Warde-Inconspicuous-Consumption.pdf.

Simmel, Georg. 1978. *The Philosophy of Money*. Boston, MA: Routledge & Kegan Paul.

Skinner, Denise, Graham Dietz, and Antoinette Weibel. 2013. "The Dark Side of Trust: When Trust Becomes a 'Poisoned Chalice.'" *Organization* 21 (2): 206–24. https://doi.org/10.1177/1350508412473866.

Strulik, Torsten. 2007. "Rating Agencies, Ignorance and the Knowledge-Based Production of System Trust." In *Towards a Cognitive Mode in Global Finance. The Governance of a Knowledge-Based Financial System*, edited by Torsten Strulik and Helmut Willke, 239–55. Frankfurt, New York: Campus.

———. 2011. "Vertrauen. Ein Ferment gesellschaftlicher Risikoproduktion." *Deliberation, Knowledge, Ethics – Forum for Deliberative Culture (Erwägen, Wissen, Ethik)* 22 (2): 239–51.

Sumpf, Patrick. 2013. "Mechanismen der Vertrauens(de)konstitution in öffentlichen Krisen – Das Beispiel EHEC O104:H4." In *Medien müssen draußen bleiben! Wo liegen die Grenzen politischer Transparenz?*, 217–35. Beiträge zur 8. Fachtagung des DFPK. Düsseldorf, 12.-14.04.2012. Berlin: Frank & Timme.

———. 2017. *System Trust – Identity, Expectation, Reassurance. With a Case Study on Trusting the Energy System*. Mannheim: PhD Thesis, University of Mannheim.

Todt, Oliver. 2011. "The Limits of Policy: Public Acceptance and the Reform of Science and Technology Governance." *Technological Forecasting and Social Change* 78 (6): 902–9. https://doi.org/10.1016/j.techfore.2011.02.007.

von Schomberg, Rene. 2013. "A Vision of Responsible Research and Innovation." In *Responsible Innovation: Managing the Responsible Emergence of Science and Innovation in Society*, edited by Richard Owen, John Bessant, and Maggy Heintz, 51–74. London: Wiley.

ZfK. 2015. "Chancen und Risiken des Smart-Meter-Gateway-Admins." *ZfK – Zeitung für kommunale Wirtschaft* 3 (2015) (March): 4.

Zucker, Lynne G. 1986. "Production of Trust: Institutional Sources of Economic Structure, 1840 to 1920." In *Research in Organizational Behavior*, edited by L.L. Cummings and Barry M. Staw, Vol. 8: 53–111. Greenwich, CT: JAI Press.

10 Shaping our energy future

The irreducible entanglement of the ethical, social, and technical realms

Rafaela Hillerbrand

Introduction

Sustainability in general is often criticized as being too broad and too imprecise a concept, permitting various different technical and social trajectories to qualify as being sustainable. With regard to the transition to a sustainable *energy* future, in contrast, there is an overwhelming consensus as to what transition amounts to, namely that renewables play a central role. And this consensus steers national policies. Driven by climate action and a limited amount of fossil fuel, most Western countries are currently enforcing a transition to more sustainable energy systems by increasing the share of energy generated from renewable sources. The European Commission (European Commission 2016), for example, aims for 27% of EU energy consumption to come from renewables in 2030. While the estimates regarding how far or on what time scale a transition to renewable energy is feasible may vary drastically,[1] the goal is largely uncontested.

Renewables, however, come with certain problems. For example, they are often accompanied by distributed and intermittent generation, i.e., electricity is generated in multiple places and only at certain times such as when the sun is shining or wind is available. This is in stark contrast to the centralized generation of electricity in the past and thus has an enormous impact on multiple aspects of the energy system. As a paradigmatic example of a sociotechnical system, the transformation of the supply and distribution side is accompanied by enormous changes on the demand-side as well. For a greener future, traditional petroleum fuels are being increasingly replaced by the use of electricity in decentralized applications like cars. All these transitions in the energy sector come with enormous challenges. Even today the increased share of renewables raises demands for new technological capacity, triggers new business models, and transforms funds (within a society or abroad). New regulatory frameworks are called for.

Following this line of reasoning, classic and now dated technological determinism has been superseded by the more complex and arguably empirically more adequate notion of the sociotechnical system. Humans are seen as an essential part and (co-)determine technological development paths in an essential way. However, putting the regulatory and thus the normative analysis at the end of a complex technical and social development threatens to undermine agency. Decision makers in government or industry would only have the possibility of reacting instead of acting, of responding arguably in multiple ways, but there is no room to genuinely shape and design our energy future. And even worse, putting the regulatory framework at the end of the process of complex sociotechnical development threatens to undermine real agency.

This chapter argues that normative analysis needs to be the starting point of a transition toward a more sustainable energy future. This implies first a need for the regulatory framework to (partially) precede the technological and societal developments so that the future paths of the latter are (partially) the result of conscious choice. (This chapter only discusses parts of the ethical aspect of such conscious decisions.) And second it means to realize that the straightforward equation of "sustainable" with "renewable" in the context of energy may be premature. At first glance the normative considerations raised in this chapter may seem to introduce more complexity into the decision-making process on already complex sociotechnical systems; but the contrary is actually true. Spelling out the normative underpinnings of the envisaged energy utopia, for example, an all-renewable generation of electricity, reduces some of the opaqueness of today's energy decision making. Among other things, normative assumptions that are usually implicit are made explicit and thus are opened for discussion, a necessary pre-prerequisite for (re-)gaining agency in complex sociotechnical systems. This contribution aims to spell out a suitable normative framework that could guide today's decision making in Western countries.

I contend that in the energy context the term "sustainability" is not yet specified well enough. In particular I will show that descriptive and evaluative elements are inseparably intertwined in a sustainability analysis. Consequently the normative underpinnings also need to be addressed, while today's discourse on sustainable energy mostly focuses on descriptive aspects. Recent social science studies seem to support this as they show that opposition to the siting of large-scale technological artifacts is fueled in part by a (perceived) inadequate acknowledgment of procedural values. The suggested normative framework for sustainability assessment aims to integrate this factor. I depict the capability approach as an ethical framework that as such, in my understanding, is necessarily to some degree paternalistic, which is compatible with the value pluralism we hold dear in modern liberal societies. In particular the capability approach is an individualist though intersubjective framework. With its help the concept of sustainability – which is commonly defined in aggregate terms only – is reinterpreted as a concept for individuals. For the sake of argument, this contribution focuses on human individuals only. I hold that the individualist footing of sustainability which the capability approach offers may help us to overcome certain motivational restraints keeping individuals from fostering a more sustainable energy future. While the third section adumbrates the capability approach as a theoretical framework, the fourth section indicates how the capability approach reduces the opacity of complex sociotechnical energy systems for the individual and how it can be used to address the topic of value uncertainty that poses a particular problem for future ethics as we can never be sure as to what future generations indeed want. The contribution concludes with a summary.

Sustainability as a concurrently normative and descriptive concept

Sustainability: the modern knighthood?

The very term "sustainability" contains both a descriptive and an evaluative element (Hillerbrand 2015; Hillerbrand and Goldammer 2018). One type of technology may score better than another with respect to certain sustainability indicators. This is a question of empirical analysis, a statement about the world and about the technology under consideration. But the statement "this technology is more sustainable" is also an appreciation, saying that more sustainable technologies are the way to go. Sustainability is meant to be good in a moral sense. Saying that something is "sustainable" entails a normative evaluation.

Sustainable thus lets us recall terms such as "brave," which we know from classical ethical analysis. Also in saying "This was a brave act," we say something about the world, that the act was in a way particular, for example when the knight risked his own life in order to save the king, and at the same time we express that this behavior is good in a normative sense. Knights were to act bravely; today we are to consume sustainably. Just the same as braveness, sustainability is thus a so-called *thick concept*, i.e., one that contains evaluative as well as descriptive elements (McDowell 2001; Williams 1985). Sustainability is a hybrid concept that is very different from a thin ethical concept such as (morally) "good" that just expresses an evaluation only. And it is also very different from mere descriptive terms that say something about the world without any evaluation as to whether something is good or not, like "high-energy density," "soft," or "blue." When referring to a technology as sustainable, speakers do not merely express their evaluation, i.e., their evaluation that in certain aspects this is a "good" technology, but also make a descriptive claim, for example that this energy technology is CO_2 neutral. The descriptive claim can be true or false in a rather straightforward way. The ethical part is more difficult to evaluate. Yet, as the very notion of thick concept highlights, the two go hand in hand and are inseparably intertwined.

While the empirical basis of sustainability analysis receives quite some attention, the evaluative basis has been much less investigated. The latter however (co-)determines the descriptive aspects of sustainability that give rise to measurable indicator sets. The desirability of the transition toward more renewable energy is hardly disputed, nor do I want to dispute it in this chapter. What I aim at is to spell out its normative assumptions. What exactly our sustainable energy future looks like and how exactly the transition should be accomplished will differ significantly for the different value bases.

Though there has been a significant refinement of the indicator sets used for sustainable energy since the Brundtland report, which still sets the agenda for our

modern thinking about sustainability, the normative basis of sustainability analysis is often not addressed, particularly when specific areas of application of sustainability analysis are being considered, such as the *area* of energy. One example
for sustainability assessment in the energy realm is the EISD, the energy indicator
set for sustainable development, from the IAEA (2005). Similar to many other
indicator sets, it is based on the three-pillar view of sustainability that famously
distinguishes an economic, an environmental, and a societal pillar of sustainability. The IAEA report claims that "good health, high living standards, a sustainable economy and a clean environment" are the most important ethical values to
consider in the discussion of sustainable energy supply. On this basis, the IAEA
identified various themes within the social, economic, and ecological domain,
such as "equity" in the first one. Then various subthemes, like "accessibility" and
"affordability" for equity, were identified, and these were then translated into
measurable indicators. For example "share of household income spent on fuel
and electricity" is used to measure affordability. In this way, the report provides
30 indicators for sustainability based on these ethical values, which are classified
into three dimensions corresponding to the three pillars of sustainability.

Though the EISD provides an excellent proxy for the sustainability of energy
conversions, it gives raise to various critiques. A very fundamental critique challenges the use of the three-pillar concept. Though these three are certainly
important themes, the focus on them as standing next to each other seems rather
arbitrary. Why is there a separate economic pillar? Are economic aspects not just
one, though very important aspect of the broader social area? Integrative sustainability concepts (Scott Cato 2009; Ott and Döring 2011; Bräutigam et al. 2015)
are an answer to these concerns. The proposition in the following sections that
the capability approach be used as a normative framework for sustainability is
not to be understood as yet another integrative sustainability concept, though it
of course shares the integrative approach. It rather addresses the preceding questions regarding normative nature. As such the proposed individualist foundation
of sustainable energy in the capability approach is an individualist development
of integrative concepts, but it is also a substantial concession.

Feasibility of ethical guidance in the light of an individual's preferences

Given the broad consensus in many Western countries on the necessity and direction of the transition toward a system utilizing more sustainable energy, namely
renewable production, the local opposition to renewable energy technologies
such as wind or hydro seems all the more astonishing and in the need of explanation. The so-called NIMBY (not in my backyard) account is often said to provide
such an explanation: People support renewable energies in principle, but when it
comes to citing issues they oppose it in their own neighborhood. Viewed in this
way, local opposition resembles very much the other social dilemmas we face in
the light of environmental issues, such as the prisoner's dilemma or the tragedy of
the commons. The question as to how to achieve sustainability is then a question
as to how to change the incentive structures in such a way that the individually
rational behavior of the utility-maximizing egoists who live in the vicinity of a

planned wind park, say, is aligned with collectively rational, i.e., ecologically sound behavior (Gardiner 2010). Institutions may play a central and important role (Ostrom 2015). Hence a large body of literature from different fields has emerged over the last decades that discusses the role of social, legal, political, or constitutional institutions in order to achieve sustainable behavior (Dovers 2001). Next to institutions that foster the right kind of individual behavior, corporate sustainability has also received quite some attention from management and organizational scholars (Montiel and Delgado-Ceballos 2014).

As diverse as these approaches are, all take an (often implicitly) top-down stance on sustainability. Individuals are seen as being in need of special guidance, nudges, or even stronger incentives to "behave" in a sustainable way.[2] Particularly the negative impact of an increasing energy consumption, including the associated environmental consequences, prompts authors of global energy studies to call for countermeasures that severely impede an individual's autonomy. Not only a feature such as a second car may come under fire; there is also a call for reducing expenditures on material goods quite generally or even for reducing birth rates, – since fewer people mean a smaller human impact on the planet. For example, the latest report to the Club of Rome in 2012 stresses China's ability to reach sustainable production and consumption because of its ability to address the population challenge (Randers 2012). This in turn is linked to China's Confucian tradition, which is reflected in meritocracy and centralized government, and is often contrasted with the alleged inability of democratic societies to react quickly to environmental problems.

Today, unlike at the beginning and in the middle of the twentieth century when considerations of eugenic health were popular, not only in Nazi Germany, decisions about the number of one's offspring are often seen as sacrosanct to institutional intervention, and quite rightly so. If realizing a sustainable energy future were to necessitate interventions into otherwise very private decisions like purchasing behavior or even choosing the number of your offspring, then we would have to carefully balance sustainability against other ethical values, such as democratic participation. As I want to argue in the following, this conflict is a result of a sustainability concept that is formulated on the aggregate level only. Following (Hillerbrand and Goldammer 2018) an individualist basis for the concept of sustainability will be formulated that alleviates this conflict.

The non-NIMBY phenomenon

The analysis in the following sections provides a conceptual philosophical analysis. In this section, however, I for now want to turn again to the social sciences and recent research that seems to hint at a way out of this dilemma between sustainability and other values in the social realm. Despite the popularity of the NIMBY explanation among policy makers, media, industry, and many scholars alike, over the past decade or so in-depth social science studies have revealed a rather different reality. Instead of venting egoistic preferences, local opposition articulates preferences that are not (solely) egoistic and often raise legitimate concerns about the decision-making process. Basta (2014), for example, investigates the local opposition against CO_2 storage in Barendrecht, Netherlands. She concludes that approaching any siting controversy as a NIMBY (not-in-my-backyard) case is not only incorrect but also dangerously instrumental. She interprets local opposition rather as an expression and reflection of nonexplicit, but retraceable, underlying ethical theories. Just like other literature on siting issues (cf. Oosterlaken 2015 for a review on the siting of wind parks), her study highlights the frequent perception of the local opposition that there has been negligence of procedural values such as transparency or procedural justice. Opposition to siting issues therefore very often cannot be interpreted as a NIMBY phenomenon. One theme that all these studies underline is that the local opposition raises legitimate concerns.

This paradigm shift in social science studies on local opposition is taken up in the current literature on participatory procedures in policy and planning (Rowe and Frewer 2005) and on participatory and constructive assessment (Joss 2002). For the current contribution these studies are important in two ways. They first show that NIMBY is not an empirically adequate description. This allows for some confidence that people do not only act egoistically and may be open to ethical argumentation. The project of an ethically sound sustainability analysis is therefore not foredoomed to fail because it cannot be implemented in practice. Second, the empirical studies indicate that people feel that procedural values (as opposed to material ones) such as transparency of the decision-making process and procedural fairness are not adequately taken into account (Taebi et al. 2014). Our analysis in the following will identify the issue of a lack of procedural values raised by the local opposition as a legitimate point.

Many of the aforementioned integrated sustainability concepts acknowledge a need to involve people who may be concerned. Civic participation becomes an essential part, however, as will be argued in the following section. The focus on articulated or indirectly revealed[3] preferences comes with certain *epistemic* and *ethical* problems (see the following section). I hence suggest making the transition from preferences that people have to values that people ought to have and thus moving the discussion from one about acceptance to one on acceptability.

From a *practical* perspective this shift offers another advantage. Per definition values provide more stable orientations for decisions than preferences do. Preferences are instable in that they may differ in different contexts. For example, the acceptance of an energy technology at a given point in time and space implies nothing about the future. These difficulties are highlighted for the special case of transport technologies in the following citation by the climatologist Jesse Ausubel:

> One hundred years ago icebergs were a major climatic threat impeding travel between North America and Europe. 1,513 lives ended when the British liner Titanic collided with one on 14 April 1912. 50 years later jets overflew liners. Anticipating the solution to the iceberg danger required understanding not only the rates and paths on which icebergs travel but the ways humans travel, too.

> (Ausubel 1995)

A prospective regulation of technological progress faces many problems. One of them is, and this is how I interpret Ausubel's citation, that we do not know the preferences of future people. By focusing on values as stable convictions as to what people ought to do can help to (partially) circumvent the uncertainty of a future generation's preferences. As such it is an essential and maybe necessary step in regaining agency in a complex sociotechnical system.

The capability approach

Criteria for sustainability

Moving from a discussion on acceptance to one on acceptability requires spelling out the underlying normative framework. Sustainability is seen by many as an important value, but it is not a simple value that cannot be further de-composed, nor is it a value in itself. Brundtland, for example, defines sustainability in terms of needs: The needs of the present generation are not to be met at the expense of future generations. Spelling out what these needs are requires some normative assumptions. For example, it seems clear that not all needs should count in the same way. But also referring to the most basic needs that we all share seems misleading as a good human life now and in the future certainly comprises much more than only the satisfaction of the most basic needs.

So what are the needs to be considered in sustainability analysis? The IAEA (2005) lists "good health, high living standards, a sustainable economy and a clean environment" as intrinsically valuable. However, to define sustainability in this way is not only circular; but – within the realm of anthropocentric ethics that Brundtland's definition of sustainability subscribes to – the environment is not an end in itself, only a means for the survival and well-being of present and future humans. The same is true of a sustainable economy. It is reasonable to consider human well-being as something of intrinsic worth that helps us to distinguish the needs whose consideration is vital in a sustainability analysis according to Brundtland's original definition.[4]

Generally speaking, we may distinguish two opposing strategies to determine what is of importance in a human life. While the first asserts that it is possible to formulate in a general way a conception of what makes for a worthy and well-lived human life, a conception that is in some sense independent of what an individual would say, the second strategy assumes that what is important in a human life can only be known by each individual person.

The latter strategy is commonly found in today's preference-based approaches to sustainable consumption. It assumes that what is important in a human life can only be known by each individual. Hence there would be no substitute for asking every person what they get out of their lives. The most common theoretical basis for this view is preference-based utilitarianism as it is commonly used in an economic cost–benefit analysis. What is valuable is each individual's utility. Current versions of utilitarianism usually take utility to be the fulfillment of subjective preferences. In other words: people gain utility if they actually get what they want or what they would *really* want if they had sufficient information about their choices and their (long-term) impact. Consequently, the possibilities of measurement and interindividual comparison, let alone those of inquiring about the satisfaction of future generations, are severely impeded, which could be devastating for assessing justice. There is a common strategy to deal with these problems, which is called a "revealed preference approach." This approach assumes that whatever people choose from a number of different alternatives is what they actually want. So on this account important information about people's preferences could for example be attained by analyzing their purchasing behavior. This is a common approach in sustainability analysis; recently QALYs (quality-adjusted life years) have also been suggested as a measure of individual utility.

This obviously does not help us in dealing with future generations, whose preferences remain opaque to us. But future generations are at the center of sustainability analysis. Of course, it might well be impossible to know anything substantial about the quality of life of people whose actual preferences one does not know. And consequently it might be true that there is no sensible and reasonable account of sustainability – but we should not be too quick to dismiss it.

Any sustainability assessment needs to consider two conflicting priorities. On the one hand, it has to be somewhat paternalistic since an ethically sustainable energy supply, for example, can only be reached by assuming that the "needs" to be addressed in sustainability analysis are somewhat universal. On the other hand, we live in a modern value-pluralistic society, and this needs to be acknowledged by any sustainability analysis (Steger and Hillerbrand 2013). Taking this value pluralism seriously seems all the more important as decisions for certain energy mixes set the risks for many without being attentive to individual risk preferences. The decision maker imposes risk on others who barely know that they are affected.

Arguably, the capability approach provides a middle ground between the paternalism of an objective account of human well-being on the one hand and the too liberal and too unrestrictive account of subjective accounts on the other hand (Robeyns 2016; Sen 1992, 2008) and as such can provide a conceptual framework for what sustainable energy amounts to (Hillerbrand 2012; Hillerbrand and Dumke 2011). According to the capability approach, the freedom to choose and to actively realize the things one has reason to value is constitutive for a good human life. By definition, a capability is the set of alternative combinations of "functionings" that can feasibly be achieved by a person. These functionings are facts about what the person is and what the person is able to do.

The value of making comparisons across alternative energy scenarios is hence peoples' freedom to choose and actively realize the things they have reason to value. One does not focus on the impact that an energy scenario has on human well-being per se, but rather on the freedom or actions it makes possible that constitute, among other things, the prerequisites for well-being. By assessing quality of life in terms of freedom and action, the capability theorist can account for the fact that human beings differ in their capacity to make use of goods and resources. By focusing on what people are actually able to do and to be, the capability theorist can thus evaluate the various elements of what is considered to be morally valuable – or less valuable – in different energy scenarios.

Capability as freedom to act

According to the capability approach, the freedom to choose and to actively realize the things one has reason to value is conducive to good human life. *Capability* is defined as the set of alternative combinations of functionings that can feasibly be attributed to the person under consideration. Her functionings are thereby defined as the facts concerning who she is and what she is able to do, a subset of all the capabilities that she actually realizes in her life. Robeyns (2005, 98) elucidates the difference between functioning and capability by taking the example of a bicycle: "[w]e are not interested in the bicycle because it is an object made from certain materials with a specific shape and colour, but because it can take us to places where we want to go, and in a faster way than if we were walking." This technical artifact allows one to move faster than when one goes anywhere on foot. The capability rests on the possibility of being able to learn to ride a bicycle. When one has learned to ride a bicycle, one has the functioning to move faster at one's disposal. This example also shows how the capabilities hinge on both personal and social characteristics. Certain mental and physical requirements must be met when learning how to ride a bike; in addition, one needs a social environment that provides access to a bike (which, in turn, requires a certain level of economic welfare), so that one can ride a bike and that it is not frowned upon that certain social groups, like women, ride bikes.

Unlike in classical utilitarian/hedonistic theory, with the capability theorists, it is not only the functionings that matter but more specifically the full set of capabilities available to a person.[5] Consider, for example, a child from a poor neighborhood who is exposed to the HighScope early childhood curriculum. Later in life, she became pregnant at a young age and did not go on to pursue higher education. However, following a capability approach for the purpose of an ethical evaluation and possibly also for the well-being of the person in question, it makes all the difference whether, through participation in the program, she at least had the opportunity to opt for higher education. The focus is therefore on capabilities in terms of what someone's life could actually have consisted of rather than being a mere evaluation of the circumstances of that same person's life. Please again note the difference to preference-based approaches. An individual may or may not find the capabilities pleasant or not. Enhanced capabilities can also be perceived as a burden.

We owe the explicit distinction between positive and negative liberty to I. Berlin, who had a great impact on Sen.

> Negative liberty is the absence of obstacles, barriers or constraints. One has negative liberty to the extent that actions are available to one in this negative sense. Positive liberty is the possibility of acting – or the fact of acting – in such a way as to take control of one's life and realize one's fundamental purposes.
>
> (Carter 2003)

Though Sen does not always clearly distinguish between the two, Sen's and other versions of the capability approach rest on a very sophisticated concept of freedom. For Sen freedom is of intrinsic value as it allows human beings to live autonomous, self-determined lives.[6] Next to negative freedoms like those of being free of suppression and violence, such freedom also encompasses the active freedom to act according one's own wishes and desires. Sen distinguishes an instrumental kind of freedom that is used to ensure and preserve such capabilities. Instrumental types of freedom are, for example, political freedom such as having the right to vote, social security, the guarantee of transparency – think of the freedom of speech or freedom that could be linked to economic institutions that ensure fair trade. The procedural values, which according to the social science studies cited in the preceding section are of core importance in sustainability considerations, thus take center stage in the capability approach.

Empirical studies show how constitutive freedom is linked to instrumental freedom and how different instrumental sorts of freedom complement and interact with each other. For example, economic welfare is an important instrumental freedom that, despite its importance, does not clearly correlate positively with life expectancy, a measure of constitutive freedom.

For Sen freedom is a normative goal, a value in itself. Though some of the capabilities can be linked to well-being, Sen's concept explicitly leaves room for people to value other things that are not related to well-being. The value of making comparisons between different decisions lies in peoples' freedom to choose and actively realize which things they have reason to value. The capability theorist does not focus on the impact that policy intervention has on human well-being as such in the way that social experiments would do. The evaluation considers instead the freedom of action it affords, which for instance facilitates the prerequisites for well-being. By assessing quality of life in terms of freedom and action, the capability approach accounts for the fact that human beings do differ *inter alia* in their ability to make use of goods and resources. By focusing on what people are actually able to do and to be, the capability theorist can then go on to evaluate the various elements of what is considered to be morally more valuable and less valuable.

Even when we only focus on the capabilities that are linked to well-being, the capability approach cannot be classified as an objective or subjective representation of well-being. The types of freedom and functioning identified in the capability approach *constitute* rather the entities that we have reason to value in life. They are not prerequisites in the way that basic goods are. This distinguishes the capability approach from resource-based approaches like J. Rawls' theory on basic goods or certain rights-based approaches. Furthermore, the capability approach does not amount to just another form of subjectivism about value. Advocates of the capability approach believe that what amounts to a morally valuable capability can, at least in principle, be determined in a nonsubjective way and can also be measured across different individuals.

Measuring the capabilities – in other words, the operationalization of the capability approach – poses particular problems. On the one hand, a multidimensional assessment is generally difficult to realize, a problem that is also faced by preference-based approaches.[7] On the other hand, in particular capabilities as the possible outcomes of the functionings that a person could have lived, but did not realize, are hard to measure. Thus existing applications of the capability approach often settle for an operationalization of functionings only. Suitable indicators for certain functionings are, for example, provided by what is known as the HDI, the Human Development Index. This welfare measure is provided by the United Nations and includes capabilities in health, education, and income. These are estimated for a given nation state on the basis of statistical figures on functionings in the following areas: life expectancy at birth, mean average years of schooling, and gross national income (GNI). Since the 1990s the UN has developed, on the basis of these figures, a comparison between various nation states according to how they score on these parameters. The precise index calculations have varied over the years; in recent years various other indices inspired by Sen's original idea have also been included, for example an inequality-adjusted HDI and the gender inequality index. Other indices inspired by the capability approach that do not make use of economic parameters like the GNI are the Human Poverty Index, the short HPI, or the MPI, the multidimensional poverty index. Robeyns (2005) lists various other studies that are influenced by the theoretical framework provided by the capability approach.

Putting the capability approach into practice

Underdetermination of the capability approach as a theory of justice

As noted above, the capability approach does not provide one unified theory. However, what all capability theorists subscribe to is a focus on the individual's areas of freedom and multidimensional assessment in terms of capabilities. All capability theorists agree that what is valuable in itself is each person's freedom to choose and act, but that the way in which this general idea is played out varies. For example, Sen's view highlights insights from social choice theory to a higher degree than Nussbaum's (2011), while the latter places more emphasis on people's skills and personality traits (Robeyns 2005). Moreover Sen connects the capabilities to individual levels of freedom and leaves further differentiation to participatory discourse. Nussbaum, however, building on for instance Aristotelian ethical virtue theory, develops ten core capabilities that all policy making must embrace if it is to form the basis for a flourishing life. These ten core capabilities have been applied successfully in relation to, for instance, poverty and inequality between men and women.

Though Nussbaum is able to cite an objective list of ten core capabilities, even in her version of the capability approach there is no clarity on how to operationalize these core capabilities, that is to say, on how to best measure physical health or integrity. Here context-dependent features may well play a role, depending on the person as well as on the circumstances. Quite generally we may assert that the capability approach is indeterminate when it comes to indicating how to operationalize capabilities.[8] Alkire (2005) argues that "operationalization is not a one-time thing" and that it is highly likely to be context-dependent. This is because people living today may have reason to strive for other functionings than people living in the future since the activities and persons that constitute a valuable life (the agent's functionings) may change over the course of time. Thus, while the capability approach provides a form of value universalism at a fundamental level, the proxies of the relevant capabilities may have plural, context-dependent instantiations. This brings the capabilities approach closer to subjectivist accounts of well-being and existing integrative sustainability concepts; the capability approach differentiates itself from more objectivist accounts like a Rawlsian account (Schlör, Fischer, and Hake 2012).

To understand the capability approach it is essential to note that "[h]uman diversity is no secondary complication (to be ignored, or to be introduced 'later on'; it is a fundamental aspect of our interest in equality" (Sen 1992, xi). Human beings are irreducibly diverse and differ as regards their "internal characteristics (such as age, gender, general abilities, particular talents, proneness to illness, and so on) as well as in external circumstances (such as ownership of assets, social backgrounds, environmental predicaments, and so on)" (Sen 1992, xi).

To Sen's mind the capability approach is also undetermined in a second way since it does not tell us which kinds of freedom are to be valued in a certain context (Hillerbrand and Peterson 2014; Hillerbrand and Goldammer 2018). This point sometimes calls for criticism, and it is said (and Sen admits it) that the capability approach does not provide a full theory of justice. But again, just as with underdetermination regarding how to operationalize the capabilities, I want, as argued elsewhere, to argue that this underdetermination feature of Sen's capability approach makes it particularly suited for policy decisions in modern democratic states.

The capability approach provides a framework for determining what counts as intrinsically valuable, that is, what enables people's capacities to first develop the concept of a good life and to then go on to live such a good life. As indicated, the capabilities provide a "metric of justice"; they tell us what needs to be taken into consideration when we reason about, for example, a certain policy intervention. However, most capability approach theorists reject a simple calculus demonstrating how to balance and trade off various fundamental kinds of human freedom. So, as far as the capability approach is concerned, the normative analysis leaves us with a multidimensional space spanned by capabilities; concrete advice as to which energy scenario is good or bad would, however, require this multidimensional space to be reduced to one cardinal value. In Sen's original account this decision as to how to weigh up and combine different capabilities is left to the democratic decision-making process. Sen's position is often criticized for only providing a mere metric of justice. That is, what we get is a value theory that tells us what qualifies as valuable, while failing to offer a full theory of justice.

The metric that the capability approach offers helps one to orient oneself in the complex space of a sociotechnical system. Consider for example hydroelectricity, wind power, and nuclear energy (see Hillerbrand 2015; Hillerbrand and Peterson 2014 for this discussion). The capability approach clearly allows us to evaluate each of these three factors with respect to reversibility, an aspect that is not recognized much in most current sustainability assessments. If future generations were to discover at some point in time that wind energy, for one reason or another, comes with unacceptable risks, it would be relatively straightforward to dismantle all wind turbines. The same does not hold true for, for example, hydroelectric power. Large hydroelectric facilities cannot be simply dismantled and the landscape not simply restored should future generations discover that a huge hydroelectric facility imposes unacceptable risks. Note that with or without geoengineering, climate change is an irreversible impact that fossil fuels have on the environment. The irreversible effects that some technologies come with reduce the capabilities (freedoms) of future generations and need to be taken into consideration from a capability perspective.

In the case of nuclear energy, highly radioactive waste poses a severe problem from the point of view of the capability approach. Even when we take into account reprocessing or the future possibility of transmutation, highly radioactive waste is something that future generations need to deal with in one way or the other. Unlike for wind energy, the risks from nuclear energy cannot be eliminated by simply withdrawing from the technology. For example, the issue of a nuclear repository is currently being very actively discussed in Germany, and despite the general disapproval of nuclear energy by the majority of the German public, 85% acknowledge a need for further research on repositories (FORSA 2013).

The capability approach highlights that the potential loss of freedom for future generations has to be taken into account in an ethical evaluation of alternative energy scenarios. But note that a technology like nuclear energy does not only come with drawbacks from a capability perspective. Technologies quite generally and most of all energy technologies enhance our freedom to act in a unique way which is something to be valued from a capability perspective. Compared to all the other energy technologies, with the exception of nuclear fusion, nuclear fission has the advantage of a high-energy density. With respect to this aspect, nuclear energy has clear advantages over renewables as the latter require vast amounts of space for the same amount of energy.

Putting the capability approach into practice 2: energy capabilities

Following Brundtland, this contribution interprets sustainability as justice between generations. It argues that what it is that is to be "distributed in a just or fair way" has not been specified well enough in the present discourse on sustainable energy. I argue that we need a normative framework and contend that the capability approach may provide a suitable basis for consideration of sustainability in modern Western societies in order to determine the future of our energy system.

The capability approach does not provide a full theory of justice, and so far many questions remain open. It is clear from our understanding of intergenerational equity that the expansion of an individual's capabilities is limited by not only other people's capabilities, but also but a future generation's capabilities.

The latter is a particularly prominent factor when considering the significant impact that (energy) technologies will exert on present and future generations. This constraint of present capabilities, however, does not give us sufficient clarification. Here Nussbaum's (2011) account can be helpful. She has formulated so-called core capabilities that are fundamental and cannot be traded-off against each other. These core capabilities are motivated by an Aristotelian ideal of humans being genuine political beings, an account that, in modern parlance, attributes central value to issues like transparency in decision-making processes. Nussbaum's fundamental or core human capabilities are *life, bodily health and bodily integrity, sense, imagination and thought, emotions, practical reason, other species, play, and control over one's environment.*

It has been specified elsewhere (Fritzsche and Oks 2018; Hillerbrand and Goldammer 2018) how these core capabilities touch upon the energy system. For the purposes of this chapter it is relevant that the core capabilities are also underdetermined and leave room for context-dependent specifications when operationalized for evaluating a particular transition path, for example. In the following, I consider the core capabilities as they become relevant for the energy system and as they were put forward in Hillerbrand and Goldammer (2018). The examples of the energy capabilities that are given aim to highlight the multifaceted ways the energy system has an impact on various capabilities and in particular to show how, for example, autonomy becomes an integral part of a sustainability concept that is based on the capability approach and is not in conflict with sustainability. For a more detailed account on the energy capabilities, see Hillerbrand and Goldammer (2018).

For the energy sector, while the core capability *life* is associated with major life-threatening accidents in the energy sector, e.g., during raw material extraction, *bodily integrity* encompasses all further effects of energy systems on human health. The latter includes many health risks that have been discussed, for example, from particle emissions from diesel engines, mercury emissions from coal power plants, but also arguably less severe and less-widely discussed impacts on health such as noise and light pollution from various elements of the energy system. Climate change, for example, impacts both the core capabilities life and bodily integrity. Note that the capability approach is well able to also acknowledge the positive impact that technology has on human lives. When considering life and bodily health, shelter, protection, and support are essential and are provided by energy technology. Even in moderate climates like those found in Europe, weather poses a great challenge to human survival and a good life. Heating or thermal insulation require large amounts of energy. The same holds for greenhouses or cold storage facilities to provide people with nutrition-rich vegetables even in the cold season. With enough energy, even clean drinking water could be provided for everybody via desalination of sea water. This is one aspect of what has become known as the "water-energy nexus."

The energy system also impacts the central human capabilities that are grouped together under the term "emotions." Accidents in power plants or extreme weather events due to climate change, for example, cause grief due to the loss of friends and family or due to loss of habitat. Climate refugees in Africa flee from water scarcity; some residents of Germany are resettled as a consequence of lignite production. Although certain fears, such as the fear of radiation emitted from a nuclear power plant or the fear of electro smog from high-voltage power lines, may overstate the actual danger, this fear may still affect people's capabilities. In contrast, energy technologies can also have positive effects at one's emotional level. A warm house not only provides protection from the cold; it also creates the feeling of security. In addition to being a highly desirable technology outcome, safety is also an important emotional state.

One of the first connections of the central capabilities that Nussbaum subsumes under *cognitive abilities* with energy-related issues is where certain aspects of an energy system are placed under a taboo. There is disagreement both in academia and the broader public as to whether climate engineering is immoral, unproblematic, or even morally necessary (Gardiner 2010), but some countries seem to have put high burdens on research in the field that may act as an implicit taboo to further investigation of climate engineering. Similar claims could be made over nuclear fission or carbon capture and storage. Such informal bans on thinking affect cognitive abilities: Political decisions about carbon capture and storage, nuclear energy, or climate engineering make it possible to hinder or prevent both education and research on these topics.

On the positive side, we can classify various energy systems by the extent to which they constructively influence Nussbaum's central capabilities of *sense, imagination, and thought.* Energy systems make human life easier and thus free up time to make more use of one's cognitive abilities. The decision to use a particular energy technology can also increase intellectual potential as it promotes research and development in that field. The promotion of renewable energy technology in Germany through the Renewable Energy Sources Act (EEG)[9] has led to improvements in renewable energy technology.

Another central human capability is *trust.*[10] In Hillerbrand and Goldammer (2018), we suggested that the continuity of the environment is an important factor that may be disrupted by resettlement due to coal mining, climate change, or hydroelectric dams. From trust we distinguished the central human capability of *connectivity*, which describes the ability to empathize and sympathize with nonhuman animals, plants, and nature in general. While large-scale ecological changes, which are partly perceived as abstract, fall under the aspect of trust, the smaller, direct environmental impact of the energy system falls under ecological connection.

The energy system has had an enormous impact on humans and their environment. The central capability of *practical reason* thus includes critical reflection on personal energy use and the preferred energy system. This is only possible if decisions in the energy sector are sufficiently transparent and citizens are sufficiently knowledgeable about the field. Information about the energy system but also (at least) basic knowledge of the natural sciences and the social sciences are needed in order to form a sound opinion about energy consumption and the desired energy system.

Affiliation refers to the capabilities for social interaction and identifying with others. In the energy system, *distributive justice* is of central importance, such as concerning questions regarding the effects of energy policy regulations on the distribution of the positive and negative impact on different parts of society. Moreover, affiliation is also about *restorative justice*. If the negative impact and benefit of the energy system affect different people in different ways, one may have to consider compensation, e.g., for those living in close vicinity of a power plant. Questions of *trade or exchange justice* also have to be considered. The contract between generations, for example, can be understood as an exchange in which we leave an intact environment and raw material reserves or equivalent energy sources for future generations, and we can expect the following generations to care for us when we get older (Höffe 1993).

Another core capability that Nussbaum mentions is named *play*. Here it is to be noted that while life becomes easier with an increased energy supply and thus provides more opportunities for relaxation, the different forms of energy generation may, for example, have an impact on the potential for leisure activities. Offshore wind power plants, for example, restrict our possibilities for sailing.

Control over one's environment in the sense of autonomy (Nussbaum uses the term *separateness*) is the central capability for living one's own life and not someone else's. In the form of electricity, energy can promote an autonomous life in a fundamental way. Note that this can cut both ways as the more I depend on the availability of useful energy, the more I depend on a complex network that involves the mining of raw materials and the generation of electricity and heat, and the less autonomous I am. Nussbaum labels a second aspect of the control over one's environment *strong separateness*. Human beings need to be able to influence their social context, e.g., via political participation. Of importance in this regard is the degree of participation that energy systems allow for various components. For example, in Germany the *Bürgerenergie* (civilian energy) currently enables local people, particularly in rural areas, to participate directly in the energy supply system (Engerer 2014).

Capability and uncertainties in decision making in complex systems

Though it has been argued in the literature that the capability approach is compatible both with deontological and consequentialist reasoning, most applications use the capability approach in the way that it has been introduced here, namely as an alternative to neoclassical economic reasoning to determine what is of intrinsic worth without leaving the realm of consequentialist reasoning. What has been said about the opportunities and challenges of these approaches when it comes to the uncertainty of the consequences of an action thus applies to the capability approach as well.[11] While in the literature the focus is often on the uncertainty of consequences, arguably as these lend themselves to the formal treatment of decision-making theory, the capability approach makes it possible to incorporate value uncertainty as well. This seems particularly crucial for a sustainability analysis because by definition it binds future as well as present generations.

The capability approach leaves room for context-sensitive considerations when operationalizing or even weighing up different capabilities. In other words, unlike in approaches based on welfare economics or in utilitarianism, the preference orders of an individual may vary in different circumstances. Following on from Sen (1992) people have various reasons – in other words, motivations, values, or goals – for making particular choices. It cannot reasonably be assumed that the actual behavior resulting from competing motivational factors can be described in all circumstances by just one preference order (Martins 2006). In this sense Sen's approach falls into the Cambridge tradition of economic thought which since Keynes has always focused strongly on uncertainty (Martins 2009, 699):

> for Sen, the multiple preference orderings that drive the human agent can be, and often are, incomplete, generating situations where there are options that are not ranked vis-à-vis each other in any way. Hence, in Sen's conception of the human agent, there will often exist what Post Keynesians term "fundamental uncertainty" concerning the choice to be made.

While the capability approach is well able to deal with value uncertainty, this ability comes at a price, namely that the value base is context sensitive. As in other sustainability concepts (Bräutigam et al. 2015), this context sensitivity shows in the operationalization of the capabilities. This context sensitivity can be interpreted as introducing yet another uncertainty; it certainly makes sustainability assessments more complex. An energy-intensive life style limits other people's central capabilities, but only careful evaluation of the context can determine whether the person in question is indeed morally blameworthy. The same holds for an appraisal of various forms of energy technology: One may be more sustainable than another, but there is clearly no black and white ranking for most energy technologies that singles out one as unethical or another as not blameworthy (for example, Hillerbrand and Peterson 2014). For example, risks from the civilian use of nuclear power can be reduced by an adequate institutional design that incorporates political institutions that monitor the nuclear waste from individual power plants in order to, for example, minimize the risk of proliferation. In a country with a stable constitutional state, nuclear power may be a morally legitimate and possibly even an imperative option, while in other countries it may be not.

Summary

Any transformation of a sociotechnical system such as the energy system necessitates societal changes that require cooperation by citizens. The change toward a more sustainable energy future is often seen as necessitating citizens to cooperate in a twofold way: Behavioral changes are needed to reduce the overall energy consumption; acceptance (particularly by the local population) is required for the siting of large-scale infrastructure installations. In the debates on sustainability the role of the citizen is often reduced to these two issues. Questions addressed in the literature include how to nudge people into sustainable behavior and whether nondemocratic states are better able to foster sustainability. In these approaches it is often wrongly assumed that the issue of what sustainability is already defined and clear for any given context. In this contribution I argue first that this is not the case, but that we rather need to carefully spell out what sustainability means. Second, in doing so I show that the concept of sustainability that is commonly used at an aggregate level can be reinterpreted in individualist terms. This issue is relevant for any democracy that seeks a shift to sustainability. By putting norma-tive considerations first, agency is regained. Agency requires us to, for example, reflect and understand the goals of technological trajectories and how they are set. Complex sociotechnical systems are often opaque in various ways. One form of such opacity disguises the reasons for making the choice to take certain direc-tions; reflection on the goals of (social-) technical development does not take place. By reclaiming a normative approach, the underlying and often implicit values are made explicit and open for debate. This provides a necessary, but cer-tainly not sufficient step for (re)gaining agency in the shift toward a more sustain-able energy future.

Notes

1　We find assessments overly optimistic that 97% of the energy for the EU27 (Jacob-son and Delucchi 2009; Greenpeace and EREC 2010) or even 100% for the whole world could come from renewable sources by the middle of this century (WWF 2011). Just as unrealistic are more conservative estimates of the world energy outlook which estimate that the share of renewables in the total power generation would amount to around 33% in 2040 (IEA 2013).

2　See also the chapter by Otto and Wittenberg in this book.

3　Common strategies here are the revealed preference approach, willingness-to-pay (WTP) or willingness-to-accept (WTA) approaches, or more recently approaches based on quality-adjusted life years (QALY). Common to all these is that they suggest measuring an individual's utility via empirical surveys.

4　There is a vast literature on the various types of happiness, well-being, or welfare and as to how these may relate to each other. For the discussion in this chapter, however, the details as well as the differences between the terms are not of importance here and for now I roughly follow a colloquial use of these terms. In this broad statement I am bracketing out many difficulties and debates.

5　As opportunities, capabilities are notoriously hard to measure. This is why most exist-ing indicator sets for estimating well-being that are based on the capability approach tend to measure the functionings instead.

6　Note that while Nussbaum's and Sen's versions of the capability approach are often discussed in the same light, Nussbaum not only argues in favor of a slightly differ-ent version of the capability approach, but her version is also based on a different rationale. Unlike Sen, who starts with the intrinsic value of certain individual types of freedom, Nussbaum refers back to the dignity of humans which makes them subject to respect.

7　See, for example, Lumer (2002) for a thorough multidimensional utilitarian analysis of climate warming.

8 For examples as to how to operationalize the capability approach for specific settings, see for example Dowding et al. (2009) or Anand et al. (2009).
9 In its original form, the *Erneuerbare-Energien-Gesetz* (EEG) ensures that electricity from renewable resources can always be fed into the grid and is guaranteed a fixed price, called the "feed-in-tariff."
10 See also the contribution by Patrick Sumpf in this book.
11 There are few applications of the capability approach to decisions concerning risk or uncertainty; see for example (Murphy and Gardoni 2012).

References

Alkire, Sabina. 2005. "Why the Capability Approach?" *Journal of Human Development and Capabilities* 6 (1): 115–35. https://doi.org/10.1080/146498805200034275.

Anand, Paul, Graham Hunter, Ian Carter, Keith Dowding, Francesco Guala, and Martin Van Hees. 2009. "The Development of Capability Indicators." *Journal of Human Development and Capabilities* 10 (1): 125–52. https://doi.org/10.1080/14649880802675366.

Ausubel, Jesse H. 1995. "Technical Progress and Climatic Change." *Energy Policy* 23 (4–5): 411–16. https://doi.org/10.1016/0301-4215(95)90166-5.

Basta, Claudia. 2014. "Risk and Spatial Planning." In *Handbook of Risk Theory*, edited by Sabine Roeser, Rafaela Hillerbrand, Per Sandin, and Martin Peterson, 265–94. New York: Springer.

Bräutigam, K.-R., J Kopfmüller, P Lichtner, B Rilling, C Rösch, V Stelzer, and N Weinberger. 2015. "Indicators for Monitoring and Assessing the German Energy Transition." Poster Presentation presented at the Science & Technology International Conference & Exhibition, Karlsruhe.

Carter, Ian. 2003. "Positive and Negative Liberty." *Stanford Encyclopedia of Philosophy.* https://plato.stanford.edu/entries/liberty-positive-negative/.

Dovers, Stephen. 2001. "Institutions for Sustainability." Australian Conservation Foundation.

Dowding, Keith, Martin Van Hees, Anand Paul, Hunter Graham, Ian Carter, and Francesco Guala. 2009. "The Development of Capability Indicators." *Journal of Human Development and Capabilities* 10 (1): 125–52. https://doi.org/10.1080/14649880802675366.

Engerer, Hella. 2014. "DIW Berlin: Energiegenossenschaften in der Energiewende." Text. DIW Roundup. July 17, 2014. www.diw.de/de/diw_01.c.470180.de/presse/diw_roundup/energiegenossenschaften_in_der_energiewende.html.

European Commission. 2016. "European Commission." 2030 Energy Strategy. https://ec.europa.eu/energy/en/topics/energy-strategy/2030-energy-strategy.

FORSA. 2013. "Forsa Umfrage Zur Kernkraft." Forsa. www.kernenergie.de/kernenergie-w Assets/docs/themen/2013-05-forsa-umfrage-kernkraft.pdf.

Fritzsche, Albrecht, and Sascha Julian Oks, eds. 2018. *The Future of Engineering: Philosophical Foundations, Ethical Problems and Application Cases.* Philosophy of Engineering and Technology. Springer International Publishing.

Gardiner, Steven M. 2010. "Is 'Arming the Future' with Geoengineering Really the Lesser Evil? Some Doubts About the Ethics of Intentionally Manipulating the Climate System." In Climate Ethics – Essential Readings, edited by Steven M. Gardiner, Simon Caney, Dale Jamieson, and Henry Shue, 284–312. Oxford: Oxford University Press.

Greenpeace, and EREC. 2010. "EU Energy [R]Evolution – Towards a Fully Renewable Energy Supply in the EU27." Greenpeace International, European Renewable Energy Council (EREC). www.greenpeace.org/eu-unit/en/Publications/2010/EU-Energy-R-evolution-scenario/.

Hillerbrand, Rafaela. 2012. "Climate Change as Risk?" In *Handbook of Risk Theory*, edited by Sabine Roeser, Rafaela Hillerbrand, Per Sandin, and Martin Peterson. New York: Springer, Dordrecht.

———. 2015. "The Role of Nuclear Energy in the Future Energy Landscape: Energy Scenarios, Nuclear Energy and Sustainability." In *The Ethics of Nuclear Energy. Risk, Justice, and Democracy in the Post-Fukushima Era*, edited by Behnam Taebi and Sabine Roeser, 231–49. Cambridge: Cambridge University Press.

Hillerbrand, Rafaela, and M. Dumke. 2011. "An Ethical Framework on How to Assess Sustainability." In *6th Dubrovnik Conference on Sustainable Development of Energy, Water and Environmental Systems*. Dubrovnik.

Hillerbrand, Rafaela, and Katrin Goldammer. 2018. "Energy Technologies and Human Well-Being. Using Sustainable Design for the Energy Transition." In *The Future of Engineering: Philosophical Foundations, Ethical Problems and Application Cases*, edited by Sascha Julian Oks and Albrecht Fritzsche. Philosophy of Engineering and Technology. Springer International Publishing.

Hillerbrand, Rafaela, and Martin Peterson. 2014. "Nuclear Power Is Neither Right Nor Wrong: The Case for a Tertium Datur in the Ethics of Technology." *Science and Engineering Ethics* 20 (2): 583–95. https://doi.org/10.1007/s11948-013-9452-5.

Höffe, Otfried. 1993. *Moral als Preis der Moderne – Ein Versuch über Wissenschaft, Technik und Umwelt*. Frankfurt am Main: Suhrkamp.

IEA. 2013. "IEA World Energy Outlook 2013." International Energy Agency. www.iea.org/publications/freepublications/publication/WEO2013.pdf.

IAEA. 2005. "Energy Indicators for Sustainable Development: Guidelines and Methodologies." Vienna: International Atomic Energy Agency. https://www-pub.iaea.org/MTCD/Publications/PDF/Pub1222_web.pdf.

Jacobson, Mark Z., and Mark A. Delucchi. 2009. "A Path to Sustainable Energy by 2030." *Scientific American* 301 (5): 58–65. https://doi.org/10.1038/scientificamerican1109-58.

Joss, Simon, ed. 2002. *Participatory Technology Assessment: European Perspectives*. London: Center for the Study of Democracy.

Lumer, Christoph. 2002. *The Greenhouse: A Welfare Assessment and Some Morals*. Lanham MD: University Press of America.

Martins, Nuno. 2006. "Capabilities as Causal Powers." *Cambridge Journal of Economics* 30: 671–85. https://doi.org/doi:10.1093/cje/bel012.

———. 2009. "Sen's Capability Approach and Post Keynesianism: Similarities, Distinctions, and the Cambridge Tradition." *Journal of Post Keynesian Economics* 31 (4): 691–706.

McDowell, John. 2001. "Non-Cognitivism and Rule-Following." *Archives de Philosophie* 64 (3): 457–77.

Montiel, Ivan, and Javier Delgado-Ceballos. 2014. "Defining and Measuring Corporate Sustainability: Are We There Yet?" *Organization & Environment* 27 (2): 113–39. https://doi.org/10.1177/1086026614526413.

Murphy, Colleen, and Paolo Gardoni. 2012. "The Capability Approach in Risk Analysis." In *Handbook of Risk Theory*, edited by Sabine Roeser, Rafaela Hillerbrand, Per Sandin, and Martin Peterson, 979–97. Dordrecht: Springer. https://doi.org/10.1007/978-94-007-1433-5_39.

Nussbaum, Martha. 2011. *Creating Capabilities: The Human Development Approach*. Cambridge, MA: Harvard University Press.

Oosterlaken, Ilse. 2015. "Applying Value Sensitive Design (VSD) to Wind Turbines and Wind Parks: An Exploration." *Science and Engineering Ethics* 21 (2): 359–79. https://doi.org/10.1007/s11948-014-9536-x.

Ostrom, Elinor. 2015. *Governing the Commons: The Evolution of Institutions for Collective Action.* Canto Classics. Cambridge: Cambridge University Press.

Ott, Konrad, and Ralf Döring. 2011. "Grundlinien einer Theorie 'starker' Nachhaltigkeit." In *Umwelt-Handeln*, 3. Aufl, 89–127. Marburg: Metropolis-Verl.

Randers, Jorgan. 2012. *2052: A Global Forecast for the next Forty Years.* White River Junction, VT: Chelsea Green Pub.

Robeyns, Ingrid. 2005. "The Capability Approach: A Theoretical Survey." *Journal of Human Development* 6 (1): 93–117. https://doi.org/10.1080/146498805200034266.

——— 2016. "The Capability Approach." Stanford Encyclopedia of Philosophy Archive Winter 2016 Edition. https://plato.stanford.edu/archives/win2016/entries/capability-approach/.

Rowe, Gene, and Lynn J. Frewer. 2005. "A Typology of Public Engagement Mechanisms." *Science, Technology, & Human Values* 30 (2): 251–90. https://doi.org/10.1177/0162243904271724.

Schlör, Holger, Wolfgang Fischer, and Jürgen-Friedrich Hake. 2012. "Measuring Social Welfare, Energy and Inequality in Germany." *Applied Energy* 97: 135–42. https://doi.org/10.1016/j.apenergy.2012.01.036.

Scott Cato, Molly. 2009. "Green Economics." Earthscan. www.gci.org.uk/Documents/128075741-Green-Economics-an-Introduction-to-Theory-Policy-and-Practice.pdf.

Sen, Amartya. 1992. *Inequality Reexamined.* Oxford: Oxford University Press.

———. 2008. "Capabilities, Lists, and Public Reason: Continuing the Conversation." *Feminist Economics* 10 (3): 77–80. https://doi.org/10.1080/1354570042000315163.

Steger, Florian, and Rafaela Hillerbrand (Eds.) 2013. *Praxisfelder angewandter Ethik: ethische Orientierung in Medizin, Politik, Technik und Wirtschaft.* Ethik und Praxis (EUP). Münster: Mentis.

Taebi, B., A. Correljé, E. Cuppen, M. Dignum, and U. Pesch. 2014. "Responsible Innovation as an Endorsement of Public Values: The Need for Interdisciplinary Research." *Journal of Responsible Innovation* 1 (1): 118–24. https://doi.org/10.1080/23299460.2014.882072.

Williams, Bernard. 1985. *Ethics and the Limits of Philosophy.* Cambridge, MA: Harvard University Press.

WWF. 2011. "The Energy Report, 100% Renewable Energy by 2050." WWF. https://wwf.be/assets/RAPPORT-POLICY/ENERGY/UK/Energy-Report-Summary-FINAL-per-pages-162204.pdf.

11 Technology and motives

The challenge of energy consumption behavior

Siegmar Otto and Inga Wittenberg

Introduction

The reduction in energy consumption is a widely discussed issue in political discourse, public dialog, and the media. Probably one of the first and most widely recognized publications in this dialog is the book *Factor four: doubling wealth – halving resource use: the new report to the Club of Rome* (Weizsäcker, Lovins, and Lovins 1998). It promotes energy and resource efficiency as the solution to most societal and environmental problems including energy consumption and climate change. It was first published in 1995 and, almost simultaneously, the "factor X debate" started (Reijnders 1998). The factor X (varying between 4 and 50) simply enhanced the discussion that started with factor 4 as a quantification of eco-efficiency or dematerialization. This discussion reflected a remarkable technological optimism. At the same time, policy makers and many other actors focused on eco-efficiency (e.g., more energy-efficient transportation, domestic heating, or household appliances) as the solution to environmental problems. For example, with the increasing acknowledgement of the anthropogenic origin of climate change, the hopes of many, including policy makers, have been to increase the efficiency of technology (Mont and Plepys 2008). To that end, in 2008 the European Union decided on the 20–20–20 strategy to be reached by 2020, which comprises: (a) reducing greenhouse gas emissions by 20% compared to 1990, (b) supporting renewable energy in order to reach a share of at least 20% energy from renewable sources in the overall energy mix, and (c) reducing the overall energy consumption by 20% by means of increased energy efficiency (Commission of the European Communities 2008).

Technological improvements, however, do not always go hand in hand with energy savings even though new technologies might be more energy-efficient. In fact, technological evolution has been a fundamental element of the sociotechnical system as a whole, i.e., a system constituted by human–technology interactions in the context of society. Such evolution plays an important societal role, but it is also the cause of perpetually increasing energy consumption, not the solution to it. The failure to reduce energy consumption solely on the basis of increased efficiency confirms the importance of having a general strategy for sustainable development as demanded in the Agenda 21, published several decades ago in the Brundtland Report (WCED 1987). In this report, improved efficiency is only one of three strategies, the others being sufficiency and consistency. Only if all three strategies are promoted simultaneously will sustainable development (and climate change mitigation) be successful (Otto 2010). Even an earlier version of the World Energy Outlook is more than clear about the efficacy of efficiency and the need for sufficiency: "The most important contribution to reaching energy security and climate goals comes from the energy that we do not consume" (IEA 2011, 2).

Increasing the energy efficiency of technologies and its consequence of possibly raising energy consumption has been widely acknowledged as the Jevons Paradox for more than one and a half centuries (Jevons 1865). The explanation of this paradox lies in the fact that people use technology to fulfill an endless number of needs and goals (Otto, Kaiser, and Arnold 2014). More generally, the phenomenon is known as rebound and is estimated in terms of the rebound effect (Sorrell, Dimitropoulos, and Sommerville 2009). The rebound phenomenon results from personal consumption which is fundamentally benefit-oriented (Ajzen 2005) and sustained by an inexhaustible amount of personal wishes and goals (Kenrick et al. 2009). Therefore, it is rather a rule than an exception that gains from efficiency such as the reduction in energy used by efficient lighting or gains resulting from energy production from renewable sources (e.g., solar panels) are used for the satisfaction of additional personal goals (Otto, Kaiser, and Arnold 2014). This illustrates the importance of considering the human factor in energy systems and the key role that people play in fulfilling the efficiency expectations placed in technological innovations. With the biface, or more symbolically, with leverage and the use of fire, i.e., the first technology to amplify human behavior – in the sense of increasing its efficiency – was invented. Use of the biface, for instance, made cutting meat and plants more efficient, and it was the first tool that was eventually used to produce more tools and weapons. The rest is history. Almost any, if not all technological interventions amplify human behavior, which is itself driven by motives. Thus, the fact that efficiency increases do not lead to reduced energy consumption is not necessarily surprising and illustrates the importance of human behavior for attaining energy efficiency goals.

Considering the human dimension, even behavior that at first glance seems economically inefficient is rational in most cases from an evolutionary perspective. For instance, buying a powerful car (e.g., a SUV) whose functional utility exceeds one's needs (e.g., for commuting every day on a paved road within a city at a 40 km/h average speed) is perfectly rational from this perspective because it simply enhances the driver's physical strength – biologically a very important competitive advantage for most animals, including humans. Even if the driver never deploys the vehicle's full strength and capabilities, it symbolizes his biological fitness – yet another motive (search for mates) which additionally underlines the rationality of buying and driving the big car. It is impressive how the share of ecologically unviable SUVs increased within the last decade despite the efforts to reduce energy consumption and CO_2 emissions.

As a consequence, the chances of reducing the energy consumption of a society (or per capita) are rather low if the focus is on increasing technological efficiency alone without taking into consideration the dominant influence of efficiency increases in a sociotechnical system, namely increasing affluence and fulfilling more human needs and goals.

Thus, we will discuss the origin and rules of our sociotechnical system from an evolutionary perspective, considering basic human needs and motives. Then we will take a closer look at the roles that technology plays in fulfilling human needs and motives and how this is related to the environment. On the basis of this, by changing the focus, we will show how a person's *intrinsic motivation to protect the environment* and the behavioral costs that depend strongly on the available technology are two core determinants of pro-environmental behavior and finally per capita energy consumption (and reduction thereof) in the sociotechnical system. Finally, against this backdrop, by illustrating that improvements in technological efficiency alone do not lead to a reduction in per capita energy use, we propose changing course in favor of the other determinant, that is, the motivation to pursue an energy-sufficient lifestyle that also attempts to reduce one's own energy consumption. In particular, we will point out how to foster the motivation for such an energy-sufficient lifestyle through nature-based environmental education.

The origins and rules of the sociotechnical system

Evolution of the sociotechnical system

To understand the development and interrelatedness of humans and technology, we have to understand behavior and its costs in the context of its biological functionality for survival and reproduction. From such an evolutionary perspective, we argue that the struggle for survival and reproduction led to a human disposition to promote behavior of ultimate utility to this struggle by advancing the likelihood of one's own survival and reproduction beyond those of others (Dawkins 2006). Humans have developed two critical means (i.e., speech and the use of technology) that have given them a major evolutionary advantage and that enable and facilitate each other respectively. Indeed, speech as an advanced and distinguished means of communication enabled humans to develop the necessary level of individual specialization that made the development and production of technology possible. In turn, technology – specifically information and communication technology (ICT) – facilitates human speech and communication in general.

The utility of technology from a biological perspective

From a biological point of view (e.g. Dawkins 2006) – guided by genetic disposition and formed by external conditions – an organism uses any means to live as (re)productively as possible. Evolution has brought forth a great diversity of organisms showing a large variety of behavioral patterns, from rather simple to highly complex ones, but all of them pursue the same ends or goals: reproduction. Hence, even the smallest species utilizes anything in their environment that helps them to reach these goals, creating an impact on the environment. By enhancing the utility of its behavior, the organism increases the likelihood of its reproductive success by producing more offspring (e.g., through a longer reproductive period and a higher frequency). It might as well reduce the chance of competitors to reproduce because it utilizes resources which are not available to them anymore. For instance, high trees in a forest fight for the resource of light: The more light one tree can harvest (through, for instance, growing higher than the others), the more energy it has for its existence and reproduction. The same holds true for the resources it draws through its roots (e.g., water and minerals). Based on the behavior and the related impact of one exemplar of a species, we can calculate the species' total impact (I) by multiplying their number (P) by an organism's impact (F), which is roughly constant throughout the whole population of a species (e.g., each bacteria of the same aerobe species will metabolize about the same amount of O_2 throughout an average lifetime). We have shown that any organism – including humans – strives to utilize as much as possible from its environment in order to reproduce, or, in other words, to gain the most utility from its behavior. For exactly the same competitive reason humans have pushed the utilization of the environment to a new level: They use technology (and organization) as an amplifier of their behavior.

As a consequence of technology, the above formula derived from evolutionary biology (Dawkins 2006, Darwin 1859) has to be modified for humans because the impact of a single individual of our species varies extremely. To calculate the environmental impact of humans, the basic formula $I = P \times A \times T$ (Ehrlich and Holdren 1971, Holdren 2000) is widely used today (e.g. IPCC 2007). This formula expands the previous one by allowing for the varying impact of individuals (F), based on their affluence (A) and the technology they use (T). In terms of CO_2, the impact ranges from 0.023 metric tons emitted per year (2007) by an average Burundi to 55.384 metric tons emitted in the same year by an average person from Qatar (source: www.worldbank.org, data for 2007). This leads to an impact magnitude (in terms of emitted CO_2) of more than 2,400 – and this is only based on national averages. These huge differences in environmental impact within one species do not exist for any animal but humans. The bottom line is that humans, like any other species, try to derive as much utility as possible from their behavior and in doing so, they use technology (and the ensuing organization of work and industrial production) to amplify their behavior.

The utility of technology from a psychological perspective

From a psychological point of view, people act to meet their personal ends, to satisfy their needs, and to fulfill their wishes and desires (Kenrick et al. 2009) – whatever these wishes, needs, desires, and ends are, wherever the reasons come from, and irrespective of whether a person can reflect on them (Bischof 1985).

Ultimately, people act because of the perceived gratifying or rewarding consequences of their deeds, and thus because behavior has *subjective utility*. In other words, behavior is a means to attain certain ends (i.e., some behavioral consequences). For example, we eat to get rid of an unpleasant sensation (i.e., feeling hungry). If hunger, proverbially speaking, is the best cook, we also learn that behavioral consequences (e.g., getting an apple) do not possess subjective utility in an absolute, pre-defining sense. They are subjectively valuable and, thus, gratifying depending on the particular circumstances a person is in. Even conspicuous conservation behavior can be explained perfectly well by psychology on the grounds of this thesis (e.g. Griskevicius, Tybur, and van den Bergh 2010).

With each transition to a more efficient form of technology (e.g., from bicycle to car and from car to airplane) people get closer to their goals and/or reduce their behavioral costs, hence, increasing their utility respectively (e.g., traveling faster, further, more conveniently). Through reduced behavioral costs people save resources – usually money or time – which they can invest in the fulfillment of any other of the less satisfied motives, increasing the utility of these as well. For instance, by switching from car to public transport they might save not only time (e.g., by reading or working on a train) but also money. These resources might be reinvested in additional consumption leading to more utility in another domain. This phenomenon is referred to as rebound, which we will discuss in more detail later in this chapter. For example, in Germany, one of the countries technologically strongly dedicated to energy efficiency, people try quite hard to save the last cent for yet another holiday, often including a long-distance flight. For these people, the rebound effect will be well beyond 100%, that is, all the gain in energy efficiency is more than compensated for by additional consumption. Generally, each switch to more efficient technology increases a person's subjective utility in at least one of the goals. Against the backdrop of these insights into the biological and psychological factors motivating behavior and several initial illustrations of the roles technology might play in this context, we will now have a closer look at the different roles that technology plays with regard to human behavior.

The function of technology for motivated behavior

Technology is omnipresent in today's affluent societies and essential to any developing society. Even the meaning of the word "developed" as used in the previous sentence – denoting a dimension used to classify societies – is connected much more to technology than to anything else, because this "development" is essentially based on technological advances. Also, just sitting here and writing these lines involves an endless chain of technology: the building, providing shelter from precipitation and wind, central heating, making it comfortably warm with currently −11°C outside; glass windows letting in the sunlight; the paper and printer for the articles cited in this book; the computer with internet connection, enabling access to an extreme amount of information and the espresso machine to increase human productiveness. Beyond that, writing and disseminating this book is only possible through our advanced means of communication (i.e., speech), which in turn is facilitated by technology (in particular ICT). In this respect, we hope that at least a few readers will consider these lines as meaningful communication. Midden, Kaiser, and McCalley (2007) have described four roles of technology as being a (a) determinant, (b) intermediary, (c) amplifier, and (d) promoter of behavior. In the following paragraphs we will show how this distinction helps to highlight important links between technology and human behavior with respect to rebound and potential improvements.

Technology as determinant

Technology *determines* the boundaries of behavioral choices. Examples are numerous and can range from small scale and often clearly determined choices to larger scale, less clearly defined boundaries. A rather complex, but reboundwise very important example is the technological determination of transport modes. Depending on the individual's perspective on time and money, public transport and individual motor vehicle traffic are two strong rivals in many European cities. Bicycling and walking can also be viable options. Even among EU member states there are large differences in the share of nonmotorized individual transport for daily activities, ranging from 34% in the Netherlands down to 7% in Luxembourg and to 3% in Cyprus (European Commission 2011, 8). Infrastructure, and thus the availability of technology, is the main reason, or in other words, the determinant of these huge differences. The availability of travel mode choices, especially those using new technology and renewable energy, plays an important role for the energy system and energy consumption and thus for the environmental impact of a society. For example, the use of electric cars can be determined by the infrastructure conditions since the charging points or stations required to recharge the vehicle are not always available (Noel and Sovacool 2016). Likewise, to reduce the environmental impact of electricity consumption in terms of CO_2 emissions, everyday behavioral options depend on the options offered by electricity suppliers, i.e., the availability of electricity based on generation from a renewable source of energy, or the possibility to install a renewable source of energy such as solar panels on the roof. Taking these two examples together, the environmental impact of electric cars will also depend on the possibility to recharge a car's battery with energy from a renewable source.

Technology as intermediary

Because technology determines the conditions for behavioral goals just by its physical presence, it also directly influences environmentally friendly behavior (Kaiser and Gutscher 2003). For each goal of a person, there is a bundle of available technological options. Once selected, technology becomes an *intermediary* between the person's goal attainment and his resource consumption. Hence, all the resources used by technology to fulfill a person's needs and goals relate directly to this person's environmental footprint. We can exemplify the intermediary function of technology by referring to the comparison of a short haul flight and a high-speed train ride, which, with respect to goal attainment can be considered fairly equal for some travel routes, especially in Europe. But CO_2 emission will vary greatly between these two alternatives in favor of the train system (Spielmann, de Haan, and Scholz 2008). In this case, the choice is easy for an environmentally conscious consumer. Hence, the promotion of (high-speed) train transport is supported widely as an environmentally friendly transport mode in comparison to the use of an individual's car and air travel. If more people switch from airplane to train, the CO_2 output will decrease – so far the popular assumption.

Also related to the determining role of technology, but much more subtle are the specific designs of technology and the way they are presented by default. According to Goldstein et al. (2008), companies miss a lot because of the inadequate default designs of their products and services. The default option of a product or service is the basic form, which customers receive unless they change it with some effort. If there were another option that would appeal much more to most customers or, even worse, if the default option were a rather useless configuration, then the product would most likely get a much worse reputation than it would get with an optimized default configuration. The same holds true for any technology that we use and that can be configured along different parameters. Whereas the availability of technology to fulfill personal goals is the first determining step, the second one – after a person has chosen one technology – is the setup of this technology, and very often the default setup is not changed. A simple example is the energy-saving settings of a notebook. Many people will not change the default setup. Hence, the default setup determines the way people use it. Furthermore, the default setup of a computer might even play a role promoting energy consumption. Imagine the computer is setup by default to remind its user to switch off an attached laser printer when the user shuts down the computer. This would save a significant amount of energy because idle laser printers (even modern models) consume 10 watts or more.

The amplifying function of technology

Picking up the comparison of a short haul flight and high-speed train travel two paragraphs above, in Switzerland, for instance, a new maglev train system has been on the agenda. Researchers analyzed the overall CO_2 output and found out that, on the basis of simple CO_2 / person × distance comparisons, the new train system would be environmentally sound. But, even with conservative assumptions, Spielmann, de Haan, and Scholz (2008) calculated a rebound effect between 11% and 114% for this specific new maglev train system because people would save time and, in the following, travel more. More generally, this rebound can be denoted as the amplifying function of technology. Likewise, Klöckner, Nayum, and Mehmetoglu (2013) found that electric car owners did not report a decrease in annual mileage except those for whom the electric car is their sole car. Electric cars were also more often used for everyday mobility, e.g., shopping or leisure activities (Klöckner, Nayum, and Mehmetoglu 2013).

There has always been progress because (efficiency) improvements and new applications have helped newer versions of technology supersede older ones. It is this *amplifying* function of technology, which, in combination with personal goals and motives, leads to rebound effects. Together with the invention of completely new technologies, efficiency improvements basically constitute the essence of technological progress. Nevertheless, in many cases the invention and breakthrough of new technologies is also enabled by efficiency improvements to essential components of the new technology (e.g., highly efficient accumulators for electric vehicles and, of course, efficient circuits and CPUs for smartphones and other mobile devices) or for its production (e.g., welding for the production of lightweight car bodies). All of these mechanisms of technological evolution had been in place long before efficiency improvements were politically discovered as the strategy for sustainable development. Unsurprisingly, the official claim labeling efficiency improvements as being ecofriendly has changed nothing in the inextricable relationship between technological efficiency improvements and technological progress in general. Therefore, efficiency and the amplifying function of technology – in other words, rebound – are still two sides of the same coin, just as always. The only variable that will make a difference is the motive behind the utilization of technological advancements and hence efficiency improvements – which is human motivation.

For example, consider social interaction or communication, which at first glance seems to be a form of action that is rather free of energy and material. This was maybe true before Alexander Graham Bell invented the telephone. Today, with computers, television, smartphones, and Web 2.0, our communication is enhanced impressively by technology. Indeed, information and communication technology (ICT) is one of the – if not the – fastest growing consumers of electric energy. ICT's share of the worldwide electricity consumption was 7.5% in 2007 (Vereecken et al. 2010). This share of total electricity consumption will rise to 15% in 2020 due to the expected annual growth of up to 12% in the different branches of ICT (e.g., PCs, TVs, and network equipment) in contrast to an increase of 2% in the overall annual consumption of electricity (Vereecken et al. 2010). Parallel to this extraordinary increase in energy consumption, ICT has one of the highest rates of energy efficiency improvements: The electrical efficiency of computation has doubled roughly every year and a half for more than six decades, a pace of change comparable to that of computer performance and electrical efficiency in the microprocessor era. These improvements in efficiency have enabled the creation of laptops, smartphones, wireless sensors, and other mobile computing devices, with many more such innovations yet to come (Koomey et al. 2011, 46). Hence, large efficiency improvements (in the case of ICT of about 66% annually) seem to be related to large increases in energy consumption.

Technology as a promoter of pro-environmental behavior

In 2008 the EU government and its national counterparts set a series of demanding targets that should be met by 2020 in order to combat climate change and increase energy security. Almost the whole strategy is based on technological energy efficiency improvements and technology that promotes pro-environmental behavior. It is widely recognized that climate change is caused by greenhouse gas emissions of anthropogenic origin. Many hope for a technological solution for reducing the energy demand and thus greenhouse gas emissions. Indeed, technological measures such as renewable energy sources (e.g., photovoltaic [PV]), energy-efficient appliances (e.g., energy-efficient fridges), or interactive technologies (e.g., a smart meter[1]) seem to be decisive, but there is increasing awareness that behavioral changes are also required.

The increase in renewable energy sources implies several new challenges for energy systems. For example, more than 1.5 million PV systems are currently registered in Germany (BSW-Solar, 2016), with a substantial proportion located in residential households. With the increasing number of PV systems feeding electricity into the grid, grid stability has become an important concern. From a technological perspective, solutions to this issue consist in technological innovations such as battery storage systems and smart grids. At the household level, batteries offer the opportunity to store electricity produced during the day for later use (e.g., in the evening), thus increasing the "self-consumption" and reducing the amount of electricity fed into the grid. Smart grids are raising interest and being discussed as solutions for energy systems. On the one hand, they can facilitate energy efficiency and energy saving in households by enabling them to manage energy generation and demand. On the other hand, the potential of smart energy systems will only be fully realized if households accept the task of actively participating by adopting the appropriate behavior (van der Werff and Steg 2016). In this respect, too, any action and behavior that is necessary prior to the final installation of a PV system introduces costs for the individual, especially in terms of the time (to read and understand special articles and communicate with experts and PV owners) needed to evaluate the unknown consequences and risks.

Given the fact that technological measures for energy efficiency in industrialized countries will at best lead to a stagnation in energy consumption (Otto, Kaiser, and Arnold 2014; for recent developments of per capita energy consumption see www.worldbank.org), one can grasp the importance of consumer behavior. In accordance with other sources such as the world energy report (IEA 2011) or Klingholz and Töpfer (2012), it can be deduced that the use of more efficient technologies alone will not be enough to reduce individual energy consumption. Potential energy savings due to technological efficiency are more or less reduced to zero by the additional consumption of energy.

Changing the focus: from technology to the human factor

The compensatory function of behavioral costs and intrinsic motivation to protect the environment

Energy efficiency is related to energy-saving behavior in daily life and to investments in technologies, e.g., energy-efficient appliances or renewable energy sources. Such pro-environmental behavior can be explained with reference to two basic determinants: behavioral costs and intrinsic motivation to protect the environment. This also applies to reactions concerning different interventions such as the operational mode of the most common measures (material and social incentives) and the evaluation of their effectiveness in consideration of the rebound phenomenon (Kaiser, Arnold, and Otto 2014). First, we will take a closer look at these two determinants. Afterwards, we will illustrate their operation with examples related to the energy transition, paying special attention to technologies which can play an important role in energy use and/or savings. Finally, we will draw conclusions for the energy transition with special attention to practical implications in terms of policy design and intervention strategies for motivating individuals or households.

In the introduction, we pointed out that energy consumption is an important issue for our society and that technological improvements increased technological efficiency but that this does not necessarily mean a reduction in overall energy consumption. To get a better understanding of this fact, we looked at the origin and rules of the sociotechnical system, adopting a psychobiological perspective on human motivation and the utility of technology in this context, followed by a presentation of the four roles that technology plays regarding human behavior and their impact on resource consumption. In the next section of this chapter, we will focus on the actual context of energy consumption, in particular in Germany, and different ways to obtain a sustainable energy system. Special attention will be given to the behavioral dimension.

Behavioral costs: what makes energy saving and environmental protection easy or difficult?

Different types of energy-saving behavior vary in terms of effort and costs, for instance the behavioral costs such as for gathering information, calculating consequences, gaining familiarity, and overcoming novelty (Kaiser, Byrka, and Hartig 2010, Miafodzyeva and Brandt 2013). For example, most people in Germany use energy-efficient lighting, which implies little effort and cost. First, light bulbs that consume a high level of energy are difficult to find in Germany nowadays, and the higher price for energy-efficient lightening is rapidly amortized by notable reductions in the electricity consumed (Umweltbundesamt 2013). Second, it has become rather common for German consumers to use energy-efficient lighting, so that this behavior nowadays corresponds to a social norm. As illustrated by the above example, all environmentally friendly behavior, including saving energy, implies behavioral costs, which are determined by factors such as technological, material, social, and other conditions. These costs are rather similar for any individual in the same context, such as the population of a specific city. For instance, inhabitants of one city have the same infrastructure (e.g., public transport, waste collection). This assumption is tested every time behavior and its costs are studied in a specific context. Several studies have supported this assumption, showing the relative stability of behavioral costs for people within the same context (e.g., Geiger, Otto, and Diaz 2014, Kaiser and Wilson 2004). The most important factors are knowledge, structural conditions, and material and social incentives.

In general, *knowledge* is a necessary condition for pro-environmental behavior (Geiger, Otto, and Diaz 2014). Depending on the knowledge and complexity of the available information in a specific situation, different forms of behavior can be related to either high or low cognitive behavioral costs in terms of assessing, selecting, and organizing available information in order to gain the required knowledge. For example, it can be necessary to consider the different characteristics of appliances in order to make decisions about a purchase and use as well as to organize the corresponding actions. Nevertheless, it is important to take the fact into consideration that specific pro-environmental knowledge, if combined with a high income, can be related to a higher consumption of resources for specific pro-environmental behaviors (Otto et al. 2016).

Moreover, the *structural conditions* under which behavior takes place and the physical effort implied in energy-saving behavior are important factors in the realm of energy consumption. In particular, material incentives or financial costs play an important role for energy-saving behavior (Abrahamse et al. 2005). For example, the acquisition costs can hinder the purchase of more expensive energy-efficient appliances. At the same time, material incentives such as subsidies can facilitate the acquisition of such appliances or of technologies such as PV systems. Furthermore, the scope of action depends on the existing infrastructure and the legal framework. In addition, technological equipment such as smart meters, which can support a frugal use of energy, goes hand in hand with financial costs and expenditures of time, especially for their use. The available technologies and the legal framework surrounding them are further important factors to be mentioned in this context.

The adoption of innovative technologies implies important financial costs, but *material incentives* are offered in several countries, e.g., in Germany, in order to reduce these behavioral costs. Material incentives come in many forms, such as subsidies, taxes, tax reductions, or free giveaways. Furthermore, according to Rogers (2003), technology itself can function as a material incentive. The diffusion of innovations theory (Rogers, 2003) innovation theory offers an interesting additional perspective for understanding the motivation behind the adoption of technologies at different stages of the diffusion of innovations. Taking the example of PV systems, early adopters, among other characteristics, generally show a keen interest in technology, report a high level of pro-environmental motivation (e.g., Wittenberg and Matthies 2016), and are also ready to take higher risks than the average population (Haas et al. 1999). Thus, they are more likely to overcome behavioral costs due to their pro-environmental motivation but maybe also due to other motives, such as that to be innovative or to engage with new technology. In going with these motives, they are also ready to inform others and to demonstrate that the technology works (Schelly 2014), which is particularly relevant with increasing the diffusion of innovations because new adopters tend to rely on such information channels (for an overview see e.g., Stern et al. 2018). In the case of the adoption of PV, information about PV from neighbors can increase interest in PV (Rai, Reeves, and Margolis 2016) and reduce the time delay for decisions on PV installation (Rai and Robinson 2013), for example. Moreover, communities of information (Schelly 2014), local electricity utilities (Palm 2016), and solar community organizations (Noll, Dawes, and Rai 2014) have been identified as important channels of information.

Social incentives also play a central role in energy consumption. For example, social norms and status can result in social reputation or, on the contrary, induce social pressure, which influences the probability of specific types of behavior (Griskevicius, Tybur, and van den Bergh 2010). In particular, this kind of influence can be expected to affect types of behavior which are easily visible or observable and are also relevant for an energy transition (Korcaj, Hahnel, and Spada 2015). For example as stated above, because energy-efficient lighting has become commonplace in Germany, it constitutes a social norm nowadays. Therefore, the use of old light bulbs that violate this social norm implies a risk of a disapproving glance or other social consequences. Complying, on the other hand, reduces the behavioral costs of energy-saving in an indirect way. In all likelihood, persons want to avoid the risk of conflict with others, e.g., family, friends, or guests, if they can fit in by using energy-efficient light bulbs. Thus, the use of energy-efficient lighting has become rather easy.

Environmental-protection attitude: who overcomes behavioral costs and adopts even difficult behavior?

Behavioral costs determine the probability of behavior. However, they do not explain why some people only adopt environmental-protection behavior that is rather easy to accept while others are willing to incur high behavioral costs in the name of environmental protection. For example, only a small number of consumers check the electricity consumption of appliances in their household by means of an ammeter or use a smart meter in order to reduce their energy consumption. To do so would imply buying a smart meter, taking the time to detect the appliances that consume a lot of energy, and reducing their consumption by means of behavioral change or investment in new energy-efficient appliances. In comparison to replacing conventional light bulbs with energy-efficient ones, the identification of appliances like older refrigerators that consume higher amounts of energy or TVs whose consumption is high in standby implies high behavioral costs. Therefore, such behavior raises questions about the reasons why some people adopt them anyway. There seems to be another determinant of behavior besides behavioral costs that leads a small number of people to adopt a behavior despite the related high effort. These people have to be motivated to such an extent that they are willing to offset the high behavioral costs. For behavior that obviously has no other advantage than saving energy and thus climate protection, it can be deduced that this is an intrinsic motivation to protect the environment (Kaiser, Byrka, and Hartig 2010).[2] Several studies provide evidence demonstrating the compensatory function of pro-environmental motivation and behavioral costs (Arnold et al. 2018).

Ways to establish a sustainable energy system: examples of energy consumption with new technology

The main goal of the European energy transition – namely, attempting to reduce energy consumption by employing more energy-efficient technology but without changing consumption behavior – corresponds to a reduction in behavioral costs. For example, a consumer can use an energy-efficient fridge as well as a conventional fridge to refrigerate food. It is easy for a consumer to reduce his or her energy consumption by taking advantage of technological improvements, thus reducing his behavioral costs. In the long term, the consumer will even save money. He or she could also reinvest the money in additional consumption or donate it, e.g., to an environmental-protection organization. This decision depends on his or her *pro-environmental motivation*, the second determinant of environmental-protection behavior, which currently receives too little attention in the context of energy transitions.

The investment in PV systems constitutes an interesting example in the context of energy consumption and renewable energies. Indeed, the acquisition of a PV system means high financial and cognitive costs and thus very high behavioral costs. Financial incentives that reduce behavioral costs are used worldwide. In Germany, the feed-in tariff for electricity production constitutes a central means for supporting investment in PV systems. In addition, investment costs have been reduced as a consequence of falling prices induced by market development (for an overview about PV in Germany, see e.g.,Wirth 2017). Nevertheless, a strong environmental-protection attitude seems to be necessary to overcome the impediment of behavioral costs. The intention to invest in a PV system (e.g., to obtain offers for a PV system) implies high behavioral costs (Kaiser and Wilson 2004), e.g., in terms of knowledge and acquisition of information. For an individual to manifest the corresponding behavior, a strong environmental-protection attitude is required to compensate for these costs. A comparison of the strong environmental-protection attitude of PV owners with a representative sample of Germans (Wittenberg and Matthies 2016) also suggests that this motivation is necessary to overcome the behavioral costs. The perception of environmental problems can motivate people to invest time to get informed about PV prior to a financial investment in a PV system (Jager 2006). Furthermore, social incentives such as social status or pressure (Korcaj, Hahnel, and Spada 2015), social networks (Jager 2006), and social norms, e.g., the diffusion of PV systems in the neighborhood (Bollinger and Gillingham 2012), play an important role in investment in PV systems as they reduce the behavioral costs. In the same line, seeing PV systems installed on nearby houses promotes interest in PV systems (Rai, Reeves, and Margolis 2016, Wolske, Stern, and Dietz 2017). Perceived social support and curiosity about the PV systems of other people can also contribute to interest in talking to a PV installer (Wolske, Stern, and Dietz 2017).

Considering the role of behavioral costs and environmental-protection attitude in the context of a PV installation on an international level makes the situation even more complex (e.g., Stern et al. 2018), but also reveals different routes to the diffusion of PV. Behavioral costs in terms of knowledge and the acquisition of information seem to be higher in the US than in Germany, while the third-party ownership option available in the US provides a means to start PV use without the high investment costs at the household level. In this case, the households lease PV systems installed on their roofs but the systems are owned and maintained by a third-party company (also optional, households purchase electricity generated by the PV systems from this company).

One strategy for raising awareness of (high) energy consumption and the underlying reasons in households is the feedback on consumption provided by smart meters, which can encourage consumers to save energy (Delmas, Fischlein, and Asensio 2013). The idea is to communicate specific information that enables users to acquire the knowledge to help them to reduce their consumption. Although smart meters provide useful information for saving energy and thus reducing behavioral costs, other behavioral costs have to be overcome. In a study by Arnold (2016), households had to (1) register, (2) log in regularly and inform themselves, and (3) on the basis of the available information identify possibilities for saving energy and put them into practice. Only some of the households that were equipped with a smart meter between 2009 and 2011 by a regional energy provider registered, hereby overcoming the first hurdle. In the end, only households using smart meters and having a strong environmental-protection attitude saved energy. Despite the fact that the behavioral costs of saving energy were reduced by smart meters, they remained at such a high level that only people whose environmental-protection attitude is strong invested time in using a smart meter to reduce their electricity consumption. Therefore, while smart meters offer an opportunity to save electricity, putting this into practice requires a strong environmental-protection attitude.

Changing course: reducing energy consumption by promoting the intrinsic motivation to protect the environment

As we have illustrated in practical examples, employing material and social incentives to reduce behavioral costs can be very effective in supporting efficient technologies and pro-environmental behavioral change. Nevertheless, this does not ensure a reduction in per capita energy consumption, since the use of material and social incentives merely reduce the behavioral costs. Consequently, the consumer saves time and money, which he or she might use for additional consumption and which increases the overall level of activities in a society.

It is only if the environmental-protection attitude is strong that the goal of reducing consumption on the individual level will help to prevent rebound. Indeed, independent of measures for increasing energy efficiency, people whose environmental-protection attitude is strong exhibit low consumption behaviors more frequently than others. In general, they use less electricity (Arnold et al. 2017), recycle more electrical appliances, more often choose to ride a bike rather than to go by car, and eat more vegetarian food (Kibbe 2017). Using and consuming less directly affects affluence (A), and thus, the environmental impact of humans, calculated with the widely used formula $I = P \times A \times T$ as described above (Ehrlich and Holdren 1971, Holdren 2000). Because affluence is a multiplier, reducing affluence directly results in a reduction of the human impact (I). In contrast, as described above, technology (T) could reduce the human impact (but does not due to rebound). A more energy-sufficient (less affluent) lifestyle is supported by a stronger environmental-protection attitude. The real challenge which needs to be addressed is thus, how to promote environmental-protection attitudes and energy-sufficient lifestyles (Otto, Kaiser, and Arnold 2014).

Although it is difficult to fundamentally change environmental-protection attitudes, as reflected in lifestyle by different behaviors, there are approaches for promoting such motivation. For example, evidence has been found that pro-environmental behaviors ranging from recycling products to renouncing holiday flights can be learned (Otto, Kaiser, and Arnold 2014). Such learning can probably be activated and strengthened by issues that are discussed in society over a long period of time, such as climate change, as well as by societal preoccupation. Furthermore, fostering environmental-protection attitudes and pro-environmental behavior through the environmental education of children and adolescents (Otto and Pensini 2017) has been the most sustainable strategy so far to encourage pro-environmental behavior without negative side effects such as rebound. This thus supports a more sustainable lifestyle.

Learning pro-environmental behavior as a chance

The prevailing Zeitgeist plays a crucial role in learning pro-environmental behavior (Otto and Kaiser 2014). If environmental issues such as climate change are widely discussed in society for several years, the related pro-environmental behavior is learned and shown more frequently. The societal relevance of an issue can take different forms. For example, it could be addressed in the mass media, integrated in education at school or university, included in funding programs, taxes, or subsidies, and brought up by citizens' groups. Supporting the presence of an issue at multiple levels is a means for fostering lifestyle changes in many people and for achieving a correspondingly large impact. Beyond adopting specific pro-environmental behavior, the purpose of an energy-sufficient lifestyle is also to reduce resource consumption. In the case of climate change, the goal is to reduce the per capita energy consumption and thus the emission of greenhouse gases. In order to reach this goal, it is necessary to educate the citizens about the emissions resulting from their behavior. Besides more conventional media, there are other means, such as calculators of CO_2 emissions (see, e.g., www.uba.co2-rechner.de). Such education should inform people about the rebound effects related to energy efficiency measures when the savings in time and money are used for further consumption.

Households with PV systems often have the opportunity to get feedback about their CO_2 savings from the consumption of solar power. In this specific case, it could be interesting to provide additional calculations concerning the mix of the total electricity consumption in order to raise the household's attention to the sufficient use of electricity. The available technologies for providing such information and their location in the household can function as both determinant and promoter in this context. It can be helpful to get such feedback in the living environment rather than in less used locations, such as a basement. The design of the technology can be decisive in promoting sufficient energy use, especially in terms of a user-friendly design that attracts interest and offers salient and easily understandable information. Changing one's lifestyle and the underlying motivations can only be achieved in middle- or long-term time spans, but they are lasting and can, combined with the required knowledge, counter rebound.

Increasing the intrinsic motivation to protect the environment and supporting an energy-sufficient lifestyle by pursuing a nature-based environmental education

A more direct and holistic approach to promoting an energy-sufficient lifestyle is to foster individual environmental competence, which consists in environmental knowledge as an intellectual component and connectedness to nature as a motivational component. Both are necessary preconditions for pro-environmental motivation and behavior and a sustainable lifestyle (e.g., Kossack and Bogner 2012, Roczen et al. 2014, Frantz and Mayer 2014). Indeed, connectedness to nature implies that damage inflicted on nature is at the same time perceived as a threat to one's self (e.g., Schultz 2002, Metzner 1999). Connectedness to nature refers to the strength of the relationship between a person and nature from the individual's perspective (Brügger, Kaiser, and Roczen 2011, Nisbet, Zelenski, and Murphy 2009, Pensini, Horn, and Caltabiano 2016) and can be supported by contact with nature and experiences in it (Pensini, Horn, and Caltabiano 2016). For example, specific experiences in nature (Mayer et al. 2009), visits to nature areas such as nature preserves but also parks (Schultz and Tabanico 2007), and the distance between home and nature (Cheng and Monroe 2012) all are linked to one's connectedness to nature and can favor it.

Thus, while environmental knowledge and connectedness to nature are necessary preconditions for a sustainable lifestyle, the question remains how both can be promoted. Nature-based environmental education has always included environmental knowledge, comprising knowledge about environmental-protection behavior in settings close to nature, which fosters a connectedness to nature at the same time (Otto and Pensini 2017). In Germany, several environmental education institutions, such as ecological farms, urban gardening projects, botanic gardens, and zoos, engage in efforts to provide environmental education. Environmental education in these institutions provides a transfer of knowledge about environmental-protection combined with experiences of nature, both for adults and especially for children. Because of the combination of knowledge and experience in nature as well as because of the focus on young target groups, they represent a crucial component for facilitating the pro-environmental motivation that underlies an energy-sufficient lifestyle, including an avoidance of rebound

(Otto and Pensini 2017). Regarding a sustainable energy system, these institutions, constituting important existing channels of communication for environmental education, can also pass on information about the use of technology such as a smart meter or a sufficient use of renewable energy. For example, they might serve as models for an energy-sufficient use of such technology or inform people about the role of PV systems in achieving a mix of sources in global electricity consumption. Moreover, such technology can represent a useful means for supporting pro-environmental education, especially ICT.

Conclusion

In summary, achieving the goal of a sustainable energy system is still challenging. Taking the perspective that energy consumption is a sociotechnical problem (1) provides useful insights into the reasons why society continues to fail in attaining the goal of a reduction of energy consumption despite achieving efficiency improvements by means of technology and (2) highlights the importance of human behavior and the underlying motivation in order to pave the way for a sustainable energy system. Deepening the motivational aspects that may lead individuals to use and improve technology as well as the four roles that technology can play for human behavior, we showed how important it is to link efficient technology with an energy-sufficient lifestyle.

Concerning the example of PV systems in private households, structural measures have been efficient in reducing the behavioral costs of investment in a PV system, especially in households with a strong pro-environmental attitude. Several studies have also revealed the importance of social incentives for overcoming the barriers of behavioral costs (see e.g., Bollinger and Gillingham 2012, Jager 2006, Korcaj, Hahnel, and Spada 2015). Nevertheless, such means only achieved the diffusion of renewable energy and energy-efficient technology. For example, investment in a PV system does not seem to be necessarily associated with a more sufficient use of energy (see Wittenberg and Matthies 2016). In particular with regard to daily behavior, such as our use of electricity, it is interesting to adopt measures focused on a perspective of long-term sufficiency, such as strengthening pro-environmental motivation by means of environmental education. Existing social networks were identified as an important factor supporting investments in PV systems (Jager 2006) and could be used to communicate environmental education. In this context, the focus should be on a sufficient use of renewable energy from the perspective of per capita consumption in order to avoid rebound. This implies attributing less importance to the use of external incentives in the management of specific measures and more to the support of an energy-sufficient lifestyle, focusing on the global impact of an individual. In this sense, effective measures providing, for example, knowledge about PV should always consider the superordinate behavior-related motivation, for example by addressing at the same time the connectedness to nature (e.g., by means of nature-based environmental education), as one of the most important predictors of an energy-sufficient lifestyle (Otto and Pensini 2017).

Although actual energy consumption is still too high despite improving technological efficiency, we focused on the determinants of energy-saving behavior, a type of pro-environmental behavior, and on the means for behavioral change. This has illustrated the ambiguous influence of technology, both hindering and facilitating sustainable energy consumption. We conclude that education on the aspects of energy consumption and a nature-based environmental education are required to foster environmental competence which includes an intrinsic motivation to protect the environment, and thus, a sustainable lifestyle. Environmental competence can help to shape the interaction between individuals and technology in a sustainable way, informing and demonstrating a sustainable use of technology. The way "back" to nature can thus help to improve the ecological outcome of technological innovations and increased efficiency in a constructive sustainable manner.

Notes

1 Smart meters are electronic appliances providing detailed data about the electricity consumption in a household.
2 The operationalization, i.e., the measure of pro-environmental motivation that we refer to in this article is based on the General Ecological Behavior scale. Other common measures of environmental attitudes or Sinus-Milieus might show a relationship with energy consumption that contradicts expectations. In other words, the energy consumption of people from Sinus-Milieus who consider the environment to be important (solely based on self-reported expressions of opinions) is frequently higher (Umweltbundesamt 2016).

References

Abrahamse, Wokje, Linda Steg, Charles Vlek, and Talib Rothengatter. 2005. "A Review of Intervention Studies Aimed at Household Energy Conservation." *Journal of Environmental Psychology* 25: 273–91. doi: 10.1016/j.jenvp.2005.08.002.

Ajzen, Icek. 2005. *Attitudes, Personality and Behavior*. Buckingham, UK: Open University Press.

Arnold, Oliver. 2016. *Verhalten als kompensatorische Funktion von Einstellung und Verhaltenskosten: Die Person-Situation-Interaktion im Rahmen des Campbell-Paradigmas*. Magdeburg, Germany: Dissertation. Otto-von-Guericke-Universität.

Arnold, Oliver, A. Kibbe, M. Vetter, M. Adler, and F. G. Kaiser. 2017. "Sustainable Travel Behavior within the Campbell Paradigm: Compensatory Effects of Environmental Attitude and the Transportation Environment." *Manuscript submitted for publication*.

Arnold, Oliver, Alexandra Kibbe, Terry Hartig, and Florian G. Kaiser. 2018. "Capturing the Environmental Impact of Individual Lifestyles: Evidence of the Criterion Validity of the General Ecological Behavior Scale." *Environment and Behavior*. 50: 350–372. doi:10.1177/0013916517701796.

Bischof, Norbert 1985. *Das Rätsel Ödipus. Die biologischen Wurzeln des Urkonfliktes von Intimität und Autonomie*. Munic, Germany: Piper.

Bollinger, Bryan, and Kenneth Gillingham. 2012. "Peer Effects in the Diffusion of Solar Photovoltaic Panels." *Marketing Science* 31 (6): 900–12. doi: 10.1287/mksc.1120.0727.

Brügger, Adrian, Florian G. Kaiser, and Nina Roczen. 2011. "One For All? Connectedness to Nature, Inclusion of Nature, Environmental Identity, and Implicit Association with Nature." *European Psychologist* 16: 324–33. doi: 10.1027/1016–9040/a000032.

(BSW-Solar), German Solar Association. 2016. Statistic Data on the German Solar Power (photovoltaic) Industry.

Cheng, Judith Chen-Hsuan, and Martha C. Monroe. 2012. "Connection to Nature: Children's Affective Attitude Toward Nature." *Environment and Behavior* 44 (1): 31–49. doi: 10.1177/0013916510385082.

Commission of the European Communities. 2008. *Energy Efficiency: Delivering the 20% Target, Communication From the Commission.* Brussels, Belgium: Author.

Darwin, Charles. 1859. *On the Origin of Species by Means of Natural Selection, or the Preservation of Favoured Races in the Struggle for Life.* London: John Murray.

Dawkins, R. 2006. *The Selfish Gene.* 30th ed. New York: Oxford University Press. Original edition, 1975.

Delmas, Magali A., Miriam Fischlein, and Omar I. Asensio. 2013. "Information Strategies and Energy Conservation Behavior: A Meta-analysis of Experimental Studies from 1975 to 2012." *Energy Policy* 61: 729–39. doi: 10.1016/j.enpol.2013.05.109.

Ehrlich, Paul R., and John P. Holdren. 1971. "Impact of Population Growth." *Science* 171: 1212–17. doi: 10.1126/science.171.3977.1212.

European Commission. 2011. Future of Transport. Analytical report. Brussels.

Frantz, Cynthia McPherson, and F. Stephan Mayer. 2014. "The Importance of Connection to Nature in Assessing Environmental Education Programs." *Studies in Educational Evaluation* 41: 85–9. doi: 10.1016/j.stueduc.2013.10.001.

Geiger, Sonja M., Siegmar Otto, and Johann Streiker Diaz. 2014. "A Diagnostic Environmental Knowledge Scale for Latin America/Escala diagnóstica de conocimientos ambientales para Latinoamérica." *Psyecology* 5: 1–36. doi: 10.1080/21711976.2014.881664.

Goldstein, Daniel G., Eric J. Johnson, Andreas Herrmann, and Mark Heitmann. 2008. "Nudge Your Customers Toward Better Choices." *Harvard Business Review* 86 (12): 99–105.

Griskevicius, Vladas, Joshua M. Tybur, and Bram Van den Bergh. 2010. "Going Green to Be Seen: Status, Reputation, and Conspicuous Conservation." *Journal of Personality and Social Psychology* 98: 392–404. doi: 10.1037/a0017346.

Haas, Reinhard, Michael Ornetzeder, Kristina Hametner, Angela Wroblewski, and Michael Hübner. 1999. "Socio-Economic Aspects of the Austrian 200 kwp-Photovoltaic-Rooftop Programme." *Solar Energy* 66 (3): 183–91. doi: 10.1016/S0038–092X(99)00019–5.

Holdren, John P. 2000. "Environmental Degradation: Population, Affluence, Technology, and Sociopolitical Factors." *Environment* 42 (6): 4–5. doi: 10.1080/00139150009604891.

IEA. 2011. *World Energy Outlook 2011. Executive Summary.* Paris: OECD.

IPCC. 2007. *Fourth Assessment Report. Climate Change 2007: Mitigation of Climate Change.* Bern: Intergovernmental Panel on Climate Change.

Jager, Wander. 2006. "Stimulating the Diffusion of Photovoltaic Systems: A Behavioural Perspective." *Energy Policy* 34 (14): 1935–43. doi: 10.1016/j.enpol.2004.12.022.

Jevons, W.S. 1865. *The Coal Question: An Inquiry Concerning the Prospects of the Nation and the Probable Exhaustion of Our Coal Mines.* London: Macmillan.

Kaiser, Florian G., Oliver Arnold, and Siegmar Otto. 2014. "Attitudes and Defaults Save Lives and Protect the Environment Jointly and Compensatorily: Understanding the Behavioral Efficacy of Nudges and Other Structural Interventions." *Behavioral Sciences* 4: 202–12. doi: 10.3390/bs4030202.

Kaiser, Florian G., Katarzyna Byrka, and Terry Hartig. 2010. "Reviving Campbell's Paradigm for Attitude Research." *Personality and Social Psychology Review* 14: 351–67. doi: 10.1177/1088868310366452.

Kaiser, Florian G., and Heinz Gutscher. 2003. "The Proposition of a General Version of the Theory of Planned Behavior: Predicting Ecological Behavior." *Journal of Applied Social Psychology* 33 (3): 586–603. doi: 10.1111/j.1559–1816.2003.tb01914.x.

Kaiser, Florian G., and Mark Wilson. 2004. "Goal-directed conservation behavior: the specific composition of a general performance." *Personality and Individual Differences* 36: 1531–44. doi: 10.1016/j.paid.2003.06.003.

Kenrick, Douglas T., Vladas Griskevicius, Jill M. Sundie, Norman P. Li, Yexin Jessica Li, and Steven L. Neuberg. 2009. "Deep Rationality: The Evolutionary Economics of Decision Making." *Social Cognition* 27: 764–85. doi: 10.1521/soco.2009.27.5.764.

Kibbe, Alexandra. 2017. *Intrinsische Umweltmotivation – Selbstbestimmungstheorie und Campbell-Paradigma im Vergleich*. Magdeburg, Germany: Dissertation. Otto-von-Guericke-Universität Magdeburg.

Klingholz, Reiner, and Klaus Töpfer. 2012. *Das Trilemma des Wachstums. Bevölkerungswachstum, Energieverbrauch und Klimawandel-drei Probleme, keine Lösung?* Berlin: Berlin-Institut für Bevölkerung.

Klöckner, Christian Andreas, Alim Nayum, and Mehmet Mehmetoglu. 2013. "Positive and Negative Spillover Effects from Electric Car Purchase to Car Use." *Transportation Research Part D: Transport and Environment* 21: 32–8. doi: 10.1016/j.trd.2013.02.007.

Koomey, J. G., S. Berard, M. Sanchez, and H. Wong. 2011. "Implications of Historical Trends in the Electrical Efficiency of Computing." *Annals of the History of Computing, IEEE* 33 (3): 46–54. doi: 10.1109/MAHC.2010.28.

Korcaj, Liridon, Ulf J. J. Hahnel, and Hans Spada. 2015. "Intentions to Adopt Photovoltaic Systems Depend on Homeowners' Expected Personal Gains and Behavior of Peers." *Renewable Energy* 75: 407–15. doi: 10.1016/j.renene.2014.10.007.

Kossack, Alida, and Franz X. Bogner. 2012. "How Does a One-day Environmental Education Programme Support Individual Connectedness with Nature?" *Journal of Biological Education* 46: 180–7. doi: 10.1080/00219266.2011.634016.

Mayer, F. Stephan, Cynthia McPherson Frantz, Emma Bruehlman-Senecal, and Kyffin Dolliver. 2009. "Why Is Nature Beneficial?: The Role of Connectedness to Nature." *Environment and Behavior* 41: 607–43. doi: 10.1177/0013916508319745.

Metzner, Ralph. 1999. *Green Psychology: Transforming our Relationship to the Earth*. Rochester, Vermont: Park Street Press.

Miafodzyeva, S., and N. Brandt. 2013. "Recycling Behaviour Among Householders: Synthesizing Determinants Via a Meta-analysis." *Waste and Biomass Valorization* 4: 221–35. doi: 10.1007/s12649-012-9144-4.

Midden, Cees J. H., Florian G. Kaiser, and L. Teddy McCalley. 2007. "Technology's Four Roles in Understanding Individuals' Conservation of Natural Resources." *Journal of Social Issues* 63 (1): 155–74. doi: 10.1111/j.1540–4560.2007.00501.x.

Mont, Oksana, and Andrius Plepys. 2008. "Sustainable Consumption Progress: Should We Be Proud or Alarmed?" *Journal of Cleaner Production* 16: 531–7. doi: 10.1016/j.jclepro.2007.01.009.

Nisbet, Elizabeth K., John M. Zelenski, and Steven A. Murphy. 2009. "The Nature Relatedness Scale. Linking Individuals' Connection With Nature to Environmental Concern and Behavior." *Environment and Behavior* 41: 715–40. doi: 10.1177/0013916508318748.

Noel, Lance, and Benjamin K. Sovacool. 2016. "Why Did Better Place Fail?: Range Anxiety, Interpretive Flexibility, and Electric Vehicle Promotion in Denmark and Israel." *Energy Policy* 94: 377–86. doi: 10.1016/j.enpol.2016.04.029.

Noll, Daniel, Colleen Dawes, and Varun Rai. 2014. "Solar Community Organizations and Active Peer Effects in the Adoption of Residential PV." *Energy Policy* 67: 330–43. doi: 10.1016/j.enpol.2013.12.050.

Otto, Siegmar. 2010. "Public Perception of Sustainable Development: What Means Sustainability and Sustainable Development?" *Oekologisches Wirtschaften* 2010 (4): 35–8.

Otto, Siegmar, and Florian G. Kaiser. 2014. "Ecological Behavior across the Lifespan: Why Environmentalism Increases as People Grow Older." *Journal of Environmental Psychology* 40: 331–8. doi: 10.1016/j.jenvp.2014.08.004.

Otto, Siegmar, Florian G. Kaiser, and Oliver Arnold. 2014. "The Critical Challenge of Climate Change for Psychology: Preventing Rebound and Promoting More Individual Irrationality." *European Psychologist* 19: 96–106. doi: 10.1027/1016–9040/a000182.

Otto, Siegmar, Alexander Neaman, Bárbara Richards, and Andrés Marió. 2016. "Explaining the Ambiguous Relations Between Income, Environmental Knowledge, and Environmentally Significant Behavior." *Society & Natural Resources* 29: 628–32. doi: 10.1080/08941920.2015.1037410.

Otto, Siegmar, and Pamela Pensini. 2017. "Nature-based Environmental Education of Children: Environmental Knowledge and Connectedness to Nature, Together, Are Related to Ecological Behaviour." *Global Environmental Change* 47: 88–94. doi: 10.1016/j.gloenvcha.2017.09.009.

Palm, Alvar. 2016. "Local Factors Driving the Diffusion of Solar Photovoltaics in Sweden: A Case Study of Five Municipalities in an Early Market." *Energy Research & Social Science* 14: 1–12. doi: 10.1016/j.erss.2015.12.027.

Pensini, Pamela, Eva Horn, and Nerina J. Caltabiano. 2016. "An Exploration of the Relationships between Adults' Childhood and Current Nature Exposure and Their Mental Well-Being." *Children, Youth and Environments* 26 (1): 125–47. doi: 10.7721/chilyoutenvi.26.1.0125.

Rai, Varun, D. Cale Reeves, and Robert Margolis. 2016. "Overcoming Barriers and Uncertainties in the Adoption of Residential Solar PV." *Renewable Energy* 89: 498–505. doi: 10.1016/j.renene.2015.11.080.

Rai, Varun, and Scott A. Robinson. 2013. "Effective Information Channels for Reducing Costs of Environmentally- Friendly Technologies: Evidence from Residential PV Markets." *Environmental Research Letters* 8 (1): 014044. doi: 10.1088/1748–9326/8/1/014044.

Reijnders, Lucas. 1998. "The Factor X Debate: Setting Targets for Eco-Efficiency." *Journal of Industrial Ecology* 2 (1): 13–22. doi: 10.1162/jiec.1998.2.1.13.

Roczen, Nina, Florian G. Kaiser, Franz X. Bogner, and Mark Wilson. 2014. "A Competence Model for Environmental Education." *Environment and Behavior* 46: 972–92. doi: 10.1177/0013916513492416.

Rogers, Everett M. 2003. *Diffusion of Innovations.* 2nd. ed. New York: Free Press.

Schelly, Chelsea. 2014. "Residential Solar Electricity Adoption: What Motivates, and What Matters? A Case Study of Early Adopters." *Energy Research & Social Science* 2: 183–91. doi: 10.1016/j.erss.2014.01.001.

Schultz, Paul W. 2002. "Inclusion with Nature: The Psychology of Human-Nature Relations." In *Psychology of Sustainable Development*, edited by Peter Schmuck and Paul W. Schultz, 61–78. New York: Kluwer. https://doi.org/10.1007/978-1-4615-0995-0_4.

Schultz, Paul W., and Jennifer J. Tabanico. 2007. "Self, Identity, and the Natural Environment: Exploring Implicit Connections with Nature." *Journal of Applied Social Psychology* 37 (6): 1219–47. doi: 10.1111/j.1559–1816.2007.00210.x.

Sorrell, Steve, John Dimitropoulos, and Matt Sommerville. 2009. "Empirical Estimates of the Direct Rebound Effect: A Review." *Energy Policy* 37: 1356–71. doi: 10.1016/j.enpol.2008.11.026.

Spielmann, Michael, Peter de Haan, and Roland W. Scholz. 2008. "Environmental Rebound Effects of High-Speed Transport Technologies: A Case Study of Climate Change Rebound Effects of a Future Underground Maglev Train System." *Journal of Cleaner Production* 16 (13): 1388–98. doi: 10.1016/j.jclepro.2007.08.001.

Stern, Paul C., Inga Wittenberg, Kimberly S. Wolske, and Ingo Kastner. 2018. "Household Production of Photovoltaic Energy: Issues in Economic Behavior." In *The Cambridge Handbook of Psychology and Economic Behaviour*, edited by Alan Lewis, 541–66. Cambridge University Press. doi:10.1017/9781316676349.019.

Umweltbundesamt. 2013. *Energiesparen im Haushalt*. Germany: Dessau-Roßlau.

Umweltbundesamt. 2016. *Repräsentative Erhebung von Pro-Kopf-Verbräuchen natürlicher Ressourcen in Deutschland*. Germany: Dessau-Roßlau.

van der Werff, Ellen, and Linda Steg. 2016. "The Psychology of Participation and Interest in Smart Energy Systems: Comparing the Value-Belief-Norm Theory and the Value-Identity-Personal Norm Model." *Energy Research & Social Science* 22 (Supplement C): 107–14. doi: 10.1016/j.erss.2016.08.022.

Vereecken, W., W. Van Heddeghem, D. Colle, M. Pickavet, and P. Demeester. 2010. "Overall ICT Footprint and Green Communication Technologies." 4th International Symposium on Communications, Control and Signal Processing (ISCCSP 2010), Limassol, Cyprus, March 3–5.

WCED. 1987. *Our Common Future*. Edited by World Commission on Environment and Development. Oxford: Oxford Paperbacks.

Weizsäcker, Ernst Ulrich von, A. B. Lovins, and L. H. Lovins. 1998. *Factor Four: Doubling Wealth-Halving Resource Use: The New Report to the Club of Rome*. London: Earthscan. Original edition, Faktor vier: Doppelter Wohlstand-halbierter Naturverbrauch: der neue Bericht an den Club of Rome.

Wirth, H. 2017. "Aktuelle Fakten zur Photovoltaik in Deutschland." Fraunhofer Institut für Solare Energiesysteme. www.ise.fraunhofer.de/content/dam/ise/de/documents/publications/studies/aktuelle-fakten-zur-photovoltaik-in-deutschland.pdf.

Wittenberg, Inga, and Ellen Matthies. 2016. "Solar Policy and Practice in Germany: How do Residential Households with Solar Panels Use Electricity?" *Energy Research & Social Science* 21: 199–211. doi: 10.1016/j.erss.2016.07.008.

Wolske, Kimberly S., Paul C. Stern, and Thomas Dietz. 2017. "Explaining Interest in Adopting Residential Solar Photovoltaic Systems in the United States: Toward an Integration of Behavioral Theories." *Energy Research & Social Science* 25: 134–51. doi: 10.1016/j.erss.2016.12.023.

Addendum

Observing sociotechnical problems

12 Observing amplified sociotechnical complexity

Challenges for technology assessment regarding energy transitions

Todd R. La Porte

Introduction

Motivation and outline

In scale and technical and organizational complexity, the program of the energy system transformation (Energiewende) is one of the most extensive and interesting efforts in technical and social change for Germany in the past several decades.[1] It has prompted a wide engagement of analytical communities – in planning and technical development and in technology forecasting and consequence assessment. Though still in earlier stages of implementation, significant aspects of the program have already been enacted and some effects are apparent, while others are taking hold. One manifestation is the growing number of organizations that are becoming involved (perhaps entangled); another is an increasing realization that its scale and demographic reach add serious challenges for public policy and behavioral analytical understanding. In addition, the energy systems of interest present an extraordinary range of complex organizational and sociotechnical phenomena to consider and try to engage.

When an invitation came to take up some of the analytical puzzles riveting the attention of the ITAS[2] staff, I was intrigued by the opportunity. They were deep in a policy mission of informing technology developments in Germany via rigorous attention to social phenomena and theoretical conceptual frames that have, in many ways, been my constant cerebral companions for years. The project we mapped out, a mix of what could be viewed as nearly basic social science research with major policy hopes, was far more compelling than I could have imagined. What follows is an essay drawn from confronting the fascinating lineaments and analytical challenges involved, considering the social and institutional evolutions inherent in the Energiewende project.[3]

The month-long series of discussions, seminars, a workshop, and many student conversations included three analytically informing frames.[4] They are discussed in turn:

- Contours of technology assessment (TA) when the technical systems are already in the early stages of deployment (Sect. 2);

- When such systems are seen, in part, through conceptions of "organization social complexity" (Sect. 3), which provoked several unexpected refinements in the resulting fine structure;
- The *challenges of knowing/discovery* when the systems of interest assume very large complex social scales and may be potentially highly hazardous across many operating generations (Sect. 4, which more explicitly takes on a TA cast and suggests two modes of progressing).

A concluding note points out seven (data/descriptive) research vectors likely to reveal potential sources of unexpected change and surprise (Sect. 5). TA readers could read these early on. The topics were much on my mind as I wrote. They would add value to the TA program. Before we dive in, the following sub-section provides additional background information.

Background: context for TA analysis, policy premises, and analytical assumptions

The Energiewende program has directives involving fundamental systemic changes: The initial withdrawal of half of the nuclear power suppliers – the rest to be retired by 2022[5] – which changed the ratios of base load to sustainable, variable load producers, raised questions about continued operational integrity (as producer facilities were phased out and nuclear waste responsibilities remained and regulatory attention was diffused.) The current situation suggests that segments of the Energiewende infrastructure have been deployed, up to some 50% of the expected new capacity. Still to be deployed is a thorough infusion of "smart distributed systems – metering and national grid." Increased emphasis on meeting regionally assigned renewable targets, with increased attention and visibility to former/newly invested operators and users/coordinators.

These changes are being deployed across all the federal states in Germany and are to be integrated in a very large-scale national system entangled in interdependences with other major infrastructures that extend throughout the EU and northern European continent.

First, the existing energy system, the result of years of interaction and operation – requiring high levels of coordination and emphasizing very reliable distribution with a second-order interest in operational safety – consists of a large number of operating (producers and users) and regulatory organizations. It has been operating in a reasonably stable equilibrium, cost levels, safety records, and public "acquiescence," even as there is continued investment in wind and solar power and natural gas generating facilities.

Second, implementing Energiewende directives produces considerable top-down initiation and pressure to alter formal organizational relations among ("path-dependently") cooperating and competing organizations that had more or less worked out rules and territories of engagement, modes of intra- and interorganizational coordination and operations.

Within the context of formal organizational schemes, pre-Energiewende system coherence (in semiequilibrium) has been due, in part, to informal operating relationships that have developed more or less organically, arising from day-to-day, season-to-season adjustments to seasonal and economic changes. This has apparently been sustained even with increasing interdependence among EU international interactions.[6]

Energiewende programs couple a major draw down of one very demanding centralized technology, such as nuclear power production and waste management, with a very significant increase in a series of diffuse sustainable energy sources – e.g., wind, solar, hydro – parallel to increases in natural gas and the continued use of coal.

This has occasioned a range of technical innovations in electrical production and distribution (dispersed solar, wind principally), as well as the expectation that technical design communities will upgrade the means of coordination and pricing via smart meters and smart grids, i.e., highly computerized smart systems still to be developed.

At the same time, national energy systems are importantly integrated into an extensive European electrical and transport grid. Revitalized in post-cold war geographies, the operators of these systems have maintained a more or less coherent organizational network of very considerable social scale.

Energiewende programs and operational systems exhibit all the manifestations of high orders of "organized social complexity" (La Porte 1975b). There are innumerable intra- and inter-producing and distributing relationships with many secondary regulatory and national security watchers and special interests that have thus far remained in the background – invisible – in the system descriptive materials.

What follows are reflections on how Energiewende organizational emergence might be ordered in terms of "organized social complexity" perspectives and how that might inform and engage TA analyses.

"Energiewende" as an object of technology assessment

Assessments of technology can range across purely technical engineering forecasts, production and/or economic analyses, sociotechnical and organizational dynamics, and vetting of the political/policy contexts and consequences of fully deployed systems. Each has particular conceptual and analytical frames to contribute; each often has intricate data sets. A full-fledged assessment would meld the conceptual frames and empirical sets, even as some of these seem incommensurable.

Governmentally stimulated TA, in which economic and public interest outcomes are equally important, may be initiated at different stages of technical development (I), deployment (II), scaling-up (III) or mature, market saturated experience. As the TA entry stage varies, so would the evaluative emphases:

TA I. Typically, proposals for assessment of novel technical promise have been focused on the early, research, demonstration, or start-up stages of economic forecast before even the initial stages of extensive demonstration. Interest is on potential and engineering feasibility in advance of serious deployment (while still in R&D or demonstration of the concept stages where initial design parameters could be modified.) Attention privileges identifying the benefits of deploying R&D, with some attention to surprise and flexible design.

TA II. Assessment projects are initiated after most of the technologies of interest have demonstrated beneficial capability. Some relatively mature systems are already partially deployed. Expected benefits are (already) represented by technical advocates or entrepreneurs and those who see opportunities for direct advantage.

TA III. Initial second-order effects are evident, as are successes in demonstrations of limited scale, widening to include interests that see direct benefits and notice from formerly inattentive groups. Market attractions may arise for some and increased completion for others. Interest from regulatory institutions is likely, along with legislative attention.

For our purposes, TA engagement with the Energiewende brackets stages II and III and shapes both analytical and evaluative attention to its technical and organizational systems.[7]

Study emphasis initially would be mostly TA-II-like, explicating *sociotechnical/ organizational dynamics* (the mission being to help avoid undue surprises associated with scaling-up widespread, nested systems of energy production, or with its use within a turbulent mix of nuclear withdrawal, the rapid growth of renewables, and the diminished role of coal in the background).

When the project calls for mixed TA II/III attention, analysis includes exploring path-dependent alternatives advocated by those seeing personal benefit, informed by the goals of interested institutions. Support and initial development of the technology is no longer problematic; systems are part way toward market saturation.

TA studies would seek to:

- Track the effectiveness of scaled-up operations (from mid-to-full market saturation), follow deployment tactics, "apraxic" trends (see below), social/ operational distortions/outcomes explicitly to be avoided, and unexpected vulnerabilities;
- Search for the unexpected, disquiet, and conditions signaling time for recalibrating, error correction, and resetting – before it is too late (see below);
- Explicate unfolding distributions of privilege/disruption/suffering. A minimalist goal could be change which is "suffering neutral," i.e., patterns of suffering have at least not gotten worse (benefit searching would already be well advanced by firms, financial institutions, and relevant agencies);
- Reveal anomalous patterns, such as societal black holes familiar to enactors but invisible to external policy or TA analysts (see Sect. 3 below).

These analytical directives, were they taken seriously, would propel TA analysts into studying sociotechnical phenomena of extraordinary complexity while the system is in considerable flux, leading to policy outcomes that could produce serious social and economic disruption and loss of public confidence. What analytical perspectives might provide guides to at least initially give some order to the skeins of organizational relationships that quickly surpass the usual scales and dynamics of public administrative studies? They take on characteristics of organized social complexity in the extreme. A view of embracing this perspective is traced out below.

On conceptualizing the energiewende through the lenses of organized social complexity

Observations and refinements

The original conversations (La Porte 1975a, 2015) resulting eventually in the organized social complexity (OSC) papers were prompted by the challenges of conceptualizing the effects of technical change on organizational dynamics. The target phenomena tacitly were existing operating systems and assumed a good deal of coherence within the systems of interest. Further, it was tacitly expected that there would likely be considerable correlation of both (elite informed) *formal authority structures* and (operator informed and usually tacit) *informal relations* facilitating demanding operations. The defining properties or variables – scale, differentiation, interdependence (S, D, I) – referred to social grouping and relationships that *actually* characterize the systems of descriptive and explanatory interest.

The distinction between formal, reporting relations and actual informal organization did not seem particularly salient for conceptual explication and was not explicitly made. Nor had we particularly considered public organizations (LaPorte 1994), for which success is importantly judged by how long into the future they can effectively operate very demanding, highly hazardous technical systems – that is, operating very reliably for many work and management generations – both hopes for energy systems in Germany and the EU.

Viewing the institutional and organizational stimuli of the Energiewende program through OSC lenses prompted at least three types of conceptual refinements:

- Calling out the unusual or unexpected organizational dynamics associated with the long-term operation of highly hazardous technologies;[8]
- The unpredictable effects of widely deployed, top-down insistence/directed changes of formal authority structure and operating stipulations upon the likelihood of *amplified and apraxic complexity*; and
- The recognition that for every major policy change, effective implementation will require requisite changes in the overall degree and character of the social complexity involved. This is implied by the types of operational changes inherent in the core technologies and the skein of social relations in the target social geographies, that is, the policy's *requisite social complexity*.

Insights on forms of complexity

The operational and governance challenges of large-scale organizations and the organization of organizations occasion increases in social effort, costs, and information requirements as organizations grow in:

- Overall *scale*, i.e., numbers of people served and of technically requisite operational staff – more individuals to engage, learn from, and motivate;
- The number of *differentiated* work and overseeing groups (as a function of variations in service populations and/or in the range of systematic knowledge and/or experience implied by core technical operating systems). As a result, there are more groups to integrate, expertise to assure, coordination to facilitate, and sometimes a wider range of regulatory awareness and errors to manage. Of particular interest here are the differential effects of novel and/or intensified technical expertise associated with reliable, safe performance;
- The number and intensity of operationally requisite, *interdependent* relationships knitting together differentiated operating groups and environmental dependents in the face of varying service demands and resource necessities. As interdependent (or only moderately asymmetric) relations grow in number and variety (see bullet point above), both superordinate knowledge and interactional requisites increase quickly for meso and senior leaders. Transaction costs mount, and there is likely to be increased skepticism from experienced operators regarding the depth of critical knowledge commanded by superordinates.

A caveat: on copacetic social complexity

If the changes noted above occur *relatively slowly in a relatively munificent resource environment*, operational adaptation to them can occur *organically* in the context of continued coherence and steady performance. The system would, in effect, have gracefully attained its *requisite level of social complexity*. The resulting experience for participants, clients, and overseers would be quite satisfactory, integrated, even energizing. Operators swept up in such *copacetic social complexity* would have a sense of coherence and achievement in the face of intense demand. Such *copacetic complexity* one might observe in the sustained aircraft movement via air traffic control in the face of oncoming turbulent weather or during the high-volume launch and recovery of a squadron-scale compliment (12–14) of combat-ready attack aircraft in air operations at sea.[9]

On the other hand, when a complex organization operating in a more or less stable organically achieved equilibrium is faced with unusually rapid changes, especially from an unexpected disruption in its external environment, the result is sometimes *radical simplification*. Resources are withdrawn, staff reduced, service obligations narrowed, and specialized groups are sloughed off. System service capacity declines. A "crisis" seems to be in the offing. The *requisite social complexity* is no longer being attained.

If in addition, externally originating changes can issue from authoritative institutional and political leaders, policy changes can occur abruptly, and resources can be diverted/enhanced to pursue imperative directives. In cases where policy initiatives intend there to be major, widely dispersed change, these initiatives often come with institutional demands for major realignments of formal organizational status and authority relationships. They may also greatly intensify potential regulatory attention and notice from formerly distant legal watchers. In extreme cases, widespread social unrest and violence is a result.

Altogether, policy proposals for such changes carry with them at least tacit obligations and responsibilities for policy planners and social leaders to *insist* on cogent estimations of the levels and character of the *requisite social complexity* implicit in the organizational expression of the anticipated technical core needed for effective operation in the settings where the systems are expected to perform.

On amplified social complexity

In a sense, such external demands, pressed insistently, force significant numbers of *formal changes* in expected subordinate relations, reporting channels, and resource flows well before internal workways and informal facilitating relations become established. Implementing efforts, then, are likely to precipitate formal changes that increase one or another of the combined properties (S, D, I)[10] we have used in typifying organized social complexity – the result being superordinately *amplified complexity and the establishment of a new, yet to be attained, level of requisite social complexity*.

Top-down insistence on rapid major technical changes – as we see, for example, in the ambitious Energiewende program – is already producing uncharted changes in each property. The objectives include very rapid withdrawal of 17 large units[11] of base load-providing nuclear power generation capacity along with the parallel, vigorous growth of widely dispersed, smaller scale sustainable energy production/consumption facilities, which is to be nationally coordinated via significance advances in developing an upgraded system of smart meters and grids.

Three hypotheses

The overall complexity is likely to be amplified due to a required increase in the overall *social scale* (1) of the eventual system, and to an explosion of *increased differentiation* (2) among system operational and producing/consuming groups, with likely additions from a wider range of regulatory watchers. The property of organized complexity likely to intensify the most will be a greatly *increased range of interdependencies* (3) within and among the proliferated established and newly differentiated groups expressing the hopes placed in energy transition across the whole country.

(1) To be sure, employment in the nuclear sector is likely to plummet, though a nuclear skills technical and social infrastructure will be needed for many years. But the expectation (and unfolding reality) of *large numbers* of "prosumers" – operators and users of sustainable, small to moderately sized energy units – is likely to replace and overwhelm the system participants of yester year. Moreover, one can imagine additional staff from regulatory and safety units as well. The *scale* of the national system is likely to be increased.

(2) Increased decentralization, geographic dispersion as well as more smaller scale organizations of new, hopefully expert practitioners and services, training and risk management units will prompt additional operational *differentiation* across the emerging national Energiewende transformation. They will be joined by an increased differentiation of overseeing and operational groups.

(3) Perhaps the major difference will be a greatly increased skein of production, use, and regulatory interaction and *interdependence*. Many more widely differentiated operating groups and organizations with wider sectors of actors and prosumers, whose relationships with the producers – *formerly mainly dependent upon central generating organizations* – are now expected to exhibit greater interdependence involving more self-organizing interaction with the overall system coordinators than before. As regulatory responsibilities grow, so will the number of intra-system interdependent relations as well. Many of these will be new experiences for those involved. This situation is likely to draw even more, probably third-party, service and consulting actors (of varying skill) into the mix.

In sum, plans and actions taken to assure a speedy transition to a world imagined by political leaders (and technical entrepreneurs) are already amplifying the complexities of the early stages and, whether or not the program is seen as successful, will surely extend and possibly confound those who live for another day.

But organized complexity amplified by insistent policy initiatives needs to be writ large in social terms in order to be aware of the conditions that bring operational equilibrium. (Analytically, this would mean explicating the levels and character of *requisite organizational complexity* implied by the policy proposal, in the context of the social properties of the geographies of implementation.) Achieving qualities of smoothly operating copacetic complexity rarely arrives with much alacrity, however hopeful are those who tipped the policy world to seek a major change. A usually tacit assumption informing such official policy dicta is that schematized and idealized views of new or altered formal status and reporting relationships – such as we see in Energiewende plans – can be realized speedily enough *within the patterns of informal operating relationships* that have facilitated reliable service (that is, accomplish this in the context of the existing levels of social complexities).

The challenge is considerable. Falling short in practice often returns stumbling systems, increasing incoherence, ungainly performance – *apraxic complexity* – with possibly surprising and unsettling outcomes.[12] Short of hopes and expectations, with disaffection of senior, expert staff ("superordinates don't know what they are doing"), there is increasing public wariness ("what's going on in those services we really depend on").

More generally, apraxic complexity arises importantly from policy planning where changes are rationalized *as if* the designer could know most of the meso-consequences of top-down imposed alterations or assumes that the consequences that are unexpected will be modest and will wash out in the daily to and fro. When the domains of interest are relatively small and the operational technologies modest and stable, such assumptions may be more or less tenable.

However, (a) the larger and more complex the operating system (more differentiated/heterogeneous the units and more interdependencies) and (b) the more numerous and widely spread the imposed changes in formal organizational, structural, and operational dicta, the more likely it is that there will be *significant surprises* within and among the affected organizations and a creeping public sense of institutional *apraxia* – an important contributor to declining public trust (LaPorte and Metlay 1996).[13]

Sensing both these lineaments of apraxic complexity and the challenges of understanding the public consequences of misestimating the requisite of complexities in policy implementation constitutes some of the central tasks and opportunities for TA efforts. This could lead to exploring the analytical aspects of: (a) increasing incoherence and *apraxic* "policy action"; (b) amplified formal complexity and potential declines in socially coherent praxis; (c) potentials for "resilient" recovery after periods of awkward, sometimes rude (crisis-like) surprise; and (d) variations in the redistribution of suffering. Other vectors could include (e) estimating the band width of minimal to excessive requisite complexities, and (f) the operational variations prompted by the uneven changes in one or another of the central properties of organizational complexity (S, D, I).

Energiewende and the challenges of TA – "Knowing" where to look, what to look for

Missing data regarding the energiewende

Major programs with wide-ranging and enduring aspirations – such as the Energiewende – entail very large-scale, increasingly entangled institutional involvement. In this case, the temporal reach and expectation of the ramp up is expected to run through 2022, then "stabilize" thereafter. Nuclear energy production is to end altogether (with continuing, long-term environmental and waste management obligations). Full-fledged, very large-scale sustainable energy supply systems and smart grid coordination are to be attained, and coal-burning power plants would be increasingly limited.

Along the way, the social scale of Energiewende organizational operations is intended to assume much larger social and technical proportions than it does at the present. This is the case within even larger matrices of social organizations, suppliers, users, and novel newcomers (prosumers) and given a proliferation of rearranging regulatory watchers throughout Germany (and the EU). Beyond this, wider, evolving consuming/producing civic cultures of everyday life have now spread well beyond Germany to the engaged national neighbors across the EU.

The *current* situations are complex and extensive with large-scale, "path-dependently" driven institutional and organizational arrangements. And these have not yet been well explicated in terms that would provide a confident basis for analyzing or assessing the potential effects of subsequent changes in major technical systems.

Then, when existing skeins or matrices of organizational interconnections *are* being stimulated to grow, how might TA analysts attempt to get a sense of the resulting behavior patterns and social footprints of disruption and rude surprise (La Porte 2007) – this in the midst of increasing complexity? Are some roots of social surprise now beyond direct notice? Two aspects of this situation are noted in the sub-sections below: (a) ways of "seeing" the likely expanding range of *newly aware noticers* (of Energiewende actors), and (b) preparing to discover *surprising anomalies*.

Observing the role of "New Noticers"

One factor in a public's response to superordinately stimulated changes in technical enterprise is the pace of that growth. When this exceeds the capacity, safely, to integrate smoothly within existing social patterns, then the number of disruptive (surprising) and sometime hazardous situations increase. Social stimuli associated with early and, then, later stages of growth become more widespread. The "technology," in a social sense, becomes present to a widening range of "others," i.e., to those outside technical circles themselves. For many, this may be the first time they notice, see, or experience the social manifestation of Energiewende technologies and associate them with the new, maybe novel, social effects of the technical enterprise to their own everyday lives. These are "newly aware noticers," emergent or *new noticers*, and sometimes regulatory "watchers."

TA and sociotechnical studies more generally could find considerable value in conceptualizing ways of "seeing" (and anticipating) the likely expanding range of "*newly aware noticers*" – for the case at hand – of the *Energiewende* infrastructure's emergence and situating them within the current institutional patterns as the sociotechnical elements and operations deploy to larger and larger social scales.

These changes in the properties of technical operations are not likely to go evenly apace, nor will their social stimuli be evenly spread. Rather TA analysts could imagine (i) geographically patchy "scale-up" in (ii) several "fits and starts," i.e., step like stages, following, say, the classical S curves of innovation, deployment, and arrival at market saturation[14] across (iii) social and political landscapes of varying character.

As these stages (of innovations, demonstration, initial scale-up to maturely scaled-up) go apace, "new noticers" become increasingly ensnared – taking notice, watching – as each expanding stage consolidates across a wider spread. Arenas of potentially new noticers stem from those who see: (i) possibilities of self-interested opportunity, either directly or indirectly via the systemic nature of the technology, or (ii) possible threats, disruptions to valued service, and in consequence, much higher costs, higher hazards and harm, or disruption of hard-won stable relationships. These would represent an accumulating layering of sympathetic or alarmed watchers, opportunists, or those disrupted.

If enough "others" (new noticers) see a potential advantage or disruption and alter their behavior, then secondary social effects become evident. The more differentiated and interdependent the existing stage becomes, the more newly aware noticers and/or watchers will come to the forefront, and the more psychic and institutional energy to "digest" the social perturbations and "re-equilibrate" the communities and regions of impact is needed.

With a bit more conceptual elaboration, at this general level, a next analytical step would be to bring into the research mix typologies of the social properties exhibited by different types of technical and infrastructural operating systems. Some of these are the social properties of deploying and operating groups and technical specializations themselves. Additional factors would include: (i) the types of external effects upon the *operating surround* intrinsic to one technical segment and/or (ii) typologies of what we might call the various "technoplexes" of integrated distinctive technical systems of interest (in our case, all the infrastructures and coordinating systems inherent in the current design of the Energiewende and the properties of the receiving political jurisdictions' social environment).

These become the empirical background when attending to the demanding *seven research vectors* noted in the concluding section. These topics would add contextual depth and demanding research targets for TA team efforts.

Observing surprising anomalies

Technology Assessment I (TA-I, compare Sect. 2) conducted prior to an R&D demonstration stage is likely to emphasize the potential benefits and barriers to development with secondary consideration of externalities (see the distinctions made above). TA bridging stages II and III of Energiewende deployment, initiated in later stages of technical deployment, where some technical elements are mature – it could be argued – have the central role of discovering and anticipating the "other" effects of technical operations. The mission is to search for early expression of the unexpected, surprises, disquiet, and disruption and to initiate recalibration, error correction, and policy resetting – before deployment has become very costly to undo.

These periods of technical and institutional flowering occasion continued, uneven growth as programs expand to the expected scale and push into (and co-opt elements in) relatively stable, established social and institutional surrounds.

Where do TA research teams look to see the early onset of disquiet? When the social scales of the phenomena overwhelm research teams, where should one's observers be posted for effective reconnaissance?

When the technologies of interest have these properties (as the Energiewende does):

- The pace of techno-institutional change is relatively rapid, "apraxic" situations should be anticipated;
- Formerly familiar social patterns are disrupted, new noticers arise, unexpected dynamics are more likely;
- Descriptive data sources are meager, and the number of TA observers is relatively few, missing data will be considerable.

These are daunting conditions for TA teams working to develop a descriptive and dynamic understanding of the technical systems and social environment into which they are being deployed. Conceptual and operational strategies are needed to focus scarce empirical and analytical resources.

Two partial strategies could facilitate such efforts: (a) ways of conceptualizing critical or interesting nexus of the interactions between emerging sociotechnical systems within complex social/economic environments that hold promise to serve as "observation" sites for advantageous description and continuous sampling of change, and (b) conceptual means for preparing to be surprised and sense the onset of that which has been unexpected.

In the first instance, (a) above, the graphic project proposed by Todd M. La Porte, "*Visualizing Socio-technical Systems:* The TOPESoCN Conceptual Framework" is an example.[15] It interactively highlights vectors of analytical/system observational awareness as these systems draw escalating responses from the wider surround, within a context of increasing social complexity.

This conceptual aid, nearing final form, shows ways of relating the interactions of a nested series of phenomena – with technical elements at its core surrounded by layers representing organization, politico-economic system, society, culture, and nature – each layer increasing complexity by adding myriad types of social actors to the whole. Cross-cutting vectors that slice through layer after layer can thus pinpoint interesting zones of intersection for inquiring about who and what is "there."

These target zones of primary interest become the nexus (or sampling circles) for careful organizational description (as in the research directions sketched out in the final section below), with dynamic patterns of interactions between, say, organizations and political-economic institutions and the wider sweep of civil society. Specific research sites could then be refined in terms of both specific policy questions and, importantly, theoretical issues of general interest and, from a TA perspective, those situations associated with large-scale, path-dependently driven institutional/organizational arrangements and their social footprints.

A second aid in sorting out analytical efforts takes a different track: TA teams *preparing themselves and agencies to be surprised*, to be sensitive to the early onset of the unexpected. In a sense, they must learn to expect to witness the unexpected.[16] This means, in part, that TA team and agency leaders must realize that forecasting and preparation, while very important, will – as the systems of interest assume greater and greater complexity, both apraxic and, less likely, copacetic – be increasingly inaccurate and that related social and organizational phenomena are likely to emerge unnoticed until severe dislocation forces harsh retrospection. Such anomalies signal the evolution of social behaviors initially outside of the categories of description – conceptual anomalies – *behaviors familiar to those who enacted them but invisible to outside analytical observers and technology assessors*. One significant implication – perhaps imperative – for technology assessors is that they must engage with those who – on the firing line – directly carry on the work of implementing and especially operate the new systems as well as remaining legacy operations.

At least two aspects of the Energiewende are candidates for such anomalies:[17]

(a) The dynamics associated with shortfalls in attaining the institutional conditions of assuring trustworthiness, institutional constancy, and highly reliable operations (LaPorte and Keller 1996).

(b) The widespread deployment of national smart meters and grids has, along with other unique institutional factors, significant potential for stimulating novel, anomalous social phenomena. Very widespread deployment of computer-based coordination and accounting systems (intrinsic to Energiewende aspirations) involves many new actors (prosumers) connected to a highly variable national web composed of a number of different production and using systems. Many of these prosumers are likely to be of only middling relative technical competence. The overall system will be very large with many computer network entry points. The number of daily intra-system transactions (both in energy flow and financially relevant data/controls) will be enormous. A great deal is continually at stake, and the perpetual risks to production reliability and financial security are extraordinary.

At least two types of "within system" adaptation (by prosumers and overseers) could result in invisible adaptive behaviors: (i) uneven understanding and maintenance of cybersecurity measures and routines, and (ii) opportunistic exploitive computer manipulation by technical insiders with the internal evolution of necessarily opaque countermeasures, increasing prosumer and "civilian" user skepticism. Adaptive, "beneath the radar" (BTR) behaviors would be likely. With internal "red team" surveillance, BTR patterns could evolve beyond current conceptual naming and remain invisible to outsiders.

A similar scenario could unfold due to the clandestine invasion of complex computer control systems from external aggressor, lone-wolf operators or other national security agencies targeting vulnerable network nodes and/or inexperienced prosumers. Again, internal adaptive patterns – while familiar to operational levels – could remain conceptually nameless and, hence, observationally invisible.

Observing what? Supporting data for descriptive research

What follows are needs for explication to observe amplified complexity:

- *First,* the array of existing operational organizations delivering energy to Germany (the power system), including the meso-level coordinating/governing institutions and the likely prosumer community, operations and networks, associational patterns and regulators.
- *Second,* the social and political geography of energy technical deployment; current distributional profiles as well as planned prospective vectors. Initially, privilege patterns comparing east vs. west federal states (Bundesländer), then socioeconomic sectors. Changes that (a) ameliorate past differences, then, (b) those that accentuate differences and latent tensions.
- *Third,* the landscape of regulatory organizations/institutions: the full range of national and regional bodies, organizations associated with each energy producing and distributing form. Descriptions of the energy form domain association/coordinating infrastructure. Estimation of comparative domain integration and associated regulatory vitality, economic and social resilience, and the likely capacity to maintain *cyber-secure operation.*
- *Fourth,* the first-cut identification of other critical infrastructures dependent on the steady uninterrupted provision of electric power (how dependent, the degree to which each has back up supply under their control). Estimation of the degree to which practiced exercise of emergency operation in the face of power loss is conducted (how robust and operative is inter-infrastructure cooperation likely to be?). Include the full range of operator coordination/control room operations and sources of crucial, largely latent interconnects/dependencies.
- *Fifth,* the development of a reasonably detailed hypothetical, straw man – cases to be disproved – descriptions of the scales and geographies of a smart grid/metering system encompassing/integrating traditional and sustainable energy sources. These would include distribution systems and hook ups/ins with other German infrastructures and arrangements within the EU grid. (This could be seen as a stage in refining the system's level of estimated requisite complexity.)
- *Sixth,* the analysis of the degree to which the deployment of computer-based smart grid/metering, communication, control, and operation is cybersecurity-ready to fend off external tampering and infiltration. Exploration of the degree to which different producing modes vary the vulnerability of the overall system as well as that within producing type and the existing institutional infrastructures of integration and governance. What latent national security matters are manifest?
- *Finally,* the explication of types/varieties of different scales and production mix/distribution. Development of a series of three or four "least-worst-case(s)" scenarios for each type. The primary goal is to provide a series of failure-related goals as central performance expectations. Failures will occur.

Plan for readiness for least-worse-case occurrence. Include indicators of "emergent noticing" – especially "newly aware noticing/noticers" activating established and coherently operating organizational actors as new systems ramp up (going to scale; relate these to logistic deployment "S curves").

In the end, many challenges for the design of stabilizing organizational dynamics and formal structures remain. Here are three:

- Avoiding technical designs and operations that confound market-assuring dynamics (else regulatory measures follow);
- Estimating the adequacy of current regulatory regimes to encompass new developments without major changes;
- Providing the incentives that assure that agencies and contractors will continually be worthy of the public's trust for generation after generation for many electoral terms (100 years plus).

Technology assessors have important opportunities (obligations?) to provide the descriptions and analyses informing the likelihood that proposed changes in the institutional status and design of energy production and smart grid coordination can meet these challenges.

Notes

1 Late in 2010, the German government, initiated by Chancellor Merkel, began a "transition [. . .] to a low carbon, environmentally sound, reliable, and affordable energy supply. [. . .] The new system will rely heavily on renewable energy (particularly wind, photovoltaics, and hydroelectricity), energy efficiency, and energy demand management. Most if not all existing coal-fired generation will need to be retired. The phase-out of Germany's fleet of nuclear reactors, to be complete by 2022, is a key part of the program." See https://en.wikipedia.org/wiki/Energiewende_in_Germany. Accessed 2018/01/16.

2 The Institute for Technology Assessment and Systems Analysis (ITAS), based at the Karlsruhe Institute of Technology (KIT), Germany, investigates scientific and technological developments with a focus on their impacts and possible systemic and unintended effects. It produces analytical knowledge and assessments of sociotechnical developments in order to provide policy and design options for decision-makers. The research covers ethical, ecological, economic, social, political-institutional, and cultural questions. www.itas.kit.edu/english/index.php [Accessed 2018/01/16].

3 The discussion skips across several of many matters that piqued analytical sensibilities and occasioned fruitful discussions with ITAS staff. These were some of the most stimulating, almost effervescent exchanges I've had with colleagues in some time. And I came to think of them as near models of what we sometimes imagine as the archetypical academic community. It was a thoroughly absorbing experience, high spirited with persistent good humor.

4 These discussions, much informed by numerous conversations with Todd M. La Porte during our simultaneous visits with ITAS, drew on his extensive experience with the US Office of Technology Assessment and his approach to teaching in the Culture, Organization, and Technology program, School of Policy, Government, and

International Affairs, George Mason University. They were extraordinary exchanges, many of them with staff and students.

5 https://en.wikipedia.org/wiki/Energiewende_in_Germany [Accessed 2018/01/16].
6 See the contribution by Kröger and Nan in this book.
7 Technology assessments could be initiated rather later as well with somewhat different intentions. Conceptually, there could be assignments for TA as Energiewende matures: TA IV. Fully deployed, in the midst of widespread operation: "What have we done? Have the outcomes been more or less what was expected?" Explicate sources of successful deployment, and disappointment. TA V. Historical retrospective. Given the technical domain of interest, now that it has been in operation for some time, what do we make of its evolution, deferred surprises and/or regrets? Which aspects are we to seek in future evolutions, and, especially, which are we to avoid?
8 These properties call out the significance of high reliability organizations (HRO) and institutional constancy imperatives as important stimuli to particular types of differentiation and interdependency (peculiar transaction costs/effects). See La Porte (1996), La Porte and Consolini (1991).
9 Other examples might be "well oiled" professional sports teams in championship play, master's level ballet and/or a philharmonic orchestra's season's performance, or, occasionally, the rapid response to a large wildfire breakout.
10 Scale, differentiation, interdependence.
11 See www.world-nuclear.org/information-library/country-profiles/countries-g-n/germany.aspx [Accessed 2018/01/16].
12 The descriptor "technological apraxia" was first suggested to me by Langdon Winner's work some years ago, where he used it to distinguish technical systems that overwhelm, stumble, and disorient (Winner 1978, 186).
13 See the contribution by Patrick Sumpf in this book.
14 For example the "diffusion of innovations" (see: https://en.wikipedia.org/wiki/Diffusion_of_innovations; accessed 2018/01/16).
15 See https://prezi.com/anvdpbzmtkmw/technology/?utm_campaign=share&utm_medium=copy; [Accessed 2018/01/17].
16 See, for example, the discussion of the "Invisibles: Anomalies" (La Porte 2012, 2016, 2018).
17 I note items that pick up themes that ran through the ITAS conversations and parallel research vectors the concluding section.

References

La Porte, Todd R. 1975a. *Organized Social Complexity: Challenge to Politics and Policy.* Princeton: Princeton University Press.

———. 1975b. "Organized Social Complexity: Explication of a Concept." In *Organized Social Complexity: Challenge to Politics and Policy,* edited by Todd R. La Porte, 3–39. Princeton: Princeton University Press.

———. 1996. "High Reliability Organizations: Unlikely, Demanding and At Risk." *Journal of Contingencies and Crisis Management* 4 (2): 60–71. https://doi.org/10.1111/j.1468-5973.1996.tb00078.x.

———. 2007. "Reflections on 'Crisis Management' Without End." In *Communicable Crises: Prevention, Management and Resolution in the Global Arena,* edited by Deborah E. Gibbons, 27–46. Charlotte, NC: Information Age Publishing.

———. 2012. "Preparing for Anomalies, Revealing the Invisible: Public Organizational Puzzles." presented at the Advanced Study of Public Organizations, Utrecht University.

———. 2015. *Organized Social Complexity: Challenge to Politics and Policy.* 2nd ed. Princeton Legacy Library. Princeton: Princeton University Press.

———. 2016. "Anomalies and Institutional Surprise: Intrinsic Challenges for Security Aspirations." Presentation presented at the Seminar on Organizing for Societal Security and Crisis Management, University of California, Berkeley, June.

———. 2018. "Preparing for Anomalies, Revealing the Invisible: Public Organizational Puzzles." *Journal of Risk, Hazard and Crisis in Public Policy* 9 (3). https://doi.org/10.1002/rhc3.12139.

——— 1994. "A State of the Field: Increasing Relative Ignorance." *Journal of Public Administration Research and Theory: J-PART* 4 (1): 5–15.

La Porte, Todd R., and Paula M. Consolini. 1991. "Working in Practice But Not in Theory: Theoretical Challenges of 'High-Reliability Organizations.'" *Journal of Public Administration Research and Theory: J-PART* 1 (1): 19–48.

La Porte, Todd R., and Ann Keller. 1996. "Assuring Institutional Constancy: Requisite for Managing Long-Lived Hazards." *Public Administration Review* 56 (6): 535–44. https://doi.org/10.2307/977252.

La Porte, Todd R., and Daniel S. Metlay. 1996. "Hazards and Institutional Trustworthiness." *Public Administration Review* 56 (4): 341–47.

Winner, Langdon. 1978. *Autonomous Technology: Technics-out-of-Control as a Theme in Political Thought.* Cambridge, MA: MIT Press.

13 Energy as a sociotechnical problem

A concluding discussion

Christian Büscher, Jens Schippl, and Patrick Sumpf

Energy challenges and interdisciplinary research

Despite the innumerable differences between countries around the world, many of the problems in their energy systems – a central determinant of economic growth and quality of life – are quite similar. For many observers, climate change is the most challenging of the global problems facing mankind, and it is deeply interwoven with the supply and consumption of energy. The reports and press releases of the Intergovernmental Panel on Climate Change (IPCC),[1] for instance, highlight the need for significant changes in the energy sector, above all cutting carbon emissions if the ongoing process of global warming is to be kept below 2° C compared to preindustrial levels. At the United Nations Climate Change Conference, COP 21,[2] held in Paris in 2015, an agreement to limit global warming was reached. In the official version of the Paris Agreement, the parties even committed to "pursue efforts to limit the temperature increase to 1.5° C" (IPCC 2015, 22). It was emphasized that decarbonization of the energy sector is an inevitable step toward achieving this objective.

Further energy-related challenges are relevant across the globe, such as providing reliable and affordable energy and transportation, a healthy environment, and a high quality of life. Challenges like these are of particular importance in light of the fast-paced and partly uncontrolled urbanization in many regions of the world (Büscher and Mascareño 2014). While these developments are largely induced by technology associated with burning carbon-intensive fossil fuels, technology simultaneously provides solutions to these problems. These solutions are often linked to the idea of sustainable development. A transition to renewable energy, a crucial element of sustainability, is usually regarded a promising way forward for the energy sector. Consequently, energy systems – in many countries – are in the midst of this transition, which entails the rise of renewable energy sources (RES) on a global scale (IEO 2017). Yet, for the German *Energiewende*, for example, combating climate change through RES deployment is not the only target; others include sociopolitical aspects such as affordability of electricity, less dependence on remote energy sources, and, specific to Germany, the phaseout of nuclear power. Analogously, Genus, Iskandarova, and Champagnie (Chap. 8) point to a multitude of sociotechnical objectives in the UK. It is widely acknowledged that far-reaching changes in infrastructures like the energy sector go far beyond the simple replacement of an old technology by a new one (see, e.g., Chaps. 1 & 2). For decades, scholars from transition research or innovation-oriented social science have accentuated our understanding of infrastructures as sociotechnical systems by demonstrating that large-scale technical change can only be understood in the context of its relationship with societal change. In a similar vein, the International Energy Agency (IEA), one of the key global players in the field, is prominently emphasizing an integrated perspective on technoeconomic and political aspects: "The global energy scene is in a state of flux. Understanding the dynamic interplay of energy markets, technology and policy has never been more critical."[3]

Against this backdrop, interdisciplinary approaches must deal with the energy complex as it is currently unfolding. The vast multitude of options, challenges, perspectives, and objectives related to changes in the energy system cannot be captured by one academic discipline alone. The very idea of this book is to propose that shared research problems be considered as a means to solidify meaningful interdisciplinary research. We consequently offered the concept of *sociotechnical problems*, i.e., issues that have to be addressed continuously during the development of large-scale infrastructure, especially if a transition is envisaged or in progress. Based on this framework, which is particularly expounded in Chap. 2 with regard to the dimensions *control, change,* and *action* (which are then the focus of Parts I – III, respectively), we have illustrated that such problems serve as instructive abstractions and reductions for achieving integrated interdisciplinary research. In the middle section of this conclusion, we will back up our optimism in this regard by providing a thorough discussion of what we have been able to learn from the authors' contributions to the respective sociotechnical problems.

The problems associated with the three sociotechnical dimensions we present in this book – *control, change,* and *action* – will never be fully resolved. Solutions always have to be adapted to new sociotechnical circumstances, be it changing societal and/or political priorities, economic objectives, or new technical developments that exert pressure on the existing system. As Arthur (2009) points out, new technology may help alleviate current problems, but simultaneously it causes cascading problems that result in the need for further technological or organizational rearrangements: "The whole moves forward in a sequence of problem and solution – of challenge and response – and it is this sequence we call structural change" (Arthur 2009, 196). This continuously ongoing cycle should attract more awareness in both the STEM (science, technology, engineering, and mathematics) and the SSH (social sciences and humanities) research communities; this is in contrast to the somewhat implicit – and sometimes even explicit – understanding of transitions as changes between two fixed states, namely the state of the art and the desirable future. Yet this desirable future, the ostensible "end state" of the transition, will encounter new sociotechnical problems that again and again will require control, change, and action at the same time.

In this regard, the drivers of transformation do not necessarily have to be outside the "system" under consideration. Internal dynamics may also constitute a destabilizing force leading to change – in a Schumpeterian sense of "industrial mutation" – that incessantly destroys the system from within and leads to renewal. In short, solutions are always followed by new problems. Academic SSH disciplines such as the philosophy of technology, science and technology studies, or technology assessment, are actually quite familiar with the idea of technology and innovation ambivalence, yet rather in the sense of unintended consequences and of their premises in the same or related sociotechnical field(s). To draw attention to this phenomenon from an interdisciplinary perspective and to demonstrate that there can be no transition without cascading consequences are important conclusions. We would like to charge STEM and SSH research with the mission of uncovering these intended and unintended consequences and premises that manifest themselves as sociotechnical problems. Such problems can serve as objects of constant scholarly monitoring of a process and guide interdisciplinary research.

Finally, the overall purpose of the book is to provide an understanding of the ongoing energy transformation as a multidimensional process in which the three analytical dimensions interact with one another in shaping future developments. The contributions in the book highlight specific problems and solutions in one of the three dimensions – control, change, and action – yet not with disregard for the other two. In doing so, the contributions illustrate in manifold ways how problem–solution nexuses in the three dimensions can be linked and that key problems have to be observed by research in all three dimensions simultaneously, in particular when support for the governance of energy transitions is at stake. For research and for policy advice, however, the notion that "everything is linked with everything" is neither helpful nor implied by the elaborations in this book. A clear focus is needed when research programs are set up or when different political or administrative units address various tasks in the process of governing energy systems. In evaluating the contributions in this book, we conclude that the formulation of sociotechnical problems is a useful way to maintain the necessary focus and clarity in interdisciplinary research programs. The dimensions of research problems introduced in this book surely exert influence on one another; however, the book shows that they are also distinct enough for guiding analysis and drawing conclusions for research and policy. The sociotechnical problems work as distinct *nuclei* to which the respective disciplinary perspectives can relate and subsequently unfold, but with regard to common reference points and directions.

Three dimensions of the energy complex

The problem of control exemplified by technical operation, social organization, and exogenous threats

In the words of von Foerster (1972, 40), the problem of control refers to the fundamental human desire to "trivialize" complex realities. The notion of systems as the object of control itself evokes the idea of "systemicy" (Beckman 1994, 311) and therefore the hope that natural, technical, and social processes are amenable to laws (e.g., of physics), possess an underlying structure, and can thus be anticipated, planned, and exploited. First of all, control, in its basic form, is a problem for the (re)production of systems in that the selective isolation of causal relationships must succeed, i.e., that only "some but not all causes that are necessary for specific effects can be employed under the control of a system" (Luhmann 1995, 20). For example, electric power plants utilize wind as a force to propel large rotor blades that are coupled to generators. Wind turbine engineers and operators are able to control specific physical causalities. However, it is not possible for them to control the weather. Atmospheric causalities are not under the system's control yet as part of its environment still influence its performance. In order to maintain control, operators therefore depend on predictions for environmental factors.

Wolfgang Kröger and Cen Nan demonstrate how large technical systems become more complicated and the organizational means more elaborate in the effort to maintain a state of control, i.e., the desired output and service, amidst a transition. All the authors in Part I of the book concur with that conclusion. The electricity system, as we observe it evolving right now, increases its organized complexity (more heterogeneous elements and relations)[4] in order to sustain itself and to keep the expected output constant even though the environment features far higher degrees of complexity, as expressed in global markets, prosumer intervention, smart technology, or atmospheric conditions for that matter. Therefore, the sociotechnical constellations that the authors analyze in their contributions to this part of the book emerge and reproduce in order to reduce environmental complexity: in the case of Wolfgang Kröger and Cen Nan with the support of sociotechnical modeling, in the case of Rolf W. Künneke by implementation of institutional settings that serve as safeguards, and in the chapter by Marcus Wiens, Wolfgang Raskob, Florian Diehlmann, Stefan Wandler, and Frank Schultmann by measures to respond to exogenous and endogenous hazards.

What Kröger and Nan report appears like a dialectic process, to borrow a philosophical term. On the one hand, we see gains in the efficiency of established technologies and a shift to a more sustainable supply of energy (at least in the domain of electricity), while on the other hand we also experience increased vulnerability to systemic events with widely spreading consequences. Tighter integration and coupling of heterogeneous elements, the ubiquitous use of computer systems for integration, communication, and control, and manifold transactions between numerous actors are only some of the features of modern energy systems. In particular, cascading events and nontechnical, behavioral variables seem to factor into all of the system reliability considerations. In this sense, Wolfgang Kröger and Cen Nan point to the need to improve modeling concepts and to predict the behavior of these sociotechnical constellations. The concept of resilience, i.e., the ability to bounce back from an endogenously or exogenously hazardous event to sustain vital services, is presented as a system design challenge and sociotechnical problem of superior order. The innovative character of such an approach is that engineering disciplines explicitly seek contact to input from the social sciences in order to account for the complexity of social systems.

In this regard, scientists put in considerable effort and computing power to analyze and predict the emergent behavior of groups, organizations, and the functional systems of society such as politics or the economy (Helbing 2012). We have to assume that all the system design, implementation, and governance efforts in the energy realm (and elsewhere) depend on the ability to predict system behavior. Thus, the generation of knowledge in this academic field affects our ability to act, such as the immediate decision making and planning by designers, operators, stock managers, and regulators.

A well-known argument is that all the liberalization, the unbundling of supply, transportation, and distribution, and the opening up of distributed RES systems or the respective inclusion of additional actors might endanger control and reliability. The reason given for this is that the competence to control all the interacting elements is not in the hand of a single organization any more, but rather split up in a fragmented value chain, with possible consequences for system performance (Mayntz 2009). In this sense, Rolf W. Künneke points to the need for social arrangements to maintain control over all of the desired transactions within energy infrastructures, especially around the dynamics triggered by energy transitions. His analysis focuses on two directions. The first is the necessity of functioning systems which is embodied in the concept of "de facto control." This condition can be observed by comparing the factual performance of the system with the preferred performance. The second direction of his research is the fact that stable expectations are required to enable a capacity to act in safeguarded transactions. Institutional economics has traditionally been interested in the issues of uncertainty in decision making and how the coordination of economic transactions can be successfully maintained. Williamson (1979, 234), for instance, claims to select the appropriate institutional setting in order to back up transactions and thus to raise the confidence in successful economic exchanges despite the risk of "opportunism." Summed up, the approach presented by Rolf W. Künneke resonates well with our attempt to expose multidimensional sociotechnical problems. Although he emphasizes *control* issues in institutional settings with regard to both technical and social requirements, his theses are relevant for the problem of *change* (reconfiguration of institutional arrangements) and *action* (uncertainty absorption and enactment through institutions).

The research group around Marcus Wiens discusses the consequences that exogenous and endogenous hazards can have for an energy system and its transformation. The most intriguing element of their contribution is their consideration of the intricate interrelations between the distinct origins of potentially harmful events. First of all, as the authors argue, modern infrastructures evolve into more and more abstract, ubiquitous, and nationally or internationally interacting entities.[5] Consequently, external shocks (like extreme weather events) might trigger cascading events or error propagation, depending on the structure of the overall energy complex. Second, if modern infrastructures serve as "enabling systems" for other vital infrastructures, then endogenous hazards in one system become exogenous hazards for others. Our curiosity leads us to raise the question as to how it is possible to avoid, prepare, respond to, or mitigate events external to one's own area of expertise and control.

Furthermore, Wiens et al. explore the learning potential for researchers, operators, or administrators by comparing two distinct enabling systems – energy and finance – and analyzing the consequences of increasing complexity, faulty designs, misleading incentive structures, and moral hazards. Overall, they conclude: "The high level of complexity and uncertainty in both systems makes it increasingly difficult for the responsible actors to assess risk scenarios and consequences" (Wiens et al. in this book, 115). Subsequently, the authors discuss the thesis that some of the features that endangered the global economy during the subprime mortgage crisis might be applicable to market mechanisms in the energy sector. In the financial markets, the combination of opaqueness, asymmetric information, and the blind trust of investors contributed to an inflation of investments in risky assets, backed by continuous affirmations by the rating agencies (Strulik 2007). Energy markets might also be susceptible to exploitation based on complicated, reflexive stock exchange and potential price collusion emerging in stock-based actor networks. Research on this topic is scarce, which is why Wiens et al. pose the question of what the consequences might be if the trend of introducing more and more economic mechanisms continues. One of the ensuing issues will be to organize the international regulation of energy markets even though infrastructures are still mostly under the supervision of national agencies.

In an ironic twist, modern society experiences the consequences of the implementation and utilization of complex sociotechnical infrastructures in the form of climate change, the deterioration of fauna and flora, and the depletion of natural resources. In addressing these consequences, the calls for change grow loud and clear. Nonetheless, we must assume that the degree of complexity will not dwindle to more manageable levels by varying the means and patterns of energy generation or by changing the way that the co-evolving domains of transportation, industrial production, research, and health care, for instance, are organized and controlled. Instead, the call for the existing systems to be transformed can also be interpreted as an invitation for society, functional systems, organizations, and individual persons to continue on their paths of growing and expanding their activities, even at the expense of continuing to utilize resources.

The problem of change exemplified by experiments, disruptive innovation, and discourse

While Audley Genus, Marfuga Iskandarova, and Leigh Champagnie as well as Gerhard Fuchs are strongly interested in the processes and mechanisms that trigger transitions, Matthias Gross focuses on the learning processes that are inevitably needed in the course of such transitions. As illustrated in the contributions in Part I (the dimension of control) and by Todd R. La Porte, the transition to renewable energy systems comes with an increase in complexity and uncertainty in the energy sector. Both new technical and new institutional structures are required to cope with this situation. A typical example is the increasing dependence on fluctuating sources, such as wind and sun; the weather is simply beyond human control. In general, better predictions as well as organizational and/or technical fallback options are needed to enable the participating actors to learn about novel circumstances and their idiosyncrasies.

Yet learning itself is a complex process. In order to "venture into the unknown" (Matthias Gross in this book, 125), those who are supposed to learn must over-come fundamental learning traps, such as only following strategies derived from past successes or discontinuing learning too early in the face of the first indica-tions of failure (March and Olsen 1995, 215ff.). But what are the conditions for conducting learning processes – including taking risks (by decision makers) or enduring dangers (by those affected) – if experiments cannot be contained in a hermetically closed facility, like in a laboratory? In order to permit technical innovation, real-world experiments must be conducted, as Gross argues, despite the considerable uncertainties attached to them. A project like the *Energiewende* cannot be pushed through against the opposition of large segments of the popu-lation. Therefore, there has to be a way for all the involved parties – such as developers, engineers, officials, local public, and everyone else – to cope with uncertainties and demonstrate their commitment.

The real-world experiment of "geothermal energy operations" that Matthias Gross analyzes emphasizes processes of *change*, yet also refers heavily to the *con-trol* dimension. Laboratory and real-world experiments establish a steep slope of complexity between bounded causalities in a laboratory situation, where all possible influences can be controlled, and experiments in geological forma-tions, where nonknowledge of factors exerting influence is still quite severe. As a consequence, Gross' analysis also bleeds into the *action* dimension in terms of how learning is possible under the circumstances of tight schedules, uncertain financial burdens, and possible hazards. The answer is not only risk distribution but mainly the interplay of the incremental steps in going back and forth from laboratory environments to the real-world setting. Every time on-site progress is stalled, engineers and developers have to retreat to a protected space – a knowledge-producing niche – to shed light on the unknowns involved in such a project.

This also holds true for the unforeseeable reactions of those affected by real-world experiments. Interaction between experts and stakeholders is a vital part of real-world experiments (Gross in this book, 131ff.), illustrating that sociotechni-cal problems present themselves as continuous challenges. As discussed in other contexts (Todt 2011), participatory exercises cannot be used as an instrument producing surefire resolutions for any kind of social conflict, as each and every situation has its own dynamics. Sticking to certain principles in decision-making processes, such as transparency and meaningful inclusion, are prerequisites for setting a basis for success in the first place. Nonetheless, this does not guarantee that dissent and conflict can be overcome. Experimenting with different forms of participation can be considered a strategy for coping with uncertainty in this regard. It is plausible that this is a problem which has to be addressed continu-ously because conflict resolution can be stable temporarily, but provides no assur-ance for a lasting settlement. In a similar vein, yet even more in the direction of actionability and agency, this topic is also addressed in Patrick Sumpf's analysis of trust relations in the energy complex as well as in the argumentation of Rafaela Hillerbrand on the value-based design of energy systems.

Change is at the very heart of the contribution by Gerhard Fuchs, as he is interested in the generic principles relevant to change in a field such as the energy sector. He tries to understand the mechanisms that change power constellations, the actor constellation, and the general practices in the field of electricity production and distribution. Transitions are shaped by the interplay between incumbents and challengers. Changes in political power in Germany led to changes in the opportunity structures that were accompanied by changing attitudes to renewable energy. The mechanisms that initiated and produced momentum and sustained the corresponding result were first of all the successful efforts at mobilization by the renewable energy actors and the delegitimization of the activities of incumbents. With the notion of legitimacy, Gerhard Fuchs addresses an important mechanism for sustaining *redundancy*,[6] i.e., legitimization in the sense of a general acceptance of actions caused by the suggestion that these actions serve a common good. Regarding the German *Energiewende*, it is especially the *withdrawal* of legitimization for large technical system design and operation (i.e., the conventional nuclear system) that triggered the search for alternative ways to supply energy. Still, the field is far from having attained a stable structure; change is about to continue, but simultaneously the incumbents are getting stronger again. Uncertainty is far from being eliminated when it comes to the future prospects of the *Energiewende*. Looking at Fuchs' line of argumentation regarding how he sees the emergence of new structures in electricity production and distribution in Germany, of utmost importance is the extent to which the mobilization and development of a broad legitimacy for renewable energy will continue and further drive the energy transition.

In applying a discourse-institutional perspective, Genus, Iskandarova, and Champagnie investigate processes of change and inertia in the UK energy complex on the basis of empirical data (interviews). They claim that institutional momentum, i.e., overcoming inertia, can be actively and purposively achieved, at least in principle. Institutions are resilient, but still susceptible to change, in particular if they are characterized by internal contradictions and uncertainties, which may motivate actors to restructure the field. Their analysis is accompanied by the concept of "institutional entrepreneurship" (Genus et al. in this book, 161). Institutions can be changed or developed by organized actors with sufficient resources. This process of change can be considered a highly discursive practice. In analogy to Gerhard Fuchs, legitimacy is affected by social discourse. Moreover, Genus, Iskandarova, and Champagnie use the idea of institutional entrepreneurship to underscore the fact that energy transitions are not necessarily uncontrollable structural drifts by society. They point out distinct social entities and assume interests and actionability. In this sense, the authors expose the role of *political actors* in instigating and sustaining energy discourses.

Their analysis reveals the variety of players in the energy field in the UK and, not surprisingly, the rather different interests these players have in relation to a transition in the energy sector. Since the authors observe a huge variety of institutional arrangements, they conclude that competing institutional entrepreneurships may have hampered the emergence of a "common meaning system." As a consequence, competing institutional logics may have limited field-level institutional change. Although the UK energy sector has changed to a certain extent, not to such an extent that would justify using the label "transition" (Genus et al. in this book, 172). The subfield of renewable energy was not able to establish an identifiable field logic of its own to provide consistent orientation within the still deeply institutionalized overall field logic of the energy sector.

The problem of action exemplified by trust, capability, and motivation

The major challenge in the action dimension is that social mechanisms like trust, the values incorporated in the design of systems, and intrinsic motivation affect one's ability to act. Patrick Sumpf conceptualizes trust as a process of attribution to social addresses, Rafaela Hillerbrand discusses capability as the possibility to attribute favorable values to the design of systems, while Siegmar Otto and Inga Wittenberg present determinants of the intrinsic motivation of individual persons. Individual persons act within the realm of the energy complex (e.g., via organizing), receive services (e.g., via consuming), and also enact change (e.g., via prosuming). The term motivation indicates, on the one hand, motives such as goals, preferences, interests, or biases and, on the other hand, some kind of action potential, i.e., a force to realize goals, to choose according to preferences, to follow one's interests, or behave according to someone's bias. Motives and preferences are shaped by socialization and therefore interact with and in distinction to others, as cultural theory has emphasized (Thompson, Ellis, and Wildavsky 1990). Most of all, competing lifestyles support different values. These values condition the approval or disapproval of actions. The value design of systems is, according to Rafaela Hillerbrand, an important motivational factor for opening up the capabilities of those affected by energy transitions to actively participate. Sumpf demonstrates that trust relations between persons, groups, or organizations are a decisive factor in decision making (and risk taking) with regard to accessing new energy-related activities. Along these lines, Otto and Wittenberg present different paths for consideration in the context of energy transitions. They ask about the possibility to be *motivated not to act*, i.e., to consider a more sufficient lifestyle and to let go of opportunities.

Trust has to do with familiar structures, and familiarity is jeopardized by a transition. The social mechanism of trust serves as an enabler of action. Lack of trust, in contrast, diminishes action potential. Mistrust or distrust functions as a motivator to look elsewhere. Therefore, risk taking, angst, and the urge to circumvent the consequences of an energy transition illustrate the broad spectrum of possible individual and organizational reactions as to how to operate under such circumstances. Patrick Sumpf goes so far as to say that in order to cope with the sociotechnical problem of action, trust might be an even more fundamental necessity than control, which refers more to knowledge about causal relationships in complicated systems. Sumpf distinguishes between the trust relations of citizens or households with corporate actors, between different organizations, and between different functional systems of society. In all three cases he assumes there are shifting "certainties," which have to be safeguarded by renewed or altered trust relationships: To which social addresses can trust be attributed in a fast changing situation with many "hidden" players? One of the more demanding remaining issues is the extent to which it is possible to work actively on trust, such as fostering trust in political transition programs or in investment schemes, while always mindful of the danger that trust relations are prone to exploitation, as Wiens, Raskob, Diehlmann et al. have discussed in their comparison of the energy infrastructure with the finance industry. This seems to be one reason why Sumpf emphasizes the balancing role that distrust plays in the sense of skepticism or requests for transparency.

The latter comparison refers to an intriguing argument about the correlation between trust and confidence in abstract systems. A positive overall level of confidence in the general state of affairs of abstract entities like economies, politics, law, or education fosters trust for de facto action situations. However, just as there is a *virtuous circle* to increase commitment in a specific situation, there is also the opposite development: a *vicious circle* instigated by the correlation of a lack of confidence and distrust with an inability to act or with a shift in motivation to other opportunities (Luhmann 1988, 104). Most prominent is the case of economic investment, which is more easily done when there is confidence in the stability of political and economic circumstances. Rafaela Hillerbrand relates to this assumption. She claims that there is a correlation between the systematic incorporation of values in the design of energy systems and the ability of individual persons to act – as boosted *agency* – in sociotechnical constellations. As she observes: "[. . .] most of all energy technologies enhance our freedom to act in a unique way which is something to be valued from a capability perspective" (Hillerbrand in this book, 212).

Agency and *actionability* are notions whose meanings differ in nuance. While actionability represents a more abstract concept, namely the pure *ability* to act in the first place, agency is more specific, referring to the ability to achieve certain goals. In addition, actionability is related to the distinction between burden (of uncertainty) and relief, whereas agency is related to the *capacity* to achieve or not achieve something desired (e.g., goal, task, or fulfill a promise). For agency, therefore, Rafaela Hillerbrand claims that the problem of decision making in the context of an energy transition demands stable and instructive premises. Otherwise such a transition cannot be envisioned in the first place. Concepts of sustainability are not enough to provide such orientation. There is the problem that the very idea of sustainability is related to the creation of favorable conditions for future generations, but it cannot be known what the preferences and attitudes of a future generation will be. Empirical work does not help in this case since preferences and attitudes may change over time or in different contexts. As a consequence, Rafaela Hillerbrand explores conditions enabling a "good life" and argues for a shift from the empirical investigation of acceptance and ventures (related to preferences and attitudes) to an ethical derivation of "acceptability" in terms of values that people ought to have. She suggests applying a "capability approach" to expose the values necessary to provide orientation for actions in the context of the *Energiewende*. She introduces ten core capabilities that should be considered in the course of changing the energy system.

This approach brings the concept of sustainability closer to the individual level and may support an individual's motivation to foster sustainability. Capabilities are thought of as rather generic values that enable individuals to lead a good life. This is not necessarily related to change. Rafaela Hillerbrand rather points at a deficit in stable orientation as impeding processes of change for achieving improved conditions of life both today and for future generations. Going into something new always brings risks and uncertainties. The capability approach may reduce these uncertainties by at least providing orientation about what is the right direction. Furthermore, it may increase the willingness of a society to take such risks as long as the risks appear worthwhile, and Hillerbrand emphasizes that this is clearly beyond a utilitarian cost–benefit analysis of individual citizens. Contradicting the NIMBY (not in my backyard) effect, she argues that people usually care about more general values and think well beyond their own cost–benefit calculations.

Referring to the sociotechnical problem of change, we can interpret the idea of core values as enabling a redundancy in energy-related activities that protects against an "overburdening" of variety. While trust is also a factor in capability approaches, Rafaela Hillerbrand promotes the value design of sociotechnical systems, based on the inclusion of a multiplicity of perspectives, values, and knowledge in transition planning. For example, engineering science needs to be informed by those affected or by philosophers and SSH research – as "outside" observers – about value variety or risk distribution (much in the sense of Todd R. La Porte's notion of "suffering"). As one consequence, the problem of complexity is reintroduced here in terms of uncertainty about values.

While Hillerbrand ruminates about the possibilities for enabling, from environmental psychology comes the issue of restricting possibilities in order to mute the impact of human activities. Motivation, as analyzed from the perspective of psychology, also has biological, cognitive, psychosocial, and technical properties, as Siegmar Otto and Inga Wittenberg point out in their contribution about technology and motives. Societal goals may clash with individual motives. Whereas limitation of the use of energy is favorable for the long-term livelihood of planetary habitats, individual behavior is concerned with the short-term quest for well-being. This includes securing access to nutrition (food and water), to shelter from the elements, and to more convenience and pleasure-oriented goods and services – all of which require energy in the life cycle of production, usage, and disposal/recycling. Otto and Wittenberg's argument is daunting: We should not hope that technological advances in the efficiency of energy use will reduce the overall demand. Efficiency may lead to stagnation, and while this is more than nothing, it does not comfort our urge to achieve an actual turnaround to sustainable ways of using energy.

Manual, managerial, and organizational skills increase the range, the quantity, and the effectiveness of human activities. Growing populations (in some parts of the world) and economies are one result. These systemic developments are complemented by individual preferences. Nowadays, in an affluent society, speed, convenience, ease of use, and comfort are predominant. All these preferences pose an obstacle to a change in lifestyle in high energy-consuming regions. A lifestyle based on the idea of sufficiency is directed at restricting the range of human activities, which renders many actions burdensome, makes life complicated, and demands reflection as well as information gathering and processing. And even if sufficiency might be enforced in some areas of modern life, there will then be more freed up resources (time and money) waiting to be utilized for even more innovative activities. All this may render gains in energy efficiency futile if not accompanied by motivational strategies. Technical innovation regarding an efficient use of energy must be complemented by education, according to Otto and Wittenberg. New individuals are constantly populating society and growing into energy consumption patterns; constantly evolving and emerging technology stimulates both shifts in behavioral patterns and the presence of new lifestyles. This promotes energy use – predominantly for reasons of convenience. Therefore, the sociotechnical problem of aligning individual motivation in the direction of sufficiency with the reality of technical innovation remains a constant challenge.

The politics of sociotechnical problems

One of the remaining questions is how the concept of sociotechnical problems can be fruitfully linked to a more governance-oriented perspective. In her contribution, Rafaela Hillerbrand (Chap. 10) emphasizes the power of the sociotechnical systems notion in comparison to technologically deterministic approaches. Her claim is representative of the intellectual efforts of all contributing authors and of a more optimistic, interventionist perspective on the development of sociotechnical systems. Yet the means for doing this differ among the authors, be it the creation of elaborate scientific models, institutional settings or learning modes, or the work on trust, on value design, or on energy education.

What lessons can be learned regarding policy making and what avenues for further research are laid bare by our proposition to analyze "energy" as a sociotechnical problem? Around the world, sustainable energy transitions have become a major topic on political agendas. But transitions are rather difficult cases for public policy since they need to be managed as long-term policy processes, which have to anticipate the different potential trajectories of technology development in its interaction with institutional and political change in "converging infrastructures." This is related to the current reorganization of knowledge in the field of energy, which has been established by engineering, computer science, and the social sciences, generating previously unknown connections. If these interactions are not taken into account adequately, failures may occur that endanger the (profitable, sustainable, secure, and socially compatible) execution of the whole undertaking. One remedy we propose is the increased use of the social sciences and humanities as a reflexive moderator of the transition process, going beyond debates over the acceptance of technology. In this way, sociologists, philosophers, psychologists, and others could help to uncover the "unknown knowns"[7] from energy actors for the sake of regulation, and to find effective ways to integrate them into the policy process of transition management.

As a consequence, establishing the necessary anticipatory capacities that are needed for the governance of energy transitions seems to be a challenge in itself. To develop such capacities, different actors have to work together, and knowledge from different backgrounds has to be combined in various spheres, such as concerning the provision, distribution, and consumption of energy. For the academic realm and research policy, we assume that the approach presented in this book can serve as a sound and innovative scheme to integrate knowledge from different sources. Research strategies have to be based on a broader set of disciplinary approaches and put together in meaningful ways. Results cannot just be added up but have to be truly integrated. During the interdisciplinary research program ENERGY-TRANS,[8] initially mentioned in the introduction, the three-dimensional approach developed for this book was still in the making and could only be applied ex post. Our suggestion is, however, that interdisciplinary projects of this kind, such as EL-TRAN or SHAPE ENERGY[9] and others to come, use this scheme from the start to see to what extent research strategies can be structured along these three dimensions from early on in the research process. This may also be applied to experiments that must accompany research, according to the contribution by Matthias Gross in this book (Chap. 6). To achieve this aim and in order to generate added value from the collected contributions (apart from accumulating individual papers), it is vital to clarify the merit of using sociotechnical problems as a distinct methodology for interdisciplinary research. This should be done at an early stage of interdisciplinary projects by highlighting its integrative function. In preparing this book, the methodology has created initial value by successfully aligning all authors on sociotechnical problems and guiding their contributions toward consideration of them. In the future, we expect much more homogeneity in individual interdisciplinary programs and are keen on developing a concrete management method for applying the concept in such settings, which is a gap in the energy research community and beyond.

The discussion in this book further emphasizes how all three dimensions must be taken into account when policy programs are being set up to induce or support energy transitions. Too much focus on *change* might undermine *stability* and/or *actionability*, such as in cases where trust relations are weakened to the point of widespread mistrust. Furthermore, the incorporation of values might fail, putting at risk the active participation of the general public in providing future energy services, which is most important when technical design considerations are produced hastily. Focusing on *stability*, conversely, may prevent *change* and the development toward societally desired objectives. In situations of great uncertainty, which is the case in a number of energy transitions around the world, and where no detailed "master plan" can be developed, the transition process has to be open to learning and adapting to surprises and new, unknown situations. Empirical research could look at the specific balance between the three dimensions and on how this balance changes over time in order to feed it into the policy process. Timing appears to be of particular importance for the relationship between stability and change: How much change is possible in what timeframe without overly undermining stability remains a question to be answered over and over again.

Furthermore, the approach presented in this book accentuates the fact that the three dimensions have to be dealt with continually since solutions always produce cascading problems that require new solutions. It can therefore be questioned if transitions, as they are unfolding right now, represent defined routes with clear-cut starting and end points. Such routes are often suggested when very specific goals are stated, specifying a targeted reduction of CO_2 by X% in a certain timeframe, for example. We are not implying that thinking in terms of targets is completely unhelpful. To be sure, normative concepts such as sustainability, linked with clear targets or roadmaps, are essential tools to provide guidance for policy making. Yet we want to raise awareness for the ongoing and (probably) never ending dynamics in sociotechnical complexes that can be addressed by referencing the three dimensions of control, change, and action, and their integrative power.

Last but not least, we think the work presented here indicates that the approach is rather generic and thus applicable to sociotechnical transitions in other fields. However, further research is needed to explore the extent to which this is the case. An appropriate example might be the transport sector, which is expected to experience a high pace of change in the years to come, driven by digitalization, battery research, and new forms of mobility. We assume that in this transition, too, the three problem dimensions serve as useful points of reference to create pertinent knowledge and to inform the governance of transition processes.

Notes

1 See www.ipcc.ch. Accessed 2018/05/07.
2 COP stands for "Conference of the Parties."
3 This sociotechnical perspective is highlighted on the IEA website for readers of the World Energy Outlook (WEO), the flagship publication of the IEA. See: www.iea. org/newsroom/news/2017/march/world-energy-outlook-2017-to-include-focus-on-chinas-energy-outlook-and-the-natu.html. Accessed 2018/05/07.
4 Referring to the concept of La Porte (2015, 6): "The degree of complexity of organized social systems (Q) is a function of the *number* of system components (Ci), the relative *differentiation* or variety of the components (Di), and the degree of *interdependence* among these components (Ik). Then, by definition, the greater Ci, Di, and Ik, the greater the complexity of the organized system (Q)."
5 See also Edwards et al. (2007, 12) on infrastructures "running from systems (centrally organized and controlled) to networks (linked systems, with control partially or wholly distributed among the nodes) to webs (networks of networks based primarily on coordination rather than control)."
6 Compare Chap. 2 for an explicit elaboration of the distinction between redundancy and variety in the change dimension.
7 Todd R. La Porte referred to this term to illustrate that dynamic transition projects involve knowledge that is known in the empirical field, yet not in the regulatory community, but is potentially retrievable through scholarly observation such as *technology assessment*. See La Porte's contribution in this book for further elaboration.
8 www.energy-trans.de/english/index.php. Accessed 2018/04/23.
9 See, for more information on both activities: https://el-tran.fi/in-english/ and https://shapeenergy.eu/. Accessed 2018/04/23.

References

Arthur, W. Brian. 2009. *The Nature of Technology: What It Is and How It Evolves*. New York, London, Toronto, Sydney: Free Press.

Beckman, Svante. 1994. "On Systemic Technology." In *Changing Large Technical Systems*, edited by Jane Summerton, 311–31. Boulder, CO: Westview Press.

Büscher, Christian, and Aldo Mascareño. 2014. "Mechanisms of Risk Production in Modern Cities." *Nature and Culture* 9 (1): 66–86. https://doi.org/10.3167/nc.2014.090104.

Edwards, Paul N., Steven J. Jackson, Geoffrey C. Bowker, and Cory P. Knobel. 2007. *Understanding Infrastructure: Dynamics, Tensions, and Design*. Ann Arbor: DeepBlue.

Helbing, Dirk. 2012. "Systemic Risks in Society and Economics." In *Social Self-Organization*, edited by Dirk Helbing, 261–84. Berlin, Heidelberg: Springer. https://doi.org/10.1007/978-3-642-24004-1_14.

IEO. 2017. "International Energy Outlook 2016-Executive Summary – Energy Information Administration." DOE/EIA-0484(2017). Washington, DC: International Energy Outlook, U.S. Energy Information Administration. www.eia.gov/outlooks/ieo/exec_summ.php. Accessed 2018/05/07.

IPCC. 2015. "ADOPTION OF THE PARIS AGREEMENT Proposal by the President Draft Decision -/CP.21." Intergovernmental Panel on Climate Change. https://unfccc.int/resource/docs/2015/cop21/eng/l09r01.pdf. Accessed 2018/05/07.

La Porte, Todd R. 2015. "Organized Social Complexity: Explication of a Concept." In *Organized Social Complexity: Challenge to Politics and Policy*, edited by Todd R. La Porte, 2nd ed., 3–39. Princeton Legacy Library. Princeton: Princeton University Press.

Luhmann, Niklas. 1988. "Familiarity, Confidence, Trust: Problems and Alternatives." In *Trust. Making and Breaking Cooperative Relations*, edited by Diego Gambetta, 94–107. Oxford: Basil Blackwell.

———. 1995. *Social Systems*. Stanford: Stanford University Press.

March, James G., and Johan P. Olsen. 1995. *Democratic Governance*. New York: Free Press.

Mayntz, Renate. 2009. "The Changing Governance of Large Technical Infrastructure Systems." In *Über Governance: Institutionen Und Prozesse Politischer Regelung*, 121–50. Schriften aus dem Max-Planck-Institut für Gesellschaftsforschung, Band 62. Frankfurt am Main, New York: Campus.

Strulik, Torsten. 2007. "Rating Agencies, Ignorance and the Knowledge-Based Production of System Trust." In *Towards a Cognitive Mode in Global Finance: The Governance of a Knowledge-Based Financial System*, edited by Torsten Strulik and Helmut Willke, 239–58. Frankfurt am Main, New York: Campus.

Thompson, Michael, Richard Ellis, and Aaron Wildavsky. 1990. *Cultural Theory*. San Francisco: Westview Press.

Todt, Oliver. 2011. "The Limits of Policy: Public Acceptance and the Reform of Science and Technology Governance." *Technological Forecasting and Social Change* 78 (6): 902–9. https://doi.org/10.1016/j.techfore.2011.02.007.

von Foerster, Heinz. 1972. "Perception of the Future and the Future of Perception." *Instructional Science* 1 (1): 31–43. https://doi.org/10.1007/BF00053969.

Williamson, Oliver E. 1979. "Transaction-Cost Economics: The Governance of Contractual Relations." *The Journal of Law & Economics* 22 (2): 233–61.

Index

Page numbers in *italics* indicate figures and in **bold** indicate tables on the corresponding pages.

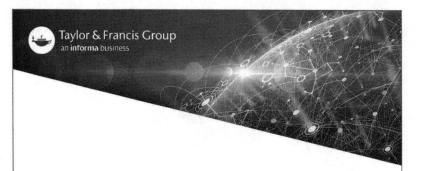